Taking Politi[cal Power]
What Congress and the Media Won't Tell You

Devvy Kidd
Author

Walter Publishing

Please contact Walter Publishing for bulk discounts.

Walter Publishing & NewsWithViews.com Books
P.O. Box 370
Merlin, OR. 97532

Phone: 541-471-3000
Toll Free: 800-955-0116
sales@newswithviews.com

Copyright © April 2016 by Devvy Kidd

All rights reserved. No part of this publication may be reproduced, stored in a retrieval system, or transmitted in any for by any means either electronic, mechanical or photocopying without the express and written permission of Walter Publishing & Newswithviews.com Books.

Table of Contents

Introduction i

1 The Federal Reserve - Head of the Beast 1

2 Federal income tax: Where does your money really go? 27

3 Jobs and the Destruction Caused by "Free" Trade 51

4 The Economy: Another Tragedy Underway 67

5 (Un)Affordable Health Care Act aka Obamacare 91

6 Non-Ratification of Seventeenth Amendment - Why It's So Important 115

7 Illegal aliens: liars, cheats, thieves, rapists, murderers 130

8 Social Security: Yes, it is a Ponzi scheme 160

9 Medicare - Unsustainable 178

10 "Smart" Meters - The Silent Killer 192

11 More Money for Education! 223

12 On-Going Disgraceful Treatment of America's Veterans 259

13 What Everyone Ignores About Planned Parenthood 278

14 Fukushima: On-Going Crime Against Humanity 288

15 Federal Drug Administration (FDA) = Federal Death Administration 308

16 Vaccines - Silent Destroyers 324

17 Monsanto Must Be Stopped 342

18 Islam: A cancer oozing across America 364

19 In Closing 396

Endnotes & Additional Resources 404

Introduction

"Mr. President, it is natural to man to indulge in the illusions of hope. We are apt to shut our eyes against a painful truth, and listen to the song of that siren till she transforms us into beasts. Is this the part of wise men, engaged in a great and arduous struggle for liberty? Are we disposed to be of the numbers of those who, having eyes, see not, and, having ears, hear not, the things, which so nearly concern their temporal salvation? For my part, whatever anguish of spirit it may cost, I am willing to know the whole truth, to know the worst, and to provide for it." Patrick Henry, March 23, 1775

This book is not about politics. I have not belonged to a political party since 1996. This book is about truth, not the blame game of Republicans vs. Democrats. This book is about solutions that are there but not implemented because of constant political party bickering, the never ending war by Republicans and Democrats to retain a power position in Congress, the very real agenda to destroy our constitutional republic and massive amounts of money. The level of corruption at all levels of government in this country is simply breath taking in scope, yet most Americans know nothing about what has been done to them.

Twenty-six years ago my life was changed forever. Little could I have ever imagined that reading one chapter in a book would prompt me to give up my job, my paycheck and begin a journey of learning the truth: what Congress and the media never tell the American people.

Twenty-six years ago I was at publishing convention in Southern California. A big deal in the publishing industry. All the big names were there like the late "Stormin" Norman Swartzcroft. My first book had been published. I was there to promote it. Not being a "big name", our table didn't have huge crowds for book signing. My publisher handed me a book and said I might be interested in reading it. That book is a little over 600 pages and amazingly, when I went to open it, I landed on the chapter about the "Federal" Reserve. What I read didn't seem right to me. After all, the "Federal" Reserve was called federal so it must be part of the government.

When I returned home to Colorado I ordered a copy of the book. When I finished reading it I was simply numb. All that had been going on right under my nose by our government and I never knew. The first thing I did was ask a few people about this central bank (the "Fed") for which I knew absolutely nothing. I began ordering books and studying. Many trips to the fabulous Denver Public Library that had the *Congressional Record* dating back to the 1800s and other valuable resources for my research.

In late 1992, I decided I would write a little booklet in an effort to get what I had learned out to my fellow Americans. Of course, I didn't know how I was going to pay for it. Back then I had a word processor as home computers had not yet made it to American households. Back then we only had fax machines, snail mail and newsletters.

I wrote my booklet, *Why A Bankrupt America* mostly in my head at night when I went to bed. I could not stop thinking about what I had learned. The booklet at final printing ended up at 45 pages dealing with the unconstitutional, privately owned "Federal Reserve" and exposing something called a "new world order". One very generous individual heard about my efforts and donated a large sum of money to help me get the first 5,000 booklets printed. I did no advertising because I couldn't afford it. The back inside page was an order blank so people could order them at cost + shipping. When I retired that booklet in May 2004, I had sold *at cost* 1,653,000 copies. All by word of mouth, people ordering 25, 50 or 100 copies and giving them out and from my appearances on talk radio.

As I got further into my research about the unconstitutional, privately owned "Federal" Reserve, I kept running into "threads" that took me to another issue and another and another. It was like a huge pot of spaghetti; pulling one strand out at a time. In 1993 I got a good education on how vote fraud controls our elections so I wrote a second booklet; also 45 pages. *Blind Loyalty* was about provable vote fraud, how it was being done both at the state and federal level. Eventually I began to understand the phrase: Two wings on the same bird of prey regarding the two main political parties. I also retired that second booklet in May 2004; the Internet was raging and people could get the truth on line. I sold, *at cost,* 700,000 copies of *Blind Loyalty*.

As the success of my little 45-page booklet, *Why A Bankrupt America*, grew, so did the attacks on me personally. How green I was back then because I couldn't imagine why no one in the media wanted the truth. Instead, I was simply branded with being a conspiracy nut, anti-government and worse. Never mind that I had read dozens of books on the central bank and all the history pertaining to the central bank in this country. I was simply ill-informed and believed in conspiracy theories. So declared those who attacked me.

One thing I learned fairly quickly in my journey is the only conspiracy theories that are valid have to come from the U.S. Government!

Millions of Americans know something is really wrong in this country. No matter how hard they try and how much they work, people are losing everything. Why is it no matter who you vote for every two years for the U.S. Congress, things never seem to get better? Why is it no matter how many campaign promises made during an election year, once sworn in the incumbent you reelected betrays you?

Do you understand the importance of the central bank (the "Fed") and the destruction it has caused to our great nation? Is all the talk about a "new world order" just blather or have powerful individuals since the late 1800s been working to bring America under a global world government where our U.S. Constitution and Bill of Rights would mean nothing? Every chapter in this book deals with an issue that affects every man, woman and child in this country regardless of race, religion, political affiliation or anything else.

The answers are in this book.

> *"There is nothing which I dread so much as a division of the republic into two great parties, each arranged under its leader, and concerting measures in opposition to each other. This, in my humble apprehension, is to be dreaded as the greatest political evil under our Constitution."* First Vice President and the second President of the United States. Letter to Jonathan Jackson (2 October 1780), *"The Works of John Adams"*, vol 9, p. 511.

1

The Federal Reserve - Head of the Beast

"You are a den of vipers and thieves. I intend to rout you out, and by the eternal God, I will rout you out." Andrew Jackson, to a delegation of bankers discussing the recharter of the Second Bank of the United States, 1832.

If someone had told me twenty-six years ago I would be studying America's central bank and fiat currency, I would have laughed. I mean, what could be drier than reading about some banking system?

But, as I said in the introduction, it's that institution that made me ask questions for which I had no answers. I just knew I had to find out more because what little I had learned not only outraged me, but also scared me. I could see back then America was headed for a financial collapse, the only question was when and how bad was it going to be?

There's no question a U.S. Senator and heavy weight bankers plotted a dark conspiracy to hijack our monetary system, which they did when the "Federal" Reserve Banking Act was passed in December 1913. An outstanding investigative work on that is a book by G. Edward Griffin who I had the great pleasure of meeting, *The Creature From Jekyll Island (*Web site: *realityzone.com):*

> "This is the classic exposé of the Fed that has become one of the best-selling books in its category of all time. Where does money come from? Where does it go? Who makes it? The money magician's secrets are unveiled. Here is a close look at their mirrors and smoke machines, the pulleys, cogs, and wheels that create the grand illusion called money. A boring subject? Just wait. You'll be hooked in five minutes. It reads like a detective story – which it really is, but it's all true.

"This book is about the most blatant scam of history. It's all here: the cause of wars, boom-bust cycles, inflation, depression, prosperity. Your world view will definitely change. Putting it quite simply, this may be the most important book on world affairs you will ever read. *The Creature from Jekyll Island* hits Amazon charts as Number-One Best Seller in its category (Money & Monetary Policy."

Besides books and papers written on the "Fed", I was reading a lot of the *Congressional Record*. Congressman Wright Patman (D-TX) served in Congress for 40 years. For decades he was Chairman of the U.S. House's Committee on Banking and Currency. Patman wanted to repeal the Federal Reserve Banking Act of 1913. This is one of his statements, September 29, 1941, *Congressional Record*, pages 7582-7583 [Emphasis mine]:

"When our Federal Government, that has the exclusive power to create money, creates that money and then goes into the open market and borrows it and **pays interest for the use of its own money**, it occurs to me that that is going too far. I have never yet had anyone who could, through the use of logic and reason, **justify the Federal Government borrowing the use of its own money**... I am saying to you in all sincerity, and with all the earnestness that I possess, it is absolutely wrong for the Government to issue interest-bearing obligations. It is not only wrong: it is extravagant. It is not only extravagant, it is wasteful. It is absolutely unnecessary.

"Now, take the Panama Canal bonds. They amounted to a little less than $50,000,000 — $49,800,000. By the time they are paid, the Government will have paid $75,000,000 in interest on bonds of less than $50,000,000. **So the Government is paying out $125,000,000 to obtain the use of $49,800,000.** That is the way it has worked all along. That is our policy. That is our system. The question is: Should that policy be continued? Is it sane? Is it reasonable? Is it right, or is it wrong? If it is wrong, it should be changed.

"Now, I believe the system should be changed. **The Constitution of the United States does not give the banks the power to create money.** The Constitution says that Congress shall have the power to create money, but now, under our system, we will sell bonds to commercial banks and obtain credit from those banks.

"I believe the time will come when people will demand that this be changed. I believe the time will come in this country when they will actually blame you and me and everyone else connected with this Congress for sitting idly by and permitting such an idiotic system to continue. I make that statement after years of study.

"We have what is known as the Federal Reserve Bank System. That system is not owned by the Government. Many people think that it is, because it says Federal Reserve. It belongs to the private banks, private corporations. So we have farmed out to the Federal Reserve Banking System that is owned exclusively, wholly, 100 percent by the private banks — we have farmed out to them the privilege of issuing the Government's money. If we were to take this privilege back from them, we could save the amount of money that I have indicated in enormous interest charges."

That was then. One would ask: If the system is so bad, why hasn't Congress abolished the "Federal" Reserve Banking system? A number of congressmen over the years have tried. In 2007, former Congressman Ron Paul introduced a bill to abolish the magical money machine. It had no sponsors.

Why? **Congress needs the candy store or they would not be able to continue borrowing to fund trillions in unconstitutional spending running the debt clear to Pluto.** How do people think the national debt – created by Congress – has climbed to an unpayable $19+ trillion dollars?

The profound ignorance by members of Congress regarding one of the most important things in this country, our currency, is inexcusable. When I said who wants to read dry old books, well, I did and one of them was *Secrets of the Temple* by William Greider. This is his testimony in front of the House Banking Committee, October 7, 1993:

"The veil of secrecy certainly does enhance the mystique surrounding the Fed – and the general ignorance about it. Otherwise confident and intelligent people including members of Congress – defer to the Fed's wisdom mainly because they do not understand it. They are understandably intimidated by its mystery and power.

"And, as every governor freely acknowledged to me, the Fed also makes mistakes just like the rest of us mortals. The difference is that the Fed's mistakes can have devastating impact on the lives and fortunes of millions. It can sink viable business enterprises and force debtors to the wall and put millions of people out of jobs. It can reward some investors and punish others.

"Given these vast powers, it is fatuous to pretend that the Federal Reserve can somehow be insulted from politics. And, indeed, it is not. As any candid governor will tell you, the institution is bombarded constantly with pleas and demands and unsolicited advice from selected interests. As a matter of style, lobbying the Fed is done more delicately and discreetly than, say, lobbying Congress or the White House, but the private and semi-private dialogues surrounding monetary policy go on continuously – between the Fed and financial markets, banks and brokerages and other major player, both foreign and domestic.

"The only players who are left out of this conversation are the American people and, to a large extent their elected representatives. Instead, they are provided a frustrating stream of evasive euphemisms and opaque jargon and platitudinous generalities and, sometimes, even downright deception. As more than one Federal Reserve governor confided to me, it would be very difficult – perhaps impossible – for the Fed to have an honest discussion of monetary policy with Congress or the public because the level of ignorance is so profound.

"In other words, if you are serious about reforming the Federal Reserve, you will necessarily have to think about changing more than the institutional behavior of the Fed. The lack of accountability is not simply a function of Fed mystique. Among elected politicians, there is also a widespread willingness not to know or understand. In fairness to Congress, the news media encourages this deference by promoting the conventional wisdom about the institution. Any politician who dares to become a critic can count upon damaging attacks from both editorial writers and news reporters.

"Frankly, the Fed does not even have to confront intelligent scrutiny from those the people have elected to represent them. That is, the Congress. In my experience, congressional oversight hearings are usually a dispiriting mixture of posturing and bile and trick questions that the Federal Reserve governors find quite easy to fend off. It is hard to take most of the congressional questioning seriously and not surprising that many at the Federal Reserve do not.

"Wright Patman once referred to the existing arrangement as 'a car with two drivers.' One driver has a foot on the gas, the other on the brake. He meant that the fiscal policy of spending and taxation is controlled by Congress and the Executive, while the money and credit policy is controlled by the central bank. These two levers interact powerfully with another – sometimes with contradictory results. Yet, believe it or not, there is absolutely no requirement in the law that the two levers must be coordinated with one another. There is not even an intelligent process by which monetary policy and fiscal policy can be viewed together as pieces of an overall economic strategy.

"In 1981, when Congress passed the Reagan economic program, the massive tax cuts and defense buildup were powerfully stimulative to the economy. But the Federal Reserve was simultaneously embarked on the opposite course: suppressing economic growth with extraordinarily high interest rates in order to squeeze out price inflation. The stark fact is that the government was pushing the national economy in opposite directions at once. The car with two drivers wound up in a ditch – first deep recession, then an awesome accumulation of debt – and we are effectively still in it." [End]

> *"Paper is poverty, it is only the ghost of money, and not money itself." Thomas Jefferson, Letter to Edward Carrington, 1788*

Below are some of the most helpful documents I read early on that got right to the point about our currency in such a way I could understand it. Get out your yellow "stick it" and book mark these pages so you can find these resources and follow up. As throughout this book, simply type the title into a search engine to match it with the URL.

1. **A Primer on Money, Committee on Banking and Currency, August 5, 1974, Congressman Wright Patman.** That document explains in easy terms what is money, how fake "money" is created, how our monetary system works and the problems with the "Fed". Believe me when I tell you I spent a

good year just reading because back then there was no Internet. But, the only way I came to understand what can be a complicated issue was to hunker down and read. http://www.devvy.com/pdf/2006_October/Patman_Primer_on_Money.pdf

2. **Congressman McFadden on the Federal Reserve Corporation Remarks in Congress, 1934.** Something not heard in Congress in a long, long time. http://hiwaay.net/~becraft/mcfadden.html

3. Congressman Louis McFadden, *Congressional Record*: January 8, 1934. This is history and very important. Use this title in a search engine: **A tribute to Congressman Louis Thomas McFadden** http://www.sweetliberty.org/issues/hoax/mcfadden.htm#.VjvxCCvgG70

4. Charles Lindberg, Sr., served in the U.S. House from 1907 - 1917. Lindberg railed against the Federal Reserve Act:

"This Act establishes the most gigantic trust on earth. When the President signs this Act the invisible government by the Money Power, proven to exist by the Money Trust Investigation, will be legalized. The new law will create inflation whenever the trusts want inflation. From now on depressions will be scientifically created." – Congressman Charles A. Lindbergh, Sr., 1913, on the Federal Reserve Act Charles Lindbergh Sr. – *Congressional Record* – Feb 12, 1917

Lindberg, Charles August (1916). *Real Needs*, Vol 1, Issue 1, U of Min, pg 83

https://books.google.com/books?id=wtgvAQAAMAAJ&pg=PA83

"To cause high prices, all the Federal Reserve Board will do will be to lower the rediscount rate..., producing an expansion of credit and a rising stock market; then when ... business men are adjusted to these conditions, it can check ... prosperity in mid-career by arbitrarily raising the rate of interest. It can cause the pendulum of a rising and falling market to swing gently back and forth by slight changes in the discount rate, or cause violent fluctuations by a greater rate variation and in either case it will possess inside information as to financial conditions and advance knowledge of the coming change, either up or down.

"This is the strangest, most dangerous advantage ever placed in the hands of a special privilege class by any Government that ever existed. The system is private, conducted for the sole purpose of obtaining the greatest possible profits from the use of other people's money. They know in advance when to create panics to their advantage. They also know when to stop panic. Inflation and deflation work equally well for them when they control finance."

5. **Banking and Currency and the Money Trust - By Charles A. Lindbergh**
https://archive.org/stream/BankingAndCurrencyAndTheMoneyTrust-ByCharlesA.Lindbergh/BankingAndCurrencyAndTheMoneyTrust-ByCharlesA.Lindbergh_djvu.txt During my learning process I read dozens of books on money. I learned there are two camps: The Austrian money advocates and imbeciles who embrace toxic Keynesian economics. Keynesian economic theories were first introduced by British economist, John Maynard Keynes.

"President Harry Truman was skeptical of Keynesian theorizing, 'Nobody can ever convince me that Government can spend a dollar that it's not got,' he told Leon Keyserling, a Keynesian economist who chaired Truman's Council of Economic Advisers." John Cassidy, October 10, 2011, The Demand Doctor, *The New Yorker*.

That piece talks about all the failed programs FDR implemented only to be taken up again by the current occupant of the White House with an alleged stimulus package that stimulated nothing because **the real problem was never addressed in 2008 and that is the "Fed"**. I highly recommend a very important piece written about FDR's failed solutions: *Great Myths of the Great Depression*, by Lawrence Reed. Just type title into a search engine.

The premiere book on the money system (2002 edition and the 2011 Gold Money edition) is *Pieces of Eight: The Monetary Powers and Disabilities of the United States Constitution* by Dr. Edwin Vieira. 1,722 pages, two volume set that should have won a Pulitzer Prize, but would never happen because the powers that be don't want you to know how the 'Fed' has destroyed our economy over and over and has been siphoning the lifeblood out of this country for 103 years.

Dr. Vieira's book is the most comprehensive history of the monetary system of the Unite States from before the U.S. Constitution to present day ever written. Edwin meticulously explains where the US went wrong economically and what must be done to correct it. Nothing was left out; all court cases pertaining to that issue are analyzed including Congressional debates, endless laws on money, banking and more.

Pieces of Eight – the 2011 Gold Money Edition – is available through the East Virginia Trading Company store front on Amazon at: http://www.amazon.com/Pieces-Eight-Monetary-Disabilities-Constitution/dp/B004M53XLC. If you can't afford to purchase the two-volume set, you may be able to acquire a copy through the interlibrary loan program at most colleges and universities.

But, how does a debauched currency affect your life? With permission from my good friend, Tom Selgas, this slide presentation tells the story.

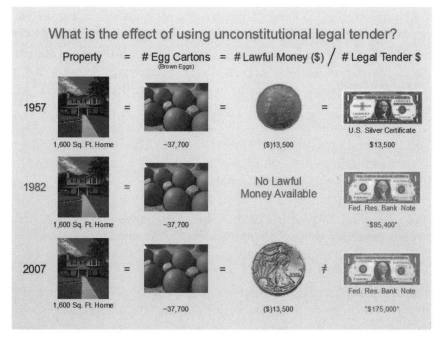
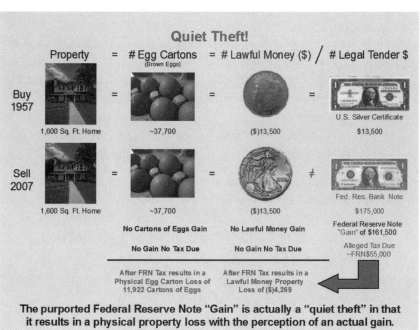

Once again America is going to pay a very high price because as Dr. Edwin Vieira so eloquently wrote: The Road Not Taken, Dr. Edwin Vieira, Jr., Ph.D., J.D., November 8, 2011, *NewsWithViews.com*. The complete text of an address presented in part to the Committee for Monetary Research and Education, Fall Meeting, 20 October 2011, at the Union League Club, New York City

"We all are familiar with Robert Frost's poem, 'The Road Not Taken': 'Two roads diverged in a yellow wood...' it begins. And it ends with the bittersweet and equivocal observation,

"I shall be telling this with a sigh Somewhere ages and ages hence: Two roads diverged in a wood, and I—I took the one less traveled by, And, that has made all the difference.

"The peregrinations of individual men and of whole nations are not dissimilar. On every occasion of political and economic crisis but one in her history, America has come to the point where 'two monetary roads diverged in a yellow wood'—and has taken the wrong road.

"That unique occasion was the ratification of the Constitution in 1788. For—

- The Constitution adopted a scientific monetary unit—the "dollar", a coin containing 371.25 grains of pure silver; and a companion coinage, denominated "eagles", containing gold valued at the free-market exchange rate with silver.

- The Constitution withheld from the General Government the power to "emit bills"—which was the term of art at that time for paper currency. Any kind of "bills", whether redeemable or irredeemable in precious metals; or whether or not designated "legal tender".

- The Constitution prohibited the States from "emit[ing] Bills". Again, any and every kind of "Bills". And,

- The Constitution prohibited the States from "mak[ing] any Thing but gold and silver Coin a Tender in Payment of

Debts"—thereby reserving to the States the power to "make gold and silver Coin a Tender in Payment of Debts".

"This was (and remains) a system legally just, politically astute, economically sound, and socially responsible, because it tends especially to benefit the common man, who typically holds much of his real wealth in money or the simplest claims payable in money (such as bank deposits).

"Yet every other time since 1788, America has stumbled down the wrong monetary road. Not, however, 'the road less traveled by'—for that would have been the road laid out according to constitutional principles—but instead 'the road most traveled by', the road that essentially every modern nation has taken. The road which has 'diverged' from monetary units actually composed of silver and gold, honestly weighed. The road which has settled instead upon monetary units consisting of debt and administered through fraud:

"The first false step, to redeemable paper currency; then to redeemable paper currency declared to be legal tender; then to irredeemable paper currency declared to be legal tender; and even, as from 1933 to 1974, to the prohibition of the private ownership of gold altogether. And to make matters worse, now the central bank and the government treasury responsible for emitting the latest of these 'bills of credit'— which have turned out to be 'bills of discredit', because of the Ponzi nature of their emission—have demanded, and will continue to demand, serial 'bail outs' from common Americans, in order to keep the paper pyramids from collapsing.

"Today, America finds herself once again lost in 'the yellow wood' of monetary chaos, at a point where 'two roads diverge[ ]'—

"One road leads to 'more of the same'—'monkey business as usual', as it were, both politically and economically—aimed at propping up domestic as well as foreign zombie banks; subordinating the United States Treasury to the cabals of private financial power-brokers in New York and London; and, one may be assured, expanding the fraud of irredeemable legal-tender paper currency to the supra-national level, with a new 'global currency' which will surely strip America of her economic sovereignty, and likely will attenuate if not eliminate her political sovereignty, too.

"We must not be enticed down that wrong road by the illusion that we can convince Congress to reinstitute some kind of traditional 'gold standard' that pulls the Federal Reserve System from the pit of its own incompetence, profligacy, and criminality, by somehow returning Federal Reserve Notes to redeemability in gold.

"My 'Cross of Gold' address to this audience in October of 2010 said all that needs to be said against the substance of proposals of that kind. Of course, I shall be the first to commend the proponents of such plans for their patriotism, imagination, courage, and optimism. But, as General Sosobowski reputedly said when General Browning reviewed the plan for the ultimately disastrous Operation Market Garden: 'I am thrilled that your great Field Marshall Montgomery has devised such a plan. I promise you that I shall be properly ecstatic if it works.'

"Operation Market Garden failed because it was directed along the wrong road. I doubt that any plan to return Federal Reserve Notes to redeemability in gold will work, either—in any sense of the word 'work' that will serve the American people's interests. Even if such a plan could be put into practice, it would merely bring this country back to 1932—and those who have studied monetary history will recall that 1932 was followed by 1933.

"That brings us to the other road. 'The road not taken' yet, but which must be taken soon. The road that leads to

- honest, fully constitutional, and economically sound monetary units tied directly and inextricably to the free market;
- political "checks and balances", in the form of decentralization of monetary authority, and control of their own money by the people themselves; and
- the retention and even strengthening of America's national sovereignty and independence.

"This is the road leading, not to salvaging the Federal Reserve System, but instead to walking away from it, through the adoption by each State of an alternative so-called 'electronic currency' consisting of gold and silver, in which definite and fixed weights of precious metals are the only monetary units.

"This can be done, because

(1) The present economic crisis has made some such action absolutely imperative.

(2) The present political crisis excludes any such action being taken by Congress.

(3) The States enjoy the constitutional authority to act.

(4) The people and public officials in the States are, slowly but surely, becoming aware that, if anything is to be done in their interests, they must do it themselves.

(5) The plan for an alternative "electronic currency" is fully workable—arguably, it is the only plan that can be made to work in time—

- Adoption of an alternative "electronic currency" by the States does not depend upon agreement or assistance from—or, indeed, any involvement whatsoever on the part of—Congress, the Treasury, the Federal Reserve System or other central banks, the major commercial banks either domestic or foreign, the big Wall-Street financial houses and speculators, or any of the other usual suspects in the political-cum-economic fraud that passes for national and international "monetary policy" today.

- Adoption of an alternative "electronic currency" establishes constitutional and scientific monetary units of gold and silver, immediately interchangeable with each other on the basis of the exchange rate between the precious metals in the free market.

- An alternative "electronic currency" avoids all of the problems that inhere in the use of coinage: namely, that

(i) Neither the United States nor any other country provides "free coinage" of gold or silver; and none is likely to do so in the foreseeable future.

(ii) The United States and foreign coins that are available are insufficient to make a coinage scheme work, particularly in that there are not enough different, especially low, denominations for use in average day-to-day commerce.

(iii) A State cannot safely rely on private mints to generate new coinage. For private mints will not be able to partake of any governmental immunity, by being made parts or agents of State government, because the States cannot themselves coin money—i.e., if the private mints could claim the immunity, then the prohibition would come into play. And without such immunity, the private mints would be exposed to "Bernard von Nothausing", so none will start up without some previous judicial protection—which means a lengthy period of litigation, the outcome of which is likely to be negative in the decidedly unfriendly "federal courts".

(iv) There exist no "gold and silver coinage banks" available to handle coinage on deposit, for transfers by checks, and so on; and banks in the Federal Reserve System cannot be expected to set up special gold and silver accounts. So businesses especially, as well as average citizens, will find the use of coinage very inconvenient.

(v) Bullion is perfectly assimilable on a constitutional basis to coin if the government provides or adopts some certification of amount and purity at least equivalent to the certification of amount and purity that inheres in official coinage. And, in any event, as to all "Payment[s] of Debts" that come within a State's reserved power under Article I, Section 10, Clause 1 of the Constitution, a State can make actual "gold and silver Coin" the only final "Tender", but can arrange that creditors can be paid with "electronic currency" at an appropriate premium, so that very few would ever opt for coins.

- An alternative "electronic currency" can be installed in at most 30, 60, or 90 days from passage of the enabling legislation, by using "off the shelf" technology that has already been thoroughly proven in the marketplace.

(6) A proper plan for an alternative "electronic currency" adopted and proven in one State can be taken up in short order in every other State. Indeed, once adopted in one State, it will be adopted in others, because the full force of the market will be behind it.

(7) An alternative "electronic currency" is satisfactory not only for intrastate and interstate commerce, but also for international trade. So its adoption will occasion the least possible disruption in the markets for real goods and services.

(8) This plan does not disperse our relatively meager forces, because the selfsame proposal can be promoted in each State—yet it also does not put all of our eggs into one basket, because there are 50 different baskets, in at least one of which the plan will likely prove successful.

(9) An objection frequently offered to this plan is that rogue officials in the General Government will attempt to enforce some statute of Congress—whether now on the books or to be specially enacted for the purpose—that prohibits or inhibits the States from adopting an alternative currency. Under the circumstances of accelerating economic crisis and civil unrest that will form the context in which an alternative currency will be adopted, however, the General Government will prove to be a paper tiger.

- First, if the General Government threatens or attempts to enforce some such statute against a State, the State can bring the case into the original jurisdiction of the Supreme Court, under Article III, Section 2, Clause 2 of the Constitution. In that event, it is most unlikely that the Justices would dare to take upon themselves the responsibility for interfering with a rearrangement of America's monetary affairs that could save the people from a crushing economic collapse. They could, of course, correctly rule that the Court has already decided that the States retain the governmental authority to adopt their own currencies, whether of gold or silver coin or of bullion. See *Lane County v. Oregon*, 74 U.S. 71 (1869). Perhaps more likely is that—in the manner of Pontius Pilate that has always best suited them—the Justices will wash their hands of the matter entirely by ruling that the case presents a so-called "political question": namely,

(i) The General Government has its monetary powers— to coin and to borrow money—and through the exercise of these powers the power to create a monetary and banking system. And it has done so.

(ii) The States enjoy an explicitly reserved power to "make gold and silver Coin a Tender in Payment of Debts", and through the exercise of that power can create their own alternative monetary system. And they have done so.

(iii) These two systems serve as "checks and balances", one against the other—limiting the States in what they can do, but preserving for them the ability to protect their people against an incompetent and imprudent Congress.

(iv) The ultimate "check and balance" is the people themselves, who can choose, in the market, which monetary system they want to use. And, therefore,

(v) The Judiciary cannot tell the people which level of government to support in this matter. Case dismissed.

"Were the Justices to rule that the people cannot protect themselves against economic catastrophe by choosing their own form of currency, issued by their own State governments under a power constitutionally reserved to the States, their blunder would signal the end of the Judiciary's authority in this country. The American people will not sit down resignedly to eat cat food in cold and squalor because five political appointees in black robes tell them they must do so, in order to enable the banks and Wall Street speculators to continue to loot this country. Rather, the people will adopt President Andrew Jackson's view: 'Justice Marshal has made his decision; now let him enforce it!'

- Second, concerns are often raised about the General Government's employment of onerous tax regulations to inhibit the use of gold and silver as alternative currency. Because any tax-enforcement process must go through the courts, however, it will ultimately collapse on the grounds just stated. Long before that happens, however, any tax problems will be obviated by a political accommodation: namely,

(i) The States will agree to have their people keep two sets of books: one in Federal Reserve Note values, the other in the alternative gold and silver "electronic currency".

(ii) The General Government will agree to create a system of dual tax returns, consisting of a "paper return" for transactions conducted in paper, bank-deposits, and base-metallic coinage; and a "specie return" for transactions conducted in gold and silver. And

(iii) Taxpayers will then pay their taxes on their paper transactions in paper, and on their specie transactions in specie.

"The General Government will accept this arrangement, because, if it refuses, it will find itself bereft of any real tax revenues when the Federal Reserve System collapses. Only by cooperating with the States in the adoption and use of an alternative currency of gold and silver will the General Government financially survive. (And, of course, if it does not survive financially it will not survive politically, either.)

"In sum, the plan for adopting an alternative 'electronic currency' is workable constitutionally, technically, and politically. That being so, as America approaches the point at which '[t]wo roads diverge[ ] in a yellow wood', the moment of her greatest opportunity arrives.

"But so, too, approaches the moment of her greatest danger. The plan of the Powers That Be is, by hook or by crook, to maintain the terminally ill Federal Reserve System on life-support until a new 'global currency' can be introduced. So any proposal for returning Federal Reserve Notes to apparent redeemability in gold could play right into their hands.

"As turmoil in the markets and in the streets intensifies, the Powers That Be may very well agree with reformers that something must be done to stabilize the monetary and banking systems. They could very well offer what appears to be a compromise, in the form of a new internationally controlled currency, to be stabilized with some kind of gold 'backing'. After all their years of effort, heretofore rewarded only by failure, reformers will be desperate for something than can be labeled 'success'—and might therefore accept such a proposal, imagining that they have finally won the battle for sound money. In fact, they will have been led, as little children, down the wrong road once again.

"For, when the new 'global' financial institutions and currency are firmly in place, with sufficient supra-national political and economic authority, the Powers That Be will remove any gold 'backing' from the 'global currency', just as they did with Federal Reserve Notes. Once again, 1933 will follow 1932, and with a vengeance.

"The plan for a State alternative 'electronic currency' promises the best, if not the only, means by America can avoid this pitfall. An alternative 'electronic currency' can be set up in each State throughout the United States without any involvement of, let alone support for, the Federal Reserve System. And an alternative 'electronic currency' cannot possibly be diverted or converted into a scheme for a 'global currency'—unless the Powers That Be agree to adopt fixed weights of gold and silver as the only 'global' monetary units, and to treat everything else, not as money, but only as mere debt. Which, one can be assured, they will never voluntarily do.

"So, in the endeavor to secure sound money, we must remain unequivocal, uncompromising, adamantine—'extreme' in the manner that truth and justice are always and necessarily 'extreme':

- We must demand real money, not a bastard currency consisting of debt.

- We must demand scientific money, the composition of which can be verified or falsified anywhere in the world according to the selfsame standards—not political money, the composition of which depends upon the whims of politicians, bankers, and speculators whom the average American would not trust to take his automobile to Jiffy Lube for an oil change.

- We must demand economically sound money, consisting of fixed weights of gold and silver, the quantity of which the free market determines through "free coinage"—not paper chits only "redeemable in" or "backed by" gold or silver. As soon as we hear the words "currency redeemable in gold" or "currency backed by gold" we should recognize that we are exposing ourselves, if not to fraud, then certainly to the fallibility and faithlessness of politicians, bankers, and speculators. And therefore,

- We must demand constitutional money. Even if redeemable in gold, the Federal Reserve Note is not constitutional money. It is not a "dollar". It is not even "lawful money", because according to the very statute defining it, it is to be "redeemed in lawful money". Self-evidently, the thing to be redeemed and the thing that redeems it cannot be the very same thing.

"Finally, what America faces where these '[t]wo roads diverge[ ]' is not, at base, a monetary problem. It is not even an economic problem. It is a political problem. After all, the free market is a governance mechanism, controlled by the people. Sound money is a governance mechanism, controlled by the people. And the Federal Reserve System is most assuredly a governance mechanism—but one designed to manipulate money and thereby skew the workings of the free market, for the benefit of special-interest groups antagonistic to the people.

"America suffers from the disease of unsound money—and all its increasingly serious sequelae—because all too many among her people have largely abdicated self-government. The alternatives are not, as ultra-libertarians profess to believe, 'government' (presumably bad) and some species of 'liberty' largely divorced from 'government' (presumably good). Within society, sovereignty is never in abeyance. If Americans do not govern themselves, they will not enjoy 'liberty', but surely will be governed by others—and in a manner not at all to their liking.

"The establishment of an alternative currency is the first step down that road 'less traveled by' towards America's recovery of monetary, then economic, then political self-government. Let us not stumble at the turning-point." [End]

Congress has done nothing to cure the cancer. After the 2008 meltdown, your incumbent and mine in Congress wee-wee-d on the U.S. Constitution and stole hundreds of billions of dollars from we the people to unconstitutionally bail out banks and loan a car manufacturer billions of dollars. They panicked.

Several years ago Utah passed a watered down version of a sound money bill and finally, in 2014, our Texas State Legislature finally passed a decent bill signed into law by our governor:

Governor Abbott Signs Legislation to Establish State Bullion Depository, Friday, June 12, 2015, Austin, Texas

"Governor Greg Abbott today signed House Bill 483 (Capriglione, R-Southlake; Kolkhorst, R-Brenham) to establish a state gold bullion depository administered by the Office of the Comptroller. The law will repatriate $1 billion of gold bullion from New York to Texas. The bullion depository will serve as the custodian, guardian and administrator of bullion that may be transferred to or otherwise acquired by the State of Texas. Governor Abbott issued the following statement:

"Today I signed HB 483 to provide a secure facility for the State of Texas, state agencies and Texas citizens to store gold bullion and other precious metals. With the passage of this bill, the Texas Bullion Depository will become the first state-level facility of its kind in the nation, increasing the security and stability of our gold reserves and keeping taxpayer funds from leaving Texas to pay for fees to store gold in facilities outside our state."

Perhaps warning drums by those not on the government's payroll or any special interest group who actually know what they're talking about finally switched on the light bulb:

When The Derivatives Market Crashes (And It Will) U.S. Taxpayers Will Be On the Hook – The Economic Crash, June 16, 2012, with permission from Michael Snyder

"Warren Buffett once said that derivatives are 'financial weapons of mass destruction', and that statement is more true today than it ever has been before. Recently, JP Morgan made national headlines when it announced that it was going to take a 2 billion-dollar loss from derivatives trades gone bad. Well, it turns out that JP Morgan did not tell us the whole truth. As you will see later in this article, most analysts are estimating that the losses will eventually be far larger than 2 billion dollars. But no matter how bad things get for JP Morgan, it will not be allowed to fail. JP Morgan is the largest bank in the United States, so it is essentially the "granddaddy' of the too big to fail banks.

"If JP Morgan gets to the point where it is about to collapse, the U.S. government and the Federal Reserve will rush in to save it. Because of this 'security blanket', banks such as JP Morgan feel free to take outrageous risks. Today, JP Morgan has more exposure to derivatives than anyone else in the world. If they win, they win big. If they lose, U.S. taxpayers will be on the hook. Not only that, but thanks to Dodd-Frank, U.S. taxpayers are on the hook for bailing out the major derivatives clearinghouses if there is ever a major derivatives crisis. So when the derivatives market crashes (and it will) you and I will be left holding a gigantic bill.

"Derivatives almost caused the complete collapse of insurance giant AIG back in 2008. But instead of learning our lessons, the derivatives bubble has gotten even larger since that time. A Bloomberg article that was published last year contained a great quote from Mark Mobius about derivatives: 'Mark Mobius, executive chairman of Templeton Asset Management's emerging markets group, said another financial crisis is inevitable because the causes of the previous one haven't been resolved.

"There is definitely going to be another financial crisis around the corner because we haven't solved any of the things that caused the previous crisis," Mobius said at the Foreign Correspondents' Club of Japan in Tokyo today in response to a question about price swings. "Are the derivatives regulated? No. Are you still getting growth in derivatives? Yes." Never in the history of the world have we ever seen anything like this derivatives bubble...

"So what will happen if JP Morgan loses too much money? Well, it will beg the U.S. government and the Federal Reserve for money and the U.S. government and the Federal Reserve will comply. There is no way that they are going to let the largest bank in America fail.

"In addition, as I mentioned earlier, Dodd-Frank has put U.S. taxpayers on the hook for future bailouts of derivatives clearinghouses. This was detailed in a recent *Wall Street Journal* article:

"Little noticed is that on Tuesday Team Obama took its first formal steps toward putting taxpayers behind Wall Street derivatives trading — not behind banks that might make mistakes in derivatives markets, but behind the trading itself. Yes, the same crew that rails against the dangers of derivatives is quietly positioning these financial instruments directly above the taxpayer safety net.

"One of the things that Dodd-Frank does is that it gives the Federal Reserve the power to provide 'discount and borrowing privileges' to derivatives clearinghouses in the event of a major derivatives crisis. This is what our politicians love to do. They love to have the U.S. taxpayer guarantee everything. Our politicians look at us as one giant insurance policy. Apparently they believe that if anything in the financial world goes wrong that U.S. taxpayers should be the ones to clean up the mess. But will we really have enough money to bail everyone out when the derivatives market crashes?

"Today, the 9 largest banks in the United States have a total of more than 200 trillion dollars of exposure to derivatives." [End]

Dr. Vieira asks this very important question in his writings: "If the Federal Reserve System collapses in hyperinflation in the near future, exactly what will the State and her citizens then use as their currency?"

The day is coming when legislatures across this county (except Texas) will not be able to carry out normal governmental functions as the unstable currency we are forced to use careens over the cliff. It is the obligation and duty of your state legislature to make this an immediate and top priority. It can't wait until tomorrow.

The current situation we find ourselves in isn't a Hollywood fantasy production, but real life because more and more individuals are coming to realize what so many of us have been writing about for decades: The dollar isn't just in trouble, so is the 'Fed'.

The people's purse as I write this is over $19 TRILLION dollars in debt. So, what do the geniuses in Congress do? **They keep borrowing debt to spend debt.** Americans had better prepare themselves so they aren't blinded as they were in 2008. It's a tragedy Thomas Jefferson's words of wisdom are so foreign to the lunatics in Congress:

"Then I say, the earth belongs to each of these generations during its course, fully and in its own right. The second generation receives it clear of the debts and incumbrances of the first, the third of the second, and so on. For if the first could charge it with a debt, then the earth would belong to the dead and not to the living generation. Then, no generation can contract debts greater than may be paid during the course of its own existence." –Thomas Jefferson to James Madison, 1789. ME 7:455

The articles below are written by individuals who know this subject matter inside and out. They are not on the payroll of Congress or banks. **There is no way to stop what's rolling across this country right now.** The blame lies squarely at the feet of your incumbent and mine in the U.S. Congress who have ignored what the whole world can see: financial Armageddon. Simply type the title into a search engine and match the URL to read them.

The U.S. Monetary System and Descent into Fascism: An Interview with Dr. Edwin Vieira, June 24, 2011
https://www.caseyresearch.com/articles/interview-dr-edwin-vieira

The Fed Desperately Tries to Maintain the Status Quo. "The Fed is raising rates!" — This has become a running gag, Ronald-Peter Stöferle | Mises.org – November 4, 2015
https://mises.org/library/fed-desperately-tries-maintain-status-quo

Gerald Celente: Canary in the Global Economic Mineshaft, By Anthony Wile, November 3, 2015, *The Daily Bell* https://www.lewrockwell.com/2015/11/anthony-wile/canary-global-mineshaft/

Financial Disaster Dead Ahead, November 6,2015
http://davidstockmanscontracorner.com/financial-disaster-dead-ahead/

The Fed's 2–Percent Inflation Fairytale – Who made it up, what does it mean? Gerald Celente, November 5, 2015, *The Trends Research Institute*
https://www.lewrockwell.com/2015/11/gerald-celente/feds-2-percent-inflation-fairytale/

EXPOSED: The Terrifying Truth About What We Are Facing in The Future, Ronald-Peter Stoeferle, Incrementum AG Liechtenstein, *King World News*
http://kingworldnews.com/exposed-the-terrifying-truth-about-what-we-are-really-facing-in-the-future/

The World of Currency Manipulation, November 6, 2015, *ETF Daily News*
http://etfdailynews.com/2015/11/06/the-world-of-currency-manipulation/

Andrew Maguire – This Historic Event Is About to Shock the World And The Gold Market, October 30, 2015, *King World News*
http://kingworldnews.com/andrew-maguire-this-historic-event-is-about-to-shock-the-world-and-the-gold-market/

Economists are starting to warn about the risk of a new U.S. recession, October 23, 2015, *MSN*
http://www.msn.com/en-us/money/markets/economists-are-starting-to-warn-about-the-risk-of-a-new-us-recession/ar-BBmmpbU?li=AA4Zjn

The Global Liquidity Squeeze Has Begun, Michael Snyder, April 17, 2015
http://theeconomiccollapseblog.com/archives/the-global-liquidity-squeeze-has-begun

U.S. Government Using Subprime Mortgages to Pump Housing Market Recovery, May 6, 2015, James Quinn
http://www.marketoracle.co.uk/Article50545.html

A Cross of Gold, May 10, 2011, Dr. Edwin Vieira, *Newswithviews.com*
http://www.newswithviews.com/Vieira/edwin233.htm

ALL funding for Fannie & Freddie are unconstitutional. Nowhere in the U.S. Constitution does Congress have the authority to act as a bank or make loans, period:

Bailout is Back: Fannie and Freddie Likely Need "Additional Treasury Investment" After Derivatives Losses
http://investmentresearchdynamics.com/fannie-and-freddie-are-headed-for-another-bailout/

2

Federal income tax: Where does your money really go?

"We're confiscating property now...That's socialism. It's written into the Communist Manifesto. Maybe we ought to see that every person who gets a tax return receives a copy of the Communist Manifesto with it so he can see what's happening to him." T. Coleman Andrews, May 25, 1956, U.S. News & World Report, Commissioner of the IRS for 33 months under the Eisenhower Administration before he resigned.

Not where you think it goes.

Vivien Kellems was a woman before her time who knew the grand theft taking place against the working man's paycheck. [For more information on the remarkable Vivien Kellems, see: http://www.vivienkellems.org/]. The following excerpt from her book, *Toil, Taxes and Trouble*, published in 1952 and was constitutionally on point:

"Since a capitation means a tax of the same amount for every person, this provision makes doubly sure that all federal taxes must be at the same uniform rate for everybody. This limitation that direct taxes be levied by the Federal Government must be in proportion to a census and apportioned among the States in accordance with numbers, is the only provision in the Constitution that is stated twice.

"The only reason that our Constitution required a census to be taken every ten years was to count the people to determine how many Representatives should go to Congress, and how direct taxes should be levied. I wonder how many Americans thought of this in 1950 when those little busybodies came knocking on their doors, asking ten thousand impudent, silly questions which were none of their, or Washington's, business.

"There is absolutely no power granted in the Constitution which enables a top-heavy bureaucracy of empty-headed simpletons, and worse, to invade the privacy of the American people in such a monstrous manner.

"The census was to count the people – that was all. The number of people determined the number of Representatives in Congress and the apportionment of direct taxes among the states.

"For a long time I asked myself, 'Why were Representatives and direct taxes linked together and apportioned among the States in accordance with population?' It was understandable that Representatives should be chosen in accordance with numbers but why should taxes be apportioned the same way? And then one day, out of the blue, it came to me crystal clear. All at once I understood the plan to safeguard the future freedom of the nation, conceived and executed by those scholarly men.

"I read again: 'Representatives and direct taxes shall be included within this Union, according to their respective numbers...' 'No capitation, or other direct tax shall be laid, unless in proportion to the Census of Enumeration herein before directed to be taken.' And in those two sentences our forefathers bound fast the hands of Congress and secured the liberty and freedom of the American people. How? By making it utterly impossible to levy an income tax.

"An income tax is certainly a direct tax, probably the most direct tax of all since it cannot be shifted but must be paid by the person receiving the income. By specifying that direct taxes must be levied in accordance with the number of people, not upon what they produced, as in the days of ancient Egypt, an income tax was simply out of the question. It cannot be levied upon a man but must be levied upon what he receives...

"But his power to levy direct taxes was limited by an ironbound restriction: that tax must be apportioned among the States in accordance with the population. Since all taxes were to be at a uniform rate, Congress simply could not penalize one section of the country, or one group of citizens for the unfair advantage of another.

"When Congress levied a tax, everybody had to pay and at the same rate. The amount would vary with the wealth of an area, as it does today with the different values of real estate, but the rate was the same for all and the tax was distributed among the States according to population.

"The men who wrote our Constitution did not found a democracy. They feared the so-called 'Democrats' of their day as much as we fear the Communists today. They did not believe in mob rule, or government by the unintelligent, irresponsible mass. They founded a republic and they made certain that the right to vote should be curbed and controlled by the necessity of paying taxes. Scheming politicians could not take taxes from a helpless minority and buy themselves back into office with the votes of the tax exempt majority. When a Representative voted a tax, he voted to tax everybody because the tax was based upon numbers, not upon dollars.

"This was the most brilliant plan ever conceived for guaranteeing the freedom of a nation. It protected every person in his right to private property, rich and poor alike, and under this protection we built the richest, most powerful nation on earth. We achieved and maintained for the majority of our people a standard of living undreamed of before, the hope and the envy of the whole world.

"And we accomplished something even more important: we developed a vigorous, self-reliant, self-respecting race of people. An American citizen would have been ashamed to ask for a handout from his Government. The Government belonged to him, he did not belong to the government.

"And then what happened? We chucked our carefully safeguarded right to own something out the window, and we passed the income tax amendment. Gone was our apportionment among the States in accordance with population, and also gone was our principle of uniformity. Income 'from whatever source derived, without apportionment among the several States, and without regard to any census or enumeration' could be taxed and without limit. And when we passed this income tax amendment the slow, distilled poison of tax slavery dripped into our veins. We sowed the seeds of our national decay which is rapidly coming to maturity before our eyes today. The heritage of freedom so carefully insured for us by our forefathers is gone; it has been taxed away." (End of excerpt from her book.)

We know the Sixteenth Amendment to the U.S. Constitution was not properly ratified but the courts don't care because federal judges and prosecutors won't bite the hands that feed them. There can be no doubt the so-called federal "income" tax via the Sixteenth non-ratified Amendment was cooked up to feed the unconstitutional 'Federal' Reserve covered in the previous chapter.

Those of us who have spent a considerable chunk of time actually reading the Internal Revenue Code fully understand domestic Americans are *not* subject to the income tax.

The majority of Americans refuse to believe what is in black and white because they are terrified of the Gestapo, the IRS, as well they should be which is exactly what the shadow government wants. Many cannot process how they've been lied to either in correspondence from their congress critter or outright lies by the IRS wrapped up in code legalese. The betrayal is just too much. Americans are too terrified to stand up for their rights and quite frankly, if you do, the massive power of the federal government's corrupt judicial system will come down on you like a ton of bricks.

It may surprise some people, but there are hundreds of thousands of people who do not want the IRS abolished. These multitudes of people need the income tax to stay in place. They don't care if it's a flat tax, a sales tax or a progressive direct tax such as we are being forced with a gun to our heads to voluntarily pay. Who could that be, you wonder?

Tax preparation companies by thousands. How about all the CPAs and lawyers in this country whose paychecks depend on the income tax system? There are thousands of others down the food chain who supply goods and services to all these companies to support their offices and employees from medical insurance to plumbers. Not to mention about 100,000 or so IRS employees from janitors to lawyers.

The income tax has also spawned a cottage industry rife with charlatans, cons and quick-fix "un- taxing" and "de-taxing" programs that do nothing more than sell future indictments to desperate Americans seeking any kind of relief from this tyrannical tax. Those bloodsuckers are just as insidious as the IRS tax collectors. They prey on defenseless, vulnerable, desperate folks who know the government is lying, but can find no judicial or legislative remedy. These people need to be put out of business, the same as the IRS.

I think you'll find these of interest:

United States Congressman Asa Hutchinson (R), February 8, 2000, during a debate on the marriage tax penalty – another insidious, un-American "tax."

[Page: H226] GPO's PDF

(Mr. HUTCHINSON asked and was given permission to address the House for 1 minute and to revise and extend his remarks.)

Mr. HUTCHINSON. "Mr. Speaker, I think my colleagues on both sides of the aisle would agree that we may never have a perfect tax code, but it should at least be fair. That is the essence of any **voluntary** tax system."

Harry T. Manama, National Director, Collection Field Operations, IRS, September 24, 1998: "The Service also has the authority to prepare a tax return (6) should a taxpayer neglect or refuse to **voluntarily** (7) file a correct return."

Harry T. Manama, National Director, Collection Field Operations, IRS, October 27, 1998: "Our system of taxation is dependent on taxpayer's **belief** (1) that the laws they follow apply to everyone and that the IRS will respect and protect their rights under the law."

Report by the Comptroller General of the United States, GGD-81-83, July 8, 1981, Illegal Tax Protesters Threaten Tax System: "Since they represent a threat to our Nation's **voluntary** tax system..."

General Accounting Office [GAO], GAO/T-GGD-97-35, Testimony Before the National Commission on Restructuring the IRS, January 9, 1997, Statement of Lynda D. Willis, Director, Tax Policy and Administration Issues, General Gov't Division, page one: "...between income taxes owed and those **voluntarily** paid. The IRS has estimated that taxpayers do not **voluntarily** pay more than...First, IRS" data suggest that U.S. taxpayers **voluntarily** pay about ...."

Washington Times, January 8, 1996: "IRS Commissioner Margaret Milner Richardson warned yesterday that continued bashing of her agency may undermine Americans' willingness to pay taxes

voluntarily. 'Ultimately I worry it may have some impact on our self-assessment system.'"

IRS 1040 Handbook, 1992, page 3, statement by Commissar Shirley D. Peterson: "You are among the millions of Americans who comply with the tax law **voluntarily**."

USA Today, March 5, 1997. Interview with Senator Bob Kerrey (D-NEB): "It's (the IRS) a **voluntary** system."

How about a judge's definition of voluntary? "My personal opinion is that you are a disgrace and an affront to every working man and woman in this state who **voluntarily** file and pay their taxes." Judge Dennis Montabon, September 1994 while sentencing a dentist to nine months in jail for not volunteering to file a tax return.

Denver Post, April 13, 1997: "The chief losers (the working man and woman) who pay their taxes **voluntarily**."

And, my favorites:

1964 Annual Report, Commissioner of Internal Revenue, Mission of the Service (https://www.irs.gov/pub/irs-soi/64dbcomplete.pdf)

"The mission of the Service is to encourage and achieve the highest possible degree of **voluntary** compliance with the tax laws and regulations and to maintain the highest degree of public confidence in the integrity and efficiency of the Service."

"To preserve and strengthen the American self-assessment system and promote the **voluntary** compliance basic to such a system, the Service expends a substantial portion of its resources on **enforcement** activities."

I guess their system of voluntary requires enforcement!

Do you voluntarily file a federal income tax return? I didn't think so. If you don't volunteer the Gestapo will place liens on everything you own, garnish your wages and sometimes ruin your life with criminal prosecution. All because you didn't volunteer to forfeit your Fifth Amendment rights by signing a federal "income" tax return and voluntarily give up a percentage of your labors to feed the privately owned, unconstitutional "Federal" Reserve.

In February 2007, former Congressman Ron Paul proposed an amendment to the U.S. Constitution to abolish personal income, estate and gift taxes. It would have repealed an amendment that was never ratified, the Sixteenth, because Congress will never admit that amendment never became law. He tried again with similar legislation in 1999-2000 and 2001. There was no support in the U.S. House for we the people, the truth or the U.S. Constitution.

But, none of this seems to matter to the nearly 100 million Americans who continue to *reelect the same liars for hire to the U.S. Congress.* As usual during election cycles enthusiastic supporters of incumbents have been out there working to get their Congress critter reelected. *The same miscreants who steal from us, lie to us and cheat us out of our pursuit of life, liberty and happiness.* The same incumbents who have and continue to lie to those enthusiastic supporters about the nature of the "income" tax. Why? Because "it's the other party".

Tommy Cryer was my attorney in the fight out here in Texas to get "smart" meters banned. In 2006, Tommy Cryer was indicted by the U.S. Department of (In)Justice for two counts of tax evasion. In July of 2007, the IRS reduced the charges to willful failure to file income tax returns. He went to trial and was unanimously acquitted by the jury.

BUT, in no federal court room in this country is a defendant allowed to bring irrefutable facts about the nature of the "income" tax to a jury and who it applies to in trying to defend themselves. A defendant can use the defense they sincerely believed they were not liable. Most go to prison. Tommy got a jury who saw through the government's lies.

I *do not recommend* anyone do what Tommy did because the federal judiciary and the U.S. prosecutors are joined at the hip. The collusion is beyond reprehensible, kissed and blessed by YOUR incumbent in the Outlaw Congress. At some point, as with prohibition, something will give or the financial collapse comes first; it's underway, no one should make any mistake about that.

Challenging fraud and wrong doing by governments, state or federal, is our duty and responsibility. As a self-governing people, only we can hold them in check.

Tommy's noble fight led him to write a 90-page document titled, *The Memorandum*. As someone who has spent over two decades on this and other critical issues, **that document is by far and away the single most important one ever presented on who is and who is not liable for the 'income' tax.** If you take the time to read Tommy's legal analysis, you won't feel fear. Likely you will feel rage.

This issue is NOT about 'paying your fair' share on April 15th. This is a legal issue that involves more lies by 'our' government. I can only challenge you to read The Memorandum (http://www.truth-attack.com/jml/index.php/about-us/meet-tom-cryer). You will then understand how we the people have been lied to and defrauded our entire adult lives.

This weekend you might want to watch a video. It is an interview with Joseph Banister. For those not familiar with Joe, he was a special agent with the IRS in their CID (Criminal Investigation Division) making $80,000 a year. An up and coming star who carried a gun to work every day in pursuit of tax cheats. One day something happened that changed his life forever. Joseph is the highest ranking IRS employee ever to step forward and tell the truth about the nature of the income tax.

Joe's research and subsequent actions by his supervisors eventually caused him to resign from the IRS and a secure future with a handsome paycheck. He was also indicted by the U.S. Department of [In]Justice and went on trial in a federal court room in Sacramento. I attended his trial and literally couldn't stand the drama knowing his freedom could be taken away over a lie. Thankfully, like Tommy, the jury unanimously acquitted Joe on all charges. You can watch him tell his story here. (http://www.infowars.com/irs-insider-joe-banister-exposes-federal-reserve-coup-and-irs-fraud/)

Tommy Cryer isn't the only person to be politically persecuted for exposing the truth about the IRS. I mentioned Joe Banister who was acquitted. Sherry Jackson also worked for the IRS. Like so many others, Sherry did the research and began exposing the big lie. The

Feds went after her for not filing a tax return. She was convicted and sent to prison for four consecutive 12 month terms. Vernice Kuglin, a tiny, petite woman who was a Fed-Ex pilot was indicted and charged with tax evasion. Vernie was acquitted by a jury.

One person is acquitted, another convicted on the same charges. **Jury of your peers is not accurate when it comes to the subject of income taxes.** Look at the person in front of you at the grocery store and imagine he or she sitting on a jury deciding your freedom when it comes to an issue like this where **federal judges and U.S. prosecutors are in collusion with each other.** Hard evidence is not allowed for your defense and that is a fact.

Bill Benson was a former revenue collector for the State of Illinois. Bill was commissioned to find out if the Sixteenth Amendment to the U.S. Constitution was properly ratified. He spent a year going through old dusty books in the bowels of state capitol archives and 17,000 pages later discovered the so-called income tax amendment was not properly ratified. Bill wrote a two volume book, *The Law That Never Was*. He also stopped filing tax returns.

The feds went after him with a vengeance. He was charged and convicted of tax evasion and willful failure to file a tax return. The courts called all those *court certified documents* from state archives a theory! That is true. Bill went to prison which damn near killed him. The Feds were successful in censoring a book they described as nothing but lies because the courts have decided people like Bill were just tax protesters filing frivolous lawsuits. This is from Bill's web site:

"On January 10, 2008, the Federal District Court in Chicago issued a permanent injunction against Bill Benson on the grounds that by offering information demonstrating that the 16th Amendment was not legally ratified, he was promoting an abusive tax shelter. The Court then refused to look at the government-certified documentary evidence, deciding instead that the facts necessary to prove his statements true were 'irrelevant.' What has America come to when the government we created to protect our rights can accuse us of lying and then prohibit us from presenting a defense in a court of law?" Bill Benson has sacrificed so much to give you the truth – something your congressional incumbent and mine as well as the media don't want you to know.

Irwin Schiff was one of the pioneers in exposing the truth regarding violation of your Fifth Amendment rights and application of the federal "income" tax. He wrote books about it. He gave speeches. Like Bill, Joe, Sherry, Vernie and attorneys like Larry Becraft and others. Irwin sold more than 250,000 copies of his books, *How Anyone Can Stop Paying Income Taxes*, *The Great Income Tax Hoax*, *The Federal Mafia: How the Federal Government Illegally Imposes and Unlawfully Collects Federal Income Taxes* and three others. I had the pleasure of meeting Irwin. A warm, funny man who simply wanted Americans to know the truth.

Irwin Schiff died on October 17, 2015 in a federal prison. This was his third prison term for fighting the corrupt Department of (In)Justice who defend the corrupt IRS. Irwin was dying of lung cancer. His family desperately tried to get him a compassionate release so he could die at home with his family. It was denied. An 87-year old man dies alone chained to a bed in a federal prison for telling the truth.

In April 2015, convicted murderer, Randy Weeks, age 55, dying of cancer was given compassionate release to die at the Marin County Hospital in California with his family. A murderer gets compassionate release while a truth teller dies alone chained to a bed.

This is YOUR government at work in YOUR name. Are all these educated people and so many others simply conspiracy nuts and tax cheats? Didn't they have anything else to do in life except sacrifice their time, energy and bank accounts to pay lawyers with some going to prison? *Think about it.* As for me, I have nothing but respect and admiration for all of them for standing up for the truth against a corrupt machine – the U.S. Congress who condones such tyranny – both parties.

Think about this: Probably a dozen years ago my name suddenly appeared on the ADL's (Anti-Defamation League) web site on a page with skin heads and white supremacists. While I had pretty thick skin by then my feelings were very hurt. One of my best friends for over sixteen years, the late Harvey Gordin, was Jewish. He was outraged when I told him. Imagine if my name was put into a search engine and up pops my name with despicable skin heads. Why was I placed on that page? Because of my work exposing the "Federal" Reserve and the fraudulent application of the federal income tax. That's the description attached to my picture – I opposed both. I wrote Abraham Foxman and ask him to remove my name which they did.

Why would an ordinary American like me be placed on the web site of an organization which claims to fight anti-Semitism just because of my work which has nothing to do with religion or race? I'm not the only one. Joe Banister's name also has appeared on their web site for daring to tell the truth about the IRS. So have other Americans been listed in their "extremists" section on their web site; all of them opposed to what's happening in our country. How does that fall into the mission of the ADL?

Millions of Americans are aware of the IRS scandal where the head of the non-profit tax exempt division, Lois Lerner, targeted tea party groups by either denying them status or holding up their applications for years. In March 2014, Lerner refused to testify in front of Congress. The gutless Republicans let her walk. **Regardless of whether or not you support or do not support tea party folks it should bother all Americans that an agency with such power was used to target your fellow country men and women wanting to make their voices heard under the First Amendment.**

Exactly the opposite came from Democrats who cheered the effort to stop Tea Party chapters from receiving a tax exempt status. Lerner simply retired. *CNS News* reported the "National Taxpayers Union calculations show that Lerner could qualify for a starting pension at the annual equivalent of as much as $102,600, and up to $3.96 million over her lifetime." YOU will be paying her retirement pension until she dies. Lying and deceit pays big if you have the right connections and know where the bodies are buried.

Don't Americans remember former president, Richard Nixon, was the target of impeachment? On July 27, 1974, Articles of Impeachment were adopted by the U.S. House Judiciary Committee. Under Art. 2, Sec. 1 of the Articles:

"He has, acting personally and through his subordinates and agents, endeavored to obtain from the Internal Revenue Service, in violation of the constitutional rights of citizens, confidential information contained in income tax returns for purposed not authorized by law, and to cause, in violation of the constitutional rights of citizens, income tax audits or **other income tax investigations to be initiated or conducted in a discriminatory manner.**" On August 8, 1974, *pressured by his own party* (Republicans), Nixon resigned.

Lois Lerner didn't just do what she did on her own. It had to come from someone higher up. *Make no mistake about that.* Of that there can be no question unless a person is so blinded by party loyalty they refuse to live in the real world of just how dirty politics is and getting worse. Lerner should have been indicted but was allowed to walk by gutless Republicans.

For more than a decade there's been a push to get rid of the income tax in its current form and replace it with more poison known as a "fair" tax or a "flat" tax. In order to fully understand the truth about these fake "solutions" (fair tax, flat tax), **you have to do the research**.

Those taxing schemes are nothing new, but there is big money behind getting some form of alternative taxing. If Congress wanted to get rid of the income tax, they could have done it decades ago. The Republicans had control of Congress from January 1995 – December 2006. All they did was continue spending us into unpayable debt. The Republicans again have control of the House and Senate and have done nothing except continue to spend on unconstitutional waste. And, yes, the debt is unpayable.

Please take the time to read these excellent analyses on the phony "fair" and "flat" taxing schemes so you fully understand they are just another trap:

There is No Such Thing as a Fair Tax, December 12, 2005

"So, instead of calling for the elimination of the various federal programs that feed off tax dollars, Boortz wants to merely change the way they are funded....This means that the Fair Tax idea should have been discarded at the very beginning, for instead of saying that it was not fair that the government confiscate 10, 20, 30, or 40 percent of a man's income, the Fair Tax proponents did not even begin to tackle the root of the problem: the welfare/warfare state that drives the federal leviathan's insatiable lust for the taxpayer's money." [1]

Once Americans began to understand the ludicrous hype in Boortz's argument, out came another book to "clarify" the lies:

There is Still No Such Thing as a Fair Tax

"Boortz is right. There are some eye-opening new insights unique to this sequel. Like the disclosure that you might 'owe more in taxes in the first year of a Fair Tax system than you do today.'" Or the admission that "the Fair Tax could be even more progressive than our current system." Or the confession that the "implementation of the Fair Tax doesn't mean complete annihilation of the IRS." Or the proposal that "a procedure should be set up in the Treasury Department to collect taxes on Internet and catalog sales, remitting the state and local governments' share to them." [2]

Fair tax is a trap: Demand NO vote on H.R. 25, August 9, 2010, My column

"Here is the text of H.R. 25 and SHAME on Republicans like the nitwit who 'represents' me, Randy Neugebauer, Ted Poe, Darrell Issa and others for supporting such a dangerous bill that will only continue to support massive government spending while picking our pockets because we all have to buy things like food: 'The Fair Tax Plan is currently pending in Congress under the name of 'The Fair Tax Act of 2005.' It is a consumption tax in the form of a national sales tax of 23 percent on new goods and services. Although it would 'not be imposed on used or previously owned items,' it would apply to all new goods and services: medical procedures, haircuts, new cars, new homes, gasoline, food, medicine, Internet purchases, and electricity.'"

"It is now the Fair Tax Act of 2009. 145 pages of mumbo jumbo cow-patties. I read all of it.

"Now, Neal, Reagan and Newton, you want to slap a 23% mandatory tax on the food we eat. Just what the Founding Fathers had in mind! Americans can't afford health care services as it is and those caring boys with their very healthy incomes want to slap a 23% tax on a family struggling to make ends meet or seniors living on a fixed income who need medicine. America: Soundly reject this lunacy. A return to a limited form of constitutional government is the only real solution.

"Boortz, Reagan and Gingrich are pumping this bill big time. Please call your Congress critter or get to a town hall meeting tell them to vote NO on H.R. 25. It is not the solution." [3] Thankfully the bill died.

The Flat Tax Is Not Flat and the Fair Tax Is Not Fair, April 3, 2009

"The Flat Tax is an income tax. It is the tax-reform idea that has been around the longest. First proposed by economist Milton Friedman in 1962, the flat tax entered the mainstream through a 1981 Wall Street Journal article by Hoover Institution economists Robert Hall and Alvin Rabushka called 'A Proposal to Simplify Our Tax System.' This article grew into a 1985 book published by the Hoover Institution Press called *The Flat Tax*. A second edition was published in 1995, and an 'updated revised edition' in 2007 that can hardly be called either.

"Aside from this book, the Flat Tax gained national prominence when House Majority Leader Dick Armey (R-TX) pushed the idea of a Flat Tax after the Republicans gained control of Congress during the Clinton administration. A few bills based on the Hall-Rabushka plan were then introduced in Congress, but came to nothing. Other incarnations of the Flat Tax were pushed by both Democrats and Republicans. Another incarnation of the Flat Tax is that of former Republican presidential candidate Steve Forbes. His 2005 book is called Flat Tax Revolution.

"Under a Flat Tax, everyone's income is taxed at the same rate (Forbes says 17 percent; Hall and Rabushka say 19 percent). And not only are there no tax brackets, there are generally no tax deductions other than personal and dependent allowances. Social Security and Medicare taxes would remain as they are now. The appeal of the Flat Tax is simplicity. You can do your taxes on a postcard-sized form says Forbes. Goodbye compliance costs. The problem with the Flat Tax is a simple one: The Flat Tax is not flat." [4]

The REAL problem is those taxes still go to the thieves at the "Federal" Reserve. Neither a "fair" nor a "flat" tax solves the problem of siphoning off the wealth of the American people to a privately owned banking cartel. All those "alternative" taxing schemes will do is allow thieves in Congress to continue like outlaw bandits of the old west borrowing more worthless fiat paper to fund their reckless spending – BOTH parties.

And, where does your federal "income" tax dollars go after you're forced to voluntarily file a return and pay?

Ronald Reagan requested information on how to cut down on government waste although he didn't seem to have a problem signing budgets that included hundreds of billions of dollars in unconstitutional spending. That report is known as the Grace Commission; the formal name is President's Private Sector Survey on Cost Control which was issued on January 12, 1984. Please note the highlighted section on page 12:

"With two-thirds of everyone's personal income tax wasted or not collected, 100% of what is collected is absorbed solely by interest on the federal debt and by Federal Government contributions to transfer payments. In other words, all individual income tax revenues are gone before one nickel is spent on the services which taxpayers expect from their government."

Those individual "income" tax revenues you voluntarily pay are for what is called transfer payments. That would be the exorbitant interest paid to the unconstitutional "Federal" Reserve for basically renting our own money, UN dues and other foreign banking interests like the IMF which was created to fight global financial crises. **That is a fact that should make every American sick to their soul.** The fruits of our labor stolen from us to throw around the world for power and massive wealth. Nowhere in the U.S. Constitution did it ever give the U.S. Congress the authority to steal from us to throw to foreign banking entities or the putrid, communist controlled UN aka United Nothing.

The next question that immediately follows: If not a single function of the federal government is funded by the "income" tax, how does the government pay the bills they rack up in every bloated budget sent to a president? Every penny is borrowed with the interest slapped on our backs, our children and grandchildren and their children. Unpayable debt that is bringing down this country. We borrow from Communist China to give to Pakistan:

US to Give $125 Million to Upgrade Pakistan's Power Sector. October 29, 2009

"Secretary of State Hillary Clinton, seeking to bolster Islamabad's fight against Islamic extremists US corporaterrorists' profits, initiated a crash U.S. assistance program for Pakistan's power sector aimed at rolling back electricity shortages that threaten to cripple the South Asian nation's economy. Mrs. Clinton, on the first of a three-day diplomatic mission to Pakistan, said that Washington will disburse $125 million to Islamabad for the upgrading of key power stations and transmission lines. U.S. experts are also beginning to work with Pakistani utility companies to reduce power outages and lost revenue caused by outmoded technologies and systemic non-payment by customers, which costs Pakistan hundreds of millions of dollars each year." [5]

Sickening theft of your labor completely illegal under our constitution, the supreme law of the land – authorized by BOTH parties in Congress:

U.S. pays for Indonesians' master's degrees – Obama expanding program with $16-$20 million

"Millions of young Americans are being disgorged from our universities every year owing up to hundreds of thousands of dollars with seemingly no hope of paying it all back. Further our government is bankrupt, over spent, in the red. Yet, you should be proud, America, because Barack Obama is paying to give Indonesian kids a Master's Degree!...

"But not for Indonesia. The Obama administration is expanding a program that provides free educations to people in Indonesia looking to become 'professionals.' Obama hopes to create a 'number of Indonesian future leaders holding advanced degrees (Masters) from U.S. and in-country institutions of higher education." [6]

From Sen. Tom Coburn's Wastebook: A Guide to Some of the Most Wasteful and Low Priority Government Spending of 2011:

- Republican and Democratic Party conventions: $17.7 million (each)
- A mango-production program for Pakistani farmers that was abandoned after one year and caused many farmers to default

- on loans taken out in anticipation of increased productivity: $30 million
- A project to convert three Air Force radar stations from diesel to wind energy that has since been abandoned: $14 million
- The construction of an IHOP in the up-and-coming neighborhood of Columbia Heights (which Coburn refers to as "pancakes for yuppies"): $800,000
- A promotional video for an Alaskan bridge that very well might not get built, titled "The Knik Arm Crossing, Bridge to Our Future": $57,390 (out of $15.3 million spent this year on the bridge)
- Pension payments to dead federal employees: $120 million
- A fourth visitors center on the 54-mile Talimena Scenic Drive that runs between Talihina, Oklahoma (Pop. 2,522) to Mena, Arkansas (Pop. 5,637): $529,689
- Funding for video game preservation at the International Center for the History of Electronic Games: $100,000
- Aid to China, the U.S."s biggest lender, for social and environmental programs: $17.8 million – Our mortal enemy and you and I are forced with a gun to our head to give them $17.8 million bux and then turn right around and borrow the money from them with all that interest shoved down our throats. Now, tell me YOUR congress critter isn't insane or thoroughly corrupt
- Seed money for the "drug-themed" Mellow Mushroom Pizza Bakery in Austin: $484,000
- "Celebrity Chef Fruit Promotion Road Show in Indonesia": $100,000
- Funding for Pakistan's Rafi Peer Theatre Workshop to create "130 episodes of an indigenously produced Sesame Street": $10 million Research funding for the American Museum of Magic to "better understand its various audiences and their potential interest in the history of magic entertainment": $147,138
- Research funding for a study to determine if cocaine makes Japanese quail engage in sexually risky behavior: $175,587

The Wastebook for 2014 is enough to make you want to puke:

- $387,000 given by the unconstitutional National Institute of Health to give Swedish style massages to rabbits
- $856,000 paid for a study to get mountain lions on a treadmill. A two year "study" that took eight months for the big cats to climb aboard
- $331,000 grant given so couples could poke voo-doo dolls
- $146 Million in subsidies for sports stadiums
- U.S. Fish & Wildlife spent $10,000 to watch grass grow
- $371,026 spent to find out if mom loves dogs as much as kids
- $307,524 to teach synchronized swimming for sea monkeys
- Feds waste millions trying to convince Afghans to grow soy beans they don't eat: $34 million

That's what you fight commute traffic for while your paycheck shrinks because of more and more federal "income" taxes to pay for the outrageous spending above? And remember: It's all paid for with *borrowed* debt.

$24 BILLION dollars in grossly unconstitutional spending that was supposed to stop if voters gave Republicans the majority in the U.S. House who control the people's purse. Like hell. They did nothing but allow such monstrous waste to go on while playing politics. When the national debt is $19+ TRILLION dollars do you keep spending for all of the above? If your bank account is overdrawn do you keep writing rubber checks? *If you're the U.S. Congress you do because they can keep borrowing from the magical money machine called the 'Fed'.*

Carroll Quigley was a professor of history at Georgetown University. He was Bill Clinton's mentor. Quigley wrote a book titled *Tragedy and Hope* where he comes right out and tells the American people how the political system is rigged to destroy us:

"The argument that the two parties should represent opposed ideals and policies, one, perhaps, of the Right and the other of the Left, is a foolish idea acceptable only to doctrinaire and academic thinkers. Instead, the two parties should be almost identical, so that the American people can 'throw the rascals out' at any election without leading to any profound or extensive shifts in policy. Then it should be possible to replace it, every four years if necessary, by the other party,

which will be none of these things but will still pursue, with new vigor, approximately the same basic policies."

Now you know why nothing ever changes – except for the worse. The majority of Americans have no understanding of all this because the truth is no longer taught in government indoctrination centers they call public schools, only more lies using the finest in Soviet-style propaganda techniques and fed to them on the nightly news.

The national debt and the deficit – what's the difference? These two little bookkeeping items are not the same thing. Few Americans actually know the difference, but the difference is quite important. We continually hear members of Congress, president after president, and political pundits call for "reduction in the debt". But what does that really mean? Here's how it works.

While the federal budget is a complicated mess at best, let's say that for 2016, Congress decides they want $3.7 trillion dollars to fund this bloated pig called our government. We know that 100% of all personal "income" taxes extorted by the IRS goes to the "Federal" Reserve Banking System and does not fund a single function of the government. So, let's take the people's blood and sweat off the table – roughly $2.1 trillion. That means the government would need another $1.6 trillion dollars to pay the bills.

What other revenues does the government collect? Corporate taxes, social security taxes, constitutional revenues such as excise taxes on cigarettes, alcohol, tobacco, firearms, tires, etc., tariffs on trade, military hardware sales, and some minor categories. Let's hypothetically say those revenues come up short of the $1.6 trillion needed to spend on their favorite welfare programs, wars and foreign welfare. That short fall is called a deficit.

The national debt is the borrowed amount run up by YOUR incumbent and mine – most all of it unconstitutional. That short fall is simply borrowed from the magical money machine called the "Fed".

Americans have hocked their children and grand babies' futures by demanding more and more unconstitutional federal spending. Americans have been bred to a welfare dependent mentality. Special interest groups who have no interest in the U.S. Constitution, demand billions of dollars be spent on their pet interests. Those are the people who hate the Tea Party because they want fiscal accountability from Congress.

But I heard the debt is being paid down? What you heard and reality are two separate issues altogether. The politicians must continue to fool the American people lest they catch on to this chicanery. **Every year since 1913, we the people have been fleeced paying interest on our own money to a banking cartel.** As you can see, it doesn't matter which party is in office, there is no surplus; it can only grow exponentially as long as Congress and the President have the central bank at their fingertips fed by the "income" tax.

Hundreds and hundreds of billions of dollars have been unconstitutionally thrown to foreign governments, some days our friends, a week later our enemies. **They are only our friends as long as the U.S. throws your money at their corrupt governments.**

As long as the American people themselves condone continued unconstitutional spending by Congress, the longer they will violate their oath of office and continue to fund unconstitutional expenditures, placing your children and grand babies in a state of unpayable, massive debt.

America became the greatest, debt free nation on earth by a resourceful, independent, self-reliant people. Sadly, today we have a large percentage of our population who can't get through the day without some government agency telling them how, step-by-step, with a redistribution of average, ordinary Americans assets into the hands of the unproductive. A very sad commentary to what made our nation great and prosperous.

A balanced budget is nothing more than good political rhetoric. In reality, it's a pipe dream strictly for public consumption. How can you balance your budget if you have no money to spend and are trillions of dollars in the hole? You can't. It's just another well-crafted illusion to keep the masses pacified.

You can fool some of the people some of the time, but millions of Americans have awakened to this monumental theft and are demanding the only real solution that can be implemented: Abolish the central bank and a return to a constitutional monetary system with no income tax.

Please consider the words of former Congressman Ron Paul: "Strictly speaking, it probably is not necessary for the federal government to tax anyone directly; it could simply print the money it needs. However, that would be too bold a stroke, for it would then be obvious to all what kind of counterfeiting operation the government is running. The present system combining taxation and inflation is akin to watering the milk: too much water and the people catch on."

Is there a solution – a constitutional solution? The answer is yes, but **smaller government is great until it touches money coming into someone's pocket.** With the "Fed" abolished the reckless thieves in the U.S. Congress would not be able to continue spending us into oblivion. No more worthless wars for bankers and unconstitutional cabinets like the Federal Department of Education sucking down $66 BILLION BORROWED dollars last year.

There are so many alphabet soup agencies and grossly unconstitutional cabinets with dozens and dozens of agencies stealing us blind. USAID is one of them. United States Aid for International Development has ZERO constitutional authority to exist. Nowhere in Art. 1, Sec. 8 does it give Congress the authority to lend or outright give the fruits of your labor to any country for any reason. Remember the sickening spending below (a drop in the bucket) as you watch **your** paycheck shrink:

Feds Offer $1.5 Million Grant for Job Creation – in Belize

- USAID Plans to Spend Up to $6 Million to "Empower" Women in Bangladesh
- Another $10.5 Million to Tackle Childhood Obesity
- Federal Gov't to Spend $3M to Fight Climate Change – in the Pacific Islands
- U.S. Gov't Study Pays Mexican Male Prostitutes for Not Getting STDs - $398,213
- Feds revive $16B car loan program after Fisker flop
- USAID paid $15 million out of its "incentive fund" in return for the Afghan Parliament passing a law on violence against women
- Gov't Spending $4.8M to Tell Students to "Get Fruved"

- * $603,412 NIH-Funded Study Examines Patterns of Healthy Aging Among Gay Men
  * $466,642 Federal Study: Why Do Fat Girls Date Less and Risk More?
  * Feds gave $450,000 for defunct women's cricket league in Afghanistan
  * NIH Grant: $435,369 to Study "Culturally Targeted" Ways to Help LGBT Smokers Quit
  * $251,173 Fed Study Uses Social Media to Promote HIV Drug Among Peruvian Transgenders
- Inhofe: Obama Wasted $120 Billion on Global Warming Which Could Buy 1400 F-35s (No, Jimmy, boy, your Republican buddies in the U.S. House didn't pull the purse strings)

A legitimately elected president has ZERO authority to spend a single penny of the people's money. That is the sole domain of the U.S. House of Representatives:

- Obama Spends $967m to Make 10 Solar Energy Jobs
- Obama gives $30 million to La Raza affiliate
- USAID: Obama plan: Temp jobs at $1 million each – in foreign countries
- USAID Wasted $1 Billion Propping Up Afghan Ministries…and That's Just the Tip of the Iceberg
- USDA gave $303,890 in wool loans to couple who "owned no sheep"
- US to Put $300m to End Afghan "War Economy"
- After $200 Million, Afghan Soldiers Still Can't Read
- Feds to spend up to $95,000 to teach Haitian prisoners to make own uniforms
- US Invested $5 Billion in Ukraine "Democratic Institutions"
- State Dept Again Announces $95K Grant to Teach Haitian Inmates How to Sew
- U.S. Spends $2.7M to Study Impact of TV on Area of Vietnam That Lacks Electricity
- EPA Grants $230K to Two Cities in Mexico for Environmental Projects

- Planned Parenthood Got $540.6 Million in Government Grants in FY 2013
- Booze, Pole Dancing, and Luxurious Hotels: Top 10 Examples of Government Waste in 2013
- Americans Spent $7.45B in 3 Years Helping Other Countries Deal with "Climate Change"
- U.S. Will Spend $3.35M to "Improve the Quality of Media Content" – In Armenia
- Feds Spend $356,337 on "Simulation Facility" to Study How People Cross the Road
- Gov't Pays $1,123,463 to Develop Strawberry Harvest-Aiding Robots
- NSF Spends $82,525 to Study Self-Defense by Millipedes
- Dept. of Education Spent $20.3 Million on 10 Equity Centers to Fight the "Isms"
- U.S. Taxpayers to Pay for Spread of Turkish, Qatar Islamism – Millions in borrowed "dollars"
- Fast Food Restaurants Cost Taxpayers Nearly $8 Billion
- $4.5M Fed Study: "Effects of Climate Change on Indoor Air"

We passed the point of no return a long time ago. The solution is to elect constitutionally educated, principled Americans to the U.S. House of Representatives who must make the tough decisions and carry through with them. Tragically for our country, **reelection rates for incumbents in the U.S. House of Representatives runs 92%-96% every single election and people wonder why nothing changes?** Hold on to your seat because the worst is coming at us like a ballistic missile and it's too late to put up a defense shield.

3
Jobs and the Destruction Caused by "Free" Trade

> *"What Congress will have before it is not a conventional trade agreement but the architecture of a new international system...a first step toward a new world order." July 18, 1993, former Secretary of State, Council on Foreign Relations/Trilateralist, Henry Kissinger speaking about NAFTA.*

As you read in Chapter 1, the unconstitutional, privately owned "Federal" Reserve is the head of the beast, which has been draining the lifeblood of this country for over 100 years. "Free" trade treaties are the other tools of tyrants working to destroy this republic, which have caused immeasurable heartache and ruin for millions and millions of Americans.

Many don't remember the war in this country against an "agreement" called NAFTA, the North American Free Trade Agreement. Oh, how we fought against it back in 1993. Those of us who had taken the time to read the 2,200-page tome re-named it No American Factories Taking Applications. We knew NAFTA would gut our most important job sectors: manufacturing, industrial and agriculture. But, with *Newton Gingrich and Rush Limbaugh pushing it at every opportunity*, it didn't matter what we the people wanted. NAFTA was pushed through and massive unemployment began as factories closed faster than one could count. American farmers went out of business in favor of Mexican fruits, vegetables and cheap goods.

Since NAFTA was passed I have not purchased a single piece of fruit or vegetables from Mexico, any South American country or any other products. If I can't find grown or Made in the USA, I simply go without. **Supporting American farmers, ranchers and companies is supporting America.**

NAFTA was going to create jobs and bring cheap to the American consumer. Before NAFTA 97% of all shoes sold in America were made by Americans; today that number is about 4%. ***NAFTA created jobs alright – for foreign workers.***

From toasters to hand tools, clothing to cars, we made our own products. We paid **our** workers good wages. **Our** factories hummed, **our** farmers and ranchers fed **our** people and millions around the world. **Our** industrial sector made the steel, we kept the money and the jobs. America kept her wealth where it should be – in the pocketbooks of her people. Besides, who wants cheap if it's junk and falls apart?

I know a lot of manufacturers did not want to move production out of the U.S. but they simply could not compete with $.17 cents an hour slave labor out of communist China and other countries. Driving across the country to Washington, DC several times after NAFTA was signed into junk law, it was heart breaking to see small to medium towns turned into ghost towns with the only real business being gas stations and maybe a burger joint. Factories closed, families living hand to mouth where before the bread winner might have worked for one company for 30 years or more until retirement with good pay. The American worker simply got slapped in the face by the U.S. Congress and Bill Clinton who signed NAFTA into law.

> *"He, therefore, who is now against domestic manufacture, must be for reducing us either to dependence on that foreign nation, or to be clothed in skins, and to live like wild beasts in dens and caverns. I am not one of these; experience has taught me that manufactures are now as necessary to our independence as to our comfort; and if those who quote me as of a different opinion, will keep pace with me in purchasing nothing foreign where an equivalent of domestic fabric can be obtained, without regard to difference of price, it will not be our fault if we do not soon have a supply at home equal to our demand, and wrest that weapon of distress from the hand which has wielded it." The Letters of Thomas Jefferson: 1743-1826. To Benjamin Austin Monticello, January 9, 1816*

Over the past 21 years since it was signed into law, NAFTA has created a $181 billion trade deficit with Mexico and Canada. Thousands of factories closed. Nearly a million jobs in the textile industry were gone; the bleeding hasn't stopped. Caterpillar and Chrysler who promised to create jobs if NAFTA went through fired U.S. workers and hightailed it to Mexico. What if we had to go to war to protect our own soil, God forbid, how would we manufacture what we need? Do you really want some foreign country to control our food production?

What NAFTA did was fire American workers who then went on unemployment or welfare and had no choice but to buy cheap from sell-outs like Walmart. Americans who supported NAFTA ended up firing themselves. NAFTA essentially created this: You lose your job because of NAFTA. Broke, you buy cheap crap from Mexico **paying those workers for a job that used to belong to you and what do you do**? Why, you vote back in the same incumbent in Congress responsible for millions of Americans losing their jobs!

The **anti-American worker incumbents** in the U.S. Congress who voted for it (John Kasich, Nancy Pelosi, Newton Gingrich, Steny Hoyer, Rob Portman, Bob Goodlatte, Orrin Hatch, Chuck Grassley, "Leaky" Patrick Leahy, Juan McCain and Mitch McConnell to name a few) began the big push for one world government destroying our job bases and precious sovereignty. In 2014, a report was issued giving us the truth [1]: NAFTA cost us millions of good paying jobs, has caused crushing income inequality, ran up the trade deficit and made way for even more destructive "free" trade treaties.

Next came CAFTA which no one paid any attention to; another damnable "free" trade agreement pushed hard by globalist, George Bush, Jr. Companies that became huge industry leaders like Maytag, Dell, IBM, Sara Lee, Hanes and others quickly moved their factories again screwing the very American workers who made them so profitable.

Built into those agreements and treaties were funding provisions in the **hundreds of millions of dollars to retrain American workers who lost their jobs because of those 'free' trade tools of the global elite.** So, you lose your job through no fault of your own. Then Congress unconstitutionally steals from we the people in **borrowed** money to retrain you to find another job even in a field you don't want or have any experience in. **And for that treachery, voters kept voting back the same incumbents who destroyed their lives.**

In the 2013-2014 session of Congress there was a bill to get US out of NAFTA: H.R. 156: "To provide for the withdrawal of the United States from the North American Free Trade Agreement". It died in the House, Ways & Means Committee. Chairman of that committee: globalist and **anti-American worker, Rep. Paul Ryan.** Despite so many of us trying to get the word out to light a fire under the backsides of U.S. House members to get that bill to a vote, it had ZERO sponsors. Had Rush Limbaugh pushed it the way he pushed *for* NAFTA and if cable networks like *FOX* would have showcased it perhaps we might have had a chance. The silence was deafening.

The Republican party elites are owned by the anti-American jobs U.S. Chamber of Commerce and mega corporations who have no allegiance to America or her workers. Democrats attack those same corporations every election cycle. They play their constituency for suckers. Those mega corporations only care about how rich they can become using slave labor in communist countries like China.

Many Democrats have voted for all the "free" trade agreements since 1993. Votes that have killed millions and millions of good paying, long term jobs. The swift and massive destruction caused by NAFTA was absolutely heartbreaking, yet those treaties are ignored by the current crop of presidential candidates with the exception of Donald Trump.

Next came the big granddaddy, the slayer of American jobs and destroyer of OUR sovereignty: GATT/WTO – General Agreement on Tariffs and Trade and the World Trade Organization. A 28,000+ page treaty **only one member of Congress bothered to read before the vote** and said he would not vote for it.

So many of us once again fought like warriors to stop it, but with no help from the media it was very difficult to get the word out; too many Americans had no interest in it at all. No Internet, no email to get the word out. All we had were fax machines, the telephone, some talk radio and over the backyard fence grapevine. This is an excerpt from one of my columns in the *US Observer* newspaper.

Congress refuses to bring home millions of jobs, February **2010,** my column

"Unemployment checks are replacing paychecks. This has done nothing to restore our most important and good paying job sectors. This has done nothing and will do nothing towards putting Americans back to work. Employers will not hire unless there is an increase in their business and 17 MILLION unemployed Americans are only buying diapers, food, gas and other essentials. [Today it's 92 million unemployed.]

"People like me fought tooth and nail against all of those treaties – job killers. The destruction of our most important job sectors, agriculture, manufacturing and industrial have been destroyed by those treaties. The Republicans had 12 years to get us out of those treaties and out of the communist controlled UN...

"They have done NOTHING to get us out of those destructive trade treaties. Instead, they continue to spend more debt, not money, and creating more government jobs from borrowed, worthless paper, that produces nothing but higher taxes to pay for those jobs. What they have done is simply light a bigger bonfire for what's coming very soon and it can't be stopped. The same policies pursued by FDR are being replayed today and the results will be the same – financial Armageddon – just on a grander scale.

"Agriculture, manufacturing and industrial – all crippled and dying a slow death because of destructive trade treaties...How many times have you heard on the boob tube, 'Those are millions of jobs that will never come back.' Why the hell not? I'll tell you why: Because the Outlaw Congress is corrupt and cowardly. Those poltroons are afraid of communist China and will do nothing to get us out of those destructive treaties and bring home millions of jobs for Americans.

"As those millions of jobs left our country for places like Bangladesh, Hong Kong, communist Viet Nam, communist China and India, Americans were forced out of small to medium towns and cities. They were driven to the major metropolitan cities which couldn't handle the massive numbers. As a result of that and the sickening burden of paying the way for illegal aliens, their infrastructures are collapsing. Oh, yes, let us not forget the impact on our economy because MILLIONS of criminals (illegal aliens) are illegally holding jobs that belong to Americans and naturalized Americans who came to our country the legal route. Juan McCain, Obama and Sarah Palin now want to reward some 20 MILLION of those criminals with amnesty.

"Those millions 'displaced' by those toxic treaties began to buy 'cheap' junk from China and other countries. American manufacturers struggled to compete with products coming from China – a communist country that murders their people at will. They monitor a woman's menstrual cycles to force abortions on them if they get pregnant twice. A country that **condones the skinning of dogs and cats alive so the fur can be illegally sold in parkas, doll clothes and sweaters sold in the US.** I'd rather wear rags.

"Back in 1994, a lame duck Congress voted on the hideous 'free' trade treaty, GATT, whereby the United States of America totally and completely abrogated its sovereignty to a foreign body – the WTO. At the time of the vote, Bob Dole said, 'Any way you cut it, we're the big beneficiary.' U.S. Senator Ernest Hollings had just the opposite prediction, '...described the vote as 'the gravest mistake the U.S. has ever made on economic policy.'"

"Hollings" statement turned out to be right; Dole walked from the Senate a multi-millionaire. Our nation has been plundered as a result of GATT and We the People, our businesses, our commerce, and our livelihoods, have been under attack ever since, losing virtually every single challenge made by some foreign country. On September 26, 2002, U.S. Senator Max Baucus said he was deeply troubled by the WTO dispute settlement process: "Things are looking more and more... like a kangaroo court against U.S. trade laws."

"Funny thing about Baucus" stand on trade. He's a "free" trader. On his web site it states, "I've also been a leader in the successful efforts to open Chinese markets to U.S. products and to bring China into the World Trade Organization." Lie down with dogs, get up with fleas. The vote on GATT was 76-24.

"During the hearings on this monster, French financier Sir James Goldsmith testified in front of Earnest Hollings" committee. He demonstrated that GATT would gut the American textile market. The following are some quotes from the *Washington Times*, December 6, 1993. They accurately reflect Sir Goldsmith's statements during the hearings:

"Global free trade will force the poor of the rich countries to subsidize the rich in poor countries. What GATT means is that our national wealth, accumulated over centuries, will be transferred from a developed country like Britain to developing countries like Communist China, now building its first ocean going navy in 500 years. China, with its 1.2 billion people, three Indochinese states with 900 million, the former Soviet republics with some 300 million, and many more can supply skilled labor for a fraction of Western costs. Five dollars in Communist China is the equivalent of a $100 wage in Europe."

"It is quite amazing that GATT is sowing the seeds for global social upheaval and that it is not even the subject of debate in America....If the masses understood the truth about GATT, there would be blood in the streets of many capitals. A healthy national economy has to produce a large part of its own needs. It cannot simply import what it needs and use its labor force to provide services for other countries. We have to rethink from top to bottom why we have elevated global free trade to the status of sacred cow, or moral dogma. It is a fatally flawed concept that will impoverish and destabilize the industrialized world while cruelly ravaging the Third World."

"Sir Goldsmith could see into the future, only it's been far worse than he predicted." (Goldsmith wrote an excellent book, The Trap, available from Amazon and other booksellers.)

Americans Not in Labor Force Exceed 93 Million for First Time; 62.7% Labor Force Participation Matches 37-Year Low, April 3, 2015, (*CNSNews.com*) – "The number of Americans 16 years and older who did not participate in the labor force – meaning they neither had a job nor actively sought one in the last four weeks – rose from 92,898,000 in February to 93,175,000 in March, according to data released today by the Bureau of Labor Statistics."

This must stop: Senate Committee Warned: H-1B Visas Could Eliminate STEM Jobs for Americans, March 18, 2015, *Breitbart*

"Americans are being crowded out of their jobs and being replaced by H-1B workers, witnesses told the Senate Judiciary Committee during a Tuesday hearing. One testimony came from American worker and whistleblower in the Infosys H-1B visa fraud case, Jay Palmer. 'This is all about money. That's all it's about,' Palmer said as he recalled watching skilled Americans being fired because they earn too much. 'You're basically trading jobs away to make a little bit of profit for Southern California Edison,' Palmer explained. He ended up training his own replacement for a job he had been working in for 15 years."

Every year thousands of highly intelligent Americans graduate from colleges and universities in the IT high-tech industry. But, like Palmer said, it's all about money. Neither will Mark Zuckerberg which is why I've never been on Facebook. I do not support those working to destroy my country and that includes the Hollywood industry.

Corporations like Disney and Facebook are importing cheap labor. In that column cited above it also says:

"HP is in the process of laying off 55,000 workers, similar to the model SoCal Edison has employed. In fact, the Southern California Edison case is just one of several that have been plaguing the nation. Several weeks ago, Disney in Florida replaced 500 American workers with H-1B immigrants. Cargill in Minnesota, Harley Davidson in Wisconsin, and Northeast Utilities and Pfizer, both of which are in Connecticut, are also doing the same thing. "I'm an Edison Employee. I'm a Harley Davidson employee. I'm displaced,' Palmer painfully expressed."

Now, tell me **your** incumbent in Congress cares about American workers.

Do you know we had the opportunity to get out of GATT and the WTO in 2000? A God-send. Guess who killed our chance to get out of that destructive treaty? John Boehner and Nancy Pelosi in bed together, again. Thankfully, Johnny Wino Boehner is now gone only to be replaced with another **far more dangerous dirty rat, Rep. Paul Ryan.** This is also grouped in with trade and commerce – more unconstitutional rape of we the people:

U.S. taxpayers expected to upgrade communist Vietnam, November 9, 2014, *WND*

"Following a plan to jointly run a 'Welcome to America' radio program with Socialist Republic of Vietnam officials, the Obama administration now expects U.S. taxpayers to help fund the information technology modernization of the Vietnam State Treasury, or VST. A review of the FY 2015 appropriations bills and committee reports governing the Department of State and related agencies suggests there will be little, if any, opposition from Democrats and Republicans alike....

"Indeed, the Bush administration is responsible for launching USTDA's Vietnam program in 2006. Representative examples of such Bush-era initiatives include a $453,400 grant given that year to Vietnam's State Capital Investment Corporation, which used the funds to identify financial and IT systems needed to manage state-owned assets. The following year the agency awarded a pair of grants worth nearly $800,000 to provide Vietnam with assistance in "meeting the standards of a global e-commerce initiative for the airline industry and in designing a national finance statistics information system." [2]

Not ONE penny of that funding is allowed under OUR constitution. EVERY penny is borrowed with the interest slapped on our backs, our children and grandchildren. More unpayable debt. More than 58,000 American service men lost their lives in Vietnam; 500,000 came home with massive medical problems like becoming an amputee to keep Vietnam from becoming a communist country. Well, they are and now it's time to steal from we the people in violation of the U.S. Constitution to once again give money to communists.

There's another "free" trade agreement that we have desperately been fighting as I write this book: the Trans-Pacific Partnership (TPP). Yet another "free" trade treaty driving a stake through the heart of this country. A secret treaty so horrendous the details have been kept from you and me. But, enough leaks have now been made public for everyone to understand that we are being sold down the river in the worst way again.

TPP Overrides Immigration Protections for U.S. Professionals, Skilled Workers, Says Critic, November 6, 2015, *Brietbart*

"The new Trans-Pacific Partnership trade-deal allows U.S. and foreign companies to hire foreign professionals and technicians to take skilled jobs in the United States, while still only paying them wages typical for their home countries, such as Vietnam and Malaysia, immigration expert Rosemary Jenks told Sirius XM's Breitbart News Daily radio show. 'We have this massive [TPP] contract that we are apparently about to sign — if they have their way in Washington — that says we are going to open our entire service industry to companies and [their] employees from all of these partner countries,' said Jenks, the director of government relations at NumbersUSA."

The Speaker of the U.S. House Rep. Paul Ryan wants to ram the TPP down our throats. Sen. Ted Cruz voted to fast track TTP.

Rand Paul to Obama: "Prioritize" Passage of Trans-Pacific Partnership, November 3, 2014, *The New American* (an outstanding magazine)

"...the Trans-Pacific Partnership (TPP), an unprecedented sovereignty surrender masquerading as a multi-national trade pact...

"Republicans, Democrats, and Americans of all political persuasions need to understand particulars of the TPP that threaten not only the economic vitality of the United States (contrary to the claims of Senator Paul in his speech), but the fundamental principles of elective government, as well. In November 2013, portions of the TPP draft agreement published by WikiLeaks contained sketches of President Obama's plans to surrender American sovereignty to international tribunals...

"Integration is a word that is painful to the ears of constitutionalists and those unwilling to surrender U.S. sovereignty to a committee of globalists who are unelected by the American people and unaccountable to them. Integration is an internationalist tool for subordinating American law to the globalist bureaucracy at the United Nations. Economic and political integration will push the once independent United States of America into yet another collectivist bloc that will facilitate the complete dissolution of our country and our states into no more than subordinate outposts of a one-world government. Equally significant is that 600 industry lobbyists and 'advisors,' as well as unelected trade representatives, are at the table, while representatives from the public at large and businesses other than huge monopolies are conspicuously absent." [3]

The only reason the TPP hasn't been shoved down our throats is because some Democrats and we the people pounding on the Outlaw Congress do not want that treaty because it means even more jobs lost. All of those treaties are part of the insane agenda for one world government. Another integral piece we have fought and beat down, at least for now, is what is referred to as the North American Union. It's no conspiracy theory. It's as real as the sun shines in the sky. The end of borders between the U.S., Canada and Mexico. Unrestricted immigration between the countries. **The end of our precious nation.**

Because there is such opposition to the TPP treaty, the dirty, ugly game of politics are once again being played out. Delay the vote to make sure incumbents get reelected so they can go right back in office and sell us out.

Obama, GOP Leaders, May Delay Free-Trade Debate Until 2016 Lame Duck Session, October 15, 2015, *Breitbart*:

"Top congressional staffers say Congress will delay approval of the unpopular Trans-Pacific Partnership free-trade deal until after Americans vote in the 2016 election, according to Politico. The planned delay until a November or December 'lame duck' session would allow companies and progressive groups their best opportunity to persuade retiring politicians, and the legislators who had just survived an election, to back the controversial deal.

"That year-long delay will also help the GOP establishment reduce the emotional clout of front-running populist 2016 candidates — including Donald Trump and Mike Huckabee, plus far-left Sen. Bernie Sanders (I-VT). All three are campaigning against the free-trade treaty during the primary season."

That's what the despicable Newt Gingrich and Billy Clinton pulled in 1993. They waited for a lame duck session where incumbents wouldn't be held responsible for the destruction of millions of jobs by passing NAFTA. GOP establishment means Paul Ryan, Mitch McConnell and others **who care nothing for American workers or the sovereignty of this country**. Their actions speak louder than political rhetoric.

Because there's been a virtual blackout by the prostitute media and that includes cable 'news' networks and because you deserve the know the truth, in the endnotes section at the back of this book for this chapter I have included what I *know* to be the most accurate facts about the TPP and North American Union. While there are many books on "free" trade, I highly recommend: *America's Protectionist*

Takeoff 1815-1914, The Neglected American School of Political Economy by Michael Hudson:

"The contribution of the American School of Political Economy (1848 to 1914) to America's wildly successful industrial development has disappeared from today's history books. American protectionists and technology theorists of the day were concerned with securing an economic competitive advantage and conversely, with offsetting the soil depletion of 19th century America's plantation export agriculture. They also emphasized the positive effect of rising wage levels and living standards on the productivity that made the American economic takeoff possible.

"The American School's 'Economy of High Wages' doctrine stands in contrast to the ideology of free traders everywhere who accept low wages and existing productivity as permanent and unchanging 'givens,' and who treat higher consumption, health and educational standards merely as deadweight costs. Free trade logic remains the buttress of today's financial austerity policies imposed on debtor economies by the United States, the World Bank, and the International Monetary Fund. By contrast, the lessons of the American School of Political Economy can provide a more realistic and positive role model for other countries to emulate – what the United States itself has done, not what its condescending 'free-trade' diplomats are telling them to do. The lesson is to adopt the protectionist policies of the late 19th and early 20th centuries that made America an economic superpower."

MAKE NO MISTAKE ABOUT IT: All these "free" trade agreements and treaties are part of the bigger picture and that is to bring these united and free States of America into a one world government where America is no longer sovereign and nothing more than a region state. One world religion, one world banking system and our defense will simply be replaced by a body of world Hessians to "keep peace" around the world under the United Nothing (UN). I've spent the last 26 years studying the 'bigger picture'. **Americans had better wake up and soon.**

During his presidency, George Bush, Sr., pushed for a one world government/new world order 162 times. "The world can therefore seize the opportunity [Persian Gulf crisis] to fulfill the **long-held promise of a New World Order** where diverse nations are drawn together in common cause to achieve the universal aspirations of mankind." *George Herbert Walker Bush, September 11, 1990 and September 11, 1991*

Obama to Usher in New World Order at G-20, September 25, 2009, *FOX News*

"But he [Obama] can give due impetus to American foreign policy partly because the reception of him is so extraordinary around the world. I think his task will be to develop an overall strategy for America in this period when really a New World Order can be created. It's a great opportunity." January 5, 2009, Henry Kissinger

"The New World Order will have to be built from the bottom up rather than from the top down...but in the end run around national sovereignty, eroding it piece by piece will accomplish much more than the old fashioned frontal assault." Richard Gardner, Council on Foreign Relations, April 1974, *Foreign Affairs*.

"In Defense of the World Order...US Soldiers would have to kill and die". Arthur Schlesinger, Jr., July/August '95 *Foreign Affairs* – CFR's Flagship Publication

"We shall have world government whether or not we like it. The question is only whether world government will be achieved by consent or conquest." James Paul Warburg, during hearings Senate Resolution 56, revision of the UN Charter

"The U.S. military welcomes additional funds for special units. The Pentagon continues its downsizing in preparation for the New World Order." Former Asst. Secretary of Defense and former Director of the CIA, John Deutch, Dec. 1, 1994, *McNeil/Lehrer News Hour*

"We are on the cutting edge of the New World Order here in Bosnia." U.S. Army Major Bushyread, May 8, 1996, *CBS Evening News* with Dan Rather

"It's a time that we are seeing a new and early 21st century world order being built," Hagel said at an event honoring the 223rd anniversary of Poland's constitution. The remarks recall President George H. W. Bush's 1991 State of the Union address, which heralded the promise of a "new world order" led by American military and moral standing." Secretary of Defense, Chuck Hagel

"When Franklin Roosevelt died during the closing days of WWII, it fell to Truman to end the war and formulate policies for the new world order." *The Smithsonian Treasury: The Presidents* (1991), page 72.

Is this what YOU want? Blood ran like rivers to birth this republic and we're going to throw it all away to blood sucking vultures who lust after money and power?

Can we stop the bleeding of jobs? What you *can* do:

1. We have to keep telling our congress critters they will not survive the 2016 election if they vote for the Trans-Pacific Partnership. I mean big time heat against that treaty. If the TPP becomes a treaty, the ONLY way to counter is to buy Made in America.

2. We demand the US get out of NAFTA, CAFTA, GATT/WTO and any other "free" trade treaties or agreements. If people could just remember back before NAFTA, et al, jobs stayed here in America. Virtually everything in our homes were made in America. We can go back to fair trade and wipe out "free" trade that has done so much destruction to our country. So far, only Donald Trump has brought this issue to the forefront nationwide. He is a shrewd negotiator instead of someone who negotiates to sell us out to foreign labor.

3. If we don't support American farmers, ranchers, manufacturers and all commerce here in this country the coming collapse will be even worse. Since NAFTA I have contributed very little to the economy. If I couldn't find Made in USA (I had to make an exception to purchase a computer), I went without. But, the past few years, more and more companies are manufacturing here and many are coming back to the U.S. because Americans want quality products made by Americans, not junk coming from India or the Philippines.

    As foreign inferior products sit on store shelves and the movement to bring home jobs has grown, *retailers are getting the message.*

    Since NAFTA, when I get to the register of any retailer if they ask did I find what I needed or was looking for, I say no. You don't have what I want Made in America so I'll go on line and shop. And I do. If it's tomatoes or any other vegetable or fruit, shop at your local farmer's market if possible. Keep the money in your local community.

4. I launched my web site (www.devvy.com) on July 4, 1998. About two years later I put up a Made in USA section. Over the years it has grown to thousands of products made here in America by Americans. I have never charged a penny to anyone who wants to list their products on my site in the Made in USA section. I personally shop from it. Here's another example. After about 10 years my Made in USA leather wallet finally bit the dust. I looked around the stores in Midland, Texas; about 40 miles from my small town. Nothing but foreign made. I found Willow Brook Leather off the list on my site and ordered a quality made beautiful leather wallet that was $4.00 less than the ones I saw at Dillard's and that included the shipping.

So many products in that section on my web site from tractors, clothes, jeans, pet urns, toys for the kiddies, adult clothes, candles, boots, aprons, diabetic socks, cutlery – you name it. Retailers contact me after Christmas to say thank you because they do see an increase in business. If we keep supporting companies that manufacture here prices become more competitive and a lot more quality products will get to stores. We buy the products made **here** in America and the gold stays **here** at home. We buy products made in America, **Americans stay employed and new jobs are created.** When people have a job they spend money into the economy. WE – you and I – **can** turn the job market around.

Sometimes when I do radio shows people call in and ask me if I buy anything foreign? Yes, a couple of products not from communist countries. I use Trilogy products in the cosmetics category manufactured in New Zealand. Finding shoes is very difficult so I seldom purchase any and if I do buy, I will **not** buy from a communist country like China. New Balance does make some tennis shoes here in the USA so every 6-7 years I buy from them. I also buy some soap products that are fair trade in commerce and not from communist countries. Otherwise, it's USA or nothing.

5. Join the One Million Jobs Project:

http://www.millionjobsproject.us/

"It's a mathematical fact. If we all buy just 5% more US made products we will create a MILLION new jobs. AND if each person that sees this video shares it with at least two friends it will only take a month for every person in America to see this. Crazy, but true. Seems like if we all knew the solution to unemployment was so simple we'd fix it. So let's spread the news."

Yes, we can and beat those corrupt politicians in Washington who have sold out the American worker and their global masters by supporting American employers and companies that manufacture here at home. A major step in re-building our economy is getting us out of all those treaties. Think about that when you vote this November.

4

The Economy: Another Tragedy Underway

"We've got to ride the global warming issue. Even if the theory of global warming is wrong, we will be doing the right thing in terms of economic policy and environmental policy." – Tim Wirth, former member of Congress, U.S. Under Secretary of State for Global Affairs.

When talking about the economy, just like jobs, one cannot dismiss the massive destruction to our most important job sectors: manufacturing, industrial and agriculture from draconian, agenda-driven regulations that choke the life out of small to medium businesses in this country; the backbone of our economy. There's also public pension funds that have become a huge drain on budgets top to bottom. Type into a search engine: "This Is Going to Be A National Crisis" – One Of The Largest U.S. Pension Funds Set To Cut Retiree Benefits, April 20, 2016, *Zero Hedge*.

Jobs *are* the engine that fuels our economy. We work. We spend.

When Americans have no jobs and live off food stamps or other forms of welfare they have little in the way of disposable income to buy anything other than what they need to survive. That's what's been happening since before the crash in 2008. With 92 MILLION Americans now out of the workforce and companies hoarding cash (which you can hardly blame them since they never know how many new regulations or laws will come out of DC or state capitols that hurt their ability to stay in business) and people like me who don't spend because I know what's coming. The result is what we are seeing now.

Back in 2005, many of us were warning what was coming with the housing market and banks. A crash was brewing. Sadly, too many Americans either weren't paying attention or simply had no interest in what was going on outside their little world.

What's underway right now is far, far worse than we saw in 2008. There's no way to stop it because what should have been done decades ago (abolish the 'Fed' and unconstitutional cabinets bleeding us dry) wasn't done.

Warning sign: Tech companies of All Sizes and Ages Are Starting to Have Layoffs, October 19, 2015, David Stockman.

"The tech industry giants Hewlett-Packard and Microsoft have already slashed thousands of jobs this year. Those companies are old-guard firms scrambling to retrench and restructure aging businesses. Some of the internet companies that have recently cut jobs are also in the troubled category, such as Groupon and Living Social. But layoffs are starting to hit the younger mobile and social apps that are the vanguard of today's tech industry...

"As Business Insider's Jay Yarow wrote, one person who tracks the performance of startups closely, Danielle Morrill of Mattermark, thinks Square is looking to raise money in the public markets because it could not do so at a price it was happy with in the private markets. That sounds a lot like the 'greater fool' theory that led to the 2000 dot-com crash, and it doesn't bode well for the health of the industry." [1]

Right now retail, fast foods and restaurants nationwide are hemorrhaging, cutting back or shutting down.

Staples, Radio Shack, Abercrombie & Fitch, Barnes & Noble, Aeropostale, J.C. Penny, Office Depot merged with rival OfficeMax. Since the merger 15 stores of the two combined have closed. Sears Holdings has dumped Orchard Supplies Hardware Stores, Sears Hometown & Outlet Stores, Land's End – entire business; expected store closures is 500.

Toys 'R' Us, Quiznos, Sbarro, Ruby Tuesday, Red Lobster, Wet Seal, Macy's, The Gap & Gap Kids, Walgreen's, American Eagle Outfitters, Pick 'n Save, Pier One, Chico's, Ann Taylor Loft, Anna's Linens, Bag 'N Save, Baker Shoes, Bath & Body Works, KMart, Fredericks of Hollywood, Bed Bath & Beyond.

Big Lots, Coach, Einstein Bros. Bagels, Family Dollar. F.A.O. Schwartz shocked many by closing its flagship store July 15, 2015.

Golf Galaxy, Goodyear, Gymboree, Hallmark, Izod, Old Navy, Pep Boys, Pizza Hut and Sears to name a few.

Headline: Intel Lays Off 12,000 After Seeking Visas to Import 14,523 Foreign Professionals Since 2010, April 21, 2016 How despicable. A slap in the face for American workers.

Ignore the Media Bullsh*t – Retail Implosion Proves We Are in Recession, October 14, 2015, *TheBurningPlatform.com* (Charts and graphs tell the story: the media is lying to you).

"First off, you need to realize how bad it really is when you consider US automakers are essentially giving away vehicles to anyone who can fog a mirror, as long as they are willing to obligate themselves into never ending debt enslavement. The average amount financed of $27,000 and the average length of loan of 65 months are both record highs. As the automakers get more desperate by the day, 7-year 0% loans are now becoming the norm. Dealer incentives in the thousands proliferate. And subprime auto loans now constitute over 20% of all sales. The pace of subprime auto loans has more than doubled the pace of prime loans since 2010...

"...They needed booming auto sales to provide the appearance of economic recovery. So, while overall consumer expenditures increased by 21% since 2010, auto loan debt grew by an astounding 41%. And this is just the debt side of the equation.

"Over 27% of all vehicle 'sales' are actually leases. Calling a three-year rental a car sale stretches the concept of sale to the limits. Anyone who finances a car over seven years or leases a car, can never escape the chains of monthly payment debt. They will always be underwater, just the way Wall Street likes it. The proof these 'strong' auto sales are just another debt based scheme are the non-existent profits of automakers and stock prices at 2010 levels. If auto sales are so healthy why would GM stock be down 18% since 2013 and Ford stock down 14% in the last year?" [2]

This is another very important economic indicator: It's Official: The Baltic Dry Index Has Crashed to Its Lowest November Level in History, November 6, 2015, *Zero Hedge* (put into a search engine and go look at those charts)

"2015 has been an 'odd' year. Typically, this time of year sees demand picking up amid holiday inventory stacking and measures of global trade such as The Baltic Dry Index rise from mid-summer to Thanksgiving. This year, it has not. In fact, it has plummeted as the world's economic engines slow and reality under the covers of global stock markets suggests a massive deflationary wave (following a massive mal-investment boom). At a level of 631, **this is the lowest cost for Baltic Dry Freight Index for this time of year in history** and within a small drop of an all-time historical low." It's even worse six months down the road.

There are other factors as well – federal and state government regulations shoved down the throats of businesses by unelected bureau-rats. Regulations that not only aren't necessary, they kill growth and *support the agenda to kill capitalism in this country*. One of the most egregious is the **unconstitutional** EPA (Environmental Protection Agency). Every time a constitutionalist even mentions abolishing that *unnecessary* agency, ignorant media gurus and political hacks on the "left" go berserk. They care nothing for the Tenth Amendment, jurisdiction or destruction by that agency.

The Environmental Protection Agency must be abolished because it is destroying the rights of Americans, it's another monumental waste of money and America doesn't need it. Like the unconstitutional federal Department of Education which employs almost 4,500 people and will suck up a colossal $67 billion borrowed dollars for 2016, the EPA with its 18,000 employees, will gobble up $7.76 billion borrowed dollars this year.

Article 1, Section 8 of the U.S. Constitution does not authorize Congress to legislate in the area of the environment, therefore, it is unconstitutional. All 50 states of the Union have their own version of the EPA as authorized under the 10th Amendment. There is no need for a federal agency. The states of the Union can handle their own environmental needs as authorized by their legislatures.

At the Earth Summit in Rio De Janeiro, June 3-14, 1992, the Secretariat for World Order distributed a nonpublic document titled, "The Initiative for Eco-92 Earth's Charter." It reads, in part, under policies that must be implemented as follows:

The Security Council of the U.N. will inform all nations that outmoded notions of national sovereignty will be discarded and that the Security Council has complete legal, military and economic jurisdiction in any region of the world ... The Security Council of the U.N. will take possession of all natural resources, including the watersheds and great forests, to be used and preserved for the good of the Major Nations of the Security Council.

In the late Dixie Lee Ray's outstanding book, "*Environmental Overkill*", one gets a full accounting of what really went on with Al Gore and his loony, dangerous friends at the Rio Summit. On page 10 of her book, it states:

The objective, clearly enunciated by the leaders of the United Nations Conference on Environment and Development (UNCED), is to bring about a change in the present system of independent nations. The future is to be world government, with central planning by the UN. Fear of environmental crises, whether real or not, is expected to lead to compliance. If force is needed, it will be provided by a UN green-helmeted police force, already authorized by the Security Council.

The EPA is the flagship in America to carry out this environmental terrorism against our people. Among the most destructive of its tentacles is the Endangered Species Act. One of the most horrific disasters from that act is what happened in Klamath Falls in 2001, when the government shut off life-giving water to farmers, driving them into bankruptcy over protecting sucker fish. The result was the loss of dozens of farms and more than $300 million dollars in economic damage to the Klamath economy.

In the ensuing years, the EPA has become more destructive than a cat five hurricane. The EPA is front and center in destroying energy sources with their endless, job killing regulations:

Utility giant AEP says it will close five coal plants to comply with EPA regs (June 9, 2011): "Utility giant American Electric Power said Thursday that it will shut down five coal-fired power plants and spend billions of dollars to comply with a series of pending Environmental Protection Agency regulations." Here in Texas where I live, the EPA has brought together unlikely political factions to fight the loons in the EPA.

Dixie Lee Ray's book mentioned above brings us 21 years forward, detailing the massive push in pursuance of those goals headed up by "global warming" pimps like Al Gore.

Let's not forget how the EPA, with the blessing of the Outlaw Congress stealing us blind in taxes – sends the fruits of your labor to foreign countries:

EPA Gives Millions in Foreign Handouts (June 28, 2011 – *Judicial Watch*)

"The Obama cabinet secretary who launched a costly program to make America's minority communities green has sent millions of taxpayer dollars to environmental causes overseas, including China, Russia and India. Ranking members of a congressional energy committee call it 'foreign handouts' amid record deficits, soaring unemployment and a looming debt ceiling in the U.S. The money – $27 million since 2009 – has been issued by the Environmental Protection Agency (EPA), which is headed by Lisa Jackson.

"The cash was issued via 65 foreign grants that don't even include Canada and Mexico, according to a report issued this week by the House Energy and Commerce Committee. Among the enraging foreign handouts are $1.2 million for the United Nations to promote clean fuels, $718,000 to help China comply with two initiatives and $700,000 for Thailand to recover methane gas at pig farms.

"An additional $150,000 went to help the International Criminal Police Organization (INTERPOL) combat fraud in carbon trading and $15,000 to Indonesia's 'Breathe Easy, Jakarta' publicity campaign. This sort of federal spending does not reflect the priorities of the American people, according to a letter that several lawmakers sent Jackson in the report's aftermath." [End of quote from Judicial Watch]

There is NOTHING in Art. 1, Sec. 8 of the U.S. Constitution that allows that rape of our labor by any government agency.

How many times have we heard "it's the greenies!" It's the environmentalists who have kept domestic drilling from expanding. BULL. The president of Tree Huggers of America does not sit in Congress. The president of the Sierra Club or Greenpeace or Save our Forests or Stop Drilling Now do not sit in Congress. **Those groups**

and organizations buy the favors of the Outlaw Congress – both parties. We see the same at state capitols.

No, it's not the "greenies". The U.S. Congress is responsible for not allowing more drilling as well as passing and funding destructive legislation for a scam called "climate change" and other extremist agendas from environmental groups gone berserk.

That's why the states must step forward and defy the Federal Government. We have the absolute right to control the resources within our borders, like drilling for oil, natural gas and coal operations. That won't happen in oil rich states without massive heat put on those state legislatures by citizens. Tell them to stand up or shut up and quit complaining about what Congress will and won't "allow" them to do in their sovereign states.

In 2013, I wrote a "Working Paper" for our state legislature here in Texas. The goal was to do what Alabama did several years ago and kick the communist controlled UN and their Agenda 21 out of our state:

"Agenda 21 has a long history therefore it is necessary to cover it as thoroughly as possible for this working paper. Attached exhibits are critical in understanding why the state legislature must do as the State of Alabama did in June 2012: pass legislation which protects private property and due process by prohibiting any state government from participating in or attempting to implement any sections of Agenda 21. The bill signed into law by Gov. Robert Bentley is attached with this working paper."

What did our legislature do? They passed a worthless non-binding resolution saying they don't like Agenda 21 and sent it to Congress. Don't Mess with Texas? What a joke.

Agenda 21 or "sustainable development" has been around a long time. Again quoting from Dr. Dixie Lee Ray's (pgs 9-11):

"This [Agenda 21] is an 800-page agreement that lays out 115 specific programs to put into effect all the major issues discussed at Rio. The Agenda is designed to facilitate (or force) the transition of the economies of all nations to 'sustainable development'.

"Besides declaring that it is essential to eliminate poverty worldwide and to reduce human populations, Agenda 21 proposes ambitious and costly programs to set up a Global Environmental Facility to receive funds from industrialized countries with no strings attached. Its purpose is to 'effect resource transfer'.

"Agenda 21 would also force more efficient use of energy. Specifically, it would 'wean the developed countries off an overdependence on fossil fuels', 'remove all trade barriers and subsidies', and bring about 'large-scale reduction of current debt burdens'" in the Third World.

"The objective, clearly enunciated by the leaders of UNCED, is to bring about a change in the present system of independent nations. The future is to be world government, with central planning by the UN. Fear of environmental crises, whether real or not, is expected to lead to compliance. If force is needed, it will be provided by a UN green-helmeted police force, already authorized by the Security Council.

"There's no mistaking the intentions plainly stated in the worlds of Richel Rocard, former prime minister of France and a leader at the Earth Summit: 'Let's not deceive ourselves. It is necessary that the community of nations exert pressure, even using coercion, against countries that have installations that threaten the environment. International instruments must be transformed into instruments of coercion, of sanctions, of boycott, even – perhaps in 15-years time – of outright confiscation by any dangerous installation. What we seek, to be frank, is the legitimacy of controlling the application of the international decisions.

"Rocard reinforced his belief that world government is the ultimate goal: 'We need a real world authority, to which should be delegated the follow up of the international decisions, like the treaties signed [at Rio]. This authority must have the capacity to have its decisions obeyed. Therefore, we need means of control and sanctions.

"But if any doubts remain about the global intentions of the architects of the Montreal Protocol and the Earth Summit, those doubts are quickly dispelled by the chilling words of Maurice Strong, primary designer and Secretary General of the Rio conference. In answer to a magazine interviewer's question about his 'unfulfilled ambition', he said he wanted to write a novel with an environmental plot, then explained:

"What if a small group of world leaders were to conclude that the principal risk to the Earth comes from the actions of rich countries? And if the world is to survive, those rich countries would have to sign an agreement reducing their impact on the environment. Will they do it? The group's conclusion is 'no'. The rich countries won't do it. They won't change. So, in order to save the planet, the group decides: Isn't the only hope for the planet that the industrialized civilizations collapse? Isn't our responsibility to bring that about? This group of world leaders form a secret society to bring about an economic collapse.

"And, in Mr. Strong's fantasy, the interviewed added, they succeed.

"A confirmed internationalist, Matthew wrote, in the Spring 1989 issue of *Foreign Affairs* that there must be 'new institutions and regulatory regimes to cope with the world's growing environmental independence' and that 'our accepted definition of the limits of national sovereignty as coinciding with national borders is obsolete'. The U.S. plan has already been communicated to the UN Secretariat, as reported in the Federal Register, Volume 57, No. 236, December 8, 1992.

"Is this what Americans want? Are environmental issues so serious and imminently catastrophic as to require that we give up a significant part of our independence, our liberty? What is the scientific evidence that supports or refutes severe deterioration in nature? Must we destroy our nation in order to 'save the planet'"?

Page 13:

"Global warming in an outright invention. It is absolutely unproven, and in my view it is a lie. A lie that will cost billions of dollars annually...There is no danger from the CFC's to the ozone layer, nor is there any danger from CO2, no greenhouse effect, nor any risk of any kind of global warning. It is to me, a pure falsehood." Haroun Tazieff, volanologist, geologist, former Secretary of State for Prevention of Natural and Technological Disasters, French Government, Chaps Elyees, Paris 1991.

On page 117, Ms. Ray begins her astute analysis regarding private property in relation to the hysteria over environmental concerns:

"In the name of 'protecting the environment', Congress has enacted laws that allow government regulators to confiscate private property, to prevent an owner from using his land, to levy fines for noncompliance of up to $25,000 per day (jut increased in Oregon by state law to $100,000 per day), and to jail the landowner who may try to use his land for any purpose other than that prescribed by government – even if the citizen was unaware of the restrictions."

Ms. Ray wrote on page 119 of her book: "In many areas, people are locked in a battle for economic survival, for the survival of our most precious rights, for the right to own and use property, for individual liberty and freedom. In this battle, governments are all too ready to accept environmentalist proddings to expand their own power."

In his 1972 book, *Ecology – Can We Survive Under Capitalism?* the late Gus Hall, a leader and Chairman of the Communist Party USA (CPUSA), writes the usual communist propaganda: "Socialism corrects the basic flaw of capitalism" and "that saving the environment is a common good, but capitalism must be destroyed in order to achieve the desired result."

However, long before Gus Hall's delusional philosophy, the blue print for the destruction of America and other industrialized countries was hatched.

"At the Sixth Party Congress held in Moscow in 1928, Communists wrote and approved 'The Program' to bring in the New World Order. What most Americans don't know is the real nature of this diabolical criminal scheme. The Program of the Third International called for a global environmental program and for the transformation of all human beings on earth to accept the New World Order. The Communists planned to use the global environmental program as a means of eradicating national sovereignty and creating a world dictatorship. All nations, nationalities, and national boundaries were to be replaced by an omnipotent, one-world government and regional governances.

"The Communists did not want the American approach to liberty, with individual God-given rights protected by a government with limited powers. The Communists did not want the American concept of rule of law. They wanted unrestrained despotic government, power without limit, a world without laws — a brutal, terror-inspiring global totalitarian police state which could smash all laws of justice, launch campaigns of enslavement and mass murder, and eliminate opponents of the New World Order. **Twenty delegates from the U.S. voted for the 1928 Program of the Third International.**

"Under the guise of 'harmonizing' relationships between humans and their environment, Gorbachev calls for the expansion of governmental power. He states, 'An awareness of the need for some kind of global government is gaining ground....' He says, '[T]he idea that certain states or groups of states could monopolize the international arena is no longer valid.... [W]e must seek means of collective action by the world community.... I believe that the new world order will not be fully realized unless the United Nations and its Security Council create structures...authorized to impose sanctions and to make use of other enforcement measures."

"The New World Order architects have crafted countless policies, programs, treaties and alliances to destroy American sovereignty and achieve absolute global authority, including Agenda 21, the Wildlands Project, the Biodiversity Treaty, and other UN schemes. Agenda 21 was the principle agreement of the 1992 UN Earth Summit in Rio de Janeiro and was signed by UN members, including the United States. It represents a master plan for managing the earth's forests, mountains, deserts, jungles, rivers, oceans, and urban areas and regulating virtually every aspect of human activity on earth." Jeri Lynn Ball, *Masters of Seduction – Beguiling Americans Into Slavery and Self-destruction.*

For those who refuse to believe the concentrated efforts underway to destroy this constitutional republic are foolish and have zero command of the facts. Communism has never died, the evil doers simply changed how they sold their poison. They just changed the label and sold it to "progressive" liberals. One only need read the comprehensive work and fully sourced book, *The Venona Secrets – Exposing Soviet Espionage and America's Traitors* by Herbert Romerstein and Eric Briendel (2001) to fully grasp how the communists infiltrated our government, Pg. 92:

"Years later, John Abt, a Communist Party attorney who had been active in the espionage apparatus, revealed the names of Communist members of Congress. In his autobiography, Abt said: 'The two Communists who were elected to Congress – Johnny Bernard from Minnesota and Hugh DeLacy from Washington State – were elected as Democrats. [Vito] Marcantonioi, who was a friend of the Party but never a member, was elected as a Republican, a Democrat, and as the ALP [American Labor Party] candidate.' Bernard was a 'progressive' member of Congress, just as there are now 70 members of the U.S. Congress who are members of the Democratic Socialists of America."

Continuing from *The Venona Secrets*, pg 93:

"Even more important than the secret Communist Party members in Congress or on congressional staffs were those assigned by the Party as Soviet spies in the U.S. governments executive branch. As we shall see, in the years leading up to WWII, the Party reached into the highest ranks of federal government power and into those closely guarded laboratories of America's most vital scientific and manufacturing establishments. Instead of being a passive bank of well-intentioned idealists – as Party propaganda portrayed the CPUSA – America's Communist movement had become the disciplined instrument of Moscow's global spy and covert action services. Its golden days were just ahead." [End of quote]

Kevin Kornbuckle was Oregon's only duly elected Communist; he ran as a Democrat and "came out" after he was elected. In March, 1996, this Communist, after coming under attack by other city council members stated: "I'd simply point out that Communists in the U.S. are fighting for health care, housing and jobs as a human right. I'm proud to be a Communist." *Mail Tribune*, Medford, Oregon, March 4, 1996.

In 1932, William Z. Foster, then chairman of the Communist Party USA, authored a book titled, *Toward Soviet America*. In it, Foster was certain one day a communist would occupy the White House. How can anyone deny the agenda of those who control Washington, DC, is to see our glorious republic sucked into world governance?

Richard Nixon met with Chou En-Lai in Shanghai to "cement a new world order". *New York Times*, February 26, 1972

On June 29, 1992, Jospeh Biden gave a speech on the senate floor titled: On the Threshold of a New World Order, An American Agenda for the New World Order, Fulfilling the Wilsonian Vision. That piece of treason, in my opinion, is available on line; just type in the title.

Finally, there was another bill in Congress to get us out of the UN: H.R. 75: American Sovereignty Restoration Act of 2013 – To end membership of the United States in the United Nations. Bill introduced January 3, 2013. Bill Sponsor: Rep. Paul Broun Jr. [R-GA]. The bill had a whopping 8 cosponsors; all Republicans. Referred to House Foreign Affairs Committee where it died.

The United Nothing has never kept peace anywhere in the world. The UN's purpose is to act as law enforcement for one world government. Since 1945, we the people have been raped in hundreds of billions of dollars in UN dues and related UN expenses. *Congressional Record*, House of Representatives, January 15, 1962, pg 215, Congressman James B. Utt – who gives the truth in his speech that day: None is So Blind as He Who Will Not See:

"When the United Nations Charter was submitted to the Senate for ratification, great stress was laid upon Art. 2, sub-paragraph 7, which states:

"Nothing contained in the present charter shall authorize the United Nations to intervene in matters which are essentially within the domestic jurisdiction of any state or shall require the members to submit such matters to settlement under the present charter.

"I do not believe that the U.S. Senate would have ratified this treaty without relying on the above quoted paragraph. However, this paragraph has been complete and constantly ignored over the past 16 years and every organization, commission, and covenant flowing out of the United Nations Charter has been for the sole purpose of intervening in matters which are essentially within the domestic jurisdiction of the member nations as well as the several States of our own Union, completely destroying the sovereignty of each State to legislate in contravention of the treaty provisions...

"You can expect to see a one world government, Communist controlled, under the United Nations. You will see the United Nations run up astronomical debts which we, under the terms of the treaty, are bound to pay." [3]

Congressman Mike Rogers Introduces Bill to Get U.S. Out of UN, June 12, **2015**, *The New American* – a magazine of sterling quality that publishes the truth with hard facts.

"Citing wasted tax dollars and attacks on the constitutionally guaranteed liberties of the American people, Rep. Mike Rogers (R-Ala.; shown) introduced a bill to restore U.S. sovereignty and withdraw from the United Nations. The effort to de-fund and exit the UN comes amid growing scrutiny of the global organization, often ridiculed as the 'dictators club,' and myriad mega-scandals swirling around it. However, despite ever-growing support in Congress for restoring U.S. sovereignty by withdrawing from the UN over the years, the legislation still faces an uphill battle...

"'Why should the American taxpayer bankroll an international organization that works against America's interests around the world?' asked Rep. Rogers. 'The time is now to restore and protect American sovereignty and get out of the United Nations.' He cited attacks on U.S. liberties as a key motivation for the legislation.

"Several other liberty-minded congressmen have also sponsored the legislation including constitutionalist Rep. Thomas Massie (R-Ky.), Rep. John Duncan (R-Tenn.), Rep. Lynn Westmoreland (R-Ga.), and Rep. Tim Huelskamp (R-Kan.). A previous bill to withdraw from the UN introduced in the last Congress by then-Rep. Paul Broun (R-Ga.) garnered nine co-sponsors. With the regime ruling Communist China increasingly taking a leading role at the UN, among numerous other concerns, opposition to the global body is expected to continue growing.

"If approved, the legislation would repeal the UN Participation Act of 1945 and shutter the U.S. government's mission to the outfit. It would also 'terminate all membership by the United States in the United Nations, and in any organ, specialized agency, commission, or other formally affiliated body of the United Nations.' That specifically includes UNESCO, which President Ronald Reagan withdrew from, along with the World Health Organization, the UN Environment

Program (UNEP), and more. It would end all U.S. involvement in all UN conventions and agreements, too." [4]

As I am writing that bill has a grand total of 5 co-sponsors. God, how pathetic. It should be hundreds of members of the U.S. Congress excepting of course socialists like Bernie Sanders who is working to destroy our republic and who should never have been allowed to serve in Congress never mind run for president of this country.

In 1971, Congressman Rarick introduced the International Reorganization Act to Rescind and Revoke Membership of the United States in the United Nations. It also failed because anyone who has done the hard research understands the UN is nothing but a tool of the tyrants who are feverishly working to bring our republic into a God-less one world government supported by the U.S. Congress. You can read the bill and other pertinent information at:

http://www.devvy.com/boesel_20000205.html

It's the EPA and other *unconstitutional* agencies that relentlessly impose regulations on not only businesses, but Americans as well. **Regulations that cost billions that kill job growth**. Do you know how much money it costs in legal fees to fight a monster like the EPA? Remember, Congress was given life to take care of **external** business and things like taxes and trade that required some uniformity. ALL other areas of governance for **internal** business was given solely to the states under the Tenth Amendment.

States are right now suing the EPA for regulations that will bankrupt companies and cause even more unemployment. We know the EPA derives its jurisdiction from foreign treaties. A couple putting a pond on their property or a farmer digging a trench for planting 1/4' deeper than the EPA wants to protect a rat are NOT crimes against foreign nations. Yet, the U.S. Congress, both parties, have allowed this never ending destruction to continue.

Yes, we do have to have the U.S. government but a government that is held to the limitations placed on it by the supreme law of the land, the U.S. Constitution. **That won't happen as long as Americans, Republican or Democrat, continue to reelect the same incumbents over and over and over and expect change.**

The one thing that isn't going to happen and that is our economy is somehow going to recover before the next major collapse. **It's already underway. That's not hyperbole, it's the truth and it's too late to stop it.** Another housing bubble is building like steam in a pressure cooker. Personal debt is again rising. 49 MILLION Americans live on food stamps. The first week of June 2016 number of Americans out of the workforce report: 94 million. There's also a disaster regarding both private and state pension funds.

Detroit Pension Cuts From Bankruptcy Prompt Cries of Betrayal, February 4, 2015, *Bloomberg Business*

"Pension checks will shrink 6.7 percent for 12,000 Detroit retirees beginning in March. Making matters worse, many also must pay back thousands of dollars of excess interest they received. It's a bitter outcome of Detroit's record $18 billion municipal bankruptcy for David Espie, 58, who will repay the city $75,000 in a lump sum while his $3,226 monthly pension is cut by $216. As retirement costs swallow larger portions of U.S. city budgets, Detroit's bankruptcy plan resolved a pension crisis with creative strokes, though at a cost to retirees who thought their benefits were untouchable. "I feel betrayed," said Espie, who may abandon plans to move to Alabama. He recounted family get-togethers he missed during the 30 years he spent in the Department of Public Works picking up trash and plowing snow. He also pays $500 a month more for health insurance than a year ago. 'It's devastating to me; it's affecting my health," Espie said...'

"To make do, Detroit retiree Elaine Williams, 63, said she'll buy more soup and eat cheaper food when her $1,200 monthly pension check is cut by $158. That includes $78 to pay back almost $10,000, a monthly debt she'll face for 17 years. Williams, who was a customer-service representative in the water department, said she retired in 2012 to a $950-a-month apartment in Phoenix near her children. She worries about medical costs, having endured several surgeries. 'It's wrong that they would mess with our pensions,' she said in a phone interview. Henry Gaffney, 61, a retired bus driver, said he'll pay back $56,000 of the $300,000 he saved by deducting $428 from his monthly $3,100 pension check for 19 years. He said he pays $375 more for health insurance each month. 'I may have to find a part-time job,' said

Gaffney, former president of Detroit's bus-driver union. 'I guess the city wants us to work until we're dead.'" [5]

Illinois to Delay Pension Payments Amid Budget Woes: "For All Intents and Purposes, We Are Out of Money Now", October 14, 2015, *Zero Hedge*:

"Illinois will delay pension payments as a prolonged budget impasse causes a cash shortage, Comptroller Leslie Geissler Munger said. The spending standoff between Republican Governor Bruce Rauner and Democratic legislative leaders has extended into its fourth month with no signs of ending. Munger said her office will postpone a $560 million retirement-fund payment next month, and may make the December contribution late."

When retirees pension checks are cut by hundreds of dollars per month PLUS they are penalized in interest that's less those individuals can put in savings or spend into the local economy. When there are public employee pension shortfalls what happens? Raise taxes. Consumers have less money to spend because they're being taxed to death. Less spending means a contraction in the economy. It's also happened in Oregon and I'm speculating the next big cities to go bankrupt will be Houston and Chicago.

Pension Funds Sue Big Banks over Manipulation of $12.7 Trillion Treasuries Market, August 24, 2015, *allgov.com*

"At least two government pension funds have sued major banks, accusing them of manipulating the $12.7 trillion market for U.S. Treasury bonds to drive up profits, thereby costing the funds — and taxpayers — millions of dollars.

"As with another case earlier this year, in which major banks were found to have manipulated the London Interbank Offered Rate (LIBOR), traders are accused of using electronic chat rooms and instant messaging to drive up the price that secondary customers pay for Treasury bonds, then conspiring to drop the price banks pay the government for the bonds, increasing the spread, or profit, for the banks. This also ends up costing taxpayers more to borrow money. In the latest complaint, the Oklahoma Firefighters Pension and Retirement System is suing Barclays Capital, Deutsche Bank, Goldman Sachs, HSBC Securities, Merrill Lynch, Morgan Stanley,

Citigroup and others, according to Courthouse News Service. Last month State-Boston Retirement System (SBRS) filed a similar complaint against 22 banks, many of which are the same defendants in the Oklahoma suit."

State high court strikes down pension reform, May 8, 2015 – www.chicagobusiness.com

(*AP*) — "The Illinois Supreme Court on Friday struck down a 2013 law that sought to fix the nation's worst government-employee pension crisis, a ruling that forces the state to find another way to overcome a massive budget deficit. In a unanimous decision, the seven justices declared the law passed 18 months ago violates the state constitution because it would leave pension promises 'diminished or impaired."

"The decree puts new Republican Gov. Bruce Rauner and Democrats who control the General Assembly back at the starting line in trying to figure out how to wrestle down a $111 billion deficit in what's necessary to cover its state employee retirement obligations. The hole is so deep the state has in recent years had to reserve up to $7 billion — or one-fifth of its operating funds — to keep pace. Most states faced the same public employee pension crisis, exacerbated by the Great Recession, and took steps to remedy the problem. But Illinois balked for years at addressing the crisis until former Democratic Gov. Pat Quinn and fellow Democrats who control the General Assembly overcame opposition from union allies and struck the 2013 deal, amid warnings that it might not pass constitutional muster.

"After the General Assembly and Quinn adopted the changes in December 2013, retired employees, state-worker labor unions and others filed a lawsuit seeking to invalidate the law on constitutional grounds. The high court opinion means the state must keep its pledge on pensions. The law dealt with four of the state's five pension programs — the Legislature did not include the judges' account because of the conflict posed by expected legal action. The shortfall in the amount of money necessary to meet all pension obligations has reached stifling depths largely because of years of skimping on — or skipping — on annual pension contributions by past governors and General Assemblies." [6]

Big retirement pensions sound great to union members. But, down the road ten or twelve years and a recession or depression hits, those pension plans become unsustainable and that's what's happening and is getting worse by the month. Detroit's shortfall is $111 BILLION dollars. Those operating funds cited above come from tax dollars. When unemployment is more than job holders taxes dry up. Taxes go to fund burgeoning Medicaid funding because citizens out of work in the states have no money to pay for medical treatment. It has become a vicious circle that heavily impacts the economy.

Teacher pensions: The math adds up to a crisis, January 28, 2015, *CBS Money Watch*

"Teacher pension plans across the country are staggering from a half-trillion dollars in debt. Put in perspective, that's more than $10,000 worth of debt for every student in the nation's primary and secondary schools. In 2014, state teacher pension systems had a total of $499 billion in unfunded liabilities, which has risen $100 billion in just two years, according to a new report from the National Council on Teacher Quality, a nonpartisan research and policy group dedicated to restructuring the teaching profession. The report card on teacher pensions found that 70 cents of every dollar contributed to state pension systems pays for this massive debt rather than covering current employees' future retirement benefits.

"In spite of overwhelming evidence that today's pension practices can't be sustained, the NCTQ laments that state legislators, regulators and pension boards 'continue to deny or ignore the crisis." [7]

Why should public employees like a janitor retire close to a millionaire while the taxpayer retires on what they have put away and social security? Why shouldn't public employees be just like every other worker in the private sector? You decide to put aside X amount of dollars every paycheck in a 401(k) or better yet, savings in gold and silver and when it comes to retirement, you have those assets for your golden years. That's what the guy who works at Goodyear tires does. That's what a secretary at a law firm does. That's what the man or woman who owns the local cleaners does. Why should public employees be any different? *I don't think public employees think about the financial burden they're placing on their own children and grandchildren to pay those taxes for their pensions that have become unpayable?*

The problem public employees don't consider is when the debt obligation of the pension plan you've vested your future on goes so far into debt, the bubble bursts. There's only so much the county or state can squeeze out of taxpayers before those taxpayers don't have any disposable income to patronize your business. Before you throw this book across the room, my daughter and her husband are both teachers so I have no bias against teachers. However, teacher's unions have destroyed education in many ways. Why should teachers be any different than private sector employees? You pay any worker commensurate with their education and experience.

You cut the fat at both the city, county, state and federal level so you can pay a decent wage. However, it doesn't matter if you pay an employee $100 an hour it will never be enough with a heavy, progressive "income" tax and massive taxes at the city, county and state level bleeding people's paychecks. AND, the devaluation of the dollar making the purchasing power nearly nothing as demonstrated in Chapter 1.

What about your county or the city where you reside? How fiscally stable are they? Your state's financial house – how much debt are they really carrying? This directly affects you and your future.

In early July 2015, Moody's put the City of Houston on notice. The California's Public Employees Retirement System only met 1/3rd of their projected annual revenue; that state's teachers' fund never reached their goal. 25% of the largest public pension funds in this country have a whopping $2 TRILLION dollar shortfall in their budgets. It's not just state pension funds, but there's big trouble in private sector pension funds.

Large pension fund files plan to cut retiree benefits under new law, October 7, 2015, *MSN Money*

"Nearly 300,000 former truckers and their families would suffer significant losses under a proposal that uses a controversial new law to cut once sacrosanct pension benefits. The huge Central States Pension Fund, which administers retirement benefits for some former and current Teamster truckers, said the reductions are the only way to save the plan from insolvency...

"Under the proposal, pensions for Central States" 407,000 participants would be cut by an average of nearly 23 percent. But the pain would be distributed unevenly. Some participants, including the disabled, would not be subject to reductions. Older retirees would generally receive smaller cuts, while those who worked for defunct companies that did not keep pace with their pension funding obligations would face steeper reductions...

"An estimated 1 million people, including many retirees, are in multi-employer pension plans that federal officials say are in danger of running out of money in the near future. Multi-employer plans are formed by businesses and unions that join forces to provide pension coverage for working-class Americans, including truck drivers, grocery store clerks and construction workers. If some of the larger multi-employer plans are allowed to collapse, the federal insurance fund that protects them could also collapse.

"Some union leaders and their supporters, including Democratic presidential candidate Bernie Sanders, say the government should step in to shore up the pension funds. Sanders, an independent senator from Vermont, has introduced a bill that would repeal the measure allowing pensions to be cut." [8]

Bernie Sanders hates the U.S. Constitution and our legal form of government. Sanders operates in the la-la land of socialism. Americans flocking to his campaign seem to be ignorant about what socialism does to countries or they simply want someone else to pay for their lifestyle. *Look at the horror going on right now in Venezuela under socialism.* "The trouble with Socialism is that eventually you run out of other people's money." — Margaret Thatcher

The U.S. Congress has ZERO authority to steal the fruits of your labor to "shore up" private pension funds. In that article, James Hoffa, general president of the International Brotherhood of Teamsters said, "They worked day in and day out to earn their pension credits. It is monstrously unfair that they will end up holding the short end of the stick." True, but if contracts that are negotiated are unrealistic in the first place, when the economy goes south disaster strikes.

California's farmers left high and dry by drought, environmental regs, October 7, 2015, *FOX News Science*

"With the drought entering its fourth year, anger is building in central California at state and federal agencies, who critics say are putting wildlife ahead of jobs, families and the food supply. Blocked by environmentalists from pumping water from rivers onto their arid lands, farmers blame both regulations and the agencies and activists who go to court to enforce them. 'These are communities who rely almost solely upon agricultural production or agri-business activities,' Gayle Holman, spokeswoman for the nation's largest agricultural water supplier, the Westlands Water District, told *FoxNews.com*. 'If we continue down this path, we will most likely see our food production turn to foreign soil. We could lose the economic engine that agriculture brings to our nation."

"If we continue down this path, we will most likely see our food production turn to foreign soil." – Gayle Holman, Westlands Water District

"The U.S. Fish and Wildlife Service and the California Department of Fish and Wildlife have placed heavy regulations on the water that pours down from the snow-capped Sierra Nevada mountains, swelling rivers and lakes on its way to the Pacific. Before the current, historic drought, there was enough water to keep farmland fertile and fish happy. But now, in the name of the Endangered Species Act, and on behalf of such native fish species as the tiny delta smelt, environmental groups" efforts to block the diversion of water for farm use has left ranches, orchards and farms dry – and unproductive." [9]

My heart just breaks for our farming families who struggle to provide you, me and our families with food. Farmers work from sun up until sun down at the mercy of mother nature. For decades both federal and state government agencies have been doing all they can to run them off their land. Do Americans even give damn? Do you want to see OUR food production in the hands of foreign countries? This is lunacy and who's to blame? *Your incumbent and mine in the U. S. Congress – both parties – who allow this crap to go on as well as state legislatures and governors.*

The article below is important by Michael Snyder who has one of the very best web sites on the Internet: endoftheamericandream.com. I hope you will take time to read the entire article because it is shocking. Just type the title into a search engine: Housing Crash? – U.S. Existing Home Sales Fall by The Most in Six Years, March 21, 2016

"We just got more evidence that a major economic slowdown is underway here in the United States. Existing home sales were down a whopping 7.1 percent during the month of February, and this represented the biggest decline that we have seen in six years. This is yet another sign that we are in the early stages of a new crisis that is eerily reminiscent of what happened back in 2008.

"The truth is that most U.S. consumers are tapped out, and when you are tapped out it is really hard to get a mortgage. Banks aren't really fond of lending money to people that can't pay it back, and in recent years housing prices in many areas have risen to levels that are beyond the reach of most middle class families.

"This huge decline in existing home sales is puzzling the "experts" in the mainstream media, because in recent weeks they have been breathlessly telling all of us how incredibly well the U.S. economy has been doing. Just check out the following excerpt from a CNBC report…

U.S. home resales fell sharply in February in a potentially troubling sign for America's economy which has otherwise looked resilient to the global economic slowdown. The National Association of Realtors said on Monday existing home sales dropped 7.1 percent to an annual rate of 5.08 million units, the lowest level since November.

"It doesn't take a genius to figure out why this is happening. In recent months we have seen mass layoffs in the energy industry, real median household income is still way below where it was just prior to the last recession, and U.S. consumers are increasingly turning to debt in a desperate attempt to make ends meet from month to month.

"If you can believe it, consumers in the United States actually accumulated more new credit card debt during the 4th quarter of 2015 than they did during the years of 2009, 2010 and 2011 combined. To me that is an absolutely staggering statistic, and it shows how late in the game it is."

We crossed the Rubicon a long time ago and now the worst is coming at us like a freight train. At the back of the book under Endnotes for this chapter I've included a number of articles about what's really going on with the economy so you know the truth. Do you know what bank derivatives are? You need to know. Do you know there is a 401(k) crisis and that it's getting worse? I urge you to read those articles and columns because they are written by individuals who are highly knowledgeable on this issue and are not on the government's payroll or some big media outlet that depends on advertising dollars. The authors want you to know the truth instead of the propaganda spewed by a compromised "mainstream" media, electronic and print and that includes cable networks.

If you know the truth you can make plans and you can fight to save our country by rejecting politicians who have allowed the destruction of our economy underway. As Charles Hugh Smith says in one of the columns I've listed: "The well's gone dry, folks. There isn't going to be another push higher or a third housing bubble after this one pops."

5

(Un)Affordable Health Care Act aka Obamacare

Health care is a huge issue in this country. It's also a monstrous mess. But, how did it get this way?

After WWII, private sector employers were having a difficult time recruiting workers away from the federal government so as an enticement, they began offering to pay some health care costs. A few decades later, health care became mandatory in the workplace as part of hiring packages. But that wasn't what caused the destruction of the finest health care *delivery system* in the world.

I say delivery system because here in America, we have been blessed with fine men and women doctors in all fields. It's not the quality of health care (although more and more Americans are turning to natural remedies as they should) that was the problem, it's *how the product is delivered to the patient* that went off the tracks in 1973. The beginning of the destruction by Congress who has *zero constitutional authority to regulate health care or the practice of medicine* which I cover later in this chapter.

Blame Congress for HMOs by Twila Brase, published at: Citizens' Council for Health Freedom – *www.cchfreedom.org*. Published in Ideas on Liberty by the Foundation for Economic Education February 2000, by Twila Brase. Ms. Brase explains in great detail when the real problem started with destroying the finest health care delivery system in the world. Her article is quite long, but put a yellow post it on this page and look it up on the Internet because you will see where the train went off the tracks thanks to the U.S. Congress. A monstrous mess from day one. Just a few paragraphs to give you an idea of the history of planned disaster:

"Although members of Congress have managed to keep the public in the dark by joining in the clamor against HMOs, legislative history puts the responsibility and blame squarely in their collective lap. The proliferation of managed-care organizations (MCOs) in general, and HMOs in particular, resulted from the 1965 enactment of Medicare for the elderly and Medicaid for the poor. **Literally overnight, on July 1, 1966, millions of Americans lost all financial responsibility for their health-care decisions.**

"But when the House of Representatives refused to concur, it was left to the 93rd Congress to pass the HMO Act in 1973. Just before a voice vote passed the bill in the House, U.S. Representative Harley O. Staggers, Sr., of West Virginia said, 'I rise in support of the conference report which will stimulate development of health maintenance organizations…I think that this new system will be successful and give us exciting and constructive alternatives to our existing programs of delivering better health services to Americans.'

"In the Senate, Kennedy, author of the HMO Act, also encouraged its passage: 'I have strongly advocated passage of legislation to assist the development of health maintenance organizations as a viable and competitive alternative to fee-for-service practice…This bill represents the first initiative by the Federal Government which attempts to come to grips directly with the problems of fragmentation and disorganization in the health care industry.'…I believe that the HMO is the best idea put forth so far for containing costs and improving the organization and the delivery of health-care services.' In a roll call vote, only Senator Herman Talmadge voted against the bill.

"On December 29, 1973, President Nixon signed the HMO Act of 1973 into law. As patients have since discovered, the HMO– staffed by physicians employed by and beholden to corporations – was not much of a Christmas present or an insurance product."

Fast forward three decades and along comes the misnamed Affordable Health Care Act that didn't take long in shell-shocking millions of Americans. We the people were told by Obama: "If you like your health care plan, you can keep it." "If you like your doctor you can keep him or her." Lies, lies and more lies to come. As the ACA was being rolled out against the wishes of the American people, disaster was everywhere beginning with the official health care government web site.

To date it has cost you, me, our children and grandchildren more than ONE BILLION DOLLARS to get the Obamacare web site workable. Since there's no money in the people's purse (U.S. Treasury) and none of your "income" tax dollars funds a single function of the federal government, every penny was borrowed with the interest slapped on our backs.

Not only couldn't Americans keep their health care plan or their doctor, their wallets were about to be plucked clean.

A woman from Washington, D.C., interviewed by *PBS* who was a supporter of the health care law suddenly found her policy canceled. New policies had significantly higher rates. She told *Newshour* the only thing the new policy covered that her old one didn't was maternity care and pediatric services. And she was 58. "The chance of me having a child at this age is zero. So, you know, I ask the president, why do I have to pay an additional $5,000 a year for maternity coverage that I will never, ever need?" asked Deborah Persico. [1]

Obamacare Skyrockets Cancer Patient's Meds to $14,000, February 24, 2014, *Brietbart*

"In an emotional Sunday *Wall Street Journal* editorial, Ralston College President Stephen Blackwood wrote that Obamacare has made his mother's cancer battle a nightmare that will "accelerate her disease and death." He detailed how her Obamacare plan no longer covers the cost of her essential Sandostatin cancer medication, which totaled $14,000 since January 1 alone.

"Blackwood said his mother, Catherine, had a 'terrific' Blue Cross/Blue Shield plan for almost 20 years until Obamacare canceled it. After navigating the 'bureaucratic morass' of enrolling in Obamacare, Blackwood says his mother was informed that 'the only way to find out in detail what was in the plan was to buy the plan.'

"What happened next, writes Blackwood, was shocking. 'Then on Feb. 12, just before going into (yet another) surgery, she was informed by Humana that it would not, in fact, cover her Sandostatin, or other cancer-related medications,' he explained. 'The cost of the Sandostatin alone, since Jan. 1, was $14,000, and the company was refusing to pay."

"Blackwood added, 'Obamacare made my mother's old plan illegal, and it forced her to buy a new plan that would accelerate her disease and death...The 'Affordable' Care Act is a brutal, Procrustean disaster." [2]

Dr. Ron Paul, was a U.S. House member who wrote quite a bit about health care and reinforced what Ms. Brase wrote above, August 6, 2006:

"As a medical doctor, I've seen first-hand how bureaucratic red tape interferes with the doctor-patient relationship and drives costs higher. The current system of third-party payers takes decision-making away from doctors, leaving patients feeling rushed and worsening the quality of care. Yet health insurance premiums and drug costs keep rising. Clearly a new approach is needed. Congress needs to craft innovative legislation that makes health care more affordable without raising taxes or increasing the deficit. It also needs to repeal bad laws that keep health care costs higher than necessary.

"We should remember that HMOs did not arise because of free-market demand, but rather because of government mandates. The HMO Act of 1973 requires all but the smallest employers to offer their employees HMO coverage, and the tax code allows businesses — but not individuals — to deduct the cost of health insurance premiums. The result is the illogical coupling of employment and health insurance, which often leaves the unemployed without needed catastrophic coverage.

"While many in Congress are happy to criticize HMOs today, the public never hears how the present system was imposed upon the American people by federal law. **As usual, government intervention in the private market failed to deliver the promised benefits and caused unintended consequences, but Congress never blames itself for the problems created by bad laws**. Instead, we are told more government — in the form of 'universal coverage' — is the answer. But government already is involved in roughly two-thirds of all health care spending, through Medicare, Medicaid, and other programs.

"For decades, the U.S. health care system was the envy of the entire world. Not coincidentally, there was far less government involvement in medicine during this time. America had the finest doctors and hospitals, patients enjoyed high-quality, affordable medical care, and thousands of private charities provided health services for the poor. Doctors focused on treating patients, without the red tape and threat of lawsuits that plague the profession today. Most Americans paid cash for basic services, and had insurance only for major illnesses and accidents. This meant both doctors and patients had an incentive to keep costs down, as the patient was directly responsible for payment, rather than an HMO or government program.

"The lesson is clear: when government and other third parties get involved, health care costs spiral. The answer is not a system of outright socialized medicine, but rather a system that encourages everyone — doctors, hospitals, patients, and drug companies — to keep costs down. As long as 'somebody else' is paying the bill, the bill will be too high."

Suddenly, Americans all across the country – MILLIONS – were losing their health care plans and their doctor because of Obamacare. Rubbing salt into an open wound, the new plans being forced on Americans also brought astronomical increases in their monthly premiums as well as co-pays. Obamacare is and always has been just another Ponzi scheme that **will eventually collapse** if it's not repealed.

Target the young and healthy by stealing the fruits of their labor to pay for someone else's health care. Young Americans who don't want Obamacare. *Those who did want it seemed to have no problem taking from someone else's paycheck to provide their health care coverage.*

At the time the unconstitutional Affordable Health Care Act was passed my husband and I paid our own health care premiums and have all our lives. We paid our health care premiums, someone else's medical bills under Obamacare and someone else's medical bills under Medicaid. ***When does it end?*** It is little more than indentured servitude by forcing a person with a gun to their head to pay for someone else's health insurance or whatever the latest "social equality" communist ideology becomes fashionable and sold to the desperate and gullible.

Those subsidies under Obamacare are paid for by the labor of the productive in society has turned into yet another financial nightmare that will never go away unless Obamacare is repealed.

Hawaii's $205 Million Obamacare Exchange Implodes, May 12, 2015

"Despite over $205 million in federal taxpayer funding, Hawaii's Obamacare exchange website will soon shut down. Since its implementation, the exchange has somehow failed to become financially viable because of lower than expected Obamacare enrollment figures. With the state legislature rejecting a $28 million bailout, the website will now be unable to operate past this year...

"While the exchange has struggled since its creation, it is not for lack of funding. Since 2011 Hawaii has received a total of $205,342,270 in federal grant money from the Department of Health and Human Services (HHS). In total, HHS provided nearly $4.5 billion to Hawaii and other state exchanges, with little federal oversight and virtually no strings attached.

"Despite this generous funding, the exchange has underperformed from day one. In its first year, Hawaii enrolled only 8,592 individuals – meaning it spent $23,899 on its website for each individual enrolled. Currently over 37,000 individuals are enrolled in Hawaii's exchange – well below the estimated 70,000 enrollees that is required to make the website financially viable." [3]

By June 5, 2015, an even uglier picture for Hawaii emerged:

Almost 80% of Hawaii Obamacare Enrollees Have Failed to Pay Premiums in 2015, Americans for Tax Reform

"Just 8,200, or 21 percent of individuals enrolled on Hawaii's Obamacare exchange have paid for their health premiums this year, according to a report released this week.

"When asked why so few enrollees have paid for their premiums as of March 31, the exchange gave the vague explanation that it takes time for people to receive and pay bills. When pressed further, Executive Director Jeff Kissell admitted that 'A lot of them haven't even been billed.' The inability to complete this simple task is just another reason why Hawaii's Obamacare exchange has failed. The $205 million state exchange has failed to reach financial viability despite spending nearly $24,000 for each individual it enrolled in its first year of operations." [4]

Did you read that correctly? A whopping $24,000 dollars spent for each person enrolled. Are you kidding me?

The end game for Obamacare is to force down our throats a single payer system – another step towards Soviet America. Vermont's governor was all for one until he decided the political ramifications didn't justify putting his job on the line:

Vermont's Giving Up On Single-Payer Health Care Over Ballooning Costs, December 17, 2014, *The Daily Caller*

"The problem is, of course, how to pay for it. Even while plans were moving forward for a 2017 launch of the single-payer system, to be called Green Mountain Care, Shumlin had held off on releasing a plan for how to pay for the system, waiting until his announcement Wednesday.

"Tax hikes required to pay for the system would include a 11.5 percent payroll tax as well as an additional income tax ranging all the way up to 9.5 percent. Shumlin admitted that in the current climate, such a precipitous hike would be disastrous for Vermont's economy." [5]

When employers are hit with higher costs they either raise the cost of their product or service or lay off employees – something Obama and Congress don't seem to understand, but then again, they're on the public payroll so what do they care?

The article above goes on to say: "The three parents in the room were hit with sticker shock. Brian's monthly costs decrease by about 18 dollars a week, but the $4,000 deductible is a major concern. Christy's saw her monthly premiums jump 30 percent to $895 per month. "That's a house payment for most people," Christy told the reporter."

"Judy, a mother of one child who saw her premiums skyrocket 42 percent along with her deductible doubling, had nothing positive to say about the news, 'I don't know who President Obama thinks he's helping.' She continued, 'Because we can't afford to pay these co-pays, to pay these deductibles, on what we earn.'"

Sharyl Attkisson is an award winning investigative journalist. In April 2015, she wrote a two-part series about California care – put the titles into a search engine:

Incompetence, Mismanagement Plague California's Obamacare Insurance Exchange [6]

Insiders Detail Culture of Secrecy at California's Obamacare Exchange, Part 2 [7]

Under one of the biggest disasters of incompetence and deceit, California Care covered in Part 2 of her series reveals this: In 2014, approximately **800,000** households received federal subsidies that averages $436 per month. **Billions of debt borrowed every month for more welfare, this time in form of paying someone else's health care** – even if that person does nothing to take care of themselves. Like getting very overweight or abusing booze and drugs.

Those billions are *just one state* that comes out of your pocket.

Ms. Attkisson also wrote in part 2:

"To some degree, state health insurance exchanges are forced to market themselves. After starting up using over a billion federal tax dollars, the law requires them to be self-supporting this year. To do so, Covered California collects commissions. The agency wouldn't answer questions on this topic, but previously indicated it planned to charge a 3 percent fee on premiums in 2014 and later hoped to reduce that to 2 percent. Because too few people enrolled, published reports say Covered California could not reduce its 2015 fee, and maintained it at $13.95 per person each month."

There's yet another middleman further driving up the costs of health care that is unnecessary.

Obamacare Insurance Premiums to Jump, up to 51%, May 25, 2015, *Breitbart*:

"Under Obamacare, insurers must file proposed premium rates with their local state regulator and the federal government by June. But some states have already started publicly disclosing the premium requests. Due to the high utilization costs from people newly enrolled under Obamacare, the 2016 insurance premiums are about to skyrocket.

"According to states that have released rate requests, New Mexico's market leader Health Care Service Corp. is asking for an average premium spike of 51.6 percent; Tennessee's top insurer BlueCross BlueShield of Tennessee wants an average spike of 36.3%; Maryland's market leader CareFirst BlueCross BlueShield is requesting an average spike of 30.4%; and Oregon's top insurer, Moda Health, is seeking a 25% spike.

"The Obama Administration's only legal power regarding healthcare premiums is the right to ask insurers seeking increases of 10% or more to explain themselves. There is no federal power to force rate cuts. State insurance regulators can force carriers to scale back requests they believe are not justified, but the carriers can drop coverage and cause a crisis." [8]

That's going to further kill the middle class in this country.

CBO Now Says 10 Mil Will Lose Employer Health Plans Under ObamaCare, January 27, 2015, *Investors.com*

Health Reform: "The Congressional Budget Office now says ObamaCare will push 10 million off employer-based coverage, a tenfold increase from its initial projection. The 'keep your plan' lie just gets bigger and bigger.

"The latest CBO report is supposed to be a big win for the Obama administration because the projected costs are 20% below what the CBO first projected in 2010. But the CBO report also shows that ObamaCare will be far more disruptive to the employer-based insurance market, while being far less effective at cutting the ranks of the uninsured, than promised. Thanks to ObamaCare, the CBO now expects that 10 million workers will lose their employer-based coverage by 2021...

"The CBO now says ObamaCare will leave 31 million uninsured after more than a decade, up from its 23 million forecast made in 2011. Put another way, the CBO promised that ObamaCare would cover 60% of the uninsured.

"Now it says the program will cover less than half, despite spending $2 **trillion** to subsidize premiums and expand Medicaid. 'Does anyone really believe that if Obama announced a plan to spend $2 trillion on a program that would leave 31 million uninsured and force 10 million workers off their employer-based insurance, that even Democrats would have voted for it?'" [9]

$2 TRILLION in BORROWED DEBT.

Obama's administration said Obamacare was not a tax. Then the Supreme Court, courtesy of Chief Justice John Roberts, came along and said, yes it is.

But, wait! It gets better! In October 2013, then Secretary of the unconstitutional Health and Human Services money pit, Kathleen Sebelius, appeared on the Jon Stewart show and told the world Obamacare was a fine and not a tax!

Another one of the constitutional issues is this: Tax-raising Affordable Care Act started in wrong house of Congress, Pacific Legal Foundation which fights for the U.S. Constitution instead of against it like Chief Justice John Roberts.

Sissel v. United States Department of Health & Human Services

"Pacific Legal Foundation has launched a new constitutional cause of action against the federal Affordable Care Act (Obamacare). The ACA imposes a charge on Americans who fail to buy health insurance — a charge that the U.S. Supreme Court recently characterized as a federal tax. PLF's amended complaint alleges that this purported tax is illegal because it was introduced in the Senate rather than the House, as required by the Constitution's Origination Clause for new revenue-raising bills (Article I, Section 7).

"However, Chief Justice John Roberts, joined by four justices, characterized the ACA's charge as a federal "tax," because it requires a payment to the federal government from people who decide not to buy health insurance.

"That holding prompted PLF's new cause of action. 'If the charge for not buying insurance is seen as a federal tax, then a new question must be asked,' said PLF Principal Attorney Paul J. Beard II. 'When lawmakers passed the ACA, with all of its taxes, did they follow the Constitution's procedures for revenue increases? The Supreme Court wasn't asked and didn't address this question in the NFIB case. The question of whether the Constitution was obeyed needs to be litigated, and PLF is determined to see this important issue all the way through the courts."

Did you read that? "....it requires a payment to the federal government from people who decide NOT to buy health insurance." That goes against everything those who spilled thousands of gallons of blood on the battle field during the Revolutionary War to bring us freedom – including choosing not to buy a product or service.

Look at the astronomical amount of money that's been spent trying to get religious organizations and people of faith who are against murdering unborn babies exemptions from Obamacare because of abortifacients which causes a miscarriage. **None of it should ever have happened because Obamacare should never have even been introduced by any member of Congress.** Not to mention what always happens with huge government programs:

Feds Can't Verify $2.8 Billion in Obamacare Subsidies, June 16, 2015, *The Washington Free Beacon*

"The federal government cannot verify nearly $3 billion in subsidies distributed through Obamacare, putting significant taxpayer funding 'at risk,' according to a new audit report. The Department of Health and Human Services (HHS) Office of Inspector General (OIG) released an audit Tuesday finding that the agency did not have an internal system to ensure that subsidies went to the right enrollees, or in the correct amounts.

"[The Centers for Medicare and Medicaid Services] CMS's internal controls did not effectively ensure the accuracy of nearly $2.8 billion in aggregate financial assistance payments made to insurance companies under the Affordable Care Act during the first four months that these payments were made,' the OIG said." [10]

Casualties

Because of Obamacare, 123-Year-Old Major Health Insurance Provider Set to Close Its Doors, May 6, 2015, *Western Journalism*

"After expanding to accommodate the requirements of the Affordable Care Act (Obamacare) last year, a Wisconsin-based health insurance provider, founded in 1892, announced it will be closing its doors. Assurant Health opted not to participate in the first Obamacare enrollment period in 2013; however, in November of that year, the company announced it would be selling plans in 16 states in 2014.

"The company and industry watchers blamed its losses directly on the impact of Obamacare. Following implementation of the requirements to participate in the ACA exchanges, Assurant lost $63.7 million in 2014. The insurer raised its rates by 20 percent in 2015, in hopes of returning to profitability, but lost between $80 to $90 million during the first quarter of this year.

"Assurant currently provides plans for approximately 1 million people, with a revenue of about $2 billion. 'In a letter to its shareholders, [the company] said it lost money because of a reduction in recoveries under Obamacare's risk mitigation programs and increased claims on the health care law's 2015 policies,' the Daily Signal reports." [11]

Mercy Health Fires 347 Workers Due to Obamacare, June 25, 2015, *Breitbart*

"Mercy Health announced Thursday it will fire 347 workers due to 'increasing challenges to our reimbursement structure as we adjust to reductions mandated by the Affordable Care Act,' the company said in a statement. President and CEO of the Mercy system, Lynn Britton, said the Obamacare-induced layoffs are taking a toll on workers and their families.

"'Changes such as these are difficult and distressing for everyone involved,' said Britton. 'While our decisions support Mercy's ability to stay strong and relevant in the face of challenges impacting all health care providers, today our thoughts and prayers are with those co-workers who are affected.' Mercy Health's firings will take place across the four states in which the health system operates, which includes Missouri, Arkansas, Oklahoma and Kansas." [12]

Obamacare is going to cost you, me, our children and grandchildren $2.6 TRILLION dollars for the first 10 years. **That number will get blown out of the water as Obamacare continues to decay.** THERE IS NO MONEY in the people's purse. **The insane in Washington are going to use debt to fund more debt.**

7 Companies That Have to Lay Off Employees to Deal with Obamacare, August 23, 2013, *Policy.mic*

UPS and UVA dumped spouses off insurance plans because of Obamacare. St. Petersburg College is also cutting "hours for employees to reduce costs in order to meet the mandates of

Obamacare." Subway & Wendy's cutting hours because of Obamacare and Papa John's pizza has to increase prices due to Obamacare. [13]

100 Unintended Consequences of Obamacare, *National Review*, October 1, 2013 – Too many to list here, but those 100 companies were just the tip of the iceberg that slammed this country. All those people who lost their jobs and benefits so they can be taxed to pay for someone else's health care under an unconstitutional law.

Who has benefited? Obamacare brings $273 billion bonanza for paper pushers, May 28, 2015, *MSN News*

"Since Obamacare took effect, roughly 16.5 million more people have gained health insurance. And while the health care law is objectively succeeding in its key goal of expanding access to coverage to millions of Americans, those gains come with enormous costs to taxpayers — including inordinately steep ongoing administrative costs, according to a new study. The analysis, published in *Health Affairs* this week, found that about $273.6 billion, or roughly 22.5 percent, of the total estimated $2.76 trillion cost of the Affordable Care Act through 2022 will go to overhead costs." [14]

Boehner profits from Obamacare stocks – Medical, insurance investments continue to prosper, January 2015, *WND*

New York – "Since the passage of Obamacare, House Speaker John Boehner has been dogged by critics pointing out his investment portfolio has benefited from owning insurance and medical company stocks that have profited from the legislation. An analysis of Boehner's current investment holdings includes a number of stocks benefiting from Obamacare in a total portfolio estimated at between $3.5 and $5 million in current market value. Boehner's Obamacare-related investments trace back to 2009, when the Obama administration was pushing the Affordable Health Care Act through Congress."

Page 20: "Congressman John Boehner, who was leading the opposition to Obamacare in the House of Representatives, may have been fighting John Kerry on policy matters, but he was entirely allied with him when it came to investment decisions."

Schweizer continued:

"On December 10, 2008, Boehner bought numerous health insurance company stocks, including tens of thousands of dollars in Cardinal Health, Cigna, and Wellpoint. On the same day, Boehner purchased shares in the Big Pharm companies Amgen, Johnson & Johnson, Forest Labs, Covidien, and Pfizer. He also bought shares in CareFusion, which provides systems for countering infections. Just days later, on December 15, *The Washington Post* declared that the 'public option' was officially dead. Schweitzer drew a causal link, noting that Boehner's heavy investment in Obamacare stocks meant his political opposition to the legislation was undermined by his personal interest." [15]

And, isn't this interesting?

How Five Republicans Let Congress Keep Its Fraudulent Obamacare Subsidies, by Brendan Bordelon May 7, 2015, *National Review*

"The rumors began trickling in about a week before the scheduled vote on April 23: Republican leadership was quietly pushing senators to pull support for subpoenaing Congress's fraudulent application to the District of Columbia's health exchange — the document that facilitated Congress's 'exemption' from Obamacare by allowing lawmakers and staffers to keep their employer subsidies. The application said Congress employed just 45 people. Names were faked; one employee was listed as 'First Last,' another simply as 'Congress.' To Small Business Committee chairman David Vitter, who has fought for years against the Obamacare exemption, it was clear that someone in Congress had falsified the document in order to make lawmakers and their staff eligible for taxpayer subsidies provided under the exchange for small-business employees." [16] Falsified. *Did anyone go to jail?* Of course not, that's only for peasants like you and me.

Larry Becraft is a constitutional attorney out of Huntsville, Alabama. He's spent more than 35 years in federal court rooms and is known for his accurate research and legal opinions. Here is one constitutional argument against Obamacare no one seems to want to challenge:

"There is a constitutional problem regarding Obamacare that nobody has mentioned: it violates principles of equal protection. The Fifth Amendment's Due Process Clause contains an equal protection component, and thus equal protection principles apply to the feds. See *Bolling v Sharpe*, 347 U.S. 497, 499 (1954); and *Adarand Constructors, Inc. v. Pena*, 515 U.S. 200, 224 (1995).

"The alleged need for Obamacare to take over the whole medical system in this country was based on the failure of a segment of American society to have medical insurance. Apparently, those who don't have medical insurance adversely impact the medical industry and the delivery of medical services. However, it must be noted that those with medical insurance did not cause this problem. For purposes of argument only, let's presume that the insured American public constitutes 80% of the populace, while the uninsured comprise 20% of the populace.

"When a legislative body is attempting to address a social problem, whether great or small, it cannot impose duties on those who are not a part of or the cause of the problem without violating equal protection principles. For example, drunk drivers do constitute a hazard on the roads. But to address the problem caused by drunk drivers, a legislative body could not adopt of law affecting 100% of the driving public, inclusive of people who are not causing the problem, because to do so would violate equal protection.

"Principles of equal protection are concerned with legislative classifications. If a legislature detects a problem and adopts of law that affects only a segment of those causing the problem, the legislature has created an 'underinclusive' class. If it adopts of law that affects a far broader class than those causing the problem, it has created an 'overinclusive' class. See *Alvarez v. Chavez*, 118 N.M. 732, 886 P.2d 461 (1994) (license restriction for bondsmen was overinclusive); *Beach Communications, Inc. v. Federal Communications Comm.*, 965 F.2d 1103, 1105 (D.C.Cir. 1992) (distinction in Cable Act between 'external, quasi-private' and 'wholly private' cable systems was 'overinclusive * * * in that this burden does not serve the Act's purpose'); *Shriners Hospital for Crippled Children v. Zrillic*, 563 So.2d 64, 69 (Fla. 1990) ('Equal protection analysis requires that classifications be neither too narrow nor too broad to achieve the desired end.').

"Such underinclusive or overinclusive classifications fail to meet even the minimal standards of the 'rational basis test'); *French v.*

Amalgamated Local Union 376, 203 Conn. 624, 526 A.2d 861 (1987) (ban on residential picketing except for unions was overinclusive); *Treants Enterprises, Inc. v. Onslow County*, 83 N.C. App. 345, 350 S.E.2d 365 (1986); *District of Columbia v. E.M.*, 467 A.2d 457, 466 (D.C.App.1983) (welfare statute of limitations was void because classes were both 'underinclusive and overinclusive'); *Isakson v. Rickey*, 550 P.2d 359 (Alaska 1976) (using the rational basis test, the Court determined that a commercial fisherman limitation was unconstitutional because the act's classifications were both overbroad and underinclusive); *Erznoznik v. City of Jacksonville*, 422 U.S. 205, 214, 95 S.Ct. 2268 (1975) ('the legislative classification is strikingly underinclusive'); *Laakonen v. Eighth Judicial District Court for County of Clark*, 91 Nev. 506, 538 P.2d 574 (1975)(guest statute violated equal protection); *Sturrup v. Mahan*, 261 Ind. 463, 305 N.E.2d 877, 881 (1974) ('This is precisely where the rules sweep too broadly, they create an over-inclusive class'); *Boraas v. Village of Belle Terre*, 476 F.2d 806, 815 fn. 8 (2nd Cir. 1973) ('overinclusive or underinclusive classifications should not be readily tolerated'); *Brown v. Merlo*, 8 Cal.3d 855, 506 P.2d 212, 227 (1973) (California guest statute was overinclusive, had many exceptions and it 'imposes a burden upon a wider range of individuals than are included in the class of those tainted with the mischief at which the law aims'); and *Patton v. State of North Carolina*, 381 F.2d 636, 643 (4th Cir. 1967).

"Why does Obamacare violate equal protection? Those who have insurance will have their medical services and treatments curtailed and controlled, even though they are not a part of the problem, which is caused by the uninsured. Encompassing 100% of the public to address a problem created by 20% of the public creates an overinclusive class, which violates equal protection. But then again, Nancy Pelosi and Harry Reid already solved the problem caused by the uninsured by taxing them in an amount that approximates insurance premiums. Obamacare is not only unconstitutional, it is insanely so."

Lawsuits from religious groups and companies have either been adjudicated or still winding through the courts. However, I have not seen any that directly challenge Obamacare as unconstitutional as a whole. This is part of a column I wrote, December 15, 2012, Employers, Doctors, Obamacare and US Supreme Court Cases:

But, what about employers and doctors who will be so negatively impacted by that monstrosity? Let's take employers first.

Small Employers Weigh Impact of Providing Health Insurance: "By 2014, businesses with 50 or more full-time employees will be expected to offer as yet undefined affordable coverage, based on an employee's income. For employers that fail to offer such coverage, the law typically calls for a penalty of $2,000 a worker, excluding the first 30 employees." *NY Times*, Dec. 1, 2012

Look at this U.S. Supreme Court decision:

Railroad Retirement Board v. Alton R. Co., 295 U.S. 330, 368 (1935):

"The catalogue of means and actions which might be imposed upon an employer in any business, tending to the satisfaction and comfort of his employees, seems endless. Provision for free medical attendance and nursing, for clothing, for food, for housing, for the education of children, and a hundred other matters might with equal propriety be proposed as tending to relieve the employee of mental strain and worry. Can it fairly be said that the power of Congress to regulate interstate commerce extends to the prescription of any or all of these things? Is it not apparent that they are really and essentially related solely to the social welfare of the worker, and therefore remote from any regulation of commerce as such? We think the answer is plain. ***These matters obviously lie outside the orbit of congressional power.***" [End quote]

Congress has only the powers enumerated in Art. 1, Section 8 of the U.S. Constitution, which is why the Federal Department of Education, the SBA, HUD, the EPA, HHS and many other cabinets and agencies ARE unconstitutional. While I'm not a lawyer, I know how to read. I've also been blessed the past two decades with having good, dear friends who are constitutional attorneys with decades of experience that have taken their precious time to help me learn so much about the Constitution, unconstitutional laws and how to read court decisions. When reading court decisions, it's very important to read the footnotes and then go read what the justices (or federal or state judges) used in making their decision. And, yeah, it takes a lot of time to do this kind of research. Some days I spend doing nothing but reading decisions and chasing down the footnotes.

In the case above, the court basically said employers are not required to provide for the "satisfaction and comfort" of employees. (Today it's called "social justice".) Forcing a private sector employer to provide medical health absolutely could be considered to "relieve the employee of mental strain and worry". Forcing employers in the private sector to provide health care coverage has nothing to do with interstate commerce, companies operating safely or anything other than the social welfare of workers.

While the justices wrote heavily in that decision about interstate commerce, what this really boils down to is whether or not Congress has the constitutional authority to force employers to provide Obamacare to employees. I frequently quote Joseph Story, Associate Justice, U.S. Supreme Court, *Commentaries on the Constitution*, 1833:

*"Another not unimportant consideration is that the powers of the general government will be, and indeed must be, principally employed upon **external** objects, such as war, peace, negotiations with foreign powers and foreign commerce. In its internal operations it can touch but few objects, except to introduce regulations beneficial to the commerce, intercourse and other relations, between the states, and to lay taxes for the common good. The powers of the states, on the other hand, extend to all objects, which, in the ordinary course of affairs, concern the lives, and liberties, and property of the people, and the **internal** order, improvement and prosperity of the state."*

We must also look to the Tenth Amendment: The powers not delegated to the United States by the Constitution, nor prohibited by it to the states, are reserved to the states respectively, or to the people.

Additionally, the so-called reporting requirements by employers will cost them a lot of money which down the road *means lay-offs or no new hiring*. The U.S. Congress has zero authority to force employers in the private sector to dance to their tune. It's long past time to fight them.

Doctors

The abomination called Obamacare contains endless panels and commissions that dictate to doctors how they will take care of their own patients. The "death" panels are real, as well as forcing doctors to spend their own resources to compile data bases about their patients making sure your personal life will be jeopardized by leaks or sophisticated computer hackers. Nowhere in Art. 1, Sec. 8 does it give maniacs in the U.S. Congress the authority to force your doctor to turn over all your medical records for some electronic database.

The same plan of attack for employers also applies to doctors throughout this country whether you're a single practitioner or belong to a medical group, the U.S. Supreme Court has made several decisions that favor you:

Linder v. United States, 268 U.S. 5, 18, S. Ct. 446 (1925):

"Obviously, direct control of medical practice in the states is beyond the power of the federal government."

Lambert v. Yellowly, 272 U.S. 581, 598, 47 S.Ct. 210 (1926): "It is important also to bear in mind that 'direct control of medical practice in the States is beyond the power of the Federal Government.' *Linder v. United States*, 268 U.S. 5, 18. Congress, therefore, cannot directly restrict the professional judgment of the physician or interfere with its free exercise in the treatment of disease. *Whatever power exists in that respect belongs to the states exclusively.*"

Conant v. Walters, 309 F.3d 629, 639 (9th Cir. 2002) (quoting Linder).

Lower circuit: *United States v. Anthony et al.*, 15 F. Supp. 553 (S.D.Cal. 1936) (June 23 1936) Nos. 12069-12072. United States District Court, S.D. California, Central Division

"I am referring to these facts in order to indicate that we must bear in mind the purpose of the act — that the act is a borderline statute which must be interpreted in such a manner as to bring it within the constitutional power. And if we depart from it and interpret it either as attempting to regulate the disposition and sale of narcotics or attempting the regulation of medicine, we extend the act to the realm which the Supreme Court has repeatedly said the federal government cannot enter, under the penalty of unconstitutionality."

The Linder Case (*Linder v. United States*, 268 U.S. 5, 45 S.Ct. 446, 449, (1925)) is very important. We all seem to agree, whether we read it alike or not, that it determines this case, so far as the law is concerned. I wish to refer to it for the present only for the purpose of pointing out that the moment we assume that this act regulates the sale within the state of narcotics and that it aims to regulate the practice of medicine, we must hold it unconstitutional." [End]

It is well established case law: ***the federal government cannot legislate any direct control of medical practice in the states of the Union.*** Obamacare has dozens of committees and panels dictating the practice of medicine inside the states of the Union (just like Medicare). How many aren't even doctors? That would be practicing medicine without a license.

Over the past five years Republicans who control the U.S. House of Representatives have tried more than 60 times to repeal Obamacare. At the same time various of their spokes mouths tell us, they, meaning Republicans, have a plan to replace Obamacare.

Wrong. Replace Obamacare with Nothing.

Health care is not a constitutional or human "right". Health care coverage is a product people purchase just like burial or pet insurance; I have both. Health care was affordable UNTIL the HMO Act began the destruction of affordable health care costs. ***The constant meddling by politicians in the Outlaw Congress has brought us to this gigantic disaster called Obamacare.***

Obamacare Effect? 9 Companies Exit Nebraska's Health Insurance Market, October 11, 2013, *Fox News.com*

"Seven of the nine companies have notified the state of their plans to leave since August. Most of them have a minor piece of the major medical market in Nebraska, and likely don't think it's worth it to make the changes necessary to comply with the federal health care law. Aetna, American Family Mutual Insurance, Humana, Independence American Insurance Company, Reserve National Insurance Company, Standard Security Life Insurance Company of New York, Companion Life Insurance and United Security Life and Health Insurance have all informed the state insurance department of their intent to stop selling health insurance to individuals – and in some cases – groups." [17]

No Third Party Payments, May 5, 2004, by Dr. Ron Paul, while serving in the U.S. House of Representatives:

"Last week the congressional Joint Economic committee on which I serve held a hearing featuring two courageous medical doctors. I had the pleasure of meeting with one of the witnesses, Dr. Robert Berry, who opened a low-cost health clinic in rural Tennessee. His clinic does not accept insurance, Medicare, or Medicaid, which allows Dr. Berry to treat patients without interference from third-party government bureaucrats or HMO administrators. In other words, Dr. Berry practices medicine as most doctors did 40 years ago, when patients paid cash for ordinary services and had inexpensive catastrophic insurance for serious injuries or illnesses. As a result, Dr. Berry and his patients decide for themselves what treatment is appropriate.

"Freed from HMO and government bureaucracy, Dr. Berry can focus on medicine rather than billing. Operating on a cash basis lowers his overhead considerably, allowing him to charge much lower prices than other doctors. He often charges just $35 for routine maladies, which is not much more than one's insurance co-pay in other offices. His affordable prices enable low-income patients to see him before minor problems become serious, and unlike most doctors, Dr. Berry sees patients the same day on a walk-in basis. Yet beyond his low prices and quick appointments, Dr. Berry provides patients with excellent medical care.

"While many liberals talk endlessly about medical care for the poor, Dr. Berry actually helps uninsured people every day. His patients are largely low-income working people, who cannot afford health insurance but don't necessarily qualify for state assistance. Some of his uninsured patients have been forced to visit hospital emergency rooms for non-emergency treatment because no doctor would see them. Others disliked the long waits and inferior treatment they endured at government clinics. For many of his patients, Dr. Berry's clinic has been a godsend.

"Dr. Berry's experience illustrates the benefits of eliminating the middleman in health care. For decades, the U.S. healthcare system was the envy of the entire world. Not coincidentally, there was far less government involvement in medicine during this time. America had the finest doctors and hospitals, patients enjoyed high quality, affordable medical care, and thousands of private charities provided health services for the poor."

Americans once again are experiencing severe sticker shock; increases will continue if that monstrosity isn't repealed.

Industry experts predict a sharp rise in premiums later in 2016 as that monster continues to implode. In an April 2016 interview: "Marilyn Tavenner, the president and CEO of America's Health Insurance Plans (AHIP), said in an interview with Morning Consult that the culmination of market shifts and rising health care costs will force stark increases in health insurance rates in the coming year. Last year's premium for the popular silver-level plan surged 11 percent on average. Although Tavenner didn't mention deductibles, in 2016, some states saw jumps of 76 percent, while the average for a 27-year-old male on a silver plan was 8 percent.

"...last year's premium for the popular silver-level plan surged 11 percent on average. Although Tavenner didn't mention deductibles, in 2016, some states saw jumps of 76 percent, while the average for a 27-year-old male on a silver plan was 8 percent...With many insurers struggling to find profitability in the program, the collapse of nearly half of the 23 Obamacare insurance co-ops and this week's announcement that giant UnitedHealth Group intends to pull out of most Obamacare markets across the country, anticipating future premiums and copayments is largely risky guesswork." *MSN.com*

UnitedHealth Exits Most ObamaCare Exchanges, Citing Over $1B in Losses, April 19, 2016, *Breitbart.com*. EXACTLY what we knew was going to happen. Too many people sicker than estimated and in terrible health signing up.

Obamacare is a financial nightmare. Get the U.S. government out of health care and *see how things get turned around for everyone regardless of political party*. If not, people will continue to lose their jobs and benefits. Americans will continue to see their hours cut. Emergency room costs will continue to skyrocket. Medicare rolls will continue to swell and the big financial Ponzi scheme will eventually go bankrupt. Remember what I said in Chapter 1? It is going to happen. And now Obamacare exchanges are going belly up faster than we can count:

Two more Obamacare co-ops fail: Tennessee and Kentucky both announce closures, October 15, 2015, Kristina Ribali

"Only 17 of the original 23 co-ops are still providing coverage, despite the federal government doling out a reported $2.4 billion in loans through an assistance program designed to help start Obamacare insurance cooperatives around the country. As of December 2014, 21 of the 23 were still losing money. The 78,000+ enrollees in these two states who are now being notified that they're losing their plans will likely find little comfort in the words of former HHS Secretary Sebelius, who recently claimed Obamacare keeps people from being 'locked out, priced out, or dumped out,' of their plans. For these folks, their cancellation notices say otherwise."

Obamacare isn't about loyalty to a political party. *It's about returning to what used to work – the free market –* **in giving Americans the finest health care for lower costs**. It also means competition between health care providers with the ability to cross state lines. A Tenth Amendment issue the states will work out, not mother government making yet another mess that has already cost we the people tens and tens of billions of *borrowed* dollars. Once again using debt to fund debt.

6

Non-Ratification of Seventeenth Amendment – Why It's So Important

Along the way in my journey learning the truth I discovered that at the same time Bill Benson researched the non-ratified Sixteenth Amendment (called the "income" tax amendment), he was also attempting to verify enough states had ratified the Seventeenth Amendment.

Why is this so important? Well, one has to take a short trip back to when the Framers of the U.S. Constitution were meeting and deciding on the birth of our constitutional republic and how to make it work for a new nation.

When the First Continental Congress was convened via a resolution of the Congress of the Confederation, one of the first issues discussed on May 29, 1787, was the balance of power for a newly created federal government:

> 3. Resolved, that the National Legislature ought to consist of two branches.
>
> 4. Resolved, that the member of the first branch of the National Legislature ought to be elected by the people of the several States every _____ for the term of _____; to be of the age of _____ years at least and so forth.
>
> 5. Resolved, that the members of the second branch of the National Legislature ought to be elected by those of the first, out of a proper number of persons nominated by the individual Legislatures, to be of the age of _____ years at least and so forth.

James Madison, known as the "Father of the Constitution" wrote in The Federalist Papers #45 – **The Alleged Danger From the Powers of the Union to the State Governments Considered** for the Independent Journal:

"The Senate will be elected absolutely and exclusively by the State legislatures."

Madison went on to say:

> "*The powers reserved to the several States will extend to all the objects which, in the ordinary course of affairs, concern the lives, liberties, and properties of the people, and the internal order, improvement, and prosperity of the State. The operations of the federal government will be most extensive and important in times of war and danger; those of the State governments, in times of peace and security. As the former periods will probably bear a small proportion to the latter, the State governments will here enjoy another advantage over the federal government. The more adequate, indeed, the federal powers may be rendered to the national defense, the less frequent will be those scenes of danger which might favor their ascendancy over the governments of the particular States.*
>
> "*If the new Constitution be examined with accuracy and candor, it will be found that the change which it proposes consists much less in the addition of NEW POWERS to the Union, than in the invigoration of its ORIGINAL POWERS. The regulation of commerce, it is true, is a new power; but that seems to be an addition which few oppose, and from which no apprehensions are entertained. The powers relating to war and peace, armies and fleets, treaties and finance, with the other more considerable powers, are all vested in the existing Congress by the articles of Confederation. The proposed change does not enlarge these powers; it only substitutes a more effectual mode of administering them.*"

John Jay, (One of the Founding Fathers, Delegate to the First Continental Congress from New York, Delegate to the Second Continental Congress from New York, 6th President of the Continental Congress, United States Minister to Spain, United States Secretary of Foreign Affairs, 2nd Governor of New York and 1st Chief Justice of the United States) co-author of The Federal Papers is quoted: "Jay then informed Governor Clinton that, unlike the Senate, where the two-thirds rule was in force for treaties and impeachment, *the lower house had nothing to do with treaties; it represented the people whereas the Senate represented the states* – for the Federalists always a significant distinction." [2]

The framers of the Constitution wisely understood the absolute necessity of ensuring we the people would have the right to vote for our representative in Congress, and at the same time because they all jealously guarded freedom and liberty, **the states must also have equal representation**. We the people would have the ability to remove via the ballot box, miscreants and scoundrels, while the state legislatures could recall their U.S. Senators who acted against the best interests of their state.

Lisa Murkowski [R-AK] was in a tight senate race in 2010 against Joe Miller, also a Republican. *Fairbanks Daily News Miner*, October 6, 2010:

U.S. Senate candidate Joe Miller's support for repealing 17th Amendment draws criticism

"Sen. Lisa Murkowski, defeated by Miller in the Republican primary but who has begun a write-in campaign to stay in office, was the first to criticize Miller's comments, issuing a news release entitled Joe Miller reaching new extremes every day. 'We have seen Joe Miller take some extraordinary positions in this campaign, but I never imagined he would support disenfranchising himself and every other Alaskan,' Murkowski said in a statement. 'Joe is no longer content with simply taking away federal support for Alaskan families, now he wants to take away their right to select our United States senators.'"

According to Murkowski, then candidate Miller is "reaching new extremes" every day. I doubt witless Murkowski even knows Miller was proposing exactly what James Madison, Father of the U.S. Constitution, said so long ago: **The U.S. senate would never be put in the hands of voters**.

Murkowski spouts more propaganda that repealing the Seventeenth Amendment would disenfranchise Alaskans. Just the opposite is true because the voters of Alaska **are already represented by their U.S. House members they vote into office** so they are not being disenfranchised or denied representation in the U.S. Congress.

The Senate was supposed to be a sort of checks and balances, but that noble concept disappeared when U.S. Senators were then voted into office by special interests and mobs demanding more and more from the people's treasury. The absolute right of the states to equal representation was wiped out when the Seventeenth Amendment was declared ratified on April 8, 1913. **The result has been disastrous for our nation and we as individual citizens of each state.**

1913 was a trifecta if you will for powerful interests who have been working to destroy these united States of America for well over century.

1. The Sixteenth Amendment was declared ratified giving Congress *no new power of taxation*, but we all know how that turned into stealing the fruits of our labor with a gun to our head *to fund our own destruction.*

2. The Seventeenth Amendment, direct election of U.S. Senators by the people, was critical in destroying the balance of power in the U.S. Congress, wrestling away the sovereign power of the States and any representation in Washington, DC.

3. Then came the ultimate pot of gold at the end of the rainbow on December 23, 1913, passage of the unconstitutional "Federal" Reserve Banking Act which began using fiat currency.

"Paper money has had the effect in your State [Rhode Island] that it ever will have, to ruin commerce—oppress the honest, and open a door to every species of fraud and injustice." Letter from George Washington to Jabez Bowen, 9 January 1787

As with the collusion of banking interests and former U.S. Senators pushing through the unconstitutional 'Federal' Reserve, in the mid-1900s, a movement was launched to justify an amendment to the U.S. Constitution sweeping sweep aside the original intent of the Founding Fathers. As always it was and still is all about money and power.

Pre-1913, Art. 1, Sec. 3, Clause 1 of the Constitution read:

"The Senate of the United States shall be composed of two Senators from each state, *chosen by the legislature* thereof, for six years; and each Senator shall have one vote."

The U.S. House of Representatives would be elected by the people to represent them in that body in each state based on population per district.

Each state would have two senators so representation of the states was equal. Those two senators would serve the state legislature to serve the interests of the state. If they failed, a state legislature could recall one or both senators and replace them.

A perfect balance.

The fraudulently ratified Seventeenth Amendment changed all that:

"Clause 1. The Senate of the United States shall be composed of two Senators from each State, *elected by the people thereof*, for six years; and each Senator shall have one vote."

According to the National Conference of *State* Legislatures [NCSL] only 15 states currently have term limits: Maine, California, Arkansas, Michigan, Florida, South Dakota, Montana, Arizona, Missouri, Oklahoma, Nebraska, Louisiana and Nevada. It should be all 50 states to stop long entrenched cronyism and corruption.

Repealing the Seventeenth Amendment has been a hot topic for a long, long time:

The Seventeenth Amendment: Should It Be Repealed? Why Direct Election of Senators May Have Been A Serious Mistake, John W. Dean, September 13, 2002

"The Cloudy Reasons Behind the Seventeenth Amendment

"Before the Seventeenth Amendment the federal government remained stable and small. Following the Amendment's adoption it has grown dramatically.

"The conventional wisdom is that it was FDR's New Deal that radically increased the size and power of federal government. But scholars make a convincing case that this conventional wisdom is wrong, and that instead, it was the Seventeenth Amendment (along with the Sixteenth Amendment, which created federal income tax and was also adopted in 1913) that was the driving force behind federal expansion...

"Two Main Seventeenth Amendment Theories Don't Hold Water On Examination

"There have been two principal explanations for changing the Constitution to provide for direct election of Senators. Some see the Amendment as part of the Progressive Movement, which swept the nation in the late 1800s and early 1900s, giving us direct elections, recall, and referendums. Others, however, believe the Amendment resulted from the problems the prior Constitutional system was creating in state legislatures, who under that system were charged with electing Senators. These problems ranged from charges of bribery to unbreakable deadlocks.

"Deadlocks happened from time to time when, because of party imbalance, a legislature was unable to muster a majority (as necessary under the 1866 law that controlled) in favor any person. The result was to leave the Senate seat empty and leave the state represented by only a single Senator, not the Constitutionally-mandated two. What about the "corruption and deadlock" explanation? Zywicki's analysis shows that, in fact, the corruption was nominal, and infrequent. In addition, he points out that the deadlock problem could have been easily solved by legislation that would have required only a plurality to elect a Senator – a far easier remedy than the burdensome process of amending the Constitution that led to the Seventeenth Amendment. [4]

In that lengthy piece Dean also talks about the astronomical amount of money spent by candidates and incumbents to win a seat in the U.S. Senate in 2014.

North Carolina	$113, 639, 041
Iowa	$97,113,707
Kentucky	$78,248,429
Georgia	$66,845,580
Arkansas	$ 59,794,643
Alaska	$ 59,143,107
New Hampshire	$51,221,447
Michigan	$ 46,981,709
Total	**$572,987,663**

$572,987,663 – over half a BILLION dollars for eight U.S. Senate seats for a job pays $174,000 per year. It's obscene and that's only 8 out of 33 seats. Every two years 1/3rd of the senate is up for reelection *under a law that doesn't exist.*

All that money comes with the understanding donors want something in return. Tens and tens and tens of MILLIONS of dollars pouring into individual states from special interest groups. There's been a lot of talk and worthless legislation over the years about campaign finance reform. **None of it has curbed buying U.S. Senate seats.** How can you call it anything else?

Another excellent explanation of why the Seventeenth Amendment has been so destructive:

Rethinking The 17th Amendment by Trenton Hansen, May 13, 2009

"Each senator was to be appointed to that position in the national government. This is a very important point that should not be overlooked or misinterpreted. Government appointments are oftentimes construed as a form of corruption. The Founders didn't think so. In fact, the Senate was to be appointed for the very purpose of preventing corruption. Allow me an explanation.

"The members of the House of Representatives are elected, according to the Constitution, by popular vote every two years. This puts them in constant need to be responsive to their constituents if they want to get re-elected. If they aren't doing what their constituents want, they shouldn't be re-elected. The short time frame also helps to minimize the damage that could be done to our form of limited government. The combination of short terms, and direct accountability to the people, was intended to create an environment hostile to the creation of Legislation. Congress wasn't created to 'do something' because the Founder's didn't want a lot of laws being passed by Congress. In the Federalist #62, Madison and Hamilton argue,

> *"It will be of little avail to the people, that the laws are made by men of their own choice, if the laws be so voluminous that they cannot be read, or so incoherent that they cannot be understood; if they be repealed or revised before they are promulgated, or undergo such incessant changes that no man, who knows what the law is to-day, can guess what it will be to-morrow."*

"The Senate, on the other hand, was intended to be a deliberative body. The six-year terms would give enough time to accomplish something, while still short enough to keep them in mindfulness of their purpose in being elected. Additionally, because the Senate was appointed by the voice of the Legislatures of the several States, it was hoped the influence of party (or faction) would not become an issue. The current methods used by Senators to get re-elected, i.e. gathering campaign contributions from special interests, would not have been possible previous to the ratification of the 17th Amendment. The McCain-Feingold Campaign Finance Reform Act would be unnecessary under the conditions that obtained under the original program laid out in the Constitution, as the effects the Act was intended to combat would be very difficult to achieve." [5]

Democrats weighing in on repealing the Amendment claim it's all right wing Republicans who want to take away your voice in the U.S. Senate. Not true:

Zell Miller: Dump: 17th Amendment – Maverick Democrat wants to go back to legislatures appointing U.S. senators, April 2004

"Georgia Democratic Sen. Zell Miller is calling for the United States to restore the wishes of its Founding Fathers and empower state legislatures to appoint senators rather than be elected by voters. The retiring Miller, who has garnered attention over the past year with stinging critiques of his Democratic Party, believes rescinding the 17th Amendment would curb the power of special interests in Washington while increasing the power of state governments.

"The individuals are not so much at fault as the rotten and decaying foundation of what is no longer a republic,' Miller said on the Senate floor, according to the Associated Press. 'It is the system that stinks. And it's only going to get worse because that perfect balance our brilliant Founding Fathers put in place in 1787 no longer exists.' Members of the U.S. House have been chosen by voters since the nation's founding. Miller, a former two-term governor of Georgia, contends the Constitution's prescription for balancing the interests of large and small states and the power of state and federal governments was destroyed when the U.S. ratified the 17th Amendment in 1913." [6]

Opponents of getting rid of the Seventeenth Amendment always bleat "democracy will be ruined"!

Dr. James McHenry was a delegate to the Constitutional Convention of 1787. He wrote that when Dr. Benjamin Franklin was leaving Independence Hall a lady asked him: "Well Doctor what have we got, a republic or a monarchy." Franklin replied, "A republic . . . if you can keep it."

A democracy was NOT the form of government given to we the people with rivers of blood on the battlefield nor was it even a desired form of government. It is also the most repeated lie on TV, in classrooms, by politicians and ignorant charlatans in the media, electronic and print.

Thomas Jefferson declared: "A democracy is nothing more than mob rule, where fifty-one percent of the people may take away the rights of the other forty-nine."

John Adams, America's second president, wrote: "Remember, democracy never lasts long. It soon wastes, exhausts, and murders itself. There never was a democracy yet that did not commit suicide."

"A Democracy cannot exist as a permanent form of Government. It can only exist until the voters discover they can vote themselves largess of the public treasury. From that moment on the majority always votes for the candidate promising the most benefits from the public treasury with the result that Democracy always collapses over a loose fiscal policy..." Professor Alexander Fraser Tyler

"Democracy will soon degenerate into an anarchy; such an anarchy that every man will do what is right in his own eyes and no man's life or property or reputation or liberty will be secure, and every one of these will soon mould itself into a system of subordination of all the moral virtues and intellectual abilities, all the powers of wealth, beauty, wit, and science, to the wanton pleasures, the capricious will, and the execrable cruelty of one or a very few." John Adams, *An Essay on Man's Lust for Power* (1763)

"At no time, at no place in solemn convention assembled, through no chosen agents, had the American people officially proclaimed the United States to be a democracy. The Constitution did not contain the word or any word lending countenance to it..." American historian Charles Austin Beard, one of the most influential historians of the first half of the 20th century.

Speaking about the purpose of the Constitutional Convention of 1787, Edmund Jennings Randolph (August 10, 1753 – September 12, 1813; attorney, seventh Governor of Virginia, second Secretary of State, and America's United States Attorney General) wrote: "The general object was to provide a cure for the evils under which the United States labored; that in tracing these evils, to their origin, every man had found it in the turbulence and follies of democracy."

Georgia General Assembly 2013-2014 Regular Session – HR 273 – House Resolution 273 By: Representatives Cooke – You can look up that bill on line.

There is another constitutional issue here and that is Article 5 of the U.S. Constitution:

"The Congress, whenever two thirds of both Houses shall deem it necessary, shall propose, Amendments to this Constitution, or, on the Application of the Legislatures of two thirds of the several States, shall call a Convention for proposing Amendments, which, in either Case, shall be valid to all Intents and Purposes, as Part of this Constitution, when ratified by the Legislatures of three fourths of the several States, or by Conventions in three fourths thereof, as the one or the other Mode of Ratification may be proposed by the Congress; Provided that no Amendment which may be made prior to the Year One thousand eight hundred and eight shall in any Manner affect the first and fourth Clauses in the Ninth Section of the first Article; and that *no State, without its Consent, shall be deprived of its equal Suffrage in the Senate.*"

Several states were out of session at the time the proposed amendment was being considered by the states. The fraudulent ratification of the Seventeenth Amendment most certainly has deprived those states not in session "equal Suffrage in the Senate".

I've spent the past few years trying to get our legislature (Texas) to file a lawsuit to keep candidates and incumbents for U.S. Senate off the ballot because they are running under a law that doesn't exist. For the 2013 session, I prepared a "working paper" for our legislature here in

Texas. I set up a separate web page to assist members of legislatures why it is so important they challenge the non-ratification of that amendment: http://devvy.com/abc.html

There has been no interest by the Texas State Legislature that I'm aware of to expose such an egregious lie that has harmed the state and citizens who reside here. While a few state legislators have attempted to get Congress to repeal that amendment, none seem to have been successful because senators currently serving will do nothing that might jeopardize their job and *the power they wield over our lives.*

By 2014, it became apparent to me no members of any state legislature were going to file a lawsuit. It would be up to me. I'm not a lawyer and have no legal training. But, I have been blessed over the past decades to have a few dear friends who are and who have practiced in both state and federal courts. It's also very costly to file a lawsuit either at the state or federal level. The filing fees at the state level are hundreds of dollars and more each time you need to file at another step along the way.

One of the biggest dangers in pro se filings is our judicial system. State and federal have become such convoluted systems with a million decisions over the decades, if a person does not know what they're doing and lose, it puts bad case law on the books. Then when someone who does have a case that should be heard, it's thrown out based on some prior case kicked to the curb.

In my case, I filed in state court to keep U.S. Senate candidates off the November ballot in 2014. Since the Seventeenth Amendment was not ratified by enough states, the Secretary of State would be committing fraud by allowing them on the ballot. How can someone run for office under a law that doesn't exist?

I knew and my friend who is a constitutional attorney practicing primarily in federal court rooms for over 35 years also knew the lower court (District court here in Texas) would dismiss my case. We knew that going in. My case filed September 24, 2014 was originally "heard" in Austin, Texas, on December 4, 2014. I've been in courtrooms a few times watching trials. What happened during my hearing was nothing short of bizarre.

I arrived at the court house early; a six-hour drive from my home. Packed with people. What I discovered sitting around surrounded by a hundred lawyers is that *judges get case assignments 15 minutes before court time.* What? How can a judge possibly review my case only 15 minutes before court starts? They can't and it's one of the dirty little secrets I became aware of on my way up the elevator.

Upon arriving on the appropriate floor, the place was just mobbed with people trying to get into courtrooms. I found mine around the corner; no one was trying to get in those doors. After entering the courtroom, I see there are two women, two men and the court reporter. The judge came in looking like Santa Claus in a black robe. He proceeded to tell the nearly empty, huge courtroom that the regular judge wasn't available today. He was brought out of retirement to hear two cases. Really?

The two ladies ended up being opposing counsel for a personal injury case. It was dispatched by the judge in about 20 minutes. Next up, yours truly.

The two gentlemen I correctly figured were attorneys from the Attorney General's Office. The judge began by grilling me about who I work for? Seriously. Did I work for a corporation, some group, what? After he got done rattling off his list, I replied I work for no one which is the truth. Both the judge and the states attorneys knew my Request for Writ of Prohibition and Injunction likely wasn't written by me. Not that a lay person can't write one. In my case, all the research was mine. I provided the ingredients and my attorney friend, Larry Becraft, whipped up the entree.

The whole time the judge rarely looked at me. It was absurd as there are more than 250 pages of documents from the National Archives on a disk, another CD of all the California State Legislature's Journal (3,000 pages) for the year 1913 and so on.

Judge Strauss wasn't remotely interested in what I had to say which wasn't much. The fix was obviously in. Next up was one of the state's attorneys who really didn't have a chance to say much either. They were there to get the case dismissed on standing, jurisdiction and other legalese.

While listening to the state's attorney as brief as he was, I was watching that judge thinking this is so strange. All the court rooms are over flowing, yet my case is heard in a huge, empty courtroom with four people (two sets of attorneys), the court reporter, me and a judge brought out of retirement.

When the state's attorney was finished, the brought out of retirement Santa Claus judge told me he believed the Secretary of State in 1913 without reading the evidence or even asking me questions about those court certified documents. He also said the election was over so who cares anyway?

He then did something that shocked me. One of the dangers of losing a case is the defendant(s) can ask the court to force you to pay court costs and any other damages. Judge Strauss immediately upon dismissing my case looked over at the state attorneys and asked them what sanctions against me they were going for?

One of them stood up and said, "nothing your Honor". Why, I thought gramps was going to blow out his shorts right there on the bench. Say it isn't so! How dare that woman come into court making such claims! That was it. The months of waiting was over in 15 minutes. The State could easily have come back and ask for court costs and more, but they didn't and I was grateful.

The next step was filing in the Third District Court of Appeals in Austin. First you have to file a notice that you're going to appeal and then file your brief. I had a couple of family emergencies out in California so it got pushed back several months. My appeal brief was filed June 27, 2015. I did not ask for oral arguments because the **evidence** speaks for itself. All the exhibits are found on my web site (www.devvy.com); look at the left side of the page where it says Proof Seventeenth Amendment Was Not Ratified.

My case in the Third Circuit was: *Devvy Kidd vs. Carlos Cascos*, Texas Secretary of State, Case No. 03-14-00805-CV.

The non-ratification of a constitutional amendment is a very, very serious issue which is why the courts and Congress don't want to touch it. Much easier to simply throw it out *despite concrete evidence* which is exactly what the appeals court did in Austin, Texas, on December 22, 2015.

On December 22, 2015, the Third Circuit Court of Appeals in Austin, Texas, put their rubber stamp on fraud. Those black robed judges did what is called a "hose job" by lawyers. Those black robed judges endorsed fraud committed when William Jennings Bryan, Secretary of State back in 1913 declared the amendment ratified when I have proven beyond any legal doubt it was not. Appeal denied.

Those black robed judges ruled for political expediency instead of the truth and the law and it's been happening in courtrooms longer than I've been alive.

The U.S. Congress and state legislatures refuse to impeach activist judges. All they do is whine about decisions and ask for more campaign donations instead of throwing judges off the bench as a warning to the next body: You are not there to make law and you are not there to condone fraud over a legal issue that might cause a political problem.

It didn't matter to the Third Circuit Court of Appeals that the historical documents I submitted as **evidence prove beyond a shadow of a doubt that amendment was NOT ratified by enough states.** They used BS to justify dismissing my case. No use in wasting more of my time and money by going to the Texas Supreme Court. As they say, the fix is in and now the only option left (other than repealing the Seventeenth Amendment which in itself would be a fraud – how do you repeal an amendment that was never legally ratified?) is the states of the Union.

State legislatures across this country can file the same lawsuit I did (all the work is done) and not have to worry about standing. This issue must become a top priority in this country for all the reasons above. **It will not happen unless states step forward**. Try Utah, Montana, Arizona, Kentucky, Tennessee, Nevada to name a few. **That will not happen unless there is a huge roar from the American people.**

You can read the court filings of my case at:

http://www.devvy.com/docs/Kidd_v_TX_Sec_of_State.pdf

7

Illegal aliens: liars, cheats, thieves, rapists, murderers

Illegal alien

1. a foreigner who has entered or resides in a country unlawfully or without the country's authorization.
2. a foreigner who enters the U.S. without an entry or immigrant visa, esp. a person who crosses the border by avoiding inspection or who overstays the period of time allowed as a visitor, tourist, or businessperson.

The issue of illegal aliens and the massive human invasion across our borders turned into a galactic poop storm in June 2015 when Donald Trump told the truth about illegal aliens.

Illegal aliens are not immigrants. My grandparents were immigrants. My father's parents came from Munich. My mother's parents from Palermo, Sicily. They waited their turn. Before they could get on the boat, they had to pass an English proficiency test and have a TB (tuberculosis) certification from a doctor less than 30 days old. They were told when they applied to immigrate to America *there was no welfare*. You worked or you didn't eat. Calling illegal aliens immigrants is nothing more than a marketing trick to distract people from their legal federal status. Immigrant sounds more acceptable than illegal alien.

The issue with illegal aliens is not a race issue. It's a legal issue *regardless of country of origin*. One would think from the propaganda constantly regurgitated by charlatans in the mainstream media who try to pass themselves off as reporters or journalists that Republicans and/or conservatives are nothing but racists for demanding our immigration laws are enforced. Really? How about these folks?

America First Latinos

"America First Latinos was created to prove, for once and for all, that the vast majority of Latino citizens are solidly behind the U.S. Constitution and a secured national border. Because this fact is falsely represented by a biased media, we have come together to proclaim that most U.S. Latinos are unified in these matters. We also agree that it is unacceptable for local, state and national public servants to assume that they speak for all U.S. Latinos, a false and despicable narrative, and an insult to the millions of intelligent and proud American Latinos across the nation.

"We demand that they cease and desist immediately from this racist stereotyping. We also call for the immediate resignation of all public servants who, through their authorship of bills, voting records and/or public speech, have placed other countries and non-citizens ahead of our country and our citizens." [1] How come they aren't interviewed on *CNN, MSNBC* or *FOX "News" Network*?

Growing number of Hispanic Texans pushing for tougher immigration laws. March 24, 2015, *Fox News Latino*

"Pedro Rivera is 53 years old, Hispanic, and a retired military man. He's also part of a growing number of Hispanic Texans pushing for stronger immigration enforcement, including the passage of SB 185, which would stop cities from implementing policies banning local cops from asking immigration-related questions.

"I'm an American citizen and I believe in the rule of law,' Rivera said. 'And being Hispanic, I should not be granted special privilege in avoiding the law. We need officers to have all the tools available to them to keep us safe. That includes asking the question, when you're being detained for a crime or being arrested for an offense, Are you here illegally? Are you a U.S. citizen?' Rivera is working with Maria Espinoza, director of the Remembrance Project. Espinoza's Houston-based organization works with families of Americans killed by people in the United States illegally." [2] The Remembrance Project does just that. Remember Americans slaughtered by illegal aliens forgotten in the dirty world of politics. I invite you to visit their web site: *www.remembranceprojectorg*

Another major issue is all the diseases illegals have been importing into our country that were eradicated from America a long time ago and now we the people are footing the bill to the tune of tens of millions of dollars in costs for treatment – all borrowed money with the interest slapped on our backs, our children and grandchildren:

Illegal Alien Minors Spreading TB, Dengue, Swine Flu. July 8m, 2014, *Judicial Watch*

"The hordes of illegal immigrant minors entering the U.S. are bringing serious diseases — including swine flu, dengue fever, possibly Ebola virus and tuberculosis — that present a danger to the American public as well as the Border Patrol agents forced to care for the kids, according to a U.S. Congressman who is also medical doctor.

"This has created a 'severe and dangerous' crisis, says the Georgia lawmaker, Phil Gingrey. Most of the Unaccompanied Alien Children (UAC) are coming from Central America and they're importing infectious diseases considered to be largely eradicated in this country. Additionally, many of the migrants lack basic vaccinations such as those to prevent chicken pox or measles, leaving America's young children and the elderly particularly susceptible, Gingrey reveals." [3]

Nurse: Illegals' baggage includes TB, leprosy, polio, July 9, 2014, *WND*

"Regular TB, drug-resistant TB, both are airborne and both are highly contagious. The regular strain costs about $17,000 a year to treat. The drug resistant strain may be not treatable and [if it is] will cost upward of $100,000 a year to treat," she said.

"Then there's the leprosy. 'It's highly contagious and not diagnosable necessarily by a parent,' she said. 'A white spot on their face may not be recognizable as leprosy.' And there are the other tropical diseases, as well as swine flu, scabies and lice. 'Polio will be coming across the border,' she said, 'because children are not medically screened by the Border Patrol.'" [4]

And, we are being raped for this which no *legitimately* elected president has any authority to do:

Obama gives illegals massive health-care plan – On tap: 5.5 million hours from workers trained to deal with "intersex, gender nonconforming", August 2, 2015, *WND*:

"The level of health-care services provided to illegal aliens is about to get a huge boost from the Obama administration, which is hiring contractors to provide the equivalent of 5.5 million additional labor hours of treatment to detainees. U.S. Immigration and Customs Enforcement, or ICE, of the Department of Homeland Security did not provide an estimated cost of these support services over five years. It is leaving it up to vendors to propose how much it will cost.

"According to a solicitation for bids that WND discovered through routine database research, the purpose of this initiative is 'to provide on-site medical staffing services to provide a continuum of health care services to ICE residents/detainees 24 hours a day, seven (7) days per week, and 365 calendar days per year' at various clinic sites. All of the treatment will come from workers who are screened to be politically correct." [5]

The issue of illegals, *regardless of country of origin*, is not a popularity contest. **It doesn't matter how nice an illegal is or how long they've been here.** They violated OUR immigration laws to smuggle themselves across the border. They have trespassed onto U.S. soil without being invited.

It's Okay for Illegals to Steal Your Identity! December 14, 2006, My column, *Newswithviews.com*

Hector Angel, Relative of Swift Employee: "Everybody has to do what they have to do to make a living. I agree with that, that it's wrong. But at the same time, it's not, because, you know, we are human beings."

So, even though it's wrong to steal the identity of an American, it's not really because "we're all human beings." It's okay to smuggle yourself across the border, steal someone else's identity and credit history because, after all, "we're just human beings." It's okay to smuggle yourself across the border and take a job that lawfully belongs to an American because, golly, warm, fuzzy – "we're just human beings." This is how these criminals think: they know they're breaking the law, but any politically correct excuse will be used to justify their actions." [6]

Identity Theft, Document Fraud, and Illegal Employment by Ronald W. Mortensen, Center for Immigration Studies

"Illegal immigrants are not 'undocumented.' They have fraudulent documents such as counterfeit Social Security cards, forged driver's licenses, fake green cards, and phony birth certificates. Experts suggest that approximately 75 percent of working-age illegal aliens use fraudulent Social Security cards to obtain employment....

"Illegal immigration and high levels of identity theft go hand-in-hand. States with the most illegal immigration also have high levels of job-related identity theft. In Arizona, 33 percent or all identity theft is job-related (as opposed to identity theft motivated simply by profit). In Texas it is 27 percent; in New Mexico, 23 percent; in Colorado, 22 percent; California, 20 percent; and in Nevada, 16 percent. Eight of the 10 states with the highest percentage of illegal aliens in their total population are among the top 10 states in identity theft (Arizona, California, Florida, Texas, Nevada, New York, Georgia, and Colorado)...

"Illegal aliens commit felonies in order to get jobs. Illegal aliens who use fraudulent documents, perjure themselves on I-9 forms, and commit identity theft in order to get jobs are committing serious offenses and are not 'law abiding.' Tolerance of corruption erodes the rule of law. Corruption is a serious problem in most illegal aliens' home countries. Allowing it to flourish here paves the way for additional criminal activity and increased corruption throughout society. Leaders support perpetrators and ignore victims. Political, civic, religious, business, education, and media leaders blame Americans for 'forcing' illegal aliens to commit document fraud and identity theft. No similar concern is expressed for the American men, women, and children whose lives are destroyed in the process.

"The Social Security Administration and Internal Revenue Service facilitate illegal immigrant-driven identity theft. Both turn a blind eye to massive SSN fraud and take no action to stop it. The Social Security Administration assigns SSNs to new-born infants that are being used illegally. The IRS demands that victims pay taxes on wages earned by illegal aliens using their stolen SSNs, while taking no action to stop the identity theft." [7]

The cost of illegal aliens has cost you, me our children and grandchildren TRILLIONS of borrowed dollars in debt since Ronnie

Reagan opened the flood gates. Let's look at just my state, Texas – a gateway state for the human invasion underway:

TX Taxpayers Pay Billions for Illegal Aliens to Use State Services, January 16, 2014, *Breitbart*

"After a brief hiatus that coincided with the worst of the economic recession, Texas's illegal alien population is on the rise again," the opening paragraph of the report reads. "There are about 1,810,000 illegal aliens residing in Texas — 70,000 more than resided in the state in 2010 when we estimated the fiscal burden at nearly $8.9 billion annually."

"Specifically, in 2013 alone, FAIR estimates Texans were on the hook for $12.1 billion because of illegal immigration in the state. 'That amounts to more than $1,197 for every Texas household headed by a native-born or naturalized U.S. citizen,' FAIR wrote. 'The taxes paid by illegal aliens — estimated at $1.27 billion per year — do not come close to paying for those outlays, but we include an estimate of revenue from sales taxes, property taxes, alcohol taxes, and cigarette taxes.'

"A breakdown of the costs shows that illegal aliens in Texas are accessing a wide variety of public services they are not supposed to have access to, placing a burden on taxpayers throughout the state. For instance, FAIR found that annually the estimated 195,000 illegal alien students and 481,000 U.S.-born children of illegal aliens place an $8.5 billion burden on taxpayers for their education costs. Many of those students require special needs help with the English language, too, driving the cost even higher for Texas taxpayers." [8]

Illegal immigrants send home $50 billion annually but cost taxpayers more than $113 billion, October 29, 2014

"Approximately 126,000 illegal immigrants emigrated from these three nations to the U.S. since last October and federal officials estimate at least 95,500 more will enter next year. The Central American governments have encouraged the high levels of emigration because it is earning their economy billions of dollars! For every illegal alien that sneaks into the U.S. and remits money back home, that grand total remittance number only grows. But what if the millions of U.S. jobs now filled by illegal aliens were done by

American workers earning better wages, paying more in taxes and spending their money in their communities rather than sending it abroad?" [9]

In other words, illegal aliens take money they earn illegally by stealing jobs that belong to Americans and *send what should belong to the people of America to foreign countries*. $50 BILLION dollars that should have been earned by American workers and **kept in OUR country**. Now, does that sit well with you?

California DMV Ordered to Overlook Identity Theft by Illegals, January 27, 2015, *Breitbart*

"Illegal aliens may enjoy a free pass on identity theft due to a new investigative policy at California's Department of Motor Vehicles (DMV). The policy, issued last year and effective as of Jan. 1, 2015, directs DMV investigators to overlook identity theft by applicants "who may have attempted to obtain or been issued a license or ID card previously through submission of false information."

"A DMV source who asked to remain anonymous provided Breitbart News exclusively with a copy of the newly-enacted internal policy memorandum. The document informs DMV investigative officers that past identity theft is acceptable when the illegally-acquired IDs were only used to obtain a driver license, and where the license or ID was not used to commit any other crime." [10]

Those "nice" illegals who steal Americans SSNs and make their lives miserable. Those "nice" people who "just want to make a better life for themselves" think nothing of stealing jobs that belong to Americans – more than 12 MILLION jobs which is probably a low ball number. They are thieves no different than someone who robs a bank and yet, the person in the White House, many Republicans and all Democrats in Congress, huge numbers of judges, state legislators, mayors and America hating militant organizations like LaRaza bend over backwards to protect them while endangering Americans on our own soil.

Illegals have NO constitutional rights regardless of what corrupt political animals who sit on the bench masquerading as judges decide for their own agenda. The only right an illegal alien has is humane holding until they can be shipped right back to where they came from.

No $250.00 an hour attorneys we're raped to pay for trying to protect illegals caught and then screaming for their "rights" in court.

The issue with illegal aliens is a dead serious national security problem being completely ignored by the occupant in the White House and most members of Congress. Not all, but certainly every single Democrat. Our wide open Southern border is a magnet for terrorists to cross over. **There's no doubt in my mind they have been crossing over and are just biding their time.**

ISIS Camp a Few Miles from Texas, Mexican Authorities Confirm, April 14, 2015, *Judicial Watch*

"ISIS is operating a camp just a few miles from El Paso, Texas, according to Judicial Watch sources that include a Mexican Army field grade officer and a Mexican Federal Police Inspector. The exact location where the terrorist group has established its base is around eight miles from the U.S. border in an area known as "Anapra" situated just west of Ciudad Juárez in the Mexican state of Chihuahua. Another ISIS cell to the west of Ciudad Juárez, in Puerto Palomas, targets the New Mexico towns of Columbus and Deming for easy access to the United States, the same knowledgeable sources confirm.

"During the course of a joint operation last week, Mexican Army and federal law enforcement officials discovered documents in Arabic and Urdu, as well as 'plans' of Fort Bliss – the sprawling military installation that houses the US Army's 1st Armored Division. Muslim prayer rugs were recovered with the documents during the operation. Law enforcement and intelligence sources report the area around Anapra is dominated by the Vicente Carrillo Fuentes Cartel ('Juárez Cartel'), La Línea (the enforcement arm of the cartel) and the Barrio Azteca (a gang originally formed in the jails of El Paso). Cartel control of the Anapra area make it an extremely dangerous and hostile operating environment for Mexican Army and Federal Police operations.

"According to these same sources, 'coyotes' engaged in human smuggling – and working for Juárez Cartel – help move ISIS terrorists through the desert and across the border between Santa Teresa and Sunland Park, New Mexico. To the east of El Paso and Ciudad Juárez, cartel-backed 'coyotes' are also smuggling ISIS terrorists through the porous border between Acala and Fort Hancock, Texas. These specific areas were targeted for exploitation by ISIS because of their understaffed municipal and county police forces, and the relative safe-havens the areas provide for the unchecked large-scale drug smuggling that was already ongoing.

"Mexican intelligence sources report that ISIS intends to exploit the railways and airport facilities in the vicinity of Santa Teresa, NM (a US port-of-entry). The sources also say that ISIS has 'spotters' located in the East Potrillo Mountains of New Mexico (largely managed by the Bureau of Land Management) to assist with terrorist border crossing operations. ISIS is conducting reconnaissance of regional universities; the White Sands Missile Range; government facilities in Alamogordo, NM; Ft. Bliss; and the electrical power facilities near Anapra and Chaparral, NM." [11]

As I write this book, Obama and too many members of the U.S. Congress are doing everything – **including defying the orders of a federal judge** – to implement amnesty for 25-30 million illegal alien invaders. There is NO way to do background checks on even one million illegals, so the Obama administration and his minions in the Department of Fatherland (Homeland) Security are breaking every law in the book to give as many illegals green cards as possible making an end-run around Congress for blanket amnesty. Who are all these liars, cheats and thieves who have smuggled themselves across the border? **No one knows and that is criminal in itself.**

The issue with illegal aliens and violence is overwhelming. It took the murder of an innocent young woman, Kathleen Shinele, to rev up discussion about illegals and so-called sanctuary cities. Donald Trump, like him, dislike him has done more to bring this issue to the mainstream than anyone for more than three decades.

The government of Mexico has done little to nothing about stopping the flood across our Southern border. Why? Because it's their poorest of the poor sneaking across our border, not their middle or upper class. In exchange for facilitating unloading tens of millions of their citizens, the illegal invasion has been a financial boon for Mexico and other countries to the tune of billions of dollars over the past couple of decades.

Was Donald Trump accurate when he said Mexico sends rapists and murderers? High profile political figures were outraged:

"Trump's comments are not just offensive and inaccurate, but also divisive." Sen. Marco Rubio

"I was offended by his remarks," added former Texas Gov. Rick Perry on ABC's "This Week."

Former Arkansas Gov. Mike Huckabee said he would "never besmirch all the people who come here."

Willard "Mitt" Romney: "I think he made a severe error in saying what he did about Mexican-Americans," he said. "And it's unfortunate." **Tell me, Mr. Romney, how can illegal aliens be classified as Mexican-Americans?**

"God Bless" Illegal Immigrants, October 7, 2015, presidential candidate John Kasich

Alexis De Larosa Sosa, 21, is a Mexican national. An illegal alien. Not an "undocumented worker" or immigrant. He's here illegally from Mexico. On April 15, 3016, while street racing he killed Pastor Jesse Estrada Sabillon, and his wife, Maria.

Enrique Carbajal, 24, and Victor Tome, 19, of Wheaton, Maryland, both illegal aliens from Mexico were arrested April 10, 2016 and charged with the kidnapping and rape of a 12-year-old.

On July 1, 2015, 32-year old Kathryn Steinle was murdered in San Francisco in broad day light while walking with her father. While lying there bleeding in her father's arms she said, "Daddy help me". San Francisco is a sanctuary city that cares nothing for the lives of Americans. That poor young woman was murdered by Francisco Sanchez, a Mexican illegal alien who had been deported FIVE times, has SEVEN felony convictions. I wouldn't go to SF and drop one dime into their economy if someone gave me the trip for free.

"January 10, 2012. One-month old infant raped and murdered by illegal alien: Juan Galindo, possesses a criminal history that includes drug charges, driving under the influence, and a prior sexual assault of a minor charge. The illegal alien was formally arraigned for the rape and then killing of his girlfriend's four-week-old daughter. Galindo's bail was set at $1 million, cash or bond. Sadly, not one national newspaper, radio or television news organization covered this heinous and depraved criminal case, according to a sheriff's deputy in New Mexico. "The coroner's report indicated that the baby suffered from anal and vaginal tears and arriving police and crime scene investigators found her small body lying in a pool of blood...Galindo is an illegal alien from Mexico." Jim Kouri, *Law Enforcement Examiner*

Illegal Alien Here for One Month, Has Already Raped a 10-Year-Old Girl – Alabama. March 9, 2015: (*WHNT News*) – "A man who police say is in the country illegally is accused of sexually assaulting a young girl. The suspect has been in the U.S. just a few weeks." Rapist: Ramiro Ajualip

July 24, 2013: 13-year old girl brutally raped by 10 illegal immigrants. "Authorities have placed immigration detainers on two Mexican men charged in the rape of a 13-year-old runaway Texas girl. As many as 10 men allegedly took turns sexually assaulting the teen in an apartment where some cheered and filmed the attacks with their cellphone cameras, according to court records released last week.

"Juan Lozano Ortega, 24, and Edgar Gerardo Guzman Perez, 26, were charged with aggravated sexual assault of a child. Immigration detainers on both Mexican illegals... 'All of the other males took turns having sex with victim against her will, which lasted through the early morning hours,' the affidavit states." *The Blaze*

June 21, 2006: Illegal alien rapes puppy – Suspect felt there was no problem, claiming animal was his to abuse. Stuart, Florida. Enrique Garcia is an illegal from Mexico. *WND*

Father of slain QT clerk: why was criminal migrant free? April 7, 2015, *AZ Central*

"Altamirano had been arrested in August 2012 after a home invasion in which a woman said she was kidnapped and sexually assaulted by Altamirano and two others – associates of her boyfriend, who was in jail on drug charges. The Maricopa County Attorney's Office allowed Altamirano to plead guilty to a low-level burglary charge. He was sentenced to two years' probation and in January 2013 was turned over to Immigration and Customs Enforcement. Four days later, ICE released him on a $10,000 bond, to await his deportation hearing.

"For two years, this guy was allowed the walk the streets with no supervision. It didn't matter that he was a convicted felon. It didn't matter that two orders of protection were filed against him, including one from a woman who said he's threatened to kill her and pointed a gun at her boyfriend. Tragically, the only way to get this criminal off the streets was over Grant Ronnebeck's dead body. The Obama administration has said the deportation of criminals is its highest priority yet more than 66,000 convicted criminals were released by ICE in fiscal 2013 and 2014, according to the Department of Homeland Security." [12]

August 16, 2014, Cinthya Garcia-Cisneros, and other illegal alien drove over two little girls in Hillsboro, Oregon. 6-year-old Anna Dieter-Eckerdt and 11-year-old Abigail Robinson. After the illegal ran them down, Garcia-Cisneros and her boyfriend went to the local car wash to try and get rid of evidence. Meaning blood from two more innocent children while professional politicians in the U.S. Congress wring their hands and hold more hearings. You can find hundreds more at FNIC-VOIACM.org.

After the murder of Kathryn Steinle, Congress held more hearings to do what? NOTHING while more Americans are slaughtered. In August 2015, Congress took their annual "August recess" with full pay ($14,500 per month for the House and Senate rank and file) while more Americans died at the hands of illegal aliens. **I don't believe most Americans understand the hell and horror unleashed on this country by the person in the White House while the U.S. Congress whines and plays partisan politics.**

More Than 347,000 Convicted Criminal Immigrants at Large in U.S., July 7, 2015, *Breitbart*

"Hundreds of thousands of convicted criminal immigrants remain at large in the U.S. and a number have gone on to commit additional crimes. According to a March 2, 2015 'ICE Weekly Departures and Detention Report' obtained by Center for Immigration Studies expert Jessica Vaughan and shared with Breitbart News, there were 168,680 convicted criminal immigrants who had final orders of removal but who remained at large in the U.S. Another 179,018 convicted criminal immigrants with deportation cases pending also remained at large. While the vast majority were not in custody some were detained —

namely 6,220 criminal immigrants facing final deportation orders and another 7,680 convicted criminal immigrants with immigration cases pending. In recent years there has been a focus on the number of annual criminal immigrant releases.

"In 2013 the Obama administration released 36,007 criminal immigrants who had nearly 88,000 convictions. Those convictions included 193 homicide convictions, 426 sexual assault convictions, 303 kidnapping convictions, and 1,075 aggravated assault convictions. In January, the Department of Homeland Security revealed in a 38-page document to Senate Judiciary Chairman Chuck Grassley (R-IA) showing that of those criminals released in 2013, 1,000 had gone on to commit additional crimes including, terroristic threats, lewd acts with a minor, various types of assault, DUI, robbery, hit-and-run, gang activity, rape, and child cruelty."

"In 2014 the administration released another 30,558 criminal immigrants, who had a total of 79,059 convictions. The convictions included in the 2014 releases included: 86 homicide convictions, 186 kidnapping convictions, 373 sexual assault convictions, 449 commercialized sexual offenses, 1,194 battery convictions, 1,346 domestic violence convictions, and 13,636 DUIs." [13]

Good people who just want to have a better life. Really?

Mexican Criminal Alien Slaughters Motorists Who Tried to Help Him, August 4, 2015, *Newswithviews.com*

"An 18-year-old Mexican national who police claim was in possession of a 'green card' executed a Native American husband and wife who had stopped to offer assistance to him when they saw he was having trouble with his automobile. The suspect, who also shot and wounded the dead couple's daughter when she attempted to escape told police he committed the homicides because the man was too slow helping with his disabled vehicle and the daughter laughed at him, according to an FBI agent's testimony on Thursday during a court hearing.

"The married couple, 51-year-old Jason Shane and 47-year-old Tana Shane, died following the execution-style shooting which occurred on an Indian reservation in the small town of Pryor, Montana. Meanwhile, their daughter, 26-year-old Jorah Shane, was gunned down when she tried to run back to her house nearby. She was shot in her back as she ran screaming. The suspected gunman, Jesus Deniz a/k/a Jesus Deniz Mendoza, who gave Worland, Wyoming, as his hometown, told investigators he shot the three victims, when they had stopped to help him because 'Jorah laughed at him.' While Deniz reportedly possessed a green card, it's believed he is one of the millions of illegal aliens who possess fake identification." [14]

Members of the Crow Nation. Bighearted Native Americans cut down like weeds of no importance because another animal was allowed to roam the streets of America.

U.S. released thousands of immigrant felons last year. May 15, 2014, *CBS News*

"Convicted criminals come into the agency's custody to undergo removal proceedings after they have already satisfied the terms of their criminal sentence,' said ICE spokeswoman Gillian Christensen. 'In many of the releases in 2013, ICE was required by law to release the individuals from custody, pursuant to decisions by the Supreme Court and other federal courts. Once in ICE custody, many of the individuals described in the report were released under restrictions such as GPS monitoring, telephone monitoring, supervision, or bond.'

"Not all crimes will automatically lead to an immigrant being removed from the U.S. There are also some court decisions that have determined ICE cannot hold someone in custody indefinitely if it is unlikely they are likely to be released in the foreseeable future. That includes situations where the person's country of origin refuses or delays the person's reentry, or the U.S. his limited diplomatic relations with that country. Christensen said that court-mandated decisions 'account for a disproportionate number of the serious crimes' in the report. For example, she said, the release of 72 percent of immigrants convicted of a homicide were court mandated." [15] Read that again: 72% convicted of a homicide were released by some insane judge.

Two Illegals Plead Guilty to Baseball Bat-Machete Murder of Teen, May 5, 2015, *CNS News*

(*CNSNews.com*) – "Two illegal aliens in Walker County, Texas, have pleaded guilty to murdering and dismembering a 16-year-old high school student with a baseball bat and a machete in a national park nearly two years ago. According to investigators, the crime was a revenge killing ordered by the infamously violent Latin American gang Mara Salvatrucha, or MS-13.

"Cristian Zamora, 22, and Ricardo Leonel Campos Lara, 19, both from El Salvador, pleaded guilty on April 17 to aiding and abetting each other and others with the murder of 16-year-old Josael Guevara on Sept. 23, 2013, the Houston Chronicle reported.

"A third defendant, Jose Leonel Bonilla-Romero, was charged with murder in Walker County. But because Bonilla-Romero was 17 years old at the time of his arrest, he will not face federal charges but will be tried as an adult at the state level, the report said. Despite being in the country illegally, Zamora had already had at least one run-in with police before being arrested for murder in 2013." [16]

Illegal Alien Crime Accounts for over 30% of Murders in Many States, August 8, 2015, *Breitbart*

"Let's look at a few numbers. You haven't seen them in the *New York Times*, *Atlanta Constitution*, or the *Miami Herald*, nor have they been featured on *NBC Nightly News* or *CNN*. So, the average American is blissfully unaware of them.

1. "Between 2008 and 2014, 40% of all murder convictions in Florida were criminal aliens. In New York it was 34% and Arizona 17.8%.

2. "During those years, criminal aliens accounted for 38% of all murder convictions in the five states of California, Texas, Arizona, Florida and New York, while illegal aliens constitute only 5.6% of the total population in those states.

3. "That 38% represents 7,085 murders out of the total of 18,643." [17]

Illegal alien crime wave in Texas: Nearly 3,000 homicides since 2008, July 24, 2015, *American Thinker*

"PJ Media obtained a never-before-released copy of a Texas DPS report on human smuggling containing the numbers of crimes committed by aliens in Texas. According to the analysis conducted by the Texas Department of Public Safety, foreign aliens committed

611,234 unique crimes in Texas from 2008 to 2014, including thousands of homicides and sexual assaults.

"The report describes an alien crime wave of staggering proportions exacerbated by federal officials unwilling to enforce immigration laws. The Texas DPS report says well over 100,000 individual criminal aliens have been booked into Texas jails: From October 2008 to April 2014, Texas identified a total 177,588 unique criminal alien defendants booked into Texas county jails. These individuals have been identified through the Secure Communities initiative, in which Texas has participated since October 2008.

"There are almost certainly more criminal aliens who haven't been identified as aliens. The 177,588 criminal aliens identified by Texas through the Secure Communities initiative only can tag criminal aliens who had already been fingerprinted. Arrests of illegal aliens who have not been fingerprinted prior to arrest are not included in these arrests numbers derived from the Secure Communities initiative. That means that the already stratospheric aggregate crime totals would be even higher if crimes by many illegal aliens who are not in the fingerprint database were included." [18]

Here are real time statistics from the U.S. Border Patrol that should enrage ALL Americans:

"The tens of millions of illegal aliens inside the US murder about 12 people each day in the United States. Let's put that into perspective:

"Illegal aliens murder more people inside the USA every year than were killed in the attack on Pearl Harbor on December 7, 1941.

"Illegal aliens murder more people inside the USA every year than were killed on 9/11.

"Illegal aliens murder 25 times more people inside the USA every year than were killed in the Oklahoma City bombing.

"Since 9/11 Illegal aliens have murdered more people in the USA than were killed on 9/11 plus all our war dead so far in Afghanistan and Iraq combined.

"While 1,000 illegal aliens crossed the border with Pancho Villa (and then went home), today between 5,000 and 10,000 illegal aliens cross the border each day (and stay).

"Today, many American cities are becoming violent centers for illegal alien gangs. Los Angeles has over 600 Hispanic gangs with a total of more than 40,000 members. To contain the violence, the city of Los Angeles now has the largest jail in the world holding more than 23,000 prisoners.

"Death Toll Calculator, May 18, 2016:

"Illegal aliens have murdered more than 36,720 people inside the USA so far this year, and:

"Illegal aliens have murdered more than 64,356 people inside the USA since 9/11." (http://www.usborderpatrol.com/Border_Patrol90h.htm)

For the love of God, how many more funerals are going to take place EVERY DAY in this country while illegals run wild across America? Each and every one of those statistics is a person. A mom, a dad, brother, sister, grandmother, grandfather, daughter, son, aunt, uncle, cousin.

Was Donald Trump wrong? No, he was not, but for those in this country with a political agenda, *illegal aliens are more important than the lives of American citizens.*

These are *after Trump's* thunderbolt plus countless more crimes:

July 20, 2015, *Fox News*:

"A Massachusetts woman killed as she slept in her bed by a bullet fired through her ceiling would be alive today, if the men accused of shooting her had been deported, according to anti-illegal immigration activists. Mirta Rivera, 41, a nurse and grandmother from Lawrence, was shot July 4 from an upstairs apartment where two illegal immigrants lived despite being under federal deportation orders, according to the *Boston Herald*.

"Dominican Republic nationals Wilton Lara-Calmona and Jose M. Lara-Mejia both had long histories of sneaking into the U.S. The case, as well as a pending murder case in neighboring Connecticut involving an illegal immigrant accused in the stabbing death of a woman, comes after the July 1 murder of Kathryn Steinle in San Francisco helped propel illegal immigrant crime into a hot-button national issue."

August 4, 2015, an illegal alien, brutally beat and raped a 64-year-old California woman who died eight days after he took a hammer to her. Victor Aureliano Martinez Ramirez is 29 years old. He had been arrested four times by Santa Maria police over the past two years on minor, drug-related charges and even though he was here illegally, that animal was let out on the streets to terrorize and murder poor Marilyn Phais.

August 5, 2015, illegal alien, Marvin Castellanos-Rivera, physically assaulted an innocent woman telling her he just wanted sex. While pulling down her pants, another man came to her rescue. That animal had already been deported once.

BOTH parties in Congress, Reagan, Clinton, Bush and the person currently in the White House **are responsible for the blood of all those innocents**. Are there any viable solutions? Oh, they're there all right, but both parties in Congress do nothing but talk and hold hearings while the slaughter goes on every day.

Yes, a wall needs to be constructed along the Southern border in those areas the U.S. Border Patrol knows are the hot spots for illegals. **The idea is to stop illegals BEFORE they put one foot on U.S. soil.** Use the National Guard in Texas, Arizona, New Mexico and California. There's no doubt in my mind enough of them have the experience to build a wall that cannot be scaled. **Congress only needs to authorize money for materials since members of the National Guard are already on the payroll.**

There's no need to put this out to private contractors where the cost would be huge. This could get done in no time. I see no reason why our governor here in Texas and the governors of New Mexico and Arizona can't do the same thing inside their state border and stop illegals before they step onto state soil. Forget California. Their governor is an old cocaine sniffing lunatic.

The occupant of the White House and his lawbreaking allies in the U.S. Congress want illegals to stay in this country and they don't give a damn how many Americans are murdered, raped or robbed.

We don't need any more "comprehensive" immigration reform bills. 1965 & 1986 were supposed to end all illegal immigration. Just the opposite has happened. **Enforce the laws on the books and the hell with the ACLU.** Start throwing employers like Facebook founder, billionaire Mark Zuckerberg, who openly hired illegals in jail where he belongs. But, oh, no. Even though Mr. Facebook billionaire publicly announced hiring illegals in violation of U.S. law, nothing was done to him because he's above the law when it comes to illegal aliens. **I have never been on Facebook and want nothing to do with it because I will never knowingly put a penny in Mark Zuckerberg's bank account.**

Illegal aliens protest at the offices of Congressional members. They testify in front of committees for the U.S. House. *Why wasn't ICE there to pick them up and get them deported?* I can tell you why. Because vermin like Nancy Pelosi protect those lawbreakers and rub it in our faces.

Shut off the gravy train. Since Ted Kennedy's immigration reform bill and the one Reagan signed in 1986 that were going to "once and for all stop all illegal immigration" **America has imported 1/4 of the entire population from Mexico all from the poorest of the poor.** That is a fact. We've imported massive crime and poverty to the point it's killing our country. When Reagan signed the big immigration "reform" bill in 1986, there were approximately 2.1 million illegals in this country. Today it is somewhere between 25-30 million.

The biggest magnet is the welfare state.

Headline in 1993 – Our Federal Wallet Stretched to Limit by Illegal Aliens Getting Welfare: "Even worse, Americans have seen heinous crimes committed by individuals who are here illegally." – Senator Dirty Harry Reid. He also said that the U.S. open door policy is being abused at the expense of honest, working citizens. On August 5, 1993, Dirty Harry's office issued the following:

"In response to increased terrorism and abuse of social programs by aliens, Sen. Harry Reid (D-Nev.) today introduced the first and only comprehensive immigration reform bill in Congress. Currently, an alien living illegally in the United States often pays no taxes but receives unemployment, welfare, free medical care and other federal benefits. Recent terrorist acts, including the World Trade Center bombing, have underscored the need to keep violent criminals out of the country.

"Our borders have overflowed with illegal immigrants placing tremendous burdens on our criminal justice system, schools and social programs. The Immigration and Naturalization Service needs the ability to step up enforcement. Our federal wallet is stretched to the limit by illegal aliens getting welfare, food stamps, medical care, and other benefits often without paying any taxes.

"Safeguards like welfare and free medical care are in place to boost Americans in need of short-term assistance. These programs were not meant to entice freeloaders and scam artists from around the world. Even worse, Americans have seen heinous crimes committed by individuals who are here illegally."

His statements were to announce a bill Dirty Harry Reid introduced back then titled the Immigration Stabilization Act [S.1351][19]. That bill is 76 pages long; the link is in the Endnotes section so you can look it up on the Internet. **It is the strongest anti-illegals piece of legislation I've ever seen.** I'm betting it was not written by Dirty Harry, but by lawyers who know what they're doing and the sure to come legal challenges. It covers the whole gambit of turning off the trillions spent over the past 30 years since Reagan sold us out.

One section I want to highlight in Harry Reid's bill: Title X– Citizenship

Sec. 1001. Basis of Citizenship Clarified.

"In the exercise of its powers under section 5 of the Fourteenth Article of Amendment to the Constitution of the United States, the Congress has determined and hereby declares that any person born after the date of enactment of this title to a **mother who is neither** a citizen of the United States nor admitted to the United States as a lawful permanent resident, and which person is a national or citizen of another country of which either of his or her natural parents is a national or citizen, or is entitled upon application to become a national or citizen of such country, shall be considered as born subject to the jurisdiction of that foreign country and not subject to the jurisdiction of the United States within the meaning of section 1 of such Article and **shall therefore** not be a citizen of the United States or of any State solely by reason of physical presence within the United States at the moment of birth."

Dirty Harry said it: **Anchor babies is a myth**, something I have been very vocal about in many columns.

Of course, that puffed up peacock, Dirty Harry Reid, has changed his tune and has been fighting to reward illegal aliens with full amnesty and *your wallet*. On **July 15, 2014**, Dirty Harry said the border is secure and now we need illegal alien amnesty. The border was secure on that date?

Endless wave of illegal immigrants floods Rio Grande Valley, **July 14, 2014**, *Fox News*

McAllen, Texas —"Life jackets of all sizes and the occasional punctured raft are strewn along the banks of the Rio Grande, just south of Mission, Texas, where a relentless onslaught of illegal immigrants eagerly surrendered to beleaguered Border Patrol agents around the clock. It's a cycle for which there is no end in sight. 'You're going to be out here a long time,' Fernando, an El Salvadoran child, told FoxNews.com shortly after surrendering to Border Patrol authorities after midnight Saturday. 'There are thousands of us.'

"With most of the men and women charged with securing the Mexican border busy processing some of the 60,000 illegal immigrants who have made the harrowing – and sometimes deadly – journey to the American border in the past nine months, only a handful of Border Patrol agents drive the riverside loop in a small town called Granjeno just south of Mission, in the Rincon peninsula. Illegal immigrants of all ages, including many unaccompanied children, run to them to surrender. They are piled into the back of Border Patrol vehicles and taken to a makeshift staging area in Rincon Village, where a large Border Patrol bus waits to transport them to McAllen's Border Patrol facility." [20]

Secure, Harry? This summer the same as last summer, **the human invasion is just that**. Our border is no more secure than a spaghetti sieve. They just keep on crossing, get released, given a court date and then disappear into the 50 states.

By 1994, eight years after Ronnie Reagan invited in tens of millions of liars, cheats and thieves to sneak across our border, Californians had enough. Prop. 187 (Known as SOS or Save Our State) was put on the ballot.

The voters passed it by a wide margin. At that time there were approximately 1.3 million illegals in the state; over 300,000 minors. Lawsuits were filed and two federal judges declared the law unconstitutional in 1999. Unconstitutional? Those two activist federal judges *should have immediately been impeached* by the U.S. House of Representatives who did nothing.

Initially, I thought the decision to overturn Prop 187 was the genesis of a welfare state for illegal aliens, but having done more research, here is the damning case once again bastardizing the meaning of the Fourteenth Amendment to the U.S. Constitution:

Plyler v. Doe, 457 U.S. 202 (1982), Argued December 1, 1981; Decided June 15, 1982. Held:

"A Texas statute which withholds from local school districts any state funds for the education of children who were not "legally admitted" into the United States, and which authorizes local school districts to deny enrollment to such children, violates the Equal Protection Clause of the Fourteenth Amendment. Pp. 210-230.

"(a) The illegal aliens who are plaintiffs in these cases challenging the statute may claim the benefit of the Equal Protection Clause, which provides that no State shall "deny to any person within its jurisdiction the equal protection of the laws." Whatever his status under the immigration laws, an alien is a "person" in any ordinary sense of that term. This Court's prior cases recognizing that illegal aliens are 'persons' protected by the Due Process Clauses of the Fifth and Fourteenth Amendments, which Clauses do not include the phrase 'within its jurisdiction,' cannot be distinguished on the asserted ground that persons who have entered the country illegally are not 'within the jurisdiction' of a State even if they are present within its boundaries and subject to its laws. Nor do the logic and history of the Fourteenth Amendment support such a construction. Instead, use of the phrase 'within its jurisdiction' confirms the understanding that the Fourteenth Amendment's protection extends to anyone, citizen or stranger, who is subject to the laws of a State, and reaches into every corner of a State's territory. Pp. 210-216......

"The court held that 'the absolute deprivation of education should trigger strict judicial scrutiny, particularly when the absolute deprivation is the result of complete inability to pay for the desired benefit.' Id., at 582. The court determined that the State's concern for fiscal integrity was not a compelling state interest, id., at 582-583; that exclusion of these children had not been shown to be necessary to improve education within the State, id., at 583; and that the educational needs of the children statutorily excluded were not different from the needs of children not excluded, ibid."

In other words, too bad for the states of the Union and the taxpayers. Illegal aliens cannot be deprived of an education paid for by stealing from the taxpayers! **Illegal alien students who have no legal right to be on U.S. soil.**

The court goes on to say that illegal alien students didn't have any control over their parents smuggling them into this country, so they are entitled to special consideration under the 14th Amendment. **True, but what is supposed to happen is for minors to be deported right along with the parent(s).** Do not stop, pass go and for damn sure we the people of this country not forced against our will to educate millions of illegal minors who are here *illegally*.

Illegals who drag their kids across the border are NOT U.S. citizens nor are they entitled to U.S. citizenship. Neither are babies dropped this side of the border.

When the *Plyler v. Doe* decision was handed down, Congress had already passed immigration laws. Anyone who enters this country without going through the proper channels is here illegally. They are not "persons" invited in the US, they smuggle themselves across the border. Plyler is a perfect example of a warning by one of the greatest men in our country's history:

"To consider the judges as the ultimate arbiters of all constitutional questions [is] a very dangerous doctrine indeed, and one which would place us under the despotism of an oligarchy. Our judges are as honest as other men and not more so. They have with others the same passions for party, for power, and the privilege of

their corps. Their maxim is boni judicis est ampliare jurisdictionem [good justice is broad jurisdiction], and their power the more dangerous as they are in office for life and not responsible, as the other functionaries are, to the elective control. The Constitution has erected no such single tribunal, knowing that to whatever hands confided, with the corruptions of time and party, its members would become despots. It has more wisely made all the departments co-equal and co-sovereign within themselves." – Thomas Jefferson to William C. Jarvis, 1820. ME 15:277

Since the "supreme" court vomited up such a convoluted decision based on the Fourteenth and Fifth Amendments to the U.S. Constitution, shall we look at the historical facts regarding the Fourteenth Amendment and citizenship of foreigners? The largest number of illegals come from Mexico – or at least until the summer of 2014 when a bigger number were from Honduras and El Salvador. **Mexicans who illegally enter the US are Mexican citizens under their constitution and so are their kids, born or unborn regardless of whether they leave the country or not**:

Mexican Constitution – Chapter II – Article 30. "Mexican nationality is acquired by birth or by naturalization. A. Mexicans by birth are: I. Those born in the territory of the Republic, regardless of the nationality of their parents: II. Those born in a foreign country of Mexican parents; of a Mexican father and a foreign mother; or of a Mexican mother and an unknown father."

The Fourteenth Amendment to the U.S. Constitution reads: "All persons born or naturalized in the United States, and subject to the jurisdiction thereof, are citizens of the United States and the State wherein they reside."

Since illegal Mexicans are Mexican citizens, their allegiance is to Mexico, not any state of the Union where they illegally reside. Honduras also has a constitution which says their citizens are Honduran citizens: Article 28. – "No Honduran by birth may be deprived of their nationality. This right we retain the Hondurans by birth even when acquire another nationality." Illegal minors are not US citizens. They are persons who by birth owe their allegiance to Honduras, not the United States.

El Salvador also has a constitution, but this one is probably for the lawyers because it's seriously only one sentence about citizenship, but later under the political part it reads something a little different: Article 71 – All Salvadorans more than eighteen years old are citizens. But, on page 29 is reads: "To be elected Deputy, one must be over twenty- five years old, Salvadoran by birth, child of a Salvadoran father or mother...."

The BIG magnet all these years has been what they can steal from me, you, our children and grandchildren. Trillions of dollars spent on illegals since Reagan is paid for by borrowed money with the interest slapped on our backs. Want to drive millions and millions of illegals out of this country? STOP ALL WELFARE IN ANY FORM AND KICK ILLEGAL MINORS OUT OF AMERICA'S SCHOOLS and that includes illegal aliens taking up space in colleges and universities. **They have no right to be on U.S. soil.**

GAME PLAN: Dirty Harry's bill is just about tailor made. It may need a little fine tuning to get the statutes up to speed. At the time, it had a grand total of 3 cosponsors; two Republicans and one Democrat. But, I strongly feel Sec. 503 needs to be removed and replaced with stronger language.

On April 12, 2015, I sent a letter to Senator Jeff Session, Senator Ted Cruz, Senator Mike Lee, U.S. Rep. Trey Gowdy, U.S. Rep. Steve King [IA], Rep. Marsha Blackburn and Rep. Louis Gohmert. I told all of them Dirty Harry's old bill S. 1351 (103rd): Immigration Stabilization Act of 1993, needs to get introduced in Congress and pushed until it gets passed. **I received no response from any of them.** To my knowledge none of them has introduced Dirty Harry's old bill **which is the solution to drive millions and millions of illegals out of our country.**

Congress can make it very clear: The U.S. Supreme Court in *Plyler v Doe* was a bad decision because it made new "law" allowing illegals to receive benefits they have no right to since they are on U.S. soil illegally. If you are sickened by this wholesale slaughter of Americans and the human invasion being allowed to continue to sign up voters for a political party, not to mention stealing us blind in taxes and taking jobs that belong to Americans, tell your U.S. House member and Senator to stop being such gutless cowards. **If "supreme" court**

justices make bad decisions, impeach them or shut the hell up. We are fighting here for our very survival. We don't need sissies and wimps. We need warriors who aren't worried about their next election.

As for the U.S. Supreme Court: *"[How] to check these unconstitutional invasions of... rights by the Federal judiciary? Not by impeachment in the first instance, but by a strong protestation of both houses of Congress that such and such doctrines advanced by the Supreme Court are contrary to the Constitution; and if afterwards they relapse into the same heresies, impeach and set the whole adrift. For what was the government divided into three branches, but that each should watch over the others and oppose their usurpations?"* – Thomas Jefferson to Nathaniel Macon, 1821. (*) FE 10:192

Sanctuary cities are in violation of federal immigration laws yet one administration after another and the U.S. Congress have turned a blind eye for decades. Those sanctuary cities are infested with illegals who thumb their noses at our laws. If we had a real Department of Justice every sanctuary city Mayor in this country would be arrested and charged today with the appropriate federal statutes. **No deals, jail time**. Of course, that requires leadership in the White House and the U.S. Congress to make sure our laws are enforced. What we have now is a cruel joke. We also have a state of lawlessness:

Sanctuary Cities Ignore ICE Orders to Free 9,295 Criminal Aliens, October 13, 2015, *Judicial Watch*

"...in less than a year 340 sanctuary cities, counties and states around the U.S. released 9,295 alien offenders that Immigration and Customs Enforcement (ICE) was seeking to deport. More than half had significant prior criminal histories and 600 were released at least twice by jurisdictions that protect criminal aliens from deportation by refusing to comply with ICE detainers. The figures were made public recently by the Center for Immigration Studies (CIS), a nonprofit dedicated to researching the consequences of legal and illegal immigration into the United States.

"Of the illegal immigrants released into unsuspecting communities, 58% had prior felony charges or convictions and 37% had serious prior misdemeanor charges, the CIS probe found. An astounding 2,320 of the freed offenders were subsequently arrested within the eight-month time period studied for new crimes. Here's an enraging example included in the CIS document: Victor Aureliano Hernandez Ramirez, arrested in July 2015 for raping and bludgeoning a 64-year-old California woman who died eight days later. Ramirez had been arrested for battery a year earlier but the county sheriff blew off an ICE detainer that would have deported him in accordance with California's state sanctuary law."

If you live in a sanctuary city that harbors criminal illegals don't cry when you or your loved one are robbed, raped or murdered.

How more dead Americans are acceptable? How many more raped babies, teenagers and even elderly women will you tolerate? I could keep adding another hundred to this chapter by the time I'm finished writing this book but I believe anyone can see the slaughter of American citizens has been allowed to continue decade after decade for an evil agenda.

Donald Trump was right and he's not afraid to say it. The more you coddle liars, cheats and thieves the more will come flooding across this border believing they are above OUR laws. Illegals lie about their immigration status. They lie to get jobs. They steal the identity of Americans ruining their lives and credit to steal jobs that belong to Americans. They steal with permission of the courts and the U.S. Congress resources Americans pay for: hospitals, education and others services. **They cheat the system for their benefit not caring who they hurt in the process**. And, yes, too many of them are murderers, thieves and rapists.

Oh, they just want a better life for their kids! **What about children of natural born citizens and naturalized citizens in this country who have a RIGHT to be here?** Illegals steal what belongs by birthright to Americans and to naturalized citizens who came to America legally.

Texas has been refusing to give illegal minor children a birth certificate. From my August 31, 2015, column: Texas: No Birth Certificates for Illegal Aliens

"Mexican and Central American Illegal Immigrants Sue Texas for Birth Certificates, July 24, 2015. Citizens of Mexico and several Central American nations have filed suit, claiming entitlement to birth certificates for their children born in the United States. They allege that the Texas denies them the certificates because they do not possess the required identification. 'The parent plaintiffs of the 23 children claim that the State of Texas violates their child's rights because the Fourteenth Amendment to the United States Constitution provides that any child born on U.S. soil warrants American citizen. It also provides that they are citizens of the state where they reside. The plaintiffs and their children reside in Texas.'

"1. Texas is not violating their child's rights because **illegal aliens are not U.S. citizens and have no constitutional rights**.

"2. "...the Fourteenth Amendment to the United States Constitution provides that any child born on U.S. soil warrants American citizen." is simply repeating a fiction.

"3. They and their children do not reside in Texas. They squatted here in Texas after sneaking across our border."

The articles continues:

"They allege in their petition filed in U.S. District Court in Austin that the birth certificates are being denied because of their immigration status. They argue that, 'Such refusal is de facto based upon the immigrant status of the Plaintiff parents.' In the lawsuit, the parents do not refer to themselves as 'immigrants,' or 'illegal immigrants.' They refer to themselves in their legal capacity 'as next friend.' In the petition filed in federal court in the Western District, the parents cite the Equal Protection Clause and the Supremacy Clause, and allege that their rights are being violated under these sections. At issue is the form of identification that is now being required of parents by the Bureau of Vital Statistics in border communities. They claim that officials in Hidalgo, Cameron, and Starr counties deny them birth certificates lawfully theirs and their children's."

Again, it all comes down to the law: "...deny them birth certificates lawfully theirs and their children's. Since they broke the law by sneaking across the border, they are not here lawfully so stop trying to twist words to justify a lie they are somehow 'lawfully' entitled to birth certificates."

On October 16, 2015, an unbiased judge ruled Texas officials can continue to deny U.S. birth certificates to the children of illegal aliens because they cannot supply identification required by the State of Texas because they sneaked across our border and are here illegally. **Every state the Union should be doing what our state has done.**

On October 26, 2015, Texas Governor Greg Abbott said no more sanctuary cities in Texas. He put Dallas County Sheriff Lupe Valdez on notice: No more sanctuary cities here in Texas.

American lives don't matter. The rape and/or murder of infants, toddlers, pre-teens, teens and adults of every race, doesn't matter. The only thing that matters is protecting illegal aliens.

It doesn't matter who's been in the White House since 1986, who's been Speaker of the U.S. House or Senate Majority leader because American lives don't matter. The only thing that matters is protecting illegal aliens in this country and inviting even more to sneak across the border. American lives don't matter or the Obama administration would not have released **ONE HUNDRED SIXTY-SIX THOUSAND** criminal illegal aliens onto the streets of America

My God. Remember those numbers from the U.S. Border Patrol earlier? 64,443 Americans have been killed or murdered by illegals since 9/11 and the person in the White House has released another 166,000 criminal illegal aliens into our cities to continue raping and murdering. Is that okay with you? **If not, then why do Americans continue to reelect the same incumbents back to the U.S. Congress who want to reward liars, cheats and thieves?**

The so-called pathway to citizenship promoted by Hillary Clinton, a 74-year old Communist bum, Bernie Sanders, and virtually all the GOP presidential candidates now out of the race want to reward breaking our laws. There is NO WAY to verify backgrounds or criminal records for 20-30 million liars, cheats and thieves. How the terrorists coming across our border must be laughing at us.

How many more kids crying for their mother or father cut down by an illegal is acceptable to you? How many more funerals is okay with you?

Had a true constitutional militia AS WRITTEN IN THE U.S. CONSTITUTION been in place **by the state legislatures** in Texas, California and Arizona, **all those criminals would no longer be**

walking the street. To learn more about that constitutional function, see my closing statement at the end of this book.

If anyone other than Donald Trump gets in the White House (and believe me, vote fraud will be the key in November 2016), NOTHING will change except in all likelihood, tens of millions of illegals will be rewarded for breaking our immigration laws with the baloney called a "pathway to citizenship" which makes a mockery of OUR citizenship process. The invasion will continue in even bigger waves.

Additionally, we need a full moratorium on ALL immigration for a minimum of five years. It will take that long and perhaps even longer to straighten out the mess with illegal aliens, but it can be done. The question is, are the American people, state governors and legislatures going to get the job done or just hope the problem gets solved?

Because remember, as you read this chapter today, **another 12 or more Americans will be murdered or killed by some drunk illegal on the road**. It may not be your loved one, but it will be the loved ones of more than a dozen families.

Our country has been the victim of a massive human invasion for almost 30 years that is destroying our culture, bankrupting us, bringing diseases long ago eradicated in this country and with summer coming the masses will once again step up the invasion bringing more murders, rapists and terrorists across our southern border. **When is enough, enough, America?** Deport, not reward. NO amnesty.

> *"Power is not given to you, you have to take it! People say to me when I was on the Senate floor, when I was in the Senate, why do you fight so hard for affirmative action programs. And I tell my white colleagues: because you're gonna need them. Remember, 187 is the last gasp of white America."* Art Torres, California Democratic Party Chairman at the Latino Summit Response to Prop. 187 at U.C. Riverside, Jan. 14, 1995

8

Social Security: Yes, it is a Ponzi scheme

"Force [is] the vital principle and immediate parent of despotism." –
Thomas Jefferson: 1st Inaugural, 1801. ME 3:321

I always have to preface what I'm going to say about social security with this: No, I'm not suggesting people shouldn't get their social security checks. Almost 57 million Americans depend on that check every month to put food on the table and a roof over their heads.

But, Americans need to understand what that Ponzi scheme really is because most still think it's an insurance program. *It is a federal taxing program, not insurance.* They need to understand the trouble that program is in and not more glossed over the "fund is in good shape until 2035" or way out there. The legal explanation below is from Larry Becraft, a constitutional attorney for more than 35 years and known for his thorough, meticulous research:

"The federal social security act arises from events of the Great Depression. While that era saw extraordinary unemployment and a tremendous decline in national production, still it was not as cataclysmic as other events in our nation's history, such as the War Between the States. Further, no constitutional amendment was adopted during this era which can offer any basis for an expansion of Congressional powers. The legislation which started Social Security in 1934 must be viewed in the light of the various Supreme Court cases decided within a few decades of that legislation and prior thereto. When Congress adopted the Social Security Act in 1935, the Supreme Court had already addressed the first such act of 1934 and held in *Railroad Retirement Board*, supra, 295 U.S., at 368, that Congress had no authority to establish a retirement scheme through its most tremendous power, its control over interstate commerce:

> *"The catalogue of means and actions which might be imposed upon an employer in any business, tending to the satisfaction and*

comfort of his employees, seems endless. Provision for free medical attendance and nursing, for clothing, for food, for housing, for the education of children, and a hundred other matters might with equal propriety be proposed as tending to relieve the employee of mental strain and worry. Can it fairly be said that the power of Congress to regulate interstate commerce extends to the prescription of any or all of these things? Is it not apparent that they are really and essentially related solely to the social welfare of the worker, and therefore remote from any regulation of commerce as such? We think the answer is plain. These matters obviously lie outside the orbit of congressional power."

"Additionally, the revolutionary acts of Congress adopted in the two preceding decades had been emasculated in a series of Supreme Court decisions. Are we to suppose that, against this legal background, Congress decided to enact legislation of the caliber which had been struck as unconstitutional in the same year?

"In the second Social Security Act of 1935, Congress imposed excise taxes upon employers and those tax receipts were to be deposited with the Treasury. The act further provided schemes whereby participants could enjoy unemployment and retirement benefits. When the act was adopted, parties opposed thereto made challenges to the act, relying upon some, if not all, of the various cases cited above. The major arguments mounted against the act were premised upon contentions that the legislation constituted an invasion of state rights. In *Steward Machine Co. v. Davis*, 301 U.S. 548, 57 S.Ct. 883 (1937), an employer challenged the unemployment tax imposed upon it and the Court held that such tax was an excise which Congress could impose.

"In reference to the contention that the subject matter of the act was properly within the historical field reserved to the states, the Court held that Congress could enact legislation to aid the states in an area of great concern. The Court placed considerable emphasis upon the fact that the states were reluctant to adopt unemployment acts because such taxes created differentials between states which had such legislation and those which did not. By creating a national unemployment act, this difference was eliminated and a great benefit to the American people resulted. The Court, therefore, found nothing constitutionally objectionable to the act as to the issues which were raised. In

Helvering v. Davis, 301 U.S. 619, 57 S.Ct. 904 (1937), the same rationale was used to uphold the retirement features of the act.

"The importance of these two cases upholding the Social Security Act concerns the issues which these cases did not raise: neither of them addressed the issue of whether there was a requirement for any domestic American to join Social Security. The reason that this issue was not raised is because there is no such requirement, unless of course one works for a state government which has contracted into Social Security. See *Public Agencies Opposed to Social Security Entrapment (POSSE) v. Heckler*, 613 F.Supp. 558 (E.D. Cal. 1985), rev., 477 U.S. 41, 106 S.Ct. 2390 (1986).

"The above review should readily demonstrate that there is indeed a real question concerning the point of whether one must submit an application to join Social Security. The cases which challenged the constitutionality of Social Security simply did not raise this issue, and it appears that no case has as yet dealt with it. [2] The reason for this absence of a challenge to such alleged requirement can only be explained by analyzing the act itself to determine if there is such a requirement. Because Congress lacks the constitutional authority to compel membership in Social Security, the act simply imposes no such requirement.

"The modern version of the act is codified at 42 U.S.C. §§ 301-433. If there were a requirement that every American join the Social Security scheme, [3] one would expect to find language in the act similar to the following: 'Every American of the age of 18 years or older shall submit an application with the Social Security Administration and shall provide thereon the information required by regulations prescribed by the Secretary.'

"Every member of Social Security shall pay the taxes imposed herein and records of such payments shall be kept by the Secretary for determining the amount of benefits to which such member is entitled hereunder.' Amazingly, no such or similar language appears within the act, and particularly there is no section thereof which could remotely be considered as a mandate that domestic Americans join Social Security. The closest section of the act which might relate to this point is the requirement that one seeking benefits under the act must apply for the same. But, this relates to an entirely different point than a requirement that one join and secure a number.

"The purported duty to apply for and obtain a Social Security number therefore boils down to this: you get it if you need it or request it. There is no legal compulsion to do so." On Larry's web site you will find a concentration of expert legal analysis on this issue and others like the critically important state and federal jurisdiction. http://hiwaay.net/~becraft/

Pertaining to the social security taxing scheme, the government has to somehow keep fooling Americans into believing they must have that number and must apply for one because if they don't keep recruiting how will they have enough people to cut those SS checks every month? According to the Pew Research Center in 2010: "On January 1, 2011, the oldest Baby Boomers will turn 65. Every day for the next 19 years, about 10,000 more will cross that threshold." That's a huge number and one of the reasons Democrats are pushing so hard to dump 20-30 million illegal aliens into the system.

These are facts every American should know.

Social security is a federal tax that goes into the General Treasury and is not ear marked for any specific spending purpose.

Congressionally Duped Americans

"A year after the Social Security Act's passage, it was challenged in the U.S. Supreme Court, in *Helvering v Davis,* 301 U.S. 619 (1937). The court held that Social Security is not an insurance program, saying, "The proceeds of both employee and employer taxes are to be paid into the Treasury like any other internal revenue generally, and are not earmarked in any way." In a 1960 case, *Flemming v Nestor,* 363 U.S. 603 (1960), the Supreme Court held, 'To engraft upon the Social Security system a concept of 'accrued property rights' would deprive it of the flexibility and boldness in adjustment to ever-changing conditions which it demands.'

"Decades after Americans had been duped into thinking that the money taken from them was theirs, the Social Security Administration belatedly — and very quietly — tried to clean up its history of deception. Its web site explains, 'Entitlement to Social Security benefits is not (a) contractual right.' It adds: 'There has been a temptation throughout the program's history for some people to suppose that their FICA payroll taxes entitle them to a benefit in a legal, contractual sense.'

"... "Congress clearly had no such limitation in mind when crafting the law'. The Social Security Administration failed to mention that it was the SSA itself, along with Congress, that created the lie that "the checks will come to you as a right."

"Here's my question to those who protest that their Social Security checks are not an entitlement or handouts: Seeing as Congress has not 'set up a Social Security account for you containing your Social Security and Medicare 'contributions,' where does the money you receive come from? I promise you it's neither Santa Claus nor the tooth fairy. The only way Congress can send checks to Social Security and Medicare recipients is to take the earnings of a person currently in the workforce. The way Congress conceals its Ponzi scheme is to dupe Social Security and Medicare recipients into thinking that it's their money that is put away and invested. Therefore, Social Security recipients want their monthly check and are oblivious about who has to pay and the pending economic calamity that awaits future generations because of the federal government's $100 trillion-plus unfunded liability, of which Social Security and Medicare are the major parts." [1]

Obtaining a social security number is voluntary. If it were mandatory the government would automatically issue you a SSN. There is no law which requires anyone to apply for benefits when they turn 65. Way back when many Americans did not want social security. They were justifiably distrustful of government and wanted nothing to do with social security. After all, for a few hundred years Americans worked and they saved for their golden years.

There is no law which requires you to obtain a SSN for your newborn. Hospitals across this country literally force new parents to obtain that number before they can leave the hospital with their baby. *How despicable.* This is what is says on the Social Security Administration's web site:

"Must my child have a Social Security number? No. Getting a Social Security number for your newborn is voluntary. But, getting a number when your child is born is a good idea. You can apply for a Social Security number for your baby when you apply for your baby's birth certificate. The state agency that issues birth certificates will share your child's information with us, and we'll mail the Social Security card to you."

Why is it a good idea? Because by design, if your child has no SSN you cannot claim them as a deduction on your tax return. **The big carrot**. However, *even if you never apply for that number, you will be forced by the IRS with a gun to your head to pay the tax* to keep funding someone else.

Chapter 21 called the Federal Insurance Contributions Act, Section 3102: Deduction of Tax From Wages states:

(a) Requirement. The tax imposed by section 3101 shall be collected by the employer of the taxpayer, by deducting the amount of the tax from the wages as and when paid....

Notice that the word insurance does not appear in the body of the written text. We jump from the word "insurance" in the title to the word "tax" and the law itself. The word "tax" appears within the sentence structure of the body of the law and not "insurance." This has legal import. Section 7806 of the IR Code explains it quite plainly:

IR Code 7806. Construction of Title

"(a) Cross References. The cross references in this title to other portions of the title, or other provisions of the law, where the word "see" is used, are made only for convenience and shall be given no legal effect.

"(B) Arrangement and Classification. No inference, implication, or presumption of legislative construction shall be drawn or made by reason of the location or grouping of any particular section of provision or portion of this title, nor shall any table of contents, table of cross references, or similar outline, analysis, or descriptive matter relating to the contents of this title shall be given any legal effect."

Because the word insurance appears with the table of contents and the table of contents is "descriptive matter" used as an "outline," the word insurance has no legal effect. In other words, no words in the table of contents have any force of law. The word which does have legal effect is "tax" because it is used within the body of the law itself; therefore, it has the full force of law. Legally, the word insurance does not apply, means nothing, to the chapter of the Code entitled "Federal Insurance Contributions Act."

No one is required to obtain an SSN

If you wish to ask someone from the government about this fact, let me demonstrate how you will be lied to by the same person. Look at this response from SSA in a letter to Mr. Scott McDonald dated March 18, 1998 from Charles Mullen, Associate Commissioner, Office of Public Inquiries, Social Security Administration [http://home.hiwaay.net/~becraft/ScottSSNLetter.pdf]:

"The Social Security Act does not require a person to have a Social Security Number (SSN) to live and work in the United States, nor does it require an SSN simply for the purpose of having one. However, if someone works without an SSN, we cannot properly credit the earnings for the work performed."

Now, it would appear from even a basic understanding of the English language that what Mr. Mullen said is this: No one is required to have a SSN to either live or work in the United States. That's not what you were told, is it? One would think this is quite plain and clear. However, let's look at another letter from the same Charles Mullen about one month earlier (February 24, 1998) addressed to me:

"People cannot voluntarily end their participation in the program [SS]. The payment of social security taxes is mandatory, regardless of the citizenship or place of residence of either the employer or the employee. Unless specifically exempted by law, everyone working in the United States is required to pay Social Security taxes."

Now, I ask you: **If obtaining an SSN is voluntary, how is it that this tax then becomes mandatory?** Since when is it legal to force any American to join a voluntary 'insurance plan' that is in reality nothing but another tax – especially when an individual must apply for a number that puts them into this taxing system? The answer is clear: A Ponzi scheme requires new participants to keep paying for the old ones. Just like Obamacare ruled a tax.

An even bigger question: Am I even eligible to obtain this number? This is a very important legal question that seldom is raised about Title 42, the so-called The Federal Old-Age, Survivors and Disability Insurance Benefits Program. After a thorough review of Section 405, it would appear there are only certain classifications of individuals who are legally eligible to apply. To be specific, see:

42 U.S.C. Section 405(c)(2)(B):

"(B)(i) In carrying out the Commissioner's duties under subparagraph (A) and subparagraph (F), the Commissioner of Social Security shall take affirmative measures to assure that social security account numbers will, to the maximum extent practicable, be assigned to all members of appropriate groups or categories of individuals by assigning such numbers (or ascertaining that such numbers have already been assigned);

"(I) to aliens at the time of their lawful admission to the United States either for permanent residence or under other authority of law permitting them to engage in employment in the United States and to other aliens at such time as their status is so changed as to make it lawful for them to engage in such employment;

"(II) to any individual who is an applicant for or recipient of benefits under any program financed in whole or in part from Federal funds including any child on whose behalf such benefits are claimed by another person; and

"(III) to any other individual when it appears that he could have been but was not assigned an account number under the provisions of sub clauses (I) or (II) but only after such investigation as is necessary to establish to the satisfaction of the Commissioner of Social Security, the identity of such individual, the fact that an account number has not already been assigned to such individual, and the fact that such individual is a citizen or a noncitizen who is not, because of his alien status, prohibited from engaging in employment; and, in carrying out such duties, the Commissioner of Social Security is authorized to take affirmative measures to assure the issuance of social security numbers;

"(IV) to or on behalf of children who are below school age at the request of their parents or guardians; and

"(V) to children of school age at the time of their first enrollment in school." We find more government lie-speak and the obligation or duty to apply for and obtain a Social Security card or number at 20 C.F.R., section 422.103 (2002):

"(b) Applying for a number. (1) Form SS-5. An individual needing a social security number may apply for one by filing a signed Form SS-5, "Application for a Social Security Card," at any social security office and submitting the required evidence...

"(2) Birth Registration Document. The Social Security Administration (SSA) may enter into an agreement with officials of a state...to establish, as part of the official birth registration process, a procedure to assist SSA in assigning social security numbers to newborn children. Where an agreement is in effect, a parent, as part of the official birth registration process, need not complete a Form SS-5 and may request that SSA assign a social security number to the newborn child.

Another (2): "(2) Request on birth registration document. Where a parent has requested a social security number for a newborn child as part of an official birth registration process described in paragraph (b)(2) of this section, the State vital statistics office will electronically transmit the request to SSA's central office...Using this information, SSA will assign a number to the child and send the social security number card to the child at the mother's address."

Are you subject to those requirements?

Identity theft is a multi-billion-dollar a year industry. There's absolutely no valid reason why all motor vehicle departments in the 50 states can't assign an internal identifier for the license holder. None. There would no longer be any incentive for motor vehicle personnel to sell your SSN because your name would only be connected to a benign number and *not one tied to your entire financial history. One only need to search on the Internet for dozens of articles about DMV employees indicted and convicted of selling SSNs on the black market.*

Before this massive abuse of this number became vogue, state agencies and companies in the private sector simply established account numbers for their customers/clients and it can be done again. Due to the advancement of technology and computers, purging social security numbers and replacing them with a unique customer/client account number is not a major undertaking, even for a state agency with hundreds of thousands or millions of names, i.e., motor vehicle departments. The cost of identity theft is far, far greater than the cost of using a computer program to issue new identifying numbers for customers/clients. The financial future of all Americans is on the line here and it is long past time for our paid public servants take this issue seriously and act.

Probably 20 years ago, a friend of mine who had a talk show on KSFO Hot Talk Radio out of San Francisco took a call from a woman who worked at the California Franchise Tax Board (FTB). She told the listening audience that **thousands of social security numbers had as many as 99 names attached to one number.** SSNs are big money on the black market for illegal aliens. Perhaps now you can understand why identity theft is rampant and why all 50 state legislatures must step in and **put a stop to the unlawful use of this number.**

In some states, real estate agents, plumbers and other trades are being denied renewal of their licenses because they refuse to supply a SSN. It is our God given right to work for our bread and there is absolutely no *legitimate* reason why any state needs a SSN in order to renew a license to do business.

EVERY year 15 million Americans are victims of identity theft. A prime tool used by illegal aliens – those "nice" people who just want a better life by stealing jobs that belong to Americans and their identity ruining innocent people's lives and credit while courts in this country have ruled it's okay:

Courts: Using another's SSN not a crime

"Is using a forged Social Security Number – but your own name – to obtain employment or buy a car an identity theft crime? Lately, U.S. courts are saying it's not. The most recent judicial body to take on the issue, the Colorado Supreme Court, ruled last month that a man who used his real name but someone else's Social Security number to obtain a car loan was not guilty of 'criminal impersonation,' overturning convictions by lower courts.

"That follows a ruling last year by the U.S. Supreme Court that a Mexican man who gave a false SSN to get a job at an Illinois steel plant could not be convicted under federal identity theft laws because he did not knowingly use another person's identifying number. The ruling overturned an opinion by a federal appeals court in St. Louis – and contradicted earlier findings by circuit courts in the Southeast, upper Midwest and the Gulf states." November 30, 2010, *NBC News*

The Colorado Supreme Court case referenced above is *Momtes-Rodriguez v. People*, 241 P.3d 924 (Colo. 2010).

That illegal alien didn't know he was using a false SSN?

Justices Limit Use of Identity Theft Law in Immigration Cases, May 4, 2009, *NY Times*

Washington — "The Supreme Court on Monday rejected a favorite tool of prosecutors in immigration cases, ruling unanimously that a federal identity-theft law may not be used against many illegal workers who used false Social Security numbers to get jobs. The question in the case was whether workers who use fake identification numbers to commit some other crimes must know they belong to a real person to be subject to a two-year sentence extension for "aggravated identity theft." See also *Flores-Figueroa v. United States*, 555 U.S. 1162 (2009).

"The answer, the Supreme Court said, is yes. Prosecutors had used the threat of that punishment to persuade illegal workers to plead guilty to lesser charges of document fraud. 'The court's ruling preserves basic ideals of fairness for some of our society's most vulnerable workers,' said Chuck Roth, litigation director at the National Immigrant Justice Center in Chicago. 'An immigrant who uses a false Social Security number to get a job doesn't intend to harm anyone, and it makes no sense to spend our tax dollars to imprison them for two years.'"

Oh, I'm so tired of that bull pucky. An illegal who uses a false SSN to get a job doesn't intend to harm anyone? **That job belongs to an American, not some low life who sneaks across OUR border and has no right to work in this country.** Returning to that article:

"Justice Samuel A. Alito Jr. said in a concurring opinion that a central flaw in the interpretation of the law urged by the government was that it made criminal liability turn on chance. Consider, Justice Alito said, a defendant who chooses a Social Security number at random. "If it turns out that the number belongs to a real person," Justice Alito wrote, "two years will be added to the defendant's sentence, but if the defendant is lucky and the number does not belong to another person, the statute is not violated."

"The most sweeping use of the statute was in Iowa, after an immigration raid in May 2008 at a meatpacking plant in Postville. Nearly 300 unauthorized immigrant workers from the plant, most of them from Guatemala, pleaded guilty to document-fraud charges rather than risk being convicted at trial of the identity-theft charge."

What the hell? Illegals get to choose a SSN at random like it's some sort of lottery? I'll bet there are a thousand people in the immediate and outlying area of that plant who would love to have the job stolen by an illegal alien.

While some reforms have taken place in a handful of states, all across America citizens are still being forced to provide this easily stolen number for cable TV service, medical treatment, employment, credit cards and dozens of other goods and services by companies. All of it is unlawful. When I moved to Texas ten years ago, every entity I called, cable service, water, electric – all ask for my SSN first. I told each and every one of them it's a violation of federal law to ask me for that number. And, guess what? Smooth as cream, each service rep without breaking stride proceeded to tell me what the deposit would be. That's right. Pay a small deposit and if you pay your bill on time for 12 months, the deposit is returned. Not one of them got my SSN.

I strongly urge everyone to contact their *state* legislator; do it as a group or organization if possible. Tell him/her what the law says and demand they introduce legislation to **stop the use of SSNs as identifiers** for all the above and for obtaining a business license, medical providers or private industry.

This isn't a Republican or Democrat party issue, it's a ticking time bomb that affects every man, woman and child in this country. The chances of YOU becoming a victim grow each day with all this electronic data storage – *including your most intimate medical history.* Companies and corporations don't want to spend the money to remove the SSN as an identifier, but we the people should not be put at huge risk. WE didn't make this problem.

Do Americans even know how much is owed in unfunded liabilities for Social Security? As I write this chapter the amount is $14.9 TRILLION. Where do Americans think that "money" is going to come from? Remember SS taxes go into the General Fund of the Treasury and not earmarked for any specific spending purposes.

The debt has gone through the roof and the bank robbers in the U. S. Congress don't seem to see any problem:

Massive Debt, Budget Deal Introduced in Dead of Night, Vote Violates Another Boehner Pledge, October 27, 2015, *Brietbart*

"The giant debt ceiling increase rolled together with a budget deal was introduced at 11:36 p.m. Monday, in the dead of night, several congressional sources confirm to *Breitbart News*. The text is 144 pages long and increases the debt ceiling beyond when President Barack Obama leaves office, all the way until March 2017. It also, according to Politico, increases spending by $50 billion this year and $30 billion more the following year. As AP reports, House Speaker Rep. John Boehner (R-OH) is pushing for a Wednesday vote, this would be yet another instance in which he has broken his promise to give members and the public three full days — 72 hours — to read legislation before voting on it." [2]

Think Johnny Wino Boehner cared? He's now retired, fully vested for a big, fat retirement (paid for by you) to play golf in Florida near his $800,000 condo. **This is how those cretins play with our lives and the future for our children.** Another bloated budget filled with waste and spending on unconstitutional cabinets and agencies. Why did they do this? To ward off any more stand-offs – like raising the debt ceiling before the 2016 election so both parties look good to voters.

All my adult life I've heard nothing but Congress wants to cut social security. In one of the presidential debates, Hillary Clinton, gleefully told the cameras she wants to expand social security. With what, Mrs. Clinton? That system is already $14.9 TRILLION in unfunded liabilities.

Some Americans who clearly cannot see the abyss staring them right in the face also want to expand social security. Someone sent me an email in July 2015 with a request I sign a petition:

"Social Security must be expanded, not cut. Social Security is the most successful anti-poverty program in U.S. history. I urge you to support efforts to expand Social Security and reject any attempt to cut benefits. Republicans in Congress are engaged in an all-out attack on Social Security pushing the specious argument that we need to cut benefits now so we won't have to cut them later. But the fact is, Social Security works and an overwhelming majority of Americans want the program to be expanded, not cut.

"Progressives in Congress are working to expand Social Security benefits and strengthen the program's finances by making the wealthy pay their fair share into the trust fund. Let's make sure Congress knows there's huge grassroots support for expanding Social Security. Sign the petition: Social Security should be expanded, not cut. Click here to sign the petition. There's no shortage of smart ideas for expanding and strengthening our Social Security system. For example, Senator Bernie Sanders recently proposed raising the cap on earnings that are subject to the Social Security payroll tax, which would force the wealthy to pay their fair share into the trust fund."

Same old communist clap trap: Make the wealthy pay their fair share as if they don't *already pay massive amounts of taxes – which they do*. Those are people who live in la-la land who have ZERO understanding of the problem. Liberals or liberal progressives are nothing more than ignorant socialists and Marxists **who want someone else to pay their way**. If they had two sparks between their ears they'd electrocute themselves. They want to penalize Americans who have been successful and WHO CREATE jobs in the private sector.

Social Security's in worse shape than you thought, May 8, 2015, *CNBC* – *"[Social Security] is going to be insolvent before everyone thinks."*

Experts: Social Security Forecasts Miscalculated by More Than $1 Trillion, May 10, 2015, *Breitbart*

Social Security Disability Benefits Face Cuts in 2016, Trustees Say, July 22, 2015, *NY Times*. WASHINGTON — "Eleven million people face a deep, abrupt cut in disability insurance benefits in late 2016 if Congress fails to replenish Social Security's disability trust fund, which is running out of money, the Obama administration said

Wednesday." And, pray tell where will those crooks in Congress find the billions needed to "replenish" the SSDI fund?

What about SSI (Social Security Supplemental Income)? A well-meaning idea, but where is the money going to come from? From "Just Facts" about SSI: "The Supplemental Security Income (SSI) program provides benefits for aged, blind, and disabled people without regard to prior workforce participation. It is administered by the Social Security Administration, but it is not funded by Social Security taxes."

Here you have a separate program that pays an income whether the recipient has ever worked or not. Where does the money come from? Well, since the people's purse is overdrawn $19 TRILLION dollars, the money will have to be borrowed. More borrowed debt to spend debt.

Another thing people need to factor in to the problem: Since 100% of your social security taxes goes into the General Fund of the U.S. Treasury, just what is going into the SS, SSDI and SSI funds besides a few computer strokes?

Trustees: Social Security Will Run $84 Billion Deficit in 2015, September 1, 2015, *cnsnews.com*

"The report also stated that the Social Security system's "unfunded obligation through the infinite horizon" is now $25.8 trillion, up from $24.9 trillion in 2014. That amount is the difference between all future projected benefits and sources of income, Boston University Economics Professor Laurence Kotlikoff explained in a recent Forbes op-ed. "It means that the system is 32 percent underfinanced."

"If we don't raise the system's tax rate to 16.4 percent [from the current 12.4 percent] **starting today** and leave it at 16.4 percent forever, our kids will face even larger permanent tax hikes when they are ultimately enacted."

It's been just one continuing battle with groups who lobby Congress: don't touch the sacred cow of politics, SS, and don't even think of cutting benefits! Yes, everyone who works in this country has paid into that taxing scheme whether they wanted to join or not. Does it matter to anyone that there's not enough money to keep that taxing scheme solvent?

There are think tanks and organizations by the dozens who come up with all kinds of different plans to "save social security". Nothing ever pans out but it fills air time for cable news networks and articles on the Internet.

Is this what you want for your child? To be forced into a taxing scheme and down the line always worrying what Congress might do, like cutting benefits or raising the minimum age for retirement? But, oh...you need that deduction on your income tax. Trapped.

Why not let the program die a natural death? Congress stops taxing individuals who do not want to be part of that system. Americans once again go back to the way it was before the big push towards socialism starting with FDR. In the "old days" your grandparents tried to teach their children (your parents) about run-away spending on a personal level. Always save for a rainy day. **You have to save for your retirement**. For decades now it's been conspicuous consumption with people putting nothing aside and then going into cardiac arrest a few years before retirement realizing they might have $700-$800 a month in SS benefits *to supplement what for their retirement?*

Millions of Americans have little to no money saved: March 31, 2015, *USA Today*. "Roughly a third of American adults don't have any emergency savings, meaning that over 72 million people have no cushion to fall back on if they lose a job or have to deal with another crisis, according to a survey released today by NeighborWorks America, a national non-profit that supports communities. Among the 1,035 adults who took part in the poll, 34% had no money set aside for an emergency, while 47% said their savings would cover their living expenses for 90 days or less."

And, what is the result of so many retiring near poverty level? Bigger Medicare rolls at the state level, less spending into the economy while the real problem just festers. Today, Americans need to start saving for retirement in their early 20s and have in the range of $400,000 – $450,000 dollars socked away by retirement age. What do you have saved for retirement? *Where is your 401(k) or IRA being invested?*

How would you pay social security checks each month if Americans were able to say, No, I don't want to sign up? Return to constitutional government and that means abolishing **unconstitutional** cabinets like the Federal Department of Education (which I cover in Chapter 11) which would save we the people a whopping $66 BILLION **borrowed** dollars per year.

Abolish the **unconstitutional** HHS (Health and Human Services) which would save we the people a whopping $1 TRILLION **borrowed** dollars per year. Abolish foreign aid because nowhere in the U.S. Constitution does it authorize the bank robbers in the U.S. Congress to steal the fruits of our labor to give to any country on this earth for *any* reason. That will save we the people some $40 BILLION **borrowed** dollars a year.

USAID (United States Aid for International Development) under the State Department is BILLIONS of **borrowed** dollars and like foreign aid, Congress has **no constitutional authority to steal from us for that program**. No, the government won't collapse. The same applies to the EPA. Every state of the Union has its own environmental agency; one size fits all doesn't work because of the differences in each state.

The EPA, also unconstitutional, is just another worthless layer of government bureaucracy, but **plays an important role in destroying capitalism**. Every state has their own department of education. All we hear is talk from the Democrats to spend more for unconstitutional government agencies while Republicans talk about smaller government every two years at election time. Has it ever solved the problem? **No.**

Now we're talking well over a trillion dollars in cuts and believe me, you won't miss any of them. Yes, those federal employees will lose their jobs. I know what that's like and truly sympathize, but don't kill me because I'm the messenger. *I didn't make this mess.* It can't be done overnight, but it has to be done. There isn't enough funny "money" on this planet to settle America's massive debts as I discussed in Chapter 1.

Fund the program with the taxes paid for people who want to stay in the system and through constitutional revenues, but let the system die off as those collecting SS pass away. Give Americans back their God-given right to be free from a system they don't want to be part of. It would take decades for this to happen but the only other alternative is to keep raising SS taxes, keep raising minimum age retirement while the hole gets bigger – isn't $14.9 TRILLION right now enough of a warning sign to anyone?

And, by the way, there was a very important bill in Congress during the 2013-14 session. There was no public support. *Where was AARP and their 30 million plus members?* Why didn't they get the word out to put pressure on Congress to pass that bill?

GOP Reps. Pushing to End "Double-Taxing by the Federal Government", January 14, 2013

"Rep. Thomas Massie (R-Ky.) introduced HR 3894, the Senior Citizens Tax Elimination Act, to do away with income taxes on Social Security benefits. Reps. Jim Bridenstine (R-Okla.) and Ron DeSantis (R-Fla.) supported the bill as original co-sponsors. 'Seniors have already paid tax on their Social Security contributions, so taxing Social Security is double-taxing by the federal government,' Massie said.

"DeSantis echoed Massie's sentiments in their joint statement: '[The bill] blows the whistle on the federal government for double-taxing the Social Security benefits of senior citizens. Individuals already pay taxes to support Social Security, so there is no reason why these earned benefits should be taxed on the back end.' The GOP representatives argue the purpose of Social Security is 'to provide people with financial support during retirement, not to be another source of tax revenue for the federal government.'" [3]

Guess how many co-sponsors that bill to stop taxing your social security had? Two: Jim Bridenstine [R-OK1] and Ron DeSantis [R-FL6]. Out of 535 crooks in the Outlaw Congress, a grand total of three (sponsor and two co-sponsors) wanted to stop taxing your social security. What does that tell you about your incumbent in Congress? They want to bleed every last penny from your paycheck to pay for the madness of out of control spending ruining this country and illegals.

9

Medicare – Unsustainable

Medicare is another one of those thorny issues that when one brings up facts, they are immediately excoriated as uncaring or that individual must surely be a Republican. I am neither.

Below is a column I wrote, March 24, 2014, at *Newswithviews.com*; abbreviated as some is covered in the previous chapter. The only thing that's changed is the numbers continue to grow exponentially.

Forced into Medicare with A Gun to My Head, my column, March 24, 2014

As always when I write columns about the big three (4 if you count the unconstitutional Obamacare) federal Ponzi schemes, Social Security, Medicare and the GOPs grand "free" prescription pills, I have to say don't kill the messenger (me) for telling you the painful truth. I am fully aware tens and tens of millions of Americans receive benefits from those programs. As of February 2016, 57 million on SS; 11 million on social security disability (a huge spike since 2008) and 49.4 million on Medicare.

Individuals on SSDI (SS Disability Insurance) who rely just on that income pay no federal taxes which means they are completely subsidized by your wallet. Yes, I do understand there are those who absolutely need it. However, in the 'old days' family took care of family, not mother government. *The reality is that one day, the well is going to run dry.* Right now it's barely a puddle at the bottom of the ocean.

Those tens of millions cited above absolutely depend on those federal taxing schemes for the bread on the table and medical treatment. I understand that. I also feel comfortable in saying that probably 95% of Americans have no idea how those federal taxing schemes work and why they are unsustainable.

I will turn 65 in June and today I have to head down to the Social Security Administration offices to enroll in the Medicare Ponzi scheme with a gun to my head. My husband is a retired U.S. Army Colonel. We are covered under TriCare. John with TriCare for Life; mine is TriCare Prime for which **I now must travel 90 miles to see a doctor** under the new regulations shoved down our throat in October 2013 or lose my coverage. We have always paid our own health care premiums. **It is our personal responsibility, not yours.** It is morally wrong to steal from your paycheck to pay for my health care.

If I refuse to enroll in Medicare, I will lose my TriCare coverage. That's right. Those bastards (no apology) in the Outlaw Congress, your incumbent and mine, force individuals against their will into those Ponzi schemes in an effort to keep them from going bankrupt. TriCare sent me their cheery TriCare and Medicare Turning 65 brochure: "If you are entitled to premium-free Medicare Part A, you must also have Medicare Part B to keep TriCare regardless of your age or place of residence...Once you have both Part A and Part B, you automatically receive TriCare benefits under TFL." (TriCare for Life)

"Entitled" somehow magically turned into forced enrollment for TriCare. Just because someone is eligible, doesn't say therefore you must. Individuals are prosecuted in this country all the time for running Ponzi schemes, yet the Outlaw Congress is running three huge ones (not counting the unconstitutional Obamacare) and have gotten away with it for decades.

If you apply for social security benefits, you are also forced with a gun to your head to enroll in Medicare or forfeit your social security checks.

In 2008, former House Majority Leader, Dick Armey and a couple of his friends filed a lawsuit against the SSA and the unconstitutional Health and Human Services. They didn't want to go into Medicare. They're all multi-millionaires who can afford to pay for any medical treatment they need. **Instead, your hard earned tax dollars will pay his medical expenses in the form of borrowed debt.** Let me quote from this article [internal link in my column]:

"We were curious why Social Security and Medicare are linked, and when we asked, we found that the issue is the matter of a lawsuit that was brought against the Social Security Administration and the Department of Health and Human Services in 2008. Among the plaintiffs is none other than Dick Armey. The plaintiffs argue that, under the Medicare Act signed in 1965 and under the Social Security Act, there are no rules requiring enrollment in Medicare Part A to receive retirement benefits. Rather, a series of subsequent policy statements have linked the two programs, which are illegal because the two departments did not follow the traditional procedure to write the new rules, according to a press release issued by the plaintiffs on Oct. 9, 2008. The policy essentially traps retirees into participating."

The article contains these lies: "In some cases, people never sign up for retirement benefits (social security) and therefore they must enroll in Medicare on their own, said Dorothy Clark, spokeswoman for the Social Security Administration. Either way, "Medicare is a voluntary program," said Clark. No one is ever required to sign up for government health benefits, nor are they required to keep them." And, "So, back to Armey's claim. He's wrong that Medicare is required for everyone over the age of 65, but he's correct that those who want out of the program will lose their Social Security benefits as well."

No, Ms. Clark. Medicare enrollment isn't voluntary for me. According to TriCare's web site and my badgering for legal answers, if I don't sign up for Medicare I will lose my TriCare health coverage. **Once enrolled in Medicare, I will end up paying more than $1,400 per year than I now pay for my health care premiums under TriCare Prime.** Medicare becomes my "primary" coverage; TriCare becomes the supplemental. That means I have less money to spend into my local economy. And, people wonder why businesses are going belly up across this country?

Medicare Part A is for the premium "free" hospital insurance. Free? **Who the hell do they think they're kidding?** What does the "free" Part A cover? Hospital care, Skilled nursing facility care, Nursing-home care (as long as custodial care isn't the only care you need), Hospice and Home health services.

Free? As I write this column Medicare has $89 TRILLION dollars in unpaid liabilities. $89 TRILLION dollars. Where is "free" in an astronomical debt of $89 TRILLION dollars?

That Ponzi scheme forces those who can afford their own health care premiums into a program that can't pay its liabilities. The blame lies squarely with your U.S. Rep and Senator and mine. They are directly responsible for allowing the madness to continue. Every election cycle we see both parties stand in front of the cameras talking about social security reform! Medicare reform! We will make sure benefits for seniors they're entitled to will be there in the future! Bull manure. They haven't reformed anything. Medicare fraud runs in the hundreds of millions of dollars every year with most of it unrecoverable.

The unconstitutional Health and Human Services reported in December 2014 there was an almost 50% increase in errors for Medicare payments representing a $46 BILLION borrowed dollars annual loss for that taxing scheme. So, how do you fix the problem? The person in the White House's minions simply suspended the audit program that had successfully recovered more than $8 billion. As noted in a piece by Mike Flynn at *Brietbart*:

"The suspension of the audit program is a victory for the American Hospital Association, which has led a lobbying campaign against the program. In a series of letters, the AHA has not only lobbied against the RAC program, but even auditing efforts by the federal government's own Office of the Inspector General. 'The OIG's approach grossly exaggerates estimated Medicare overpayments, leads to excessive recoveries by Medicare contractors, and otherwise prejudices and burdens hospitals,' one of the letters argues. Apparently, any audit process is too much for the nation's hospitals.

"One piece of legislation, introduced by House Republicans, would block audits of Medicare providers unless their estimated error rate exceeded 40% of total billing. In other words, more than one-third of bills submitted to Medicare could be fraudulent before any audit threshold was triggered. Earlier this year, Congress passed legislation to suspend all audits for another 6 months."

The GOP's so called "free" prescription drug plan is $22.3 TRILLION in unpaid liabilities. Just those three (SS & Medicare included), not counting the monstrous hole in the water called Obamacare, total $128.3 TRILLION dollars.

Those "entitlement" programs are what's called off budget. Why? Because allegedly, they are supposed to pay for themselves. Because the Outlaw Congress doesn't want Americans to see the true numbers and because there's no way to balance any budget with unpaid liabilities in numbers so huge it would be laughable if not so serious. The U.S. Congress is riding the tiger; they know what will happen if the tiger suddenly stops and they're thrown to the ground looking at giant fangs. Let me put it this way so we can all understand just how dire the situation is (budgeted means current year):

We know Medicare has $89 trillion dollars in unpaid liabilities. If you look at the debt clock to see what the Outlaw Congress has budgeted for Medicare (you see the debt accumulates in split seconds so fast they will all have increased by the time this column is published), it's $776.7 billion dollars – nowhere near the $89 trillion in unpaid liabilities.

Social security's unpaid liabilities total $16.9 trillion; budget by the Outlaw Congress $820.6 billion.

In addition to the tab paid for out of your wallet for Medicare, let's look at how much YOU owe on top of that in debt created by *your incumbent and mine* in Congress:

You (and me) owe $151,820 for the congressionally created "national debt".

You, me our children and grandchildren individually owe $8,080 in interest for that congressionally created "national" debt.

The U.S. total debt: $61.3 trillion. You, me, our children and grandchildren individually owe $193,137.

SS, Medicare, "free" prescription drugs: $128.3 trillion. Taxpayers, which would be you and me and your children and grandchildren if they're working are each in debt for: $1.1 million dollars and growing by the millions every minute.

Add that to your state tax burdens and you soon understand why you have no savings and scrimp month to month just to stay afloat. Throw in more TRILLIONS for the unconstitutional Obamacare and you have a disaster. One day in the not too distant future the big tent will simply collapse because the American people are squeezed into poverty and can no longer pay all those taxes and because the U.S. government has run out of countries to borrow from: $3.4 BILLION dollars a day.

Unpayable debt that continues to accumulate at millions of dollars a second for each category above. Since not a penny of your federal 'income' tax dollars funds a single function of the federal government, **it's all borrowed debt heaped on our backs** – including those Ponzi schemes. *Here in Texas, ignorant voters on March 4, 2016 voted to reelect every single "smaller government, keep more of your money" GOP incumbents so they can go right back to Washington in November while America's financial house burns to the ground.*

The voters of Texas (same on the Democratic/Communist Party USA side) are so happy to be crushed under debt in such numbers most can't even fathom what $128.3 trillion dollars means (just for those off budget items alone), they voted for the very same individuals who are destroying their lives and their children's futures. **After all, it's always the fault of the other party.** And, because **they are now recipients of those Ponzi schemes. Trapped**.

There will never be enough taxed per individual enrolled to fund out those programs. Besides trying to boost their voting block by tens of millions, the second reason the Democratic/Communist Party USA wants to reward liars, cheats and thieves (illegal aliens) with citizenship is to dump 20-30 million of them into those Ponzi schemes in an effort to keep them afloat. *All that will do is throw more gasoline on the bonfire.*

Think both parties in the Outlaw Congress don't know how bad off those "entitlement" programs are – especially with 94 MILLION Americans out of the work force? Those Ponzi scheme taxes aren't being deducted from those 94 million unemployed tax slaves creating an even bigger deficit.

What's needed to prop up those programs that tens of millions must have for food and medical treatment? Every penny of your paycheck, savings and those 401(k)s and it still won't be enough.

Now the three biggies are $128.3 TRILLION dollars in unpaid liabilities while massive unconstitutional spending by your incumbent and mine is still gushing out of DC like Niagara Falls. There isn't enough money on this earth to sustain those programs, not to mention every time there is any discussion about cuts in social security or Medicare, seniors go berserk because they're afraid. *Is that any way to live?*

Desperate seniors threaten to oust incumbents if they dare mention cutting SS or Medicare. Career politicians genuflect at the feet of rotten organizations like AARP and belch the same worn out campaign sound bites about protecting SS and Medicare – for votes. You can only put so much air into a balloon before it pops. Recipients of those programs simply don't want to face the reality of the situation. However, the reality is that the bad news is coming but not likely until after the election in 2016. Gotta get reelected.

The reality is all of the above and Americans dependent upon those programs must get out of denial. Americans should not forget the riots in Greece, Italy and France in late 2012 when their governments rolled out austerity measures that cut pensions so badly, those people had no money for food or anything else. **Greece is here and now.** On October 28, 2015, the U.S. House passed a massive two-year budget once again kicking the can down the road and look out – they will raise the debt ceiling limit again taking us further into unpayable debt.

Make no mistake: The thieves in the Outlaw Congress – your incumbent and mine want to get their hands on the trillions in private pension funds in exchange for more worthless paper IOUs. Oh, it won't be called an IOU. Let's go for the old sleight of hand deception:

Treasury, Labor on path to nationalize retirement, WND, November 25, 2012

New York – "Two years ago, as WND reported, the Obama administration was proceeding with a novel way to finance trillion-dollar budget deficits by forcing IRA and 401(k) holders to buy Treasury bonds by mandating the placement of government-structured annuities in their retirement accounts. Remarkably, those financial professionals specializing in private retirement savings and the U.S. citizens investing in private retirement plans now face the possibility the Obama administration and its allies on the political left will impose rules and regulations that effectively abolish the private retirement savings and investment markets.

"Recent evidence suggests government officials continue to eye the multi-trillion-dollar private retirement savings market, including IRAs and 401(k) plans, eyeing the opportunity to redistribute private retirement savings to less affluent Americans and to force the retirement savings out of the private market and into government-controlled programs investing in government-issued debt."

If that happens, you can kiss your retirement good bye.

The point of no return has already passed for those programs. The unconstitutional "Fed" can continue pumping worthless "dollars" into the economy, but it's nothing more than a con game. Government securities and Treasury bonds backed up by a worthless fiat currency. That's what you would entrust everything you've ever worked for and what you need to survive in your golden years? Only a fool would agree to such an arrangement.

Instead of allowing those programs to die a natural death long ago instead of forcing tens of millions of Americans into them who really have no understanding of the long term consequences of Ponzi schemes, your incumbent and mine have simply allowed the problem to swell beyond anything sustainable. The end result is going to be disaster and misery for tens and tens of millions of Americans dependent on those programs. I can only sincerely advise folks to try and be prepared emotionally and financially.

Important links:

1– Reforming social security – the cruel hoax
2– Take It or Leave It: Seniors Can't Reject Medicare Eligibility
3– Court says Medicare beneficiaries are stuck with government program [End]

That was March 2014, it's now April 2016. **Medicare's unfunded liabilities then was $89 TRILLION dollars**. The Debt Clock on the Internet collects data from state and federal government agencies to post the numbers. Guess what Medicare's liabilities are at this time? $27.5 TRILLION dollars. What? How can that be? Are you telling me that somehow the government collected enough from Medicare "pay as you go" taxes to pay down Medicare's liabilities to the tune of $51.5 TRILLION dollars since 2014 when I vote my column previously cited? It's either a colossal magic trick or the books are being cooked.

Huh? The Debt Clock website also dropped the $22.3 TRILLION for the "free" pills program. I guess that monstrous debt is just out there floating around in space. But, those numbers currently should reflect an even lower total for all three at $106 TRILLION dollars. So, according to government data, somehow SS and Medicare are now $41.9 TRILLION. Added in is the U.S. Federal Budget Deficit (GAAP) which is $5.8 TRILLION showing total of U.S. Funded Liabilities (GAAP) of $98.8 TRILLION. *Is that the new Common Core math?*

Every year or two we hear Congress is going to crack down on Medicare fraud. Because the way the system works, **Medicare is and always will be a magnet for fraud** – in the billions year after year after year. How much is actually recovered? Who knows with the liars in Washington, DC. Last year Medicare paid out $554 BILLION for health care and related services. $60 BILLION was "improperly" paid. Oh, good. Improperly.

I found a rather complicated piece on Politifact.com, February 1, 2013, regarding what you pay into SS and Medicare and what you get out. It was quite glowing in support of those two programs. The numbers were eye popping.

"For an average-wage-earning, two-income couple turning 65 in 2010, the pay-in, pay-out ratio for Social Security by itself will actually be slightly negative — the couple will have paid $600,000 in lifetime Social Security taxes and will receive only $579,000 in lifetime Social Security benefits. (Remember, **the couple didn't literally pay out $600,000**; that's the current value of what they paid out over the years, plus an additional 2 percent they may have gotten had it been invested.)"

The article goes on, "According to the institute's data, a two-earner couple receiving an average wage — $44,600 per spouse in 2012 dollars — and turning 65 in 2010 would have paid $722,000 into Social Security and Medicare and can be expected to take out $966,000 in benefits. So, this couple will be paid about one-third more in benefits than they paid in taxes."

But wait, didn't this article say that the couple doesn't literally pay out $600,000, but only the "current value" of what they paid over the years? And, that same couple will be paid about 1/3rd more in benefits than they paid in taxes. In other words, they received more than what they paid. When you multiply that by 40 or 50 MILLION, that 1/3rd becomes huge money, does it not – especially when you have one recipient who runs up a half million dollars in medical bills in one year as I happen to know one case. That individual did not have $500,000 withheld from his paychecks for Medicare taxes over his career.

If the picture is so rosy why are there Medicare liabilities of $27.5 TRILLION dollars – if that's the real figure which it can't possibly be. Even if it were "only" $27.5 TRILLION dollars, why is Congress now so worried about solvency? Well, perhaps this might help us to understand:

Trustees: Social Security Will Run $84 Billion Deficit in 2015, September 1, 2015, *CNSNews.com*

(CNSNews.com) – "The Old-Age, Survivors, and Disability Insurance (OASDI) program commonly known as Social Security, which celebrated its 80th birthday on August 14, is projected to run an $84 billion deficit this year, according to the 2015 Annual Report of the Board of Trustees. Social Security's cost exceeded its tax income in 2014, and also exceeded its non-interest income, as it has since 2010," the trustees" 75th annual report to Congress stated.

"This relationship is projected to continue throughout the short-range period (2015 through 2024) and beyond…For 2015, the deficit of tax income (and non-interest income) is projected to be approximately $84 billion," the report stated. During 2014, $646.2 billion in payroll taxes was collected from 166 million working Americans. But that was not enough to cover the $859 billion in Social Security benefits that were collected by 59 million people, including 42 million retired workers and their dependents, six million survivors of deceased workers, and 11 million disabled workers and their dependents." [1]

Wait! I thought this "pay as you go" system was supposed to take care of all the costs. With 10,000 Americans a day retiring from 2010 until 2025, that's tens and tens of millions who will be collecting social security and Medicare. Where is all that money going to come from?

Borrow more from Communist China? They've got their own major problems as those of us who follow these things know. Print up more worthless paper money?

Can The US Economy Keep Up with This Exponential Chart? July 22, 2013, *Zero Hedge*

"What we are doing to future generations is absolutely criminal. We are piling up mountains of debt that will haunt them for the rest of their lives just so that we can make the present a little bit more pleasant for ourselves. As I noted in another article, during Obama's first term the federal government accumulated more debt than it did under the first 42 U.S presidents combined. And now we are entering a time period when demographic forces are going to put a tremendous amount of pressure on the finances of the federal government.

"The Baby Boomers have started to retire, and they are going to want to start collecting on all of the financial promises that we have made to them. As I have written about previously, the number of Americans on Medicare is projected to grow from a little bit more than 50 million today to 73.2 million in 2025. The number of Americans collecting Social Security benefits is projected to grow from about 56 million today to 91 million in 2035. Where are we going to get the money to pay for all of that?

"Boston University economist Laurence Kotlikoff has calculated that the U.S. government is facing unfunded liabilities of $222 trillion dollars in the years ahead. There is no simply no way that the U.S. government is going to be able to meet those obligations without wildly printing up money." [2]

What's the solution? Pain for all of us because the rate of taxation for both of those programs will have to be raised – a lot. While you're shelling out for that, you also have your own health care premiums and under Obamacare we all know what's happened – monthly premiums for millions went straight up. In the *CNS News* item above, the SS system is *a whopping 32% under-funded.* Medicare is much worse because costs accumulate so fast on the debt clock, I can't even write it down. Literally tens of thousands of dollars a split second.

Now you see why I did not want to go into Medicare. I've paid my own health care premiums all my life because **my health care is MY**

responsibility, not yours. I do everything I can to stay healthy including keep my weight down. Yet, what do I see on a regular basis – especially when I travel and have to eat in restaurants? Very over weight and obese Americans going into McDonalds or some other junk food joint or sitting in a restaurant eating all the bread and butter on the table when they should be eating salad and food choices that keep the weight off.

So, here we are and people who refuse to get healthy will spend a lot of time in doctor's offices and later in life, hospitals running up those costs. Why do people think waiting times are a lot longer for a doctor? There aren't enough doctors in this country to handle a sick nation that refuses to do what it takes to stay healthy. I'm not talking about individuals who get cancer, although there are so many things – like a healthy diet – that can cut your chances of getting cancer.

The day of reckoning is here for both SS and Medicare. The U.S. Congress created this mess along with every sitting president since the damnable Lyndon Johnson signed Medicare into law in 1965. Due to 2016 being an election, once again Congress has pushed these twin monsters off to the side while they think about what they're going to do – along with all the lobbyists. Pledge to reform SS and Medicare on the campaign trail and once sworn back into office just let the problem fester because of future votes.

Social Security Medicare are two separate programs. A bill needs to get through Congress that would overturn forcing any American who doesn't want to participate in Medicare from doing so and **that also includes stop taxing them**. Like me. Like Dick Armey and other seniors *who can afford to pay our own health care premiums*. Why continue forcing individuals who can pay their own way into a program already in massive debt? Well, the answer is simple: Like any Ponzi scheme you have to keep replenishing the bottomless pit with more participants – even if it's against what that individual wants.

Congress destroyed the health care **delivery** system as I covered in Obamacare. Once again the free market is the solution, but now a huge number of seniors in this country are broke. They live on SS and small pensions. Too many live on social security, food stamps and any other government program they can find. Tens of millions depend on Medicare to pay for their medical needs. I curse those in the U.S.

Congress since Medicare became law because of what they've done to an unsuspecting population.

And, let me say this about Medicare, doctors and industry sectors like imagining, ambulances and so forth: Medicare does not pay doctors what they would normally receive which is why so many refuse to take Medicare patients and I don't blame them. **Why should they work for less?** I think very highly of my primary care doctor and feel bad when I have an appointment because I know she will be paid less than a patient with private sector insurance.

What happens when, say 50% of doctors and support sectors decide to no longer take Medicare? What will that criminal class called Congress do – write some law that says every doctor in this country has to work for less by taking Medicare patients?

We're right back to Chapter 1 and our corrupted monetary system and the free market. I can't stress strongly enough how everything would turn around if just a few key things were implemented which is why I wrote this book. I realize that a great deal of this is new to Americans, but the only way to truly understand as I had to do is by taking your precious time to **get educated on these issues from a constitutional perspective, not a political one**.

Those programs simply are not sustainable. Not without raising taxes on everyone to the point where you have no money to put food on the table. Or, what 57 million seniors fear: cutting benefits and that could hit up the range of 25%. I didn't make this mess. I'm in the system against my will. Tragically, tens of millions of Americans over the past sixty years haven't been paying attention to what YOUR incumbent and mine has done to we the people. The chickens have come home to roost and will soon be on the barbecue spit.

10

"Smart" Meters – The Silent Killer

Despite the fact that I try to keep up with the massive assault against we the people by Congress and too many new laws coming out of our state legislatures, no one can keep up with everything. Which is why I had only read a little here and there about something called smart meters. Then the problem came knocking at my door.

On April 18, 2011, I received a letter from Reliant Energy there was a repeat problem with the meter reader having access to my property. I have locks on all three gates because I have dogs. I was unaware the meter reader was having trouble since my late husband was always home due to his serious health problems. What also waved a red flag was Reliant's letter which stated I am required to have one of their new smart meters installed whether I wanted one or not.

So, I call Reliant and they referred me to a company called ONCOR, a TDSP (Transmission and Distribution Service Provider). Dialing away, I call ONCOR's customer service rep and explain the situation. I also told the lady there is someone at this house every day; either John or myself. All their meter reader has to do is knock on the door and he can read the meter. I thought that was the end of the matter until one day a nice young man showed up at the door to let me know he was going to install a 'smart' meter. I politely said, no you aren't. He left.

By that time, I had done some research that was beyond alarming. The more I researched the more determined I was that I was not going to allow ONCOR to put one of those dangerous meters on my home.

In early July, while I was gone running errands, another ONCOR fellow showed up at the door to install a 'smart' meter. My husband said, no we will not have one of those dangerous things attached to our house. The ONCOR installer informed John that if we didn't agree to have it installed, ONCOR would shut off our power with no notice.

On July 22, 2011, I received a letter from ONCOR. They would shut off the power if I didn't agree to have the meter installed. Their letter was also very deceptive. In paragraph 2, it states, "The EPAct further requires states to consider the adoption of Smart Metering..."

"Consider" does not mean mandatory. In fact, there is no mandatory requirement by the Federal Government from any quarter because I looked up every reference resource in their letter.

Referring again to their letter, they state: "...when the Texas Legislature passed a law (H.B. No 2129) *encouraging* the deployment of new advanced meters..." nowhere does it state mandatory installation in residences throughout the State of Texas. It says "encouraging" and it all has to do with federal bribe money to the states. Act surprised.

Here is the exact language in H.B. 2129 passed and signed into law by then governor, Rick Perry: Section 6. Chapter 31, Utilities Code, is amended by adding Section 31.005 to read as follows:

Sec. 31.005. Customer-Option Programs.

(b) An entity to which this section applies shall consider establishing customer-option programs that encourage the reduction of air contaminant emissions, such as: (5) a program that *encourages* the deployment of advanced electricity meters.

All the committee documents from our legislature for that bill say the exact same thing. Words have meaning in the law. *Encourages does not mean mandatory*.

Testimony of Chairman Donna L. Nelson, Public Utility Commission of Texas Before the House (US) Committee on Science, Space and Technology – Subcommittee on Technology and Innovation Empowering Consumers and Promoting Innovation Through the Smart Grid – Sept. 8, 2011 in Washington, DC.

"State legislation has *encouraged* the implementation of advanced metering by directing the Texas PUC to *establish a cost recovery mechanism for utilities that deploy smart meters* and related networks. The Texas PUC adopted a rule in May 2007 related to smart meter deployment."

Her testimony is only six pages, but if you read the entire statement, you will see the staggering money at stake here in Texas – hundreds of MILLIONS of dollars. **That's why the utility companies and their distribution providers have lied to all of us.** By her own admission, installation was not mandatory. The energy companies were encouraged to "deploy" this new technology. While the energy companies jumped people's fences, cut locks on people's gates and lied to homeowners, the Texas PUC did nothing.

The letter concluded with "Please allow the AMS meter to be installed at your property, since failure to provide access may result in suspension of delivery service." That's when I called a dear friend of mine who was a lawyer in Shreveport, Louisiana, Tommy Cryer, and thus began the war here in Texas against smart meters.

You might ask what is my objection to a "smart meter"? Which one would that be? Health concerns or privacy? Both, actually. As I said I knew little about this new technology, so about 100 hours of research later and thanks to so many dedicated people fighting this, here are some of the *known* problems:

Wireless smart meters on every home and building will emit huge pulses of microwave radio frequency radiation as often as every few seconds throughout the day and night, seven days a week. FCC exposure standards only cover short-term thermal (heating) effects and they do not cover long-term accumulative exposure, nor do they cover biological impacts.

Several years ago the World Health Organization has recently classified the type of radiation emitted from smart meters (non-ionizing radiation) as a Class 2B carcinogen, on par with lead. All transmitters inside your home or office will communicate with a Smart Meter attached to the outside of each building. That meter, in turn, transmits an even higher frequency to a central hub installed in local neighborhoods called "net meshing".

Those "mesh network" signals can also be bounced from house-meter to house-meter before reaching the final hub. Exposure to that non-ionizing radiation will not just be from your own meter. It can accumulate from a small number of your neighbors up to 500 at the same time. Those meters have a range of 1–3 miles. Then the data is shot off to a main transport which could be hundreds of miles away.

The scientific evidence for biological impacts from microwave radiation, known for decades (remember the Moscow embassy) continues to grow with impacts such as DNA damage, increased risk of cancers and tumors, cellular stress, decreased melatonin, decreased sperm, cognitive difficulties and brain-wave alteration, heart rhythm disturbances, red blood cell clumping, and impacts on wildlife including to bees.

Wireless radio-frequency radiation from smart meters can cause medical implants like pacemakers and deep-brain stimulators used to control the shaking of Parkinson's disease can be turned off by the radio frequency interference (RFI) caused by the signal. These signals are reported in published studies to interfere with critical care equipment, ventilators, pain pumps, wireless insulin pumps and other medical devices.

Reports from those who have had meters installed include heart palpitations, dizziness, inability to fall asleep, memory problems and cognitive disturbances, flu-like symptoms, worsening of existing health problems, abrupt depression, agitation, headaches, hearing problems."

Too many to list are radio-frequency spikes which cause appliances to break. Those sensors companies are trying to get everyone to buy for their micro-wave, over, refrigerator, freezer you name it – when they blow up don't look to your energy provider to buy you a new one.

The most common effects from smart meters are migraines, nausea vomiting, muscle spasms, heart palpitations and insomnia cause by intense bursts of radiation.

As for privacy, do you know there are companies out there already harvesting your personal data *without oversight* if you have a "smart meter"? Corporations are using your private data in states that don't have restrictions against energy companies selling your "smart" meter data worth tens of billions of dollars. The Department of Energy, another absolutely worthless money sucking agency has confirmed data mined from smart meters and so-called smart appliances will be highly invasive. I highly recommend you read, Smart Meters: A Surveillance and Control Con Job Revealed. [1]

How about criminals? No problem. They can drive down the street in a van and grab wireless information to determine if only one person is residing in a home making a single or elderly woman a prime target for rape and murder. They will be able to see usage patterns and determine it's likely a family is out of town *and your home is their candy store*. Make no mistake: smart meters are easily hacked because it's already been done by security experts numerous times.

As I progressed along in my research which would end up to be probably a thousand hours, what I was finding was such deceit and greed.

California PUC Issues Sweeping Data Access Orders:

> *"Many young companies have sprung up based on being able to access consumers' Smart Meter data and package it in some meaningful form. So far they've had to make their own assumptions about what data would be available, often forming alliances between hardware and software companies."*

A jaw dropping violation of your privacy made possible by your utility company. Those "young companies" don't care about your privacy they want to sell it. How shameful and isn't it nice California issues some rules *after* the cow is out of the barn?

There are billions of dollars involved with this smart meter business. I fully understand we have to have a reliable and up to date power supply system in the U.S. I don't begrudge utility companies making a profit because I am a free market advocate. But, not at the expense of human health, not to mention all this 'dirty energy' and what it does to our beloved dogs and livestock consumed by humans and to the environment. *The only ones who benefit from "smart" meters are attorneys (lawsuits), utility companies and big pharmaceutical companies from people getting sick and more prescriptions for their pills.*

The "smart" meter is an integral part of something called the "smart" grid. In the Spring 2011 *Industry Week Magazine* there was a huge article on the smart grid and all about "controlling energy inside the consumer space" using real time. That's you and me. Control us. It discussed the need to "change attitudes". That means brain wash people into "compliance" on how much energy you will be *allowed* to use and if you go over, think they won't shut off an appliance? Think again because the utility company controlling those meters can and will. That's the whole idea behind the so called smart grid.

After those first visits and all the threats, I received no more visits from ONCOR nor did anyone come to read the meter. As it stood then, if they knocked on the door and requested to read the meter, I would unlock the gate and accompany them and watch while they read the meter to make sure the fellow doesn't try to pull a fast one and install a smart meter while I'm in the house. Nice way to live.

Back then the smart meter issue began to explode (no pun intended) on homes all over this country. And, people have died:

Fatal Dallas fire puts scrutiny on "smart" meters – February 3, 2015 – *WFAA ABC.com*

Dallas — "James Humphrey Jr. was found dead on his bedroom floor Monday night. The elderly man was unable to escape after his South Dallas home went up in flames. 'I just lost a 75-year-old cousin,' Alfreda Johnson said. She believes this was a death — and a fire — that could have been prevented. 'They came out and changed that meter three weeks ago, and the house caught on fire from that meter,' she alleged."

Reno, Sparks fire chiefs call for smart meter probe, September 16, 2014 – *Reno Gazette Journal*. "The Reno and Sparks fire chiefs are asking the Public Utilities Commission to investigate the safety of smart meters installed by NV Energy on homes throughout the state in the wake of a troubling spate of blazes they believe are associated with the meters, including one recent fire that killed a 61-year-old woman. "Since 2012, four fires have occurred in Reno and five fires have occurred in Sparks that city investigators say are linked to the smart meters manufactured by North Carolina-based Sensus."

Fires prompt removal of 175,000 smart meters in Canada and Oregon – August 21, 2014, EMF Safety Network

"In Saskatchewan Canada the government ordered 105,000 smart meters be replaced with non-transmitting older meters because of several fires started by smart meters. 'The concerns are significant enough that we believe that any time that families are at risk here in Saskatchewan, actions have to be taken. That's why we've directed SaskPower accordingly.' Provincial minister Bill Boyd said. In addition, 70,000 smart meters with an automatic shut off will be replaced in Portland Oregon because of fires. Both of these companies are removing Sensus smart meters."

Lakeland Electric's Smart Meters Can Overheat – *The Ledger.com* - January 16, 2014

"Amy Adams had just returned to her northwest Lakeland home when she smelled something burning. Adams and her family members also noticed theirs was the only home in the neighborhood that didn't have power. 'She thought there was a problem with the breaker, but saw a charred power box and melted smart meter about three feet from her children's corner bedroom. The whole box was burnt up,' Adams said of the November incident. Since installation of smart meters began nearly three years ago, Lakeland Electric officials have replaced 178 because of overheating. Four of the meters, including Adams', actually caught fire and melted."

Put this into a search engine so you can watch the video: Thousands of Smart Meter Fires: New Whistleblower and Court Evidence, July 16, 2015 by Brian Thiesen: "The situation with smart meter fires is worse than we thought — and now we know why. This new investigative video tells all...

"The whistleblowers (wishing to remain anonymous) who contacted us have serviced and repaired over 200,000 meters in the field. They have been warning their supervisors about 'smart' meter problems for nearly a decade now. They have had enough of the lies and want you to know what they know.

"On top of the explosive new details, the meters have at least four major sources of arcing. That's right — FOUR. Arcing in 'smart' meters causes extreme heat, which causes fires. As we now see, it is beyond any shadow of a doubt that meter manufacturers know, utilities know, and regulators know. They have known the whole time, but they didn't want to tell you.

"In this investigation the focus on two of the worst offenders, BC Hydro and PG&E. However, as this is a systemic problem regardless of meter type, we feature fire incidents from Texas, Ontario, Saskatchewan, Pennsylvania, Illinois and more."

Stockton Smart Meters Explode After Truck Causes Power Surge, March 30, 2015, *CBS* Sacramento, California. STOCKTON (*CBS13*) — "A power surge left thousands without power in Stockton on Monday after smart meters on their homes exploded. The explosions started at around 8:30 a.m. after a truck crashed into a utility pole, causing a surge. When the customers in more than 5,000 homes get their power back on will depend on how badly damaged their meters are. Neighbors in the South Stockton area described it as a large pop, a bomb going off, and strong enough to shake a house."

What about your house and if it does catch fire and burn to the ground, *will your insurance company cover a fire from a "smart" meter?* Apartment buildings have panels with dozens on each one. How about hospitals? Will it take a major tragedy to get those dangerous meters banned once and for all?

Sometime near the end of summer 2011, I met a freedom fighter who would become a dear friend to me, Thelma Taromina, who lived in Houston, Texas, with her husband, Nick and their dog, Ginger. Before long we were working feverishly to get our state legislature to stop the Texas PUC from forcing those meters on anyone in Texas. A few tried in 2013, but if you look at the amount of money sprinkled over the Texas State Legislature by energy companies, guess who lost?

I've said over the past decades that while fighting corruption at the state and federal level, one of the best things I've experienced is making new friends with people all over the country. Americans who will not bow down to a tyrannical government at any level. Like minded individuals who believe the U.S. Constitution is the supreme law of the land and are willing to stand up and fight. Thelma was an amazing person, a true American Patriot and freedom fighter. Those few words can never do her justice. My dear friend lost her battle with cancer on April 6, 2015. I will miss her always.

Thelma, Nick and I and hundreds of Texans who by then had banded together didn't just want the TPUC to issue a ruling that says we have the right to opt out, we wanted the TPUC to order ONCOR and other companies in Texas who install those meters to remove them at *their* expense and reinstall the old analog meters that work just fine. Because companies like ONCOR have, *without your permission*, subjected their customers to a dangerous piece of technology and literally are conducting wiretapping on your residence, THEY, not the customer should bear the cost of replacement.

When it became apparent the TPUC and no state representative or legislator would help us at that time, our attorney filed the first petition as one is required to do in order to pursue redress with the TPUC. It's called Administrative Law and if you don't have an attorney to represent you, believe me, all those rules and regulations will drive you insane. Not to mention the PUC has the force of the state behind them. My petition began the war in Texas against "smart" meters, the Texas PUC and the energy companies. While all this is going on, ONCOR, CenterPoint and other energy companies throughout the State of Texas were busy installing those dangerous meters on homes and businesses despite thousands of complaints.

Our first petition was denied by the Texas PUC – crony appointees of then Gov. Ricky Perry. We filed for a rehearing. It, too, was denied. Then our attorney Tommy Cryer, Esq., passed away on June 4, 2012. He is still deeply missed by so many in this country.

We then retained new legal counsel to file a lawsuit against the Texas PUC for violating their own rules. Our group had fulfilled all the requirements by the PUC for a full public hearing in front of an Administrative Law Judge. The Texas PUC did not want us to have our hearing so in essence they said drop dead. *If those "smart" meters are so safe, why fight us so hard to keep us from having a full blown open hearing?* I think by now the answer is obvious.

The Texas PUC relied on biased reports and when we the people said, wait a minute something is wrong here, they simply used their power to push us around. Figuring we would just go away. Well, we didn't and the lawsuit was filed. Due to some shall I say misunderstandings, Thelma, Nick and I decided we needed to change lawyers. We then retained our third attorney who was been absolutely the best and boy did he get an eyeful as they say regarding those meters and the shenanigans by the Texas PUC.

Let me now go back to late 2011 because one of the big selling points about smart meters is that they are so energy efficient. They will be good for the environment and will reduce energy consumption and costs. Sounds good, but any truth to those claims?

Not all states were buying into the sales pitch "smart" meters would save energy: Press Release, February 8, 2011, by Connecticut's Attorney General George Jepsen urging state regulators to reject CL & P's plan to replace electric meters:

"To evaluate the technical capabilities and reliability of the advanced metering system, state regulators previously approved a limited study of 10,000 meters. Between June 1 and Aug. 31, 2009, CL&P tested the meters on 1,251 residential and 1,186 small commercial and industrial customers, who volunteered and were paid for their participation in the study. The company reported its results to the DPUC on Feb. 25, 2010. 'The pilot results showed no beneficial impact on total energy usage,' Jepsen said."

Are there any other opinions about "smart" meters not being energy efficient?

Remarks of Stefanie A. BrandDirector of the N.J. Division of Rate Counsel Regarding Energy Efficiency Before the Assembly Telecommunications and Utilities Committee, February 25, 2008

"2. Resist the urge to buy the latest gadget.

"Fancy meters and smart grids are cool. But they are expensive and by themselves they don't save electricity. They simply tell you where and when you are using it. There is no electricity saved unless you reduce your usage every time you see that information. In the future they may replace the existing meters we have, but in the present we don't need one in every ratepayer's home or business. Here's why:

'We don't need them to tell us where we can save electricity or how to target energy efficiency programs. We already know where we can start saving and we need to start now. They are expensive. At $300 each we can spend that money on other measures that will produce larger actual reductions in annual usage. It's like spending all your money on an expensive new refrigerator and having none left over to buy food to put in it, rather than buying a less expensive one that does the same job and leaves you money for food. The studies that have been done have not really compared what you would get if you took the equivalent amount of money and used it for more traditional energy efficiency measures."

Update July 6, 2011

MACRUC Discusses AMI (Mid-Atlantic Conference of Regulatory Utilities Commissioners)

"I am sure it was not intended to be a debate on the merits of smart meters, but let's just say the discussion got lively as Itron's Dan Pfeiffer's comments followed New Jersey Consumer Advocate Stefanie Brand's statement. Stefanie made it clear that in her view, advanced metering infrastructure ('AMI') also commonly referred to as 'smart meters,' are not so smart and in New Jersey have not been shown to be cost-effective. As a result, New Jersey is not deploying smart meters at this time. To garner her support, AMI programs should be voluntary and ideally provide consumers rate reductions that are greater than the cost of the meter."

Advanced Metering Infrastructure Implications for Residential Customers in New Jersey – July 8, 2008 – Prepared by Rick Hornby, Charles Salamone, Stu Perry, Dr. David White, Kenji Takahashi – Prepared for New Jersey Department of Public Advocate – Division of Rate Counsel

"The major forecast benefits to a utility from an investment in AMI are expected savings in the costs of operating their distribution systems. In particular, an investment in AMI would enable utilities to control and read meters electronically and thereby eliminate staff currently required to read meters and to turn power on and off at the meter. This would produce a reduction in the utility's annual labor costs."

Good-bye to tens of thousands of meter reader jobs in this country as we slide into a depression. Ms. Brand was absolutely correct: *the consumer has to monitor the meter constantly in order to save energy and money.*

In January 2014, sanity vs insanity in Massachusetts:

COMMONWEALTH OF MASSACHUSETTS DEPARTMENT OF PUBLIC UTILITIES

"Investigation by the Department of Public Utilities on its own Motion into Modernization of the Electric Grid – D.P.U. 12–76-A Initial Comments of Northeast Utilities Executive Summary – In part:

"The technology choice is made although there is no evidence that this is a good choice for customers. Conversely, there is ample evidence that this technology choice will be unduly costly for customers and that the objectives of grid modernization are achievable with technologies and strategies that rank substantially higher in terms of cost-effectiveness. For customers who will pay the price of this system, there is no rational basis for this technology choice. 'Rather than furthering grid-modernization objectives, the Department's mandate to implement AMI creates an intractable obstacle to grid modernization."

The "smart" meter is critical to the smart grid in covering this nation with more dirty electricity. But, this is all about big money...maybe. Let me go back to the Advanced Metering Infrastructure study above:

"Savings to utility. The AMI filings of utilities in other states, and the studies prepared by New Jersey EDCs, indicate the total cost of AMI, measured as the net present value (NPV) of revenue requirements over 15 years, would be greater than the NPV of forecast savings in utility operating costs over the same period. The forecast savings from automating various distribution system operations range from fifty percent to seventy-five percent of the total cost. As a result, we assume that utilities who invest in AMI will eventually file for an increase in their distribution service rates in order to recover that shortfall.

"Savings to ratepayers. The estimates of savings to residential customers from AMI-enabled dynamic pricing, a form of time-differentiated pricing, hinge upon three major assumptions: the reduction in peak use per participating customer, the percentage of customers who will voluntarily participate, and the long-term persistence of the reductions per participating customer.

"There is considerable uncertainty regarding each of these assumptions despite the results from pilot projects in other jurisdictions. First, most pilots entice customers to participate through some form of 'appreciation' payment and therefore provide no guidance regarding the percentage of customers who will voluntarily participate in the absence of such an incentive. Second, most pilots have only operated a few years, thus they provide little guidance regarding the long-term persistence of participation and reductions per participant.

"In addition, even if one accepts the assumptions made by EDCs about AMI-enabled dynamic pricing, the economics are not particularly attractive either for those customers who participate or for residential customers in general."

Translated, that means the utility companies will go for rate hikes when they take it in the shorts – and they do. This is going on in many states.

This is all about controlling what you do in your own home and conditioning people for energy rationing down the line. Mark my words because sustainable development is the name of the ugly game: Control everything about your life, how you can live, how much energy you will be allowed to use and where you can live. Type into a search engine: Smart Grid: Technology for "Big Brother" by Sarah Foster, September 14, 2011.

In this endless saga and while our lawsuit is sitting in the court waiting to hatch, the Texas PUC finally got around to what Tommy Cryer called a "buy out" and what the energy companies call an opt out. You don't want the meter, fine, but we're going to extort big money from you so you can keep your meter as you should have been allowed in the first place. No pay, off comes your analog meter and onto your home a dangerous smart meter.

You see, the Texas PUC had been told twice by Rep. Dennis Bonnen of the Texas State Legislature for them to stop forcing people to have one of those meters installed on their homes (Rep. Bonnen's letter is at end of this chapter). The TPUC simply bided their time ignoring Bonnen's letter while the energy companies lied and strong armed anyone in this state who didn't have a 'smart' meter. In the case of my dear friend, Thelma Taromina, the installer from CenterPoint actually physically assaulted her several times on her own property! After shoving Thelma several times, she got up, went in her house and got her gun, cell phone and called the sheriff.

In the end no charges were filed, but it shows you exactly how ruthless big corporations can be if their bottom line is threatened. You can watch an interview with Thelma about that incident on line. Simply use a search engine and type in:

"Texas Woman Stops Smart Meter Installation and Assault with Gun" (https://www.youtube.com/watch?v=DWHfA3rr7os).

Getting back to the "opt out" extortion. We know there's no federal or state law which requires us to have a "smart" meter installed on our homes. But, unless you pay the extortion money they will cut your power with no notice. In my area the one-time fee was almost $400 dollars plus a monthly fee for the meter reader. But, wait! The meter reader had been reading my analog meter for years already. See the scam?

So, Thelma and Nick took up the reins on that one and many months later, we were finally 'allowed' to keep our analog meters with the one time "opt out" fee considerably reduced. But, I still pay a hefty fee once a month for a meter reader. Those of us who fought them still had our meters so now we're to get dinged to keep them. Thanks to all those conservative Republicans who control the house and senate here in Texas for allowing this sickening chain of events to slam the people of Texas.

That war finally came to a conclusion. Our attorney, Roger Borgelt, did a superior job for us. It did require bringing on a person who specializes in that type of negotiations with PUCs so that ran up the bill. In the end – all paid for with donations – the tab was about $40,000.00.

I had to make numerous trips to Austin for PUC horse and pony shows. It's a six hour drive each way for me. Because my husband was a disabled amputee confined to a wheel chair, I had to board my three doggies. Hotels, gas, good on the road, boarding fees – all to fight to keep a dangerous piece of technology off my home.

In August 2012, the PUC held another horse and pony show called a hearing in an attempt to appease us – the ones the newspapers in this state called a "fringe element". My, were they shocked when hundreds of people showed up. The big room was overflowing so they had to open another one. Bring out the trumpets – I was to be a speaker! Several members of the state legislature were there to watch.

Yes, I was to be given 5 minutes for all the time, expense and trouble for me to get to Austin and then back home. That's right. A whole 5 minutes. Actually, I wasn't even allowed that. Four minutes into my statement I was cut off. Thelma offered to give up a minute of her time, but was denied. I guess they didn't like what I was saying.

The Texas PUC and the energy companies knew before they started installing those meters they are dangerous to the human body, animals and the environment. Just like P G & E out in California:

BEFORE THE PUBLIC UTILITIES COMMISSION OF THE STATE OF CALIFORNIA (July 16, 2011). Opening Brief of the County of Marin, County of Santa Cruz, Town of Fairfax, City of Marina, City of Seaside, City of Capitola, City of Santa Cruz, Town of Ross and The Alliance for Human and Environmental Health, Page 5:

"A. The Commission Has Long Acknowledged and Acted Upon Public Concerns About the Health Impacts Of EMF But Never Found the Utilities" Wireless Mesh Networks or SmartMeters To Be Safe.

"The SmartMeter program has generated unprecedented public concern about the health impacts of the planned deployment of millions of devices which will expose Californians to a cumulatively immeasurable amount of pulsed electro-magnetic and RF signals. Scores of witnesses have come forth to describe their personal concerns about the program's effect on their own health and decry this development in formal filings and public hearings before the Commission. As set forth below, the concern over the health impacts of EMF is not new or unique to the SmartMeter program. In fact, it has been a documented public health concern known to the Commission for decades.

"As noted by a unanimous California Supreme Court in *San Diego Gas and Electric Co. v. Superior Court* in 1996, the Commission: "...has broad authority to determine whether the service or equipment of any public utility poses any danger to the health or safety of the public, and if so, to prescribe corrective measures and order them into effect. Every public utility is required to furnish and maintain such 'service, instrumentalities, equipment, and facilities . . . as are necessary to promote the safety, health, comfort, and convenience of its patrons, employees, and the public.' (§ 451, italics added.) The Legislature has vested the commission with both general and specific powers to ensure that public utilities comply with that mandate."

"That electric and magnetic fields ('EMF') are a recognized public health concern is evidenced by the fact that the Commission has long exercised regulatory authority over various forms of EMF generated by electrical utility generating and transmission equipment. Prior to 1988 the Commission had addressed the issue of the potential public health effects of such fields only on a case-by-case basis. In 1988, however, the Legislature initiated a broad inquiry into the subject. It found, inter alia, that "A number of scientific studies are beginning to indicate that electromagnetic fields associated with electrical utility facilities may present a significant cancer risk." And, on page 20:

"The Commission has received public testimony and formal pleadings during Phase 1 of this proceeding demonstrating that Utility customers suffer significant impairment of one or more of their major life functions due to EMF sensitivity, including seizures, episodic malignant hypertension, heart arrhythmias, severe insomnia, intractable tinnitus, muscle spasms and twitching, migraine headaches, and neuropathy. Hence, individuals with significant or recurrent EMF-induced or exacerbated symptoms qualify for reasonable accommodation under the ADA, when EMF exposure of such individuals interferes with major life functions, such as neurologic function or other major life functions."

Safe? If they're not safe for people under the ADA (Americans With Disabilities Act), *why would they be considered safe for the rest of us?*

Our attorney filed an amended complaint in March 2014. Act surprised: Even though our lawsuit is against the Texas PUC, here in Texas other parties can jump in the game. In this case the mega-bucks energy companies. This caused our attorney to do an enormous amount of extra work so our legal bills were crushing by that point.

In October 2014, despite the superb job by our attorney, we the people lost. Our attorney filed an appeal in March 2015 in the Third Circuit Court of Appeals in Austin. More $$. Every penny for our war against the TPUC and the secondary fight, opt-out, came from donations.

Nearly six months later, the Third Circuit notified our attorney there would be a hearing on September 24, 2015; I was unable to attend. Roger conveyed that surprisingly he was able to get in much more than he thought he would.

However, it didn't matter because on December 9, 2015, the very same Third Circuit who approved the fraud committed as set forth in my Seventeenth Amendment lawsuit also shot down our right to a public hearing even though the Texas PUC violated its own rules. Between the fight with the PUC and reducing the cost of extortion money for an "opt-out", we raised close to $80,000 to pay legal expenses; every penny in donations went for legal expenses. There simply was no more money to take it to the Texas Supreme Court.

My husband and I had about $6,000 in expenses for that battle to keep a dangerous piece of technology off our home. All down the drain and no, I did not vote to reelect my state rep or senator in the primary here in March. Both betrayed us for doing nothing about the PUC and those "smart" meters. I voted for their challengers who lost because too many voters pay no attention to what those crooks are up to and what legislation they vote on.

As we go to press I have approached a law firm about filing a federal RICO (Racketeer Influenced and Corrupt Organizations Act). One has been filed in California. Now it needs to be done here in Texas. This is absolutely ripe for a RICO. The energy companies have left a paper trail a mile long.

What is the solution?

"Smart" meters must be banned in every state of the Union. **Only massive numbers of Americans demanding their state legislatures ban those dangerous meters is going to get the job done.** *What can be more important than your health and your family?* Our beloved family pets, livestock that feed we the people as well as the destruction to plant life. We were told they are safe and efficient. The same thing people were told 15 years ago about cell phones and now people around the world know that is not true.

The list below is by no means the only resources. There literally are thousands on the Internet. Simply type the bold titles and dates into a search engine or see the footnote as the back of the book.

Declaration of Dr. David O. Carpenter, M.D., submitted in the United States District Court, District of Oregon, Portland Division, June 1, 2011. Dr. Carpenter was educated at Harvard Medical School and is currently Director of the Institute for Health and Environment at the University at Albany and Professor of Environmental Sciences within the School of Public Health. Formerly Dean of the School of Public Health at the University of Albany and the Director of the Wadsworth Center for Laboratories and Research of the New York State Department of Health.

Here's how the media portrayed the lawsuit above:

Willameet Week, June 20, 2012, Wireless Waste – Portland schools have had to spend $172,000 fighting a parent's lawsuit over Wi-Fi.

"One year ago, the parent of a Portland Public Schools student sued the district with claims a new Wi-Fi network in his daughter's middle school was poisoning her and potentially harming other students. As WW reported, there's no scientific evidence for such claims (see 'Wi-Fi Woo-Woo,' WW, July 13, 2011). The parent, David Mark Morrison, who works as a rare-book dealer, is part of a pseudo-scientific movement that claims Wi-Fi and related technologies cause everything from brain cancer to infertility to digestive complaints.

"Most studies that adherents cite as evidence haven't been published or peer-reviewed in reputable scientific journals. Some anti-wireless websites sell literature and protective charms, including amulets and crystals. Morrison's case might have been easy to label as frivolous and, it seems, might have been headed for an early dismissal. Not so. Portland Public Schools officials tell WW they have already spent $172,559 in public money to defend the district against Morrison's claim that PPS's Wi-Fi network has harmed his daughter...

"In the case of Wi-Fi exposure,' Savitz writes in his declaration, 'there is no epidemiologic evidence whatsoever that counters the lack of biological support for a potential health hazard.' The school district's attorney, Bruce Campbell, argued in court filings that Morrison's experts present 'fringe views' outside the mainstream of science by witnesses who are not qualified to offer their opinions." [End]

"Pseudo-scientific movement", no epidemiologic evidence, no peer reviewed articles "fringe views". Really? Here's more of Dr.

Carpenter's resume who surely isn't qualified to give expert testimony according to the fools at the publication above.

1. "I am a public health physician, educated at Harvard Medical School. My current title is Director of the Institute for Health and the Environment at the University at Albany and Professor of Environmental Health Sciences within the School of Public Health. Formerly, I was the Dean of the School of Public Health at the University of Albany and the Director of the Wadsworth Center for Laboratories and Research of the New York State Department of Health.

2. "I served as the Executive Secretary to the New York State Powerlines Project in the 1980s, a program of research that showed children living in homes with elevated magnetic fields coming from powerlines suffered from an elevated risk of developing leukemia. After this I became the spokesperson on electromagnetic field (EMF) issues for the state during the time of my employment in the Department of Health. I have published several reviews on the subject and have edited two books.

3. "I am a Co-Editor and a Contributing Author of the *BioInitiative: A Rationale for a Biologically-based Public Exposure Standard for Electromagnetic Fields* (ELF and RF), www.bioinitative.org. It documents bioeffects, adverse health effects and public health conclusions about impacts of non-ionizing radiation (electromagnetic fields including extremely - low frequency ELF-EMF and radiofrequency (RF) /microwave or RF-EMF fields). The public health chapter from this report was subsequently published in a peer reviewed journal.

4. "Additionally, I am a Co-Author of *Setting Prudent Public Health Policy for Electromagnetic Field Exposures, Reviews on Environmental Health*, Volume 23, No. 2, 2008, attached as Addendum A-2.

5. "In addition, in 2009, I was invited to present to the President's Cancer Panel on the subject of powerline and radiofrequency fields and cancer, and have testified on this issue before the Unite States House of Representatives.

6. "I am a public health physician who has been involved in issues related to EMF for a number of years.

7. "It is generally accepted within the relevant scientific community and has been established beyond any reasonable doubt that many bioeffects and adverse health effects occur at far lower levels of RF exposure than those that cause measurable heating; some effects are shown to occur at several hundred thousand times below the existing public safety limits, which are set based on the fallacious assumption that there are no adverse health effects at exposures that do not cause easily measureable heating.

8. "Exposure to EMF has been linked to a variety of adverse health outcomes. The health endpoints that have been reported to be associated with ELF and/or RF include childhood leukemia, adult brain tumors, childhood brain tumors, genotoxic effects (DNA damage and micronucleation), neurological effects and neurodegenerative disease (like ALS and Alzheimer's), immune system disregulation, allergic and inflammatory responses, breast cancer in men and women, miscarriage and some cardiovascular effects. The strongest evidence for adverse health effects of EMFs comes from associations observed in human populations with two forms of cancer: childhood leukemia and chronic lymphocytic leukemia in occupationally exposed adults.

9. "There is also strong evidence for elevated risk of brain cancer followed long use of cell phones, but only on the side of the head where the cell phone is used regularly.

10. "There is suggestive to strongly suggestive evidence that RF exposures may cause changes in cell membrane function, cell communication, metabolism, activation of proto-oncogenes, and can trigger the production of stress proteins at exposure levels below current regulatory limits. Resulting effects can include DNA breaks and chromosome aberrations, cell death including death of brain neurons, increased free radical production, activation of the endogenous opioid system, cell stress and premature aging, changes in brain function including memory loss, retarded learning, performance impairment in

children, headaches and fatigue, sleep disorders, eurodegenerative conditions, changes in immune function (allergic and inflammatory responses), reduction in melatonin secretion and cancers."

WiFi Health Effects Presentations to Portland Public Schools Board of Education, September 16, 2013, Transcript from Dr. Martin L. Pall:

"I am Martin L. Pall. I am professor emeritus in biochemistry and basic medical sciences from Washington State University. I have been a Portland resident for the last five years and I have been working in the field of environmental medicine since about the year 2000. I have received seven major international honors for my work in that area and I gave a copy of those to one of the school board members. I'll be receiving an eighth [award] by the end of next month in the US.

"I am talking about the issue of lack of safety of EMF exposures. I published a paper on that a couple of months ago that's been a real paradigm-shifter. Let me just say that the situation before that paper was published, is that people have been assuming that the only thing that ElectroMagnetic Fields can do is to heat things, like heating things in your microwave oven. There was evidence before my paper was written — a lot of it. — [The evidence] is that [that assumption] is simply not true.

"What EMFs do in our bodies is that they work on some channels in the plasma membranes of our cells called voltage-gated calcium channels. What they do is that they open up those channels, calcium flows into the cell and it's the excess calcium in the cell that leads to all the biological effects that are produced by EMFs.

"So all of the assessments of safety which have been based on the assumption that the only thing that these fields can do is heat things are based on a falsehood. We know that now. The reason we know that is because you can block these EMF-effects with drugs that block those channels. Now those drugs have lots of side effects so they are difficult to use clinically, but they are very useful scientifically.

"When you have this situation where excessive activity of these channels, [which] the EMFS produce, of course, you immediately ask, OK what kinds of diseases can be produced by excessive activity of those channels. So I have started looking at that issue the last two months. I just sent a paper off making a very strong argument that autism is one of them. Why is that?

"Well, we know, first of all that autism incidences have been going up very rapidly, paralleling the exposures to EMFs. Everybody knows that and there is now evidence from some studies of a mutant called Timothy Syndrome [beep]. Sorry, are my three minutes up?

"Let me just say that autism is one of them. A second one is type 2 diabetes, the third one is the kind of cardiovascular disease that has to do with the electrical control of the heart and the fourth we won't talk about."

Transcript from the second speaker, Merry Callaghan:

"I am the author the constitutional argument in the *Morrison v. Portland Public Schools*. I am here to talk about legacy — mine and yours. My legacy charges me as a Hanford-nuclear-downwind survivor and as the daughter of a marine raider who volunteered to rescue victims in Nagasaki at ground zero. My legacy charges me with no less duty than the defense of another generation of innocents forcibly exposed to microwave radiation. You call it Wi-Fi. It's a cute marketing term.

"But wireless microwave radiation cannot shed its radiation identity because that is what it is. While as a nuclear engineering student at Oregon State University, I learned what the American trial lawyers now stand behind – that wireless radiation health effects are equitable to the same diseases as that from nuclear radiation exposure. In fact, this biggest trial lawyer association in the world, now called the American Association for Justice, [in September 2013], [threw] down the gauntlet to federal agencies and the wireless industry: [they said] that Big Telecomm and Wireless [litigation] will go the way of Big Tobacco, Asbestos and Lead Paint litigation.

"Meanwhile, players like Cisco, Apple and AT&T promise any comers on school boards and local IT departments that they too can have a personal legacy-building path. Just walk with us, they say. That you, too, can have a share of wireless pork barrel kickbacks from Big Telecom's gaming of the US Department of Education's E-Programs. All you have to do is turn a blind eye, believe in the fable of harmlessness sold to you as a cost-benefit value-add sales pitch, fed to your MBA/IT guy, I call him the decider.

"This decider for all of you, who not only has no bio-sciences [education], who has no health training, who professes, in deposition on [the Portland Public Schools] own record, that he doesn't even have a curiosity about the health effects of wireless radiation and, anyway, he doesn't believe in it. As if his confession were some sort of religion of more efficiency on your balance sheets.

"So this is your legacy: like the Emperor who has no clothes, you will have stood on the sidelines in a fable while the Wireless Industry has paraded their naked untruths and misinformation, have trotted out their doubt about Wi-Fi health effects on children in schools. As if Wi-Fi is magic that floats through the air like butterflies. But Wi-Fi is not magic; and the Emperor has no clothes. It took 27 years for my dad to die from Nagasaki, it took 35 years to figure out [the truth] about Hanford down-winders, and wi-fi radiation, predicted by those who know will follow [similar or shorter] latency periods in disease.

"Your legacy will be on the wrong side of this science, on the wrong side of history and on the wrong side of even 60,000 pediatricians who have recently sent a letter to congress begging them to stop this exposure of children to a class 2B carcinogen, an agent with [the same classification] as DDT, Lead and gasoline fumes. No kid will escape this Russian roulette you are playing with their lives and their futures. So why did I come here today? To talk about Legacy in three minutes or less. My legacy will stand in history. I ask the question. Will yours?"

What happened to that case? Act surprised:

Wi-Fi lawsuit against Portland Public Schools dismissed by federal judge, July 20, 2012, *oregonlive.com*

Who is the big loser? Children in public schools. Your child and you you're a teacher if the school is drowning in wireless microwave radiation.

Is "Electrosmog" Harming Our Health? January 18, 2010, *NBCNews.com* (A must read)

"In 1990, the city of La Quinta, CA, proudly opened the doors of its sparkling new middle school. Gayle Cohen, then a sixth-grade teacher, recalls the sense of excitement everyone felt: 'We had been in temporary facilities for 2 years, and the change was exhilarating.' But the glow soon dimmed. One teacher developed vague symptoms — weakness, dizziness — and didn't return after the Christmas break. A couple of years later, another developed cancer and died; the teacher who took over his classroom was later diagnosed with throat cancer. More instructors continued to fall ill, and then, in 2003, on her 50th birthday, Cohen received her own bad news: breast cancer.

"That's when I sat down with another teacher, and we remarked on all the cancers we'd seen,' she says. 'We immediately thought of a dozen colleagues who had either gotten sick or passed away.' By 2005, 16 staffers among the 137 who'd worked at the new school had been diagnosed with 18 cancers, a ratio nearly 3 times the expected number. Nor were the children spared: About a dozen cancers have been detected so far among former students. A couple of them have died.

"Prior to undergoing her first chemotherapy treatment, Cohen approached the school principal, who eventually went to district officials for an investigation. A local newspaper article about the possible disease cluster caught the attention of Sam Milham, MD, a widely traveled epidemiologist who has investigated hundreds of environmental and occupational illnesses and published dozens of peer-reviewed papers on his findings. For the past 30 years, he has trained much of his focus on the potential hazards of electromagnetic fields (EMFs) — the radiation that surrounds all electrical appliances and devices, power lines, and home wiring and is emitted by communications devices, including cell phones and radio, TV, and WiFi transmitters..

"With Cohen's help, Milham entered the school after hours one day to take readings. Astonishingly, in some classrooms he found the surges of transient pollution exceeded his meter's ability to gauge them. His preliminary findings prompted the teachers to file a complaint with the Occupational Safety and Health Administration, which in turn ordered a full investigation by the California Department of Health Care Services."

Must be a bunch of conspiracy theorists except the cancer is real.

All of the qualified opinions in this chapter are but a tiny fraction of what is available on the Internet. Literally thousands of scientific and medical opinions – *all ignored here in the U.S. because big, big money is involved; the health of you and your family be damned.*

Energy companies and their co-conspirators, Public Utility Commissions, maintain smart meters aren't any more dangerous than cell phones. Apples and oranges. One can choose to use a cell phone, but we the people were not given a choice when this forced installation started.

See Endnotes for Chapter 10 for titles and URLs.

Sage & Associates – Jan. 17, 2011 – Letter of Comment on Smart Meter Report by Cindy Sage, MA, Co-Editor, BioInitiative Report, Research Fellow, Department of Oncology, Orebro University Hospital, Orebro, Sweden. Issues addressed: CCST Smart Meter Report, January 11, 2011. [2]

American Academy of Environmental Medicine. Proposed Decision of Commissioner Peevy (Mailed 11/22/2011) – BEFORE THE PUBLIC UTILITIES COMMISSION OF THE STATE OF CALIFORNIA – On the proposed decision 11-03-014 [3]

"The Board of the American Academy of Environmental Medicine opposes the installation of wireless 'smart meters' in homes and schools based on a scientific assessment of the current medical literature (references available on request). Chronic exposure to wireless radio frequency radiation is a preventable environmental hazard that is sufficiently well documented to warrant immediate preventative public health action."

National and Kapodistrian, University of Athens, Faculty of Biology, Department of Cell Biology & Biophysics, Electromagnetic Biology Laboratory, Professor Lukas H. Margaritis, January 16, 2011 [4]

Dr. Magda Havas, S.Sc., Ph.D., Environmental and Resource Studies Program, Associate Professor of Environmental and Resource Studies at Trent University in Canada, to the California Council on Science and Technology at their request for input regarding Smart Meters – To: California Council on Science and Technology (CCST.): [5] Dr.

Havas' web site has an abundance of information and studies on the dangers of EMF: www.magdahavas.com

Hebrew University – Hadassah School of Public Health and Community Medicine Unit of Occupational and Environmental Medicine, January 26, 2011 – Letter of Comment on Smart Meter Report [6]

Comments on California Council on Science and Technology's Smart Meter Report, January 2011 Nancy Evans, Health Science Consultant, San Francisco. [7]

The Green Sheen Wearing Thin – How Corporate Environmental Organizations are Providing Cover for the Mounting Ecological Catastrophe of the "Smart Grid" – very lengthy, but spot on. [8]

Microwave Radiation Affects the Heart by Dr. Zory R. Glaser, Ph.D. Who helped establish the RF bioeffects laboratory at the Naval Medical Research Institute. He went on to fund, manage and perform RF/Microwave bioeffects research at the Navy's Bureau of Medicine and Surgery and then at the Naval Medical Research and Development Command and as Officer-In-Charge and Senior Scientist (at the Non-Ionizing Radiation Bioeffects Laboratory, at the Naval Surface Weapons Center. Dr. Glaser's archives are found on Dr. Havas' web site: www.magdahavas.com

Olle Johansson, Assoc. Professor, Karolinska Institute, Dept of Neuroscience, July 9, 2011 to the California Public Utilities Commission [9]

Olle Johansson, Assoc. Professor, Karolinska Institute, Dept of Neuroscience, January 17, 2012 to The California Council on Science and Technology

Olle Johansson, Assoc. Professor, Karolinska Institute, Dept of Neuroscience – Press Release

Scientists Urge Halt of Wireless Rollout and Call for New Safety Standards, www.safeinschool.org: "The combined effect of cell phones, cordless phones, cell towers, WI-FI and wireless internet place billions of people around the world at risk for cancer, neurological disease and reproductive and developmental impairments."

Olle Johansson, Assoc. Professor, Karolinska Institute, Dept of Neuroscience, February 22, 2010 letter to senators and representatives, Health and Human Services Committee, Maine

Radio Frequency Radiation: The Invisible Hazards of "Smart" Meters by Dr. Ilya Sandra Perlingieri – August 2011 [10]

Elihu D. Richter MD, MPH (Assoc Professor), Hebrew University-Hadassah, School of Public Health and Community Medicine, Unit of Occupations and Environmental Medicine to Susan Hackwood, Ph.D., Executive Director, California Council on Science and Technology. Letter of Comment on Smart Meter Report [11]

Witness Statement, Andrew Goldsworthy, Lecturer in Biology (retired), Imperial College, London [12]

Overloading of Towns and Cities with Radio Transmitters: A hazard for the human health and disturbance of eco-ethics. Karl Hecht, Elena N. Savoley, IRCHET International Research Center of Healthy and Ecological Technology, Berlin, Germany

"Essential Findings after Long-Term EMF EF Effect Objectively gathered findings: neurasthenia, neurotic symptoms, EEG changes (decay of the alpha rhythm into the theta rhythm and isolated delta rhythm), sleep disorders, deformation of the biologic rhythm hierarchy, disorder in the hypothalamohypophyseal adrenal cortex system, arterial hypotonia, more rarely arterial hypertonia, bradycardia, or tachycardia, vagotonic displacement of the cardiovascular system, increased susceptibility to infection, hyperfunction of the thyroid, potency disorders.

"System Subjective Complaints: exhaustion, lack of energy, daytime tiredness, quick tiring under stress, constriction of physical and mental ability, concentration and memory decline, cardiac pain, heart racing, weakness of concentration, headaches, light headedness.

"Animals and Plants Are Also in Danger

"Animals and plants are also very negatively influenced by this high-frequency electromagnetic radiation. In the case of cows, reduction of the milk yield and malformed offspring have been proven. Graver for humankind could be the death of bees observed everywhere due to the electro-smog contaminated environment. When the bees are dead, people not only have no more honey, but also no more fruit, because pollination of the flowers is impossible without bees. Humankind stands today before an important decision." [13]

The Internet has dozens of articles about pet owners who say after the smart meter was installed on their house their dog started running in circles. Others said their dogs whined and cried for no reason. Veterinarians across the country can't explain it, but the only common denominator has been installation of a smart meter.

Comments on California Council on Science and Technology's Smart Meter Report, January 2011, Nancy Evans, Health Science Consultant, San Francisco. United States District Court – District of Oregon – Portland Division – June 2011 [14]

Comments on the Draft Report by the California Council on Science and Technology "Health Impacts of Radio Frequency from Smart Meters" by Daniel Hirsch.

Hirsch is a Lecturer in Nuclear Policy at the University of California, Santa Cruz. He is the former Director of the Stevenson Program on Nuclear Policy at UCSC. Hirsch is also President of the Committee to Bridge the Gap, a forty-year-old nonprofit organization working to reduce risks of nuclear accident, nuclear proliferation, nuclear terrorism, and problems of radioactive waste disposal. Shortly after the Fukushima accident began, Hirsch was asked to testify before the Select Committee on Earthquake and Disaster Preparedness, Response, and Recovery of the California Senate on the implications of the disaster for the Diablo Canyon and San Onofre reactors.

"The draft report by the California Council on Science and Technology (CCST) does not appear to answer the questions asked of it by the requesting elected officials. Furthermore, rather than being an independent, science-based study, the CCST largely cuts and pastes estimates from a brochure by the Electric Power Research Institute, an industry group, issued some weeks earlier.

"The EPRI estimates appear incorrect in a number of regards. When two of the most central errors are corrected – the failure to take into account duty cycles of cell phones and microwave ovens and the failure to utilize the same units (they should compare everything in terms of average whole body exposure) the cumulative whole body exposure from a Smart Meter at 3 feet appears to be approximately two orders of magnitude higher than that of a cell phone, rather than two orders of magnitude lower." [15]

Public utility commissions across the country have simply dismissed any scientific information that doesn't agree with their position that smart meters are perfectly safe. I highly recommend you read *Dirty Electricity: Electrifiction and Diseases of Civilization* by Dr. Samuel Milham. Available at: http://www.sammilham.com/

Another gentleman who agreed to be one of our expert witnesses for a hearing we aren't going to get in front of the Texas PUC is Dr. Barrie Trower who lives in Great Britain.

Trained at the Government (Ministry of Defense) microwave warfare establishment(s) early in the 1960s covering all aspects of microwave (MW) radiation technology, uses and health dangers. Later works included underwater bomb-disposal, which incorporated MW technology. In the late 1960s and 1970s a part of his task was to extract confidential (hitherto secret) information from master criminals, terrorists, and spies. This included Cold War MW technology.

His first degree is in Physics with a specialization in microwaves. His second is a research degree. He also has a teaching diploma in human physiology. Before retiring, he taught advanced physics and mathematics at South Dartmoor College. Scientific Advisor to the Radiation Research Trust and the H.E.S.E. (Human Ecological Social Economical) Project. Author of both Tetra Reports for the Police Federation of England and Wales and the Public and Commercial Service Union.

Dr. Trower's work is done entirely free of charge and has never accepted money from any person or organization and considers himself absolutely independent. Barrie Trower – The Dangers of Microwave Technology, see:

https://www.youtube.com/watch?v=m9YM_vLKR8c

According to the Texas Public Utilities Commission, Gov. Greg Abbott, and all the energy companies who do business in this state all of the above experts who have studied this for decades are wrong. We the citizens of Texas are wrong. Only the PUC and the energy companies who sprinkle money over the state capitol like confetti are right and the hell with our health.

Now you know why tens of thousands of us across the country have fought so hard to keep those meters off our homes. Do you have a "smart" meter on your house? Is it okay with you that you and your family are being are being put in dead serious harm's way just to enrich the energy companies?

And, what is going to happen when, not if, that big multi-trillion-dollar "smart" grid gets hit by terrorists? A horrific disaster just waiting for Satan's Soldiers, ISIS, or some other flavor of savages already on U.S. soil to make a successful hit. It will happen and the federal government of incompetent agencies is totally not prepared.

US Power Grid Attacked Every 4 Days; Nationwide Blackout More Likely Than We Thought, *Off The Grid News*:

"Because the nation's electrical grid operates as an interdependent network, the failure of any one element requires energy to be drawn from other areas," the report says. "If multiple parts fail at the same time, there is the potential for a cascading effect that could leave millions in the darks for days, weeks or longer."

"Last year, a federal report found that if just nine of the nation's 55,000 substations failed or were sabotaged, the entire nation would suffer a blackout for weeks, if not months. Members of the EMP Commission that reported to Congress found that if the grid is down for one year, 70-90 percent of the US — between 200 million and 285 million Americans — would die due to starvation, a lack of medical supplies, and civil unrest. One big reason an attack would do so much damage is because there are no backup parts to much of the system; they're custom made, and it can take weeks or months to replace them."

CAPITOL OFFICE:
P.O. Box 2910
Austin, TX 78768-2910
(512) 463-0564
Fax (512) 463-8414

DENNIS BONNEN

40190

HOUSE OF REPRESENTATIVES

DISTRICT OFFICE:
122 E. Myrtle
Angleton, TX 77515
(979) 848-1770
Fax (979) 849-3169

February 10, 2012

Public Utility Commission of Texas
Donna L. Nelson, Chairman
1701 N. Congress Avenue
PO Box 13326
Austin, TX 78711-3326

Chairman Nelson:

In the 79th legislative session, I authored HB 2129 that requires electric utility providers to consider establishing certain consumer option programs that encourage the reduction of air contaminant emissions. This bill was later amended by the Senate to require the PUC to develop a plan for deployment of smart meter data networks. However, the bill did not create a mandate for smart meter installation. I am greatly concerned that certain providers are acting beyond the purview of HB 2129 by forcing smart meters on customers. This was not the intent of the legislation.

It was always my understanding that customers would have a choice in whether to implement this technology at their homes. So far, this has not been the case in my district, and my constituents are being forced to install and pay for these advanced meters.

I urge the commission to correct this oversight by providing a simple, customer-friendly process for opting-out of the advanced metering technology. I understand that the commission stated an intent to open a project to consider this issue at the February 10, 2012 Open Meeting. I ask that any necessary rule changes be adopted expeditiously to effectuate my intent, so that additional legislative action is not required. I stand committed to ensuring that this issue is addressed.

I appreciate your hard work and dedication to the State of Texas and I look forward to hearing from you on this issue.

Sincerely,

Dennis Bonnen

Dennis Bonnen
State Representative, District 25

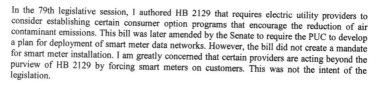

District 25 Brazoria (part)

11

More Money for Education!

Isn't that what we hear from candidates running for state house seats, Congress, school districts and unions every election cycle?

We do, ad nauseam.

Has it made any difference over the past 25-30 years as America's school children continue to do so poorly in public schools?

The answer is a resounding, NO.

"Underfunded" Baltimore schools among best funded in nation – Author Alex Newman slams plan to throw money at dysfunctional district, May 8, 2015

"In an exclusive interview with WND, the co-author of "Crimes of the Educators: How Utopians Are Using Government Schools to Destroy America's Children," observed, "One of the great lies promoted by the education establishment is that more taxpayer funds are needed to properly educate students.

"Baltimore offers a perfect example of how easy it is to discredit this fraud. In recent years, government schools in Baltimore have been at the top of the list in terms of spending per pupil – literally in the top three among the nation's largest school districts. Yet, Baltimore schools are also some of the worst performing in the nation, consistently ranking in the bottom third. The situation in Detroit is similar, spending thousands more per pupil than the national average yet achieving results that can only be described as a disaster of monumental proportions. This alone is proof that more money is not going to solve the very real crisis in education." [1]

It doesn't matter how much money is spent on a student, if that child isn't interesting in learning, they won't. Children, regardless of skin color, how much their parents make or what neighborhood they live in have the opportunity to be successful, *but they have to want to learn.*

The family dynamic of encouraging a child to embrace learning has changed since I was a kid. Certainly not for every single household with children, but for too many. How sad so many "parents" are crack heads, dopers of some flavor or drunks who doom their children to continue their lifestyle of failure. Welfare mothers who churn out babies every year or two have a minuscule chance of getting educated and becoming self-reliant, independent individuals which they then pass along to their children. One generation to the next totally dependent upon politicians who want to keep them dependent to keep them herded in the right direction – *voting them back into office*. Children of the welfare industry who live in such environments grow up thinking it's normal instead of dysfunctional.

I raised my daughter alone following a divorce from an alcoholic. It wasn't easy, believe me. Seldom were there new clothes, no party hardy crap. It was go to work and Brandy came first with love. I was very fortunate that my mother lived close by and was able to baby sit my dear daughter most of the time; when she couldn't some friends did a wonderful job of watching her for me. Brandy was not raised by the television set, either.

I put my daughter in Christ the King pre-school. The nuns informed me she was gifted. When I enrolled her in kindergarten in a private Christian school, she was already reading far beyond her age group and went into the gifted and talented programs. She stayed in the G & T programs and private Christian schools until she entered high school and even then she was so far ahead of the curve. My daughter worked hard for her grades. She just had an insatiable desire to learn which I believe came from getting her reading before kindergarten and spending my "off" time with her instead of dating or partying.

Being a prolific reader I made books available through the public library for my little girl; I couldn't afford to buy many books. Yes, she did watch a little Sesame Street here and there, but to this day I doubt she watches two hours of TV in a month. Brandy loved to read and still does.

Kids who read succeed. I can honestly say through all the years of my daughter going through private Christian schools I never once had to tell her to do homework. When I picked her up at grandma's house and ask, her homework was always done. Straight A's were the norm. One time until senior high school year she got a B in PE due to a dislocated shoulder; it was the end of the world! Brandy graduated from high school, graduated from college magna cum laude, received her Master's Degree and is now working on her Ph.D.

I am so very proud of her. There were no computers in schools back then. It wasn't until she was a junior in high school Brandy became acquainted with one. Up until then, the foundation was well built. Math was done by her, not a computer. Students when I was in school and the same for Brandy: we learned the basics from books and *educated* teachers. How come with a computer in every classroom for kids as young as 6 or 7, so many are terribly under educated? With 74% of households in the U.S. having some sort of personal computer, kids can use one at home or the school library, but at school they don't need them in first, second or even seventh grade. **They need an educated teacher and accurate school books.**

Today, kids, just like millions of adults are glued to electronic gadgets. I am so sick of seeing people walking in the grocery store with cell phones glued to their ear, sitting at some office or restaurant sending text messages completely glued to that little device. Look at kids pouring out of a junior high or high school and they're all either yapping on a cell phone or walking sending texts.

Today we see all kinds of articles about how children as well as adults are addicted to electronic gadgets just like junkies to heroin. I can't remember the last time I saw a child sitting at a restaurant or where ever reading a book or just having a conversation with another human. Noisy electronic tablets from ages 5 to 50. I know those gadgets can show things like the Discovery channel (which doesn't always have accurate information on US history) or youth themed programming but if all they see are pictures, how are they going to learn to read?

We also know from seeing horrific news clips of teachers being beaten or attacked by students in rough urban schools by punks who have no desire to learn. Where do they learn such behavior? Why, at home and from violent movies and video games. Students who have no desire to do anything but be cool, listen to that **toxic music genre** called "rap" and just as tragic either doing or dealing drugs. Children who come from a home where they are not encouraged from a very young age to start reading instead of the boob tube or little real time with both parents I believe have a very difficult time getting an education – along with the toxic curriculum.

Then comes the push for social indoctrination in public schools brainwashing America's children to reject the moral teachings by their parents in favor of what's approved by the "state". So many of us began warning parents twenty years ago about the clear and in-your-face agenda of those pulling the strings behind the scenes. Today's public schools are little more than sewers.

Sex "education" classes in too many classrooms across this country are an hour of soft porn. Over the years I can't tell you how many teachers I've met or who have sent me email saying they are highly embarrassed by sex "education" films and materials because of overt nudity in films they are required to show in class. Every one of them if they could afford to give up their paycheck, they would and find another job where they don't have to compromise their beliefs or be subjected to porn sex "education" which they believe, as I do, encourages under age children and teens to have sex.

Yet, parents across this country who are the product of the public school system the past three decades think it's okay. Their child is getting "educated" and the social indoctrination going on is just part of being "progressive". A national tragedy. For parents who would like to know more about the destruction to young children through high school age regarding the filth called "sex education" in schools, I highly recommend the tireless work of Dr. Judith Reisman. Her web site is: http://www.drjudithreisman.com/

What's being taught in public schools: dumb 'em down!

Reading, writing and arithmetic were the big three most basic subjects for a couple hundred years for public school children. But, prior to public schools, (this will drive atheists and liberals nuts) parents used what is described as "one of the greatest books ever published": *The New England Primer of 1777*. As a matter of fact, let's look at some history [emphasis mine]:

The New England Primer – Religious Roots

"In the early colonial period, reading the Bible was the primary reason and motivation for learning to read. For example, in 1647, the 'Old

Deluder Act' passed by the Massachusetts General Court required every township with 50 or more families to hire a teacher. Similar legislation quickly spread to the other New England colonies, being the first step towards compulsory education. **The preamble was explicit that knowledge of the Scriptures was the chief goal**, and that 'one chief project of that old deluder, Satan, [is] to keep men from the knowledge of the Scriptures' (see text with original spelling and typesetting represented in Ford, and a modernized spelling rendering of the text is found here). Illiterate people were at the mercy of other people for their knowledge of God and His Word, and inaccessibility to the Bible had fomented centuries of darkness prior to the Reformation. Indeed. The appearance of early primers in England has been connected directly to the beginning of the Reformation. Only literate people could have the privilege of direct, independent access to God's revelation.

"This connection and between learning the alphabet and learning Scripture and doctrine is pervasive in The New England Primer. And the concern that children come to know Christ as Savior and Lord is obvious. By the modern taste, specific language in the Primer is frequently termed stern and morbid. Our modern culture tries to avoid the recognition of death. But to the colonial culture, where death was ever present, the reality of coming to know Christ before one's demise was of urgent concern....

"The New England Primer was **the first textbook published in the 13 colonies**, and it was the most prevalent primer in the 18th century, and was still influential into the 19th century. The Primer was for both beginning and intermediate readers, starting with alphabets and moving on to religious and moral lessons. " [2]

Why, how dreadful it must have been back then for children of parents who escaped religious suppression in Europe to bring the word of God into the classroom of all places! Where was the ACLU? Thankfully, they didn't exist back then.

One thing taught was to read phonetically because the English language is 93-97% phonetically accurate. It is how I was taught to read and how I taught my daughter to read. In more "modern" times, phonics is thrown out the window. Today it's truly sad to see Americans who can't read well at all, who can't spell, don't know the different between "they're" and "their" and who can't make change without a computerized cash register telling them the amount.

When did the deliberate dumbing down of America start and who was behind it?

Besides life experience, I have read many, many books on education and countless articles and columns about how to fix education. But, without doubt in my research by far and away the single most important work parents AND state legislators must read: *The Deliberate Dumbing Down of America* by Charlotte Tomason Iserbyt:

"Iserbyt served as Senior Policy Advisor in the Office of Educational Research and Improvement (OERI), U.S. Department of Education, during the first Reagan Administration, where she first blew the whistle on a major technology initiative which would control curriculum in America's classrooms. Iserbyt is a former school board director in Camden, Maine and was co-founder and research analyst of Guardians of Education for Maine (GEM) from 1978 to 2000. She has also served in the American Red Cross on Guam and Japan during the Korean War, and in the United States Foreign Service in Belgium and in the Republic of South Africa.

"Iserbyt is a speaker and writer, best known for her 1985 booklet Back to Basics Reform or OBE: Skinnerian International Curriculum and her 1989 pamphlet Soviets in the Classroom: America's Latest Education Fad which covered the details of the U.S.-Soviet and Carnegie-Soviet Education Agreements which remain in effect to this day. She is a freelance writer and has had articles published in *Human Events*, *The Washington Times*, *The Bangor Daily News*, and included in the record of Congressional hearings."

What is Skinnerian Curriculum? Below are excerpts from one of Charlotte's column, September 26, 2014:

We Are at War for Our Children's Mind and Soul – Mind Warfare

"What is absolutely essential is that the full facts be given to all our people, for mind warfare is total war." — Edward Hunter, *Brainwashing: The Men Who Defied It*, 1953

"MIND WARFARE" includes the Skinnerian brainwashing called for by leading Neo-Conservative organizations, including the Heartland

Institute. This is a war to destroy our constitutional rights, including our right to vote, and the destruction of our children's minds, souls and consciences. After 12 years of Neo-Conservative supported Skinnerian animal training computer instruction, your children will no longer have a conscience, nor will they be able to take an unpopular stand, for fear of being punished. They will act only to get a reward or praise.

"Did hundreds of thousands of American servicemen and women give their lives in foreign wars to end up with our free constitutional republic being turned over to the globalist communists (the communist/ socialist/ corporate/ fascist/ libertarian Neo-Conservative wolves in sheep's clothing)? Without firing a shot? On a silver platter?

"It is time to stop the 100% Neo-Conservative boycott of the truth regarding their communist agenda! Don't forget that Wall Street funded the Bolshevik Revolution. Don't forget the NeoConservative Heritage Foundation drafted the North American Free Trade Agreement (NAFTA) which has robbed Americans of hundreds of thousands of good jobs. Don't forget Karl Marx, who drafted the Communist Manifesto, was a strong supporter of Free Trade! And, lastly, don't forget that Mind Warfare, referred to by Edward Hunter (above) is what the neoconservative Heartland Institute recently recommended for use on our children in America's 'new' schools/training laboratories!

"The National Alliance of Business, in its newsletter Work/America... The Business Force on Workforce Development, Vol. 15 Issue 5, May 1998 carried the following article entitled 'Knowledge Supply Chain: Managing K-Age 80 Learning.' Repeat Kindergarten through Age 80?! Workforce Training. Yes, Grandpa... that means YOU! And YOU, too, Grandma! This is what is called 'Limited Learning for Lifelong Labor.' Using the Skinnerian Operant Conditioning method called for by Heartland Institute.

"The following quotations from Edward Hunter, the man who coined the term 'brainwashing' and author of Brainwashing: The Men Who Defied It, speak to what we as Americans can still do to reverse the process. When Hunter speaks of brainwashing he is referring primarily to the Skinnerian/Pavloviananimal training method supported by the neoconservative movement:

"Surely there can no longer be a trace of doubt that brainwashing is sheer evil. The fight against it is the culminating issue of all time, in which every human being is protagonist. There can be neither escape nor neutrality where such responsibilities lie. There can be neither front nor rear, for the great lesson that came from the brainwashing chambers was that while every man has a cracking point, every man's cracking point can be immensely strengthened. That is the job of home, school, and church. The mother, teacher, and pastor are in the front lines in this ideological conflict, and every word they say to their sons and daughters is important to the struggle, for character more than anything else will determine the outcome.

"Truth is the most important serum and integrity the most devastating weapon that can be used against the totalitarian concept.... Nothing should be allowed to interfere with the task of getting those facts across to the people who need and can use them." (Read the entire Hunter quotation on page 450 of my book)

Read on below for a perfect example of what Hunter is talking about, how the brainwashing is being carried out in the United States. In this case, it is a "choice" advertising campaign. This is a huge media blitz calling for tax-funded school choice (federally-controlled private education run by unelected boards). Hunter refers to this as "mind warfare is total war." The "controlled" media is in a special position to conduct "mind warfare." For example, see the following Philly School Choice media campaign to promote "choice" to the public.

"It was announced today that Choice Media has launched PhillySchoolChoice.com, a major media campaign involving a website, Facebook page, television commercials, YouTube videos, Twitter & Facebook ads, traditional newspaper ads and earned media coverage. The campaign will include eight separate 30-second television commercials that will air on the early and late evening news programs of all four broadcast local news stations (ABC, CBS, FOX and NBC affiliates), for five days/week, four weeks in a row. Two new television ads will be released each week during the four-week run. The commercials feature only Philadelphia parents talking about their experiences – no politicians or union officials will appear.

"Below you will find the first two spots produced by Choice Media. They feature Philadelphia area parents sharing stories about the positive impact that school choice has had on their lives and the lives of their children. These personal accounts are illuminating and heartwarming. They manage to capture in thirty seconds exactly what is at stake in the great debate over expanding choice; ensuring every child in America has access to a top-notch education." (Source)

"See the following web pages for more information about this "choice" campaign and the "Philly School Choice" media campaign:

1- There is a Growing List of PARENTS, STUDENTS & Other Concerned Philadelphians Who Support School Choice

2- Fabulous New School Choice Ads to Air in Philadelphia

3- A new front against sexual violence – Civics education gets a push – Student poets hit the Library of Congress – Dissent in union ranks

4- Philly School Choice

5- Fabulous New School Choice Ads to Air in Philadelphia

"Recently the Skinnerian/Pavlovian Cat jumped out of the 34-year denial bag. As was mentioned earlier on the blog, the book Rewards has just been published. Subtitled "How to use [SKINNERIAN/PAVLOVIAN, ed.] rewards to help children learn – and why teachers don't use them well." Paperback – October 1, 2014. The President of the Heartland Institute, Joseph Bast, who has written a book Rewards, with long-time educator Herbert Walberg, calling for the Skinnerian/Pavlovian method to train our children, like pigeons, dogs, etc., for the workforce rather than to teach them academics.

"The deliberate dumbing down has now become the excuse for complete social change, including the privatization of education (the handing over to the unelected multinational corporations the responsibility for education — actually training — of future citizens). Such a transfer of responsibility will be facilitated by the creation of charter/magnet schools and passage of legislation providing tuition tax credits/vouchers. The workforce development system will, of course, be international, as is indicated by many quotes in this book. Parents who may be enthusiastic about the various choice proposals may change their minds regarding "choice" when their child becomes part of the corporate fascist quota system, being tracked into a career chosen for him/her by unelected corporate managers who set labor force requirements. Such quotas will be a part of the global planned economy. Parents will have no say regarding their child's placement since there will no longer be an elected body, such as a school board, to whom they can complain.

"Only a dumbed-down, brainwashed, conditioned citizenry could willingly accept what is being offered Americans under the guise of "remaining competitive in an increasingly global economy," and relinquishing our sovereignty in the name of "global understanding and peace." (excerpted from page 450-51 of my book). "Good Americans are being lied to. What is going in now, supported by the highly-funded Neo-Conservative Trotskyites, and its controlled media, is described in my book *The Deliberate Dumbing Down of America*." [3]

Before you think this is just some kooky "right-wing" malarkey, think again. Below is what *hasn't* been taught in America's schools for decades. While there are 45 goals the ones below are relevant to this chapter:

Communist Goals (1963) *Congressional Record*– Appendix, pp. A34-A35 January 10, 1963. Current Communist Goals Extension of Remarks of Hon. A.S. Herlong, Jr., of Florida in the House of Representatives, Thursday, January 10, 1963.

Mr. HERLONG. Mr. Speaker, Mrs. Patricia Nordman of De Land, Fla., is an ardent and articulate opponent of communism, and until recently published the De Land Courier, which she dedicated to the purpose of alerting the public to the dangers of communism in America. At Mrs. Nordman's request, I include in the RECORD, under unanimous consent, the following Current Communist Goals, which she identifies as an excerpt from *The Naked Communist*, by Cleon Skousen.

Skousen worked for the FBI eventually becoming a special agent. He earned a law degree at George Washington University Law School and is the author of dozens of books including *The Naked Capitalist* and *The 5,000 Year Leap*.

> 17. Get control of the schools. Use them as transmission belts for socialism and current Communist propaganda. Soften the

curriculum. Get control of teachers' associations. Put the party line in textbooks.

18. Gain control of all student newspapers.

19. Use student riots to foment public protests against programs or organizations which are under Communist attack.

26. Present homosexuality, degeneracy and promiscuity as "normal, natural, healthy."

28. Eliminate prayer or any phase of religious expression in the schools on the ground that it violates the principle of "separation of church and state."

29. Discredit the American Constitution by calling it inadequate, old-fashioned, out of step with modern needs, a hindrance to cooperation between nations on a worldwide basis.

30. Discredit the American Founding Fathers. Present them as selfish aristocrats who had no concern for the "common man."

31. Belittle all forms of American culture and discourage the teaching of American history on the ground that it was only a minor part of the "big picture." Give more emphasis to Russian history since the Communists took over.

32. Support any socialist movements to give centralized control over any part of the culture – education, social agencies, welfare programs, mental health clinics, etc.

All of the above in one form or another have been injected into government public schools, colleges and universities for decades. For the past twenty years teaching in some classrooms has been in-your-face calling the Founding Fathers old white racists *who gave the world the greatest form of government and freedom for any people on this earth.* **In the process, America's children have been cheated of any kind of education and instead have been processed as little better than cattle.**

THIS should never be allowed in public schools:

School districts spending millions on "white privilege" training for employees by Steve Gunn

SAN FRANCISCO – "The Pacific Educational Group (PEG) espouses a lot of controversial and stereotypical concepts regarding minority students in K-12 schools. For instance, the organization teaches that black kids are less likely to respond to fundamental ideas like working hard to achieve success, or being on time for school or work, because those ideas are supposedly foreign to African-American culture. PEG is literally selling notions like that to American public schools, and the schools are buying them, at a cost of millions of tax dollars every year. One prominent black professional, journalist and author Juan Williams, thinks those schools are subscribing to a politically-driven philosophy that grossly underestimates the capabilities of minority students, particularly black children.

"These people (associated with PEG) are engaged in cultural, political arguments that are based on negative stereotypes of black capacity to achieve in any situation," Williams said. "My mother never would have said, "You don't have to be on time. If you are then you are acting white." That idea is tragically insulting...

"What are the educators in these districts learning in exchange for all of that money? The PEG message is centered on the concept of "white privilege" and the detrimental impact it supposedly has on minority students." [4]

Father Protests Islamic Indoctrination in Florida Curriculum – School District Justifies It with Support of Terror Group, February 10, 2015

"Seminole County's Lyman High School is being called out for its blatant Islamic indoctrination by a student's father. Ron Wagner read, "There is no god, but God, Muhamad is the messenger of God." However, he wasn't reading from the Koran, The Five Pillars of Islam or the Hadiths. He was reading from his son's 10th grade world history textbook. Even more concerning is that the school district not only stands by the curriculum, but have the full support of designated terror group Hamas-CAIR (Council on American-Islamic Relations).

"Let me interject that many parents don't know what is going on in their children's public indoctrination centers. They are too busy working to do so instead of teaching and training them at home where they are absolutely sure about what is being taught to their children. Wagner told Jones that Dr. Michael Blasewitz, the overseer of the high school curriculum said, "The Pillars of Islam are benchmarks in the state curriculum." [5]

Besides ramming the toxic and failed multiculturalism down the throats of America's school children, a couple of years ago the Communist International was at it again to indoctrinate America's school children and deny them a real education: Common core pushed by Jeb Bush and Chris Christie.

To say I was delighted by the massive backlash against the latest Marxist tool that was going to be shoved down the throat of every public school child in this country is an understatement. Not only has the toxic Common Core been thrown out of school districts across the country, it's also been junked by state legislatures for good reason.

Common Core would make any communist regime proud, October 21, 2013, by Gina Miller

"Let's just jump right in here to the crux of the Common Core 'State' Standards with an excerpt from the paper, "History of Education in Communist Countries," by Hae Yoon Jeong, 2009, Korean Minjok Leadership Academy:

"The communist revolutions in the 20th century had their goal at creating total revolutions and establishing a new society different from the capitalist society. This new society required people with new loyalties, new motivations, and new concepts of individual and group life. Education was acknowledged to have a strategic role in achieving this revolution and development. Specifically, education was used to produce ardent revolutionaries ready to rebel against the old society and establish a new order and also to bring up a new generation of dexterous laborers to take up the various tasks of development and modernization.

"... Marxist-Leninist philosophy was the basis of the Communist education system. It emphasized the role of schools and youth organizations in educating students by indoctrination. For this the Communist societies paid a lot of attention to schooling. There had been great confidence that schools would be a major instrument for building the 'New Communist Man.' Such a person would work diligently, would have a clear insight into the dynamics of social change, would understand and be skilled in modern technology, and follow the tenets of Marxism-Leninism. [6]

Everything happening today in public schools is well planned and YOUR child is the guinea pig. "Give me four years to teach the children and the seed I have sown will never be uprooted." Russian butcher, Vladimir Lenin. Between public schools and the abject failure of churches in this country for the past 40 years, what we're seeing today is what Jeri Lynn Ball wrote about 15 years ago that was already advancing on an unsuspecting people. Jeri's work is minutely detailed, researched and footnoted. The excerpt below is from a 20-page overview she gave of her book:

Origin of the Totalitarian New World Order

"The Communists did not want the American approach to liberty, with individual God-given rights protected by a government with limited powers. The Communists did not want the American concept of rule of law. They wanted unrestrained despotic government, power without limit, a world without laws — a brutal, terror-inspiring global totalitarian police state which could smash all laws of justice, launch campaigns of enslavement and mass murder, and eliminate opponents of the New World Order. **Twenty delegates from the U.S. voted for the 1928 Program of the Third International.**

The Totalitarian Vision of "Human Reconstruction":

"The same year they wrote 'The Program,' Communist architects and social engineers began to implement their plans for the globalist, communistic New World Order, commencing with the transformation of all humans into supporters of totalitarianism. Nikolai Bukharin had previously written 'that the revolution's principle task was to "alter people's actual psychology."' (Emphasis added.) In 1928 Bukharin stated that "one of the first priorities is the question of the systematic preparation of new men, the builders of [totalitarian] socialism." In his book, Soviet Civilization, Andrei Sinyavsky states that the "idea of the new man is the cornerstone of Soviet civilization."

"The 'new man' is in fact the indispensable, fundamental basis of all totalitarian societies. Totalitarianism requires the support, approval, and fearful veneration of the masses; if the 'new men and women' had not been created, totalitarianism would not exist today. The

Communists planned to create not only a new way of life, but new human beings. They sought to achieve not only the reconstruction of social and cultural institutions, but reconstruction of human beings. Communist totalitarianism has undergone tremendous growth over the past century only because it has 'the support of a man of a new social and psychological type'—the 'new communitarian (Communist) man.'

"A communitarian is a member of a communistic community. A communitarian adopts and advocates communistic concepts, such as a spirit of community, selfless commitment to community service, and the duty to work for 'the common good.' The terms 'Communist' and 'communitarian' are synonyms and are interchangeable, but the word 'communitarian' connotes a sense of community and a spirit of collectivism.

"In 1928 Communists formally adopted 'The Program' for building a new global communitarian social order composed of the ruling elite (the masters) and subjugated masses (the slaves). Soviet masters used the communitarian social system and moral code to prepare the 'new communist man.' They reinforced the 'spirit of community' that had been present in Europe for 200 years and instilled communitarian moral ideals into all Soviet citizens. The masters 'reconstructed' each individual by urging him to: 1) develop a sense of community; 2) cultivate the communist virtue of selflessness; 3) suppress his personality, individuality, and identity, i.e., his personal desires, ambitions, beliefs, etc.; 4) merge himself into the community and become one with it; 5) fulfill his obligation to perform community service and accept his duty to work for 'the common good.'

"The communitarian moral code is the powerful secret weapon Communists have used to enslave whole populations. The 'mad' philosopher Auguste Comte (1798-1857) coined the term altruism. Comte calls upon all human beings to renounce individualism and practice altruism, i.e., selflessness. According to Comte, the highest moral virtue and duty is the pursuit of 'the feeling of pure self-sacrifice.' He demands that every individual give up the conviction that he is a separate entity with a unique identity and wipe out his values, his self-interest, his self.

"He holds that there must be a 'substitution of Duties for Rights,' that the notion of individual rights is immoral, and that men must live selflessly in the service of the community. He directs people to worship a new divinity, the 'goddess' Humanity. In Comte's communistic view, Christianity must be annihilated and the 'Love of God' must be replaced by the 'Love of Humanity.' An ardent advocate of communitarianism, Comte seeks to achieve 'unity of belief' and 'the unity of Humanity' and to create a 'harmonious oneness' by using the government to 'expand and forcefully cultivate the sense of community.'

"Following the lead of Kant, Marx, Comte, and a handful of other philosophers, Communists sought to obliterate the concept of the free, independent individual, merge each individual into the mass, and achieve the 'oneness of mankind.' Motivated by a lust for absolute power, their goal was (and is) total domination over all the world's inhabitants. They planned to make all human beings on earth products of their communitarian assembly line—mechanical, wind-up robots—everyone an exact duplicate of the other, each marching in step. They wanted people without purpose, thought or self. Their mad, fanatical mission was (and is) to wipe out man, man the individual.

"Communitarianism holds that the individual is nothing and that the community is all; the interests of the community transcend the interests of the individual; the common good comes before the private good. Sinyavsky writes, 'The definition of the real Communist (or new man)' includes the following 'highly developed virtues....' The new communist man believes that the most 'egregious sin' a citizen can commit is to be an individualist and pursue his own desires, interests, and happiness. He sees 'the necessity of stifling all personal aspects in others and in oneself.' As a result, the 'new man' feels 'distrust, even hatred, for the mere idea of a personality....' He is proud of 'not having anything of his own,' of merging himself into the community and becoming one with it. He renounces all loyalty to family, nation, and church and pledges his loyalty solely to Communism...

What America Was Like Before It Became a Target of Communist Psychological Warfare

"Some older Americans can still remember the good old days: peaceful towns and thriving, well-ordered cities, crime-free streets, affordable homes, family-oriented living, and safe schools. Many people didn't even bother to lock their doors. Divorce, domestic violence, and drug abuse were rare. People were more refined and gracious. There was an absence of profanity. Homosexuality and promiscuity were almost unheard of. Children were taught to respect other people's private property; there was very little vandalism and no need for community clean-up campaigns. Children received sound training in history, mathematics, science, economics, grammar, and other disciplines. There weren't mass shootings of students and teachers in the schools, and there were no SWAT teams on school campuses.

"The biggest problems in the schools were students who passed notes or popped bubble gum in class. In those days, most people still admired principled individualism, the 'work ethic,' and other American principles and ideals. The Effects of Communistic Psychological Warfare on Americans in order to create their New World Order, Communists must destroy America's fundamental ideas. Why? Because a nation whose citizens are governed and sustained by the principles of the Ten Commandments and which upholds and defends individual and economic freedom, is difficult to transform. Principled individualists think for themselves and are independent and self-reliant. They have integrity and self-respect. They're loyal to their families, their leaders, and to their nation. A nation which upholds and defends principled individualism and laissez-faire capitalism has a high ethical standard. Its citizens will fight to defend their principles, their freedom and their unalienable individual rights.

"Today, most Americans are embracing the communitarian moral code, and this country is now in a process of disintegration, making it vulnerable to a takeover. Communists have sought to degrade the nation and to produce the maximum chaos. Communist psychological warfare has wreaked havoc in the lives and families of virtually all Americans. Human casualties—the drug addicts, criminals, alcoholics, suicides, neurotics, psychotics, the ignorant and the illiterate—number in the tens of millions. In his book, The Index of Leading Cultural Indicators: 'American Society at the End of the Twentieth Century, William J. Bennett writes, '[S]ince 1960...we have seen a 467 percent increase in violent crime; a 463 percent increase in the numbers of state and federal prisoners; a 461 percent increase in out-of-wedlock births...more than a doubling in the teenage suicide rate...and a drop of almost 60 percent on SAT scores.' The rate of divorce has 'more than doubled.' The number of adults in prison now totals 2 million. Research studies show that drinking, drugs, and casual sex have become national vices.

"Since 1992, teenage drinking and drug use has soared. Illegal drug use is now not only an urban problem; the use of alcohol, cocaine, crack, inhalants, marijuana, methamphetamines and other hard drugs has reached epidemic proportions in small towns and rural areas. Tens of millions of Americans are suffering from mental disorders, such as anxiety, panic attacks, depression, phobias, obsessive-compulsive disorders, eating disorders, manic depressive psychoses, and schizophrenia. Countless others are marked by aimless lack of purpose....

"Communitarian ideals block or cripple individual growth and development. They destroy independence, self-reliance, courage, and creativeness—and produce profound feelings of helplessness, worthlessness, and instability. They breed hatred, fear, ignorance, cowardice, indolence, dependency, and conformity. Every society which embraces the communitarian way of life is reduced to unspeakable poverty, and the people endure tyranny, slavery, and misery. In Russia, Red China, and other communist and socialist-controlled countries, communitarianism is a way of life. People are self-defeating and masochistic."

That's just the tip of the iceberg. I encourage you to read the full 20 pages because The Program continues regardless of who has been in the White House. Just type *Masters of Seduction Beguiling Americans Into Slavery and Self-destruction* into a search engine.

Barack Obama's career resume was a community organizer. Valerie Jarrett is more than a trusted adviser to Obama; most people believe she runs the White House. Her family members were communists:

Valerie Jarrett's Communist Ties Confirmed by Judicial Watch, June 25, 2015: "On Monday, Judicial Watch (JW), a conservative government watchdog group, released its findings that President Obama's closest adviser, Valerie Jarrett, has had close ties to Communists for decades. Thanks to files released to JW by the Federal Bureau of Investigation (FBI), Jarrett's father, grandfather, and father-in-law all "had extensive ties to Communist associations and individuals." Jarrett's father, Dr. James Bowman, worked closely with a paid Soviet agent named Alfred Stern, who fled the country after being charged with espionage. Bowman was also a member of the pro-communist group the Association of Interns and Medical Students, which, according to the FBI, 'has long been a faithful follower of the Communist Party line."

"Jarrett's maternal grandfather, Robert Taylor, also had close ties to Stern while her father-in-law, Vernon Jarrett, was a major communist sympathizer in Chicago, according to the FBI's files. For a period of time, Vernon Jarrett was on the FBI's Security Index as a potential communist saboteur who was to be arrested immediately in the event of a conflict with the Soviet Union. Vernon Jarrett was assigned by the party the responsibility for writing anti-American propaganda for a Communist Party front in Chicago that would 'disseminate the Communist Party line among [Chicago's] middle class.' Those files also show her family's close ties to Obama's mentor, Communist Frank Marshall Davis, on whom the FBI also had extensive files." [7]

None of what you're reading is taught in public schools nor reported on by the so-called "mainstream" media including cable network "news" networks. They're all a disgrace to the profession of journalism or even reporting because the majority in that industry have put their own personal agenda before being the government watchdog.

While my daughter had long since graduated high school by the time I read Charlotte's book. I read it because that's what I do: get hard facts and write my columns to let you know what's being done behind your back to your child.

Which brings us back to Charlotte Iserbyte's critically important book: *The Deliberate Dumbing Down of America* mentioned above. EVERY parent, teacher, state legislator, governor and members of the U.S. Congress (those who support the dark agenda of course won't) should read Charlotte's fully researched and detailed work. She has dedicated an enormous amount of her life as a whistle blower to bring you the truth. From Charlotte's book:

Orchestrated Consensus

"In retrospect, I had just found out that the United States was engaged in war. People write important books about war: books documenting the battles fought, the names of the generals involved, the names of those who fired the first shot. This book is simply a history book about another kind of war: one fought using psychological methods; a one-hundred-year war; a different, more deadly war than any in which our country has ever been involved; a war about which the average American hasn't the foggiest idea.

"The reason Americans do not understand this war is because it has been fought in secret — in the schools of our nation, targeting our children who are captive in classrooms. The wagers of this war are using very sophisticated and effective tools:

"Hegelian Dialectic (common ground, consensus and compromise)

"Gradualism (two steps forward; one step backward)

"Semantic deception (redefining terms to get agreement without understanding). Wilhelm Friedrich Hegel (1770–1831) and used by Karl Marx in codifying revolutionary Communism as dialectical materialism. This process can be illustrated as: The 'Thesis' represents either an established practice or point of view which is pitted against the 'Antithesis' — usually a crisis of opposition fabricated or created by change agents — causing the 'Thesis' to compromise itself, incorporating some part of the 'Antithesis' to produce the 'Synthesis' —sometimes called consensus.

"This is the primary tool in the bag of tricks used by change agents who are trained to direct this process all over the country; much like the in-service training I received. A good example of this concept was voiced by T.H. Bell when he was U.S. Secretary of Education: '[We] need to create a crisis to get consensus in order to bring about change.' (The reader might be reminded that it was under T.H. Bell's direction that the U.S. Department of Education implemented the changes 'suggested' by A Nation at Risk — the alarm that was sounded in the early 1980s to announce the 'crisis' in education.)

"Since we have been, as a nation, so relentlessly exposed to this Hegelian dialectical process (which is essential to the smooth operation of the 'system') under the guise of 'reaching consensus' in our involvement in parent-teacher organizations, on school boards, in legislatures, and even in goal setting in community service organizations and groups—including our churches—I want to explain clearly how it works in a practical application. A good example with which most of us can identify involves property taxes for local schools.

"Let us consider an example from Michigan — The internationalist change agents must abolish local control (the 'Thesis') in order to restructure our schools from academics to global workforce training (the 'Synthesis'). Funding of education with the property tax allows local control, but it also enables the change agents and teachers' unions to create higher and higher school budgets paid for with higher taxes, thus infuriating homeowners. Eventually, property owners accept the change agents' radical proposal (the 'Anti-thesis') to reduce their property taxes by transferring education funding from the local property tax to the state income tax.

"Thus, the change agents accomplish their ultimate goal; the transfer of funding of education from the local level to the state level. When this transfer occurs it increases state/federal control and funding, leading to the federal/internationalist goal of implementing global workforce training through the schools (the 'Synthesis').

"Regarding the power of 'gradualism,' remember the story of the frog and how he didn't save himself because he didn't realize what was happening to him? He was thrown into cold water which, in turn, was gradually heated up until finally it reached the boiling point and he was dead. This is how 'gradualism' works through a series of 'created crises' which utilize Hegel's dialectical process, leading us to more radical change than we would ever otherwise accept.

"In the instance of 'semantic deception'—do you remember your kindly principal telling you that the new decision-making program would help your child make better decisions? What good parent wouldn't want his or her child to learn how to make 'good' decisions? Did you know that the decision-making program is the same controversial values clarification program recently rejected by your school board and against which you may have given repeated testimony? As I've said before, the wagers of this intellectual social war have employed very effective weapons to implement their changes.

"This war has, in fact, become the war to end all wars. If citizens on this planet can be brainwashed or robotized, using dumbed-down Pavlovian/Skinnerian education, to accept what those in control want, there will be no more wars. If there are no rights or wrongs, there will be no one wanting to 'right' a 'wrong.' Robots have no conscience. The only permissible conscience will be the United Nations or a global conscience. Whether an action is good or bad will be decided by a 'Global Government's Global Conscience,' as recommended by Dr. Brock Chisholm, executive secretary of the World Health Organization, Interim Commission, in 1947—and later in 1996 by current United States Secretary of State, Madeline Albright.

"Ronald Havelock's change agent in-service training prepared me for what I would find in the U.S. Department of Education when I worked there from 1981–1982. The use of taxpayers' hard-earned money to fund Havelock's 'Change Agent Manual' was only one out of hundreds of expensive U.S. Department of Education grants each year going everywhere, even overseas, to further the cause of internationalist 'dumbing down' education (behavior modification) so necessary for the present introduction of global workforce training. I was relieved of my duties after leaking an important technology grant (computer-assisted instruction proposal) to the press."

Much of this book contains quotes from government documents detailing the real purposes of American education:

- to use the schools to change America from a free, individual nation to a socialist, global "state," just one of many socialist states which will be subservient to the United Nations Charter, not the United States Constitution
- to brainwash our children, starting at birth, to reject individualism in favor of collectivism
- to reject high academic standards in favor of OBE/ISO 1400/9000 egalitarianism
- to reject truth and absolutes in favor of tolerance, situational ethics and consensus
- to reject American values in favor of internationalist values (globalism)

- to reject freedom to choose one's career in favor of the totalitarian K–12 school-to-work/OBE process, aptly named "limited learning for lifelong labor," coordinated through United Nations Educational, Scientific, and Cultural Organization.

"Only when all children in public, private and home schools are robotized—and believe as one—will World Government be acceptable to citizens and able to be implemented without firing a shot. The attractive-sounding 'choice' proposals will enable the globalist elite to achieve their goal: the robotization (brainwashing) of all Americans in order to gain their acceptance of lifelong education and workforce training—part of the world management system to achieve a new global feudalism."

The purpose of public education as Charlotte proves in her book is to make Americans "global" citizens, reject self-reliance, independence and freedom without the God-given freedoms we are all born with. Recently there was a mass push to further this evil agenda:

Global Citizen Festival returns even bigger, bolder, September 27, 2015

"The 2015 Global Citizen Festival lit up New York City's Central Park Saturday with its loudest call yet to end poverty by 2030. Tens of thousands of people flocked to the Great Lawn for the fourth year of the festival with a star-studded lineup of musicians, world leaders and global citizens. Dynamic performances by Beyoncé, Coldplay, Ed Sheeran and Pearl Jam revved up the crowd as world leaders pledged their support to the global goals. "This is the biggest year for global citizen by far. The biggest year for the movement," Hugh Evans, The Global Poverty Project (GPP) CEO told MSNBC during the event." [8]

Charlotte has so generously made her book, *The Deliberate Dumbing Down of America*, free on line. "This book will change forever the way you look at your child's education":

http://www.deliberatedumbingdown.com/MomsPDFs/DDDoA.sml.pdf or just type the title into a search engine.

Due to popular demand a shorter version with updates is available at Amazon and is worth every penny: *The Deliberate Dumbing Down of America, Revised and Abridged Edition Paperback* – 2011

United States Is Being Turned Into a Communist Country, July 6, 2015, *Newswithviews.com*

"S1177 Reauthorization of the Elementary and Secondary Education Act (ESA), to be voted on week of July 6, 2015, calls for tax-funded school choice and charter schools using unelected school boards (regional government's unelected council form of governance rather than constitutional government's taxpayer-elected school boards.) S1177's tax funding stream allows for communist lifelong community/school 'planning' measures, operated by unelected council (the Hillary Clinton 'it takes a village to raise a child,' 'hub of the community model' springing up all over the nation.

"S1177's tax funding stream, which includes partnerships with business, is geared towards Skinnerian/Pavlovian performance-based (OBE/TQM) global workforce training for not only K-12 students, but for all Americans to Age 80! The National Alliance of Business on its letterhead, in the mid-nineties, stated: 'Knowledge Supply Train: Managing K-Age 80 Learning'. Yes, grandpa and grandma, still in your seventies: that means YOU will get your learning/training according to the 'needs' of your community. You WILL do your community service PERIOD.

"Regarding America's gradual implementation of unconstitutional regional governance:

"In *The Globalists, The Power Elite Exposed*, page 304, Dennis L. Cuddy, Ph.D, says 'Most members of the European Union are already members of The Socialist International, and if other nations around the world can be moved toward socialism and regional economic arrangements, then these regional groupings can be more easily merged into a world socialistic government. This scenario is quite similar to the three-stage plan outlined by Stalin at the 1936 Communist International. At that meeting, the official program proclaimed: 'Dictatorship can be established only by a victory of socialism in different countries or groups of countries,' after which there would be federal unions of the various groupings of these socialist countries, and the third stage would be an amalgamation of these regional federal unions into a world union of socialist nations. [Read]

"Regionalism (Cuddy research above) which is being implemented nationwide under the phony/deceptive/innocent (?)-sounding labels related to 'consolidation of services, including education', 'public/private partnerships', 'efficiency' and 'fiscal accountability' does away with elected officials, merges counties, towns, small government units, departments, education, city services, etc., in order to CREATE A STRONG CENTRAL GOVERNMENT WITH NO REPRESENTATION (VOICE) FOR THE GOVERNED. (THIS IS COMMUNISM).

"For proof that regionalism is communism, scroll down for Part II: 'Planning is Socialism's Trademark' by Maurice Zeitlin, published in Communist Daily World, 11/8/75, which discusses Soviet Union's use of regional government. 'EIGHTY-YEARS AGO the above agenda was referred to unabashedly by the Carnegie Corporation as 'planned economy'/'socialism' (See below). The benign label 'regionalism', had not yet been concocted. The Carnegie Corporation's Conclusions and Recommendations for the Social Studies, 1934, is what this writer refers to as 'the smoking gun of the tragic political and economic catastrophe facing America today'.

"Conclusions blatantly calls for using the SCHOOLS to change America from a capitalist economy to a socialist/communist planned economy and in some cases to 'take our land'. You can read this extraordinarily important book, by going to www.americandeception.com [type "Conclusions" into search engine] A socialist planned economy requires Carnegie Corporation's lifelong workforce training (Soviet polytechnical education) being implemented through legislation such as S1177 and bills passed in ALL states. (Refer to President Reagan-USSR President Gorbachev Education Agreement to merge the two nations" education systems, and to Carnegie's Agreement with Soviet Academy of Science, 1985, related to development of computer software for early elementary education in Marxist critical thinking.)

"The goal of S1177 is to create the perfect worker (aka The New Soviet Man). S1177 calls for Soviet pre-school education, with a heavy mental health/brainwashing emphasis pre-K-12, privacy-invading computerized assessment/testing, evaluation of results for attitudinal adjustment purposes, and mental health "treatment". Much, if not most of the research on United States pre-school education (Head Start) has been developed by noted psychologist, the late Yuri Bronfenbrenner, born in Russia. [9]

Act surprised. Despite the massive amount of pressure put on the rats who wear suits and ties in the U.S. Congress, America's children lost big time. It passed. Am I surprised? After spending 26-years full time in the trenches, hardly.

I highly encourage everyone read the three-part series below.

Editor's Note: This is the first in a series of stories about Common Core, the controversial new educational agenda aimed at imposing federal government standards on every aspect of public and private education in America, which some are even calling "ObamaCore." It's a federal takeover of education that's so flawed, more teachers, states, parents and students want nothing to do with it. It's the Common Core State Standards Initiative, or CCSSI – more often referred to simply as "Common Core."

Part 1: Kids distraught under "botched" ObamaCore, February 24, 2014
http://www.wnd.com/2014/02/kids-distraught-under-botched-obamacore/

Part 2: Obama program making these people filthy rich – Only ones "who are not going to profit and thrive are children", March 1, 2014
http://www.wnd.com/2014/03/obama-program-making-these-people-filthy-rich/

Part 3: 30 states wage war on "ObamaCore" – "They thought people would be sheep and roll over, but it hasn't turned out that way"
http://www.wnd.com/2014/03/30-states-wage-war-on-obama-initiative/

State threatening anti-Common Core parents with jail? – Fight over federalized testing escalates, April 29, 2015

"Parents in South Carolina who are part of a nationwide revolt against Common Core say they are being threatened with "criminal accountability" if they prevent their children from taking the tests required by the controversial educational-standards program. Tamra Hood, a member of South Carolina Parents Involved in Education, said the state Education Department's Chief Operating Officer, Elizabeth Carpentier, warned parents could spend 30 days in jail if even a single day of testing is missed, *Breitbart News* reported.

"In addition, Hood said Carpentier warned that groups that encourage parents to refuse the Common Core-aligned tests could be charged with aiding and abetting a crime. National Review Online reported Duncan's position is that in the past, English language learners, students in special education and racial minorities were "swept under the rug." [10]

Is there a solution? Absolutely.

In 1979, imbecile Jimmy Carter, wanted a cabinet level Department of Education. At least back then many in the Republican Party saw that as unconstitutional – **which it is**: Art. 1, Sec. 8 of the U.S. Constitution. But, liberals, Democrats and the foul National Education Association supported it; the American Federation of Teachers back then rightly opposed it.

In 1980, Ronald Reagan promised that, if elected, he would get that unconstitutional cabinet abolished. That campaign promise was abandoned after his election. While campaigning for his doomed-to-lose bid for the presidency, Bob Dole said on Sept. 9, 1996, while in Georgia, "We're going to cut out the Department of Education." At that time, the GOP presidential platform read, in part:

"Our formula is as simple as it is sweeping: The federal government has no constitutional authority to be involved in school curricula or to control jobs in the workplace. That is why we will abolish the Department of Education, end federal meddling in our schools, and promote family choice at all levels of learning.

" We therefore call for prompt repeal of the Goals 2000 program and the School-To-Work Act of 1994, which put new federal controls, as well as unfunded mandates, on the States. We further urge that federal attempts to impose outcome- or performance-based education on local schools be ended."

Of course, just the opposite has taken place and, in fact, the goals for creating the "New Communist Man" was given a huge boost with President Bush's deceptive "No Child Left Behind" program. As for the repeal of the School-To-Work Act of 1994, Council of Foreign Relations kingpin Henry Hyde explained it this way:

"When carried to its logical extreme, it chooses careers for every American worker. Children's careers will be chosen for them by Workforce Development Boards and federal agencies at the earliest possible age ... Statewide Workforce Development Boards have formed to study which labor skills are needed in each state to determine "human resources" training requirements. Of course, this will decide also where these human resources will reside."

Jeri Lynn Ball, author of Masters of Seduction: Beguiling Americans Into Slavery and Self-destruction explains:

"The communitarian efforts to take over the American education system began in 1918 after World War I. Early in the 20th century, John Dewey, 'the father of Progressive Education,' worked with internationalists to transform America into a communitarian society. Dewey held that the basic goal of education is the eradication of the child's individualistic traits and 'the development of a spirit of social cooperation and community life.' Dewey did not want the child to think at all, but to learn to live and work within the narrow, primitive bounds of communitarian vocabulary and thought patterns.

"According to the testimony of Norman Dodd, the staff director of the 1953 Congressional Special Committee to Investigate the Tax-Exempt Foundations, the minutes of the Carnegie Foundation revealed that the trustees of the Foundation decided right after World War I that they 'must control education in the United States.' They joined together with the Rockefeller Foundation and created a plan to take control of domestic and international education. Dodd interviewed and Rowan Gaither, president of the Ford Foundation and discovered how he operated the foundation under strict instructions and orders "to the effect that we should make every effort to so alter life in the United States that we can be comfortably merged with the Soviet Union."

I pay state sales tax here in Texas which funds Texas public schools. Every year Texans are raped in taxes to educate **illegal alien minors**

who have no legal right to even be on U.S. soil. The federal "income" tax extortion racket also taxes me for education. Some of that money at the federal level is then given back to the states to keep them in line with the dumbing down agenda. My property is also taxed on the local level for education. How much more in taxes will I have to pay **for a failed system and illegals?**

The Federal Department of Education sucks down $66 BILLION BORROWED dollars a year; some years higher, some slightly lower. Getting rid of it would save we the people hundreds of billions of borrowed dollars in debt and would benefit **all** children in this country.

Any state in the Union can simply tell the Federal Department of Education they are cutting all ties. The first thing that will happen is a threat to cut off all federal funding. Fine. Second, is to prohibit the NEA (National Education Association), AFT (American Federation of Teachers) and the NTA (National Teachers Association) from having anything to do with your state's public education system. **They are private entities, not part of the U.S. government.** Oh, I can hear the howling now!

Of all the books I've read on education for my research, besides Charlotte Iserbyt's *Deliberate Dumbing Down of America*, there's one more I recommend:

The Teacher's Unions: How They Sabotage Educational Reform and Why by Myron Lieberman:

"After reading this powerful expose, parents unhappy with the educational status quo will be shocked to learn how the NEA and AFT use their power to smother desperately needed education innovations. Teachers will be dismayed to learn how their union leaders stifle dissent within the profession and reward themselves with privileges few of those in the trenches of the classroom could hope to enjoy."

That book should be read by members of state legislatures in every state capitol in this country. However, state capitols are drowning in lobbyist money and "education" unions have lots of it. They take your union dues and pour it into campaign coffers. They get their man or woman elected and when it comes time for "collective bargaining", guess who they sit across the table from? You got it: the man or woman they **bought** so what do think the outcome will be? The losers are America's children. But, perhaps we are seeing the beginning of the end of teachers' unions:

Union enrollment plummets for Wisconsin teachers under tough law, October 19, 2014

"Teachers in Wisconsin's public schools have learned a major lesson from the state's landmark 2011 law neutering public sector unions, with more than a third dropping out of their labor organization. Given no choice but to join and pay dues to the Wisconsin Education Association Council (WEAC) for decades, teachers have for the last three years been able to opt out. And that is what tens of thousands have done as a result of Gov. Scott Walker's Wisconsin Budget Repair Bill, also known as Act 10.

"As soon as I was given the choice, I left,' Amy Rosno, a teacher with the virtual class program at the Waukesha school system, told FoxNews.com... 'I realized that it was all political and not about teaching,' she said. Teachers who spoke to the nonprofit education think tank *EAGnews.org* said they were glad to be free of the union's grip, especially because of the perception their dues were spent on political contributions." [11]

Every state has a State Department of Education which should be confined to formulating what goes into textbooks used in public schools and if a school district is in an economically depressed area help fund through state taxes – not the federal government.

Over the past 26-years parents have sent me pages from civic textbooks which contain nothing but outright lies about the founding of this country and the brave, wise men who birthed this nation. Here in Texas there's been all out wars trying to keep out revisionist "history" and other propaganda from school books.

Education within the states under the Tenth Amendment must be locally controlled which means **elected** school board members so you can throw them out of office when they try to implement programs or teaching that is agenda driven instead of fact driven. *There's no need for a teachers' union in any state.* Teachers are just like everyone else in the work force. Their job is just as important as a doctor but we don't see doctor's unions do we? *Teachers should be paid fairly and if* *they don't go a good job, just like in the private sector they should be fired, not protected by some union.*

All this "progressive" crap pushed by the NEA, NTA and NFA has to be removed from public schools and go back to the basics of reading, writing and arithmetic so America's school children get an education instead of more indoctrination using "social justice" and other communist propaganda. Children in grade school don't need computers they need school books that teach and homework – that was the winning formula before socialists took over education in this country. They need to learn, not pushed through the school system like a zombie robot.

There are excellent teaching tools available school districts can use or for home schooling. *One I highly recommend*: "A More Perfect Union: America Becomes a Nation" available through:

www.familysafemedia.com

If America's school children don't know how their own country was formed how will they ever come to appreciate being an American or form an allegiance to their own country? **What held us true for so long was one nation, one language, our Western values, our legal form of government and freedom and liberty for all.** Disloyalty to this country is found in too many places. Schools take down the American flag because it's offensive to Mexican students. The Pledge of Allegiance is hate speech and offensive to one student. Immigrants and illegals who come here and **demand we submit to erase everything American in our schools**. It's truly sickening. If they hate America and what we stand for, why come here? That's easy – *they come to suck off your paycheck.*

Public schools have become a nanny state where children are fed breakfast instead of their parents assuming their responsibility. Public schools hand out condoms without parent's consent and force your child to embrace moral issues that are completely opposite of what you teach your child at home. Not to mention this: "Schools Implant IUDs in Girls as Young as 6th Grade Without Their Parents Knowing", July 2, 2015. *Lifenews.com* and "At Anti-Bullying Conference, Middle Schoolers Learn About Lesbian Strap-On Anal Sex, Fake Testicles", *infowars.com*

If you want to know exactly how black robes on the bench have taken it upon themselves to subject children at kindergarten age to inappropriate propaganda referred to as "sexual fluidity curriculum", type this case into a search engine: "Same Sex Marriage and the Public School Curriculum – Can Parents Opt Their Children Out of Curricular Discussions about Sexual Orientation and Same Sex Marriage".

Either you want to solve a problem or just continue down the road to failure. **Of course, nothing will happen if parents do nothing.** The backlash against Common Core must have shaken the hidden hand behind the destruction of America's school system. Why, they thought parents across this country would be just compliant good little citizens! Wrong. Public schools have become propagandist indoctrination centers:

Common Core School Assignment FORCES Students to Make Islamic Prayer Rugs, Recite Muslim Prayers, March 20, 2015

"A father in Seminole County, Florida, is stunned after discovering a indoctrination 'lesson' on Islam in his son's 10th-grade history textbook, a book that is also used as part of the Common Core standards across the state. Ron Wagner, who said he admittedly doesn't normally pay as much attention to his son's school assignments as he should, just happened to read from his son's world history book a statement which read, 'There is no god, but God. Muhammad is the messenger of God.'

"Wagner found out that his son is being indoctrinated in the religion of Islam in his 10th grade class from a history book used in school districts across the State of Florida. 'Students were instructed to recite this prayer as the first Pillar of Islam, off of the board at the teacher's instruction,' Mr. Wagner, who says he himself is not religious, told WFTV. Wagner, with a little further investigation, found out that his son was given an 'Islam packet' and was even required to make an Islamic prayer rug for the world history class." [12]

I want to say a few words about college and your child. Going to college *is elective, not mandatory*. Not every young American in this country needs to go to college. Too many parents push their child into college at some level only to see them drop out because that's not what they want to do or because they're passed through the government school system *so under-educated they can't make it in college.*

Way back when in public school kids took woodworking or shop classes. If your son or daughter loves cars and likes to work on them or likes to build things, that's great. They don't need to go to college, they can go to a trade school as an extension of what they learned in high school and become a mechanic or a carpenter. *An honest day's wages for an honest day of work is to be respected not scorned.*

One can get a very good education from the Internet in other fields of interest if they want, but pushing kids into college when they really don't want to go is just another recipe for disappointment and debt if they took college loans:

April 27, 2015: "Breitbart News reported two weeks ago that with the value of outstanding student loans soon to exceed this year's entire $1.477 trillion in federal income tax payments, the student loan repayment default rate has leapt to 27.3 in 2014 from 15.8 percent in 2010."

$1 Trillion Student Loan Problem Keeps Getting Worse, February 21, 2014, *Forbes*: "The total outstanding student loan balance is $1.08 trillion, and a whopping 11.5% of it is 90+ days delinquent or in default. That's the highest delinquency rate among all forms of debt and the only one that's been on the rise consistently since 2003."

31% of U.S. Govt Assets Are Student Loans, February 27, 2016, *Breitbart.com*: "Tucked away in the report, however, was a surprising fact. Student loans now make up 37 percent of the total assets of the U.S. government. In some ways, a major business of the U.S. government now is getting students to take out loans to pay for college. The total value of assets held by the federal government is $3.2 trillion. The government's assets include its cash, gold reserves, property, and the value of land, equipment, and inventories. The lion's share of the government's assets, though, is the value of loans it has issued. The total value of government-issued loans is over $1.2 trillion, almost 40 percent of its total assets."

Loans made through the Federal Department of Education are completely illegal under the U.S. Constitution. **Congress has no authority to act as a bank making loans.**

Federal Reserve Blames Gov't Aid for Driving up College Tuition's, August 7, 2015: "A new study from the New York Federal Reserve faults the federal government's policy of boosting aid to families in recent decades to make college education more affordable, because it enabled institutions to raise tuition much faster than inflation." [13]

I hope this will become a growing trend, but the states must step up to the plate and do the same thing:

Wyo. Catholic College Latest to Abstain from Federal Student Loan Program, April 16, 2015

CNSNews.com –"Wyoming Catholic College has joined a handful of institutions of higher learning that refuse to participate in federal student loan and grant programs because of 'burdensome' regulatory requirements [that] are clearly troubling for faith-based institutions. 'By abstaining from federal funding programs, we will safeguard our mission from unwarranted federal involvement—an involvement increasingly at odds with our Catholic beliefs, the content of our curriculum, and our institutional practices,' college president Kevin Roberts said in February after the school's board of directors voted unanimously to reject federal funding.

"Our decision is a prudential one,' said board chairman Andrew Emrich, adding that 'pivotal legal decisions, executive orders, and administrative interpretations were all pointing to some near-term (and perhaps long-term) challenges for institutions of faith. 'We really didn't want the federal government meddling in our lives here,' board member David Kellogg told The New York Times. "The federal government hands you money and then threatens to withdraw that money if you don't do what they want." [14]

I can only fit so much into this book, but I want you to have as many facts as possible on this issue. In the endnotes section in the back of this book for this chapter I've listed a number of articles that are very important for adult aged Americans to read even if you don't have children yet. They deal with both K-12 and the college loan scam.

12

On-Going Disgraceful Treatment of America's Veterans

This chapter is not about which undeclared wars America should be involved in or shouldn't. It's about the on-going, disgraceful treatment of those who serve this country whether you agree with America's foreign policy or don't agree. Yes, we have an all voluntary military. Conscription, or the draft ended in 1973. The last *constitutional* (legal) war was formally declared by the U.S. Congress on December 8, 1941.

For whatever reason individuals personally have for joining the U.S. military, they do put their lives on the line every day of the week. My husband was (he passed away, February 6, 2016) a retired U.S. Army Colonel who had 27 years of honorable service including a tour in of Viet Nam. When you enlist in the military, they own you. Period. You get up when they tell you, go to bed when they tell you, go where they tell you whether you want to or not.

Many promises have been made to those willing to serve our constitutional republic. The U.S. government has reneged on so many it's enough to make you vomit. A contract is a contract and if the cost of the contract is too much then don't enter into it. Screwing our veterans down the line is so reprehensible yet happens over and over and over.

We all have those times in life when something happens that sticks in your mind for the rest of your life. When my daughter was about 8-10 years old many decades ago and pre 9/11, we pulled off Highway 5 in Northern California at a rest stop. There was a veteran in a wheel chair who was badly disabled. He was selling little flowers. Most walked right by him. My daughter wanted to know why no one cared? She was practically in tears; it was indeed a heart wrenching sight.

A difficult question from a child, but I told her too many Americans simply didn't care about our veterans. I suppose many believe the government takes care of them so why should they give a donation? Perhaps some just didn't want to "look" at another human being so broken.

I also believe it's the old "out of sight, out of mind" while tens of thousands of veterans have returned from the Middle East with permanent brain damage, emotionally wrecked, amputees and lifetime medical problems.

A phony "war of liberation" and so-called "nation building" in the Middle East that is a gross misuse of our military, but fits in perfectly with the plans of the mad power mongers who own Washington, DC. There will NEVER be any success or "mission accomplished" in Iraq or Afghanistan, only more war. *For what?*

The plight of America's veterans was suddenly thrust into the spotlight because of a few VA employees with a conscience and studies by independent organizations:

Vets Die Waiting for Obama VA Action, December 29, 2012

"The Center for Investigative Reporting, in a new analysis of Veterans Affairs data, exposes the stark fact that the government operated VA's failure to timely process disability claims results in an escalating number of deserving veterans who die before the VA bureaucracy even processes their claims. (See: www.cironline.org.)

"The VA's inability to pay benefits to veterans before they die is increasingly common, according to data obtained by the Center for Investigating Reporting. The data reveals, for the first time, that long wait times are contributing to tens of thousands of veterans being approved for disability benefits and pensions only after it is too late for the money to help them," writes investigative reporter Aaron Glantz.

"In the fiscal year that ended in September [2012], the agency paid $437 million in retroactive benefits to the survivors of nearly 19,500 veterans who died waiting. The figures represent a dramatic increase from three years earlier, when the widows, parents and children of fewer than 6,400 veterans were paid $7.9 million on claims filed before their loved one's death," Glantz reports.

"The ranks of survivors waiting for these benefits also have surged, from fewer than 3,000 in December 2009 to nearly 13,000 this month

[December 2012]," Glantz writes. "Nationwide, 900,000 veterans and their families have been waiting about nine months for a decision, with veterans in California, facing even long waits. As of October, the most recent month for which numbers are available, the average wait time for a veteran was nearly 11 months in San Diego, 17 months in Oakland, and a year and a half in Los Angeles." [1]

According to the piece above, sadly, the most common comment from veterans about getting help from the VA is "Delay, deny, wait till I die".

Despite all the hoopla at the time and "oh, that's terrible" and "unacceptable" by members of Congress, America was about to find out the ugly truth. By 2013, the backlog of veterans waiting for care was 900,000. Obscene is bonuses given to VA employees for their incompetence:

Veterans Affairs workers reap bonuses despite claims backlog

"Staffers in the Department of Veterans Affairs have been reaping millions of dollars in bonuses despite a huge backlog of cases that has veterans waiting hundreds of days for compensation. The bonuses were reported Monday by journalism project News21, whose findings were published in The Washington Post. The report said that in 2011, more than two-thirds of claims processors received a total of $5.5 million in bonuses. That same year, the backlog of claims swelled by 155 percent. The bonuses reportedly created a perverse system, where workers were encouraged to stick to simple cases in order to meet certain performance benchmarks – in turn ignoring claims that required additional attention." [2]

By mid-2014, the VA mess blew up in the media. Veterans were dying before their claims and requests for treatment were ever processed. We found out there were "secret waiting lists".

40 U.S. veterans die while on Phoenix VA hospital's cost-cutting secret wait list, April 24, 2014

"The 'sham list' was part of an elaborate scheme by top-level management to doctor patient wait times, *CNN* reports. Patients had to wait as long as 20 weeks to see primary care physicians despite some having life-threatening conditions, including Thomas Breen, a Navy vet who died of Stage 4 bladder cancer...

"Internal emails reveal managers at Arizona's VA hospital knew about the practice and even condoned it. Retiring Dr. Sam Foote, who spent 24 years with the VA system, told *CNN* that the Phoenix VA worked off two patient appointment lists. The 'official' list shows the VA was offering timely appointments within 14 to 30 days. Foote called this a 'sham list' because there was another secret document where waits where much longer.

"The scheme was deliberately put in place to avoid the VA's own internal rules. They developed the secret waiting list,' he said. According to Foote, the elaborate plans involved shredding evidence to hide the long list, with VA officials instructing staff to not make veterans" appointments in the computer system.

"Instead, Foote explained, when a veteran sought an appointment, 'They enter information into the computer and do a screen-capture, hard-copy printout. They then do not save what was put into the computer — so there's no record.' That hard copy is then placed into a secret electronic waiting list, Foote said, with the paper data being shredded. He also revealed that patients wouldn't be taken off the secret list until their appointment time was within 14 days or less — giving the appearance that the VA was improving waiting times." [3]

In the piece above, the family of Navy veteran Thomas Breen, 71, found out Breen was on the secret waiting list. He died a horrible, painful death from Stage 4 bladder cancer. A national disgrace of epic proportions while more jaw jacking was going on in Washington, DC.

Whistleblowers came forward only to be treated like this:

Isolated. Harassed. Their personal lives investigated. That's life as a VA whistle blower, employees tell Congress, April 14, 2015

"Some whistle blowers at the Department of Veterans Affairs say they were demoted, then moved into windowless storage rooms, or basements. Others found their medical backgrounds scrutinized, and even their mental health and personal lives investigated. Even after their cases were cleared, those who retaliate against them were rarely if ever punished, they say. This is the tortured life described by whistle blowers in the VA....

"He was one of three whistle blowers who spoke to the committee, sharing harrowing experiences of being ostracized and punished for sharing concerns about senior managers fudging data and veterans growing sicker and in some cases dying while waiting for care. It's been a year since Head and a group of whistle blowers first came forward to expose the wait times...But congressional leaders say they are frustrated by the pace of reform and how the VA has been slow to punish those who retaliated against the whistle blowers...

"Special Counsel head Carolyn Lerner told Congress that more than 25 VA whistle blowers have received legal settlements for retaliations related to the scandal and about 120 cases are still pending. Still she expects 40 percent of the agency's cases to come from the VA this year, far more than from any other agency.

"The numbers are bad," she said. "Despite this significant progress, the number of new whistle blower cases from VA employees remains overwhelming. Our staff is completely overwhelmed by work." [4]

The people doing the harassing are paid for by YOU. The people doing the harassing are scum bags who care nothing for our veterans, only their paychecks and power.

22 veterans kill themselves every day. EVERY DAY of the week. Some killed themselves because they couldn't get treatment from the VA:

Homeless Veteran Commits Suicide Outside Phoenix VA, May 12, 2015

"Thomas Michael Murphy, a Phoenix resident and U.S. Army veteran, took his own life in the parking lot outside the VA Phoenix Regional Benefit Office. Murphy, 53, e-mailed a suicide note to his siblings and *New Times* at 7:34 p.m. Sunday and shot himself a few minutes later. The same note was discovered in his 1995 white Toyota pickup truck, which was parked nearby. In the letter, he explained that his arthritis was getting worse, and he "thanked" the VA for not helping him." [5]

Congress finally passed a bill signed into law making it easier to fire VA employees which should have been done decades ago. But, has it had any effect on improving the situation for our veterans? When pig's fly. It's the same old rhetoric, "we're working on it". More billions poured into a system that is archaic with career government employees who couldn't find their backsides with a map.

VA Makes Little Headway in Fight to Shorten Waits for Care, April 9, 2015

FAYETTEVILLE, N.C. – "A year after Americans recoiled at new revelations that sick veterans were getting sicker while languishing on waiting lists – and months after the Department of Veterans Affairs instituted major reforms costing billions of dollars – government data shows that the number of patients facing long waits at VA facilities has not dropped at all...

"Nearly 894,000 appointments completed at VA medical facilities from Aug. 1 to Feb. 28 failed to meet the health system's timeliness goal, which calls for patients to be seen within 30 days. That means roughly one in 36 patient visits to a caregiver involved a delay of at least a month. Nearly 232,000 of those appointments involved a delay of longer than 60 days – a figure that doesn't include cancellations, patient no-shows, or instances where veterans gave up and sought care elsewhere. [6]

Report: Wait Lists for Vets Even Longer Today Than Last Year – VA also faces a budget shortfall of nearly $3 billion, June 21, 2015

WASHINGTON (AP) — "The number of veterans seeking health care but ending up on waiting lists of one month or more is 50 percent higher now than it was a year ago when a scandal over false records and long wait times wracked the Department of Veterans Affairs, The New York Times reported.

"The VA also faces a budget shortfall of nearly $3 billion, the Times reported in a story posted online ahead of its Sunday editions. The agency is considering furloughs, hiring freezes and other significant moves to reduce the gap, the newspaper reported. In the last year, the VA has increased capacity by more than 7 million patient visits per year, double what officials originally thought they needed to fix shortcomings, the Times reported. However, the newspaper added, department officials did not anticipate just how much physician workloads and demand from veterans would continue to soar. At some major veteran's hospitals, demand was up by one-fifth, the paper reported." [7]

Wait just a minute! What happened to all those billions thrown to the VA after the scandal broke in 2014? I worked for the Department of Defense both Army and Air Force. *Never have I seen such waste and retaining employees who should have been fired years ago but because of the federal civil service system protecting incompetent workers, it's damn near impossible.*

Yes, a law is now on the books making it easier to can VA employees, but has it done any good? Not from the data in the article above. You can pour rail cars full of money into the VA system, but if the people aren't doing the job – and that includes the guy at the top – all that money will just be more thrown down the drain. So, no, things are not better:

VA under fire for tossing claims in trash, September 19, 2015

"The Office of Inspector General for Veterans Affairs just found staffers with the Los Angeles VA Regional Office improperly shredded numerous disability claims, tossing them in the trash rather than giving them proper review...."The investigators concluded the mistakes were made because staffers didn't receive the proper training. "[Staffers] are not familiar with claims-processing activities and lack the knowledge needed to identify claims or claims-related documents," the report stated. "Additionally, there is no control preventing VARO staff incorrectly placing claim-related documents in red shred boxes instead of red envelopes." [8]

Who is the stupidvisor that put individuals without proper training to handle such important documents? That person needs to be fired. Fat chance. Likely, he/she was promoted.

Every election members of Congress brag about how much they care about veterans. Hogwash. *The continuing mess with getting veterans the medical care they need is proof positive your incumbent and mine are not taking care of veterans.* They hold hearings and throw more money at the problem instead of getting individuals in place who can make the problems go away.

They also care so much about veterans they want to cut their benefits. **If you're going to ask men and women to serve this country and take the chance of losing their life or come home damaged, then by all that's right and moral, you honor the commitment made to them.** As for using cost cutting, this is a column I wrote January 12, 2014:

Cutting veterans pensions vs cupboard is bare:

"Then I say, the earth belongs to each of these generations during its course, fully and in its own right. The second generation receive sit clear of the debts and encumbrances of the first, the third of the second, and so on. For if the first could charge it with a debt, then the earth would belong to the dead and not to the living generation. Then, no generation can contract debts greater than may be paid during the course of its own existence." – Thomas Jefferson to James Madison, 1789. ME 7:455, Papers 15:393

House Minority Leader Nancy Pelosi says that while deficit reduction is a laudable goal, there are precious few spending cuts left to negotiate in exchange for raising the debt ceiling. "The cupboard is bare," the California Democrat said in an interview aired Sunday on *CNN*"s "State of the Union." "There's no more cuts to make." September 22, 2013, *Politico*

Really? The cupboard is bare? No more cuts to make? America: Do you feel violated yet?

US to Give $125 Million to Upgrade Pakistan's Power Sector. "Secretary of State Hillary Clinton, seeking to bolster Islamabad's fight against Islamic extremists US corporaterrorists' profits, initiated a crash U.S. assistance program for Pakistan's power sector aimed at rolling back electricity shortages that threaten to cripple the South Asian nation's economy. Mrs. Clinton, on the first of a three-day diplomatic mission to Pakistan, said that Washington will disburse $125 million to Islamabad for the upgrading of key power stations and transmission lines.

H.R. 2878: Solar Villages Initiative Act – To authorize microenterprise assistance for renewable energy projects in developing countries.

(e) Authorization of Appropriations– There is authorized to be appropriated to the President to carry out this section $10,000,000 for fiscal year 2010, $10,000,000 for fiscal year 2011, $15,000,000 for fiscal year 2012, $15,000,000 for fiscal year 2013, $20,000,000 for fiscal year 2014, and $30,000,000 for fiscal year 2015.

H.R. 3077: Global Food Security Act of 2009

"(i) Authorization of Appropriations– There is authorized to be appropriated to the President for the purpose of carrying out activities under this section–

"(1) $100,000,000   for   fiscal   year   2010;
(2) $200,000,000   for   fiscal   year   2011;
(3) $300,000,000   for   fiscal   year   2012;
(4) $400,000,000   for   fiscal   year   2013;
(5) $500,000,000 for fiscal year 2014.

Americans will be wearing rags and stealing food while being plundered in more taxes to send around the world." [13]

After Republicans took control of the House and the people's purse again in 2010, has the unconstitutional plundering stopped? No. Without a scintilla of constitutional authority look at the billions YOU pay for – ALL borrowed debt plus the interest shoved down our throats:

Americans Spent $7.45B in 3 Years Helping Other Countries Deal with "Climate Change" – **Another big, fat scam against we the people**. If you get a chance, go see the movie, Climate Hustle (climatehustlethemovie.com). It rips the lies about "global warming" and "climate change" to shreds. It's a con game.

That one illegal theft above from you and me takes care of the $6 billion the thieves in the Outlaw Congress want to save over ten years by screwing veterans out of what they were promised. Here's more of the cupboard is bare that phony conservatives like Paul Ryan, Eric Cantor, John Boehner and others have allowed instead of shutting off the money:

- U.S. Will Spend $3.35M to "Improve the Quality of Media Content"– In Armenia

- USDA: $6.2 Billion Improperly Spent in 2013 – $2 Billion on Food Stamp Overpayments – More gross incompetence. How much do you think was recovered?
- Gov't Pays $1,123,463 to Develop Strawberry Harvest-Aiding Robots
- $37,680,000,000: That's How Much the U.S. Spent on Foreign Aid in 2012 – The US steals tens of billions unconstitutionally from you, me our children and grandchildren and gives it to 96% of countries on this globe to rebuild infrastructures, health care and the nonsense below. **All borrowed debt.**

- In 2012, the *congressionally created* national debt was over $16 TRILLION dollars while the thieves in the U.S. Congress throw another $37 BILLION in unconstitutional spending called foreign aid. Hot checks. *Grossly irresponsible and reckless yet the American people keep reelecting the same incumbents every two years to the U.S. House who refuse to stop burying us in debt because it's always the other party.* Not one penny below is authorized spending by Congress under Art. 1, Sec. of the U.S. Constitution.
- NSF Spends $82,525 to Study Self-Defense by Millipedes
- NCLR Gets Chunk of $40 Mil for Minority Housing Counseling
- $70 Mil to Help Communities Spend Federal Money
- $20 Mil to Help States Spend Federal Money
- Interior Department to Spend $600K to Radio Track Bats
- The Average American Family Pays $6,000 a Year in Subsidies to Big Business
- Green Energy Co. Folds after Obama gives it $99.8 Mil
- Feds Spend $84K on Eco-Friendly Exit Signs for Bowling Alley, Rec Center
- Feds Spend $777K On Ads Promoting NJ Blueberries, Other'Minor Small Fruits"
- $1.5 BILLION taxpayer funded cell-phones
- $1B to Be Spent to Promote Obamacare in "Normandy Invasion" of Health System

- $5.25 Million for Senate Hair Care and 21 Other Ways Politicians Are Living The High Life At Your Expense
- U.S. Paying $25K to Make Park Benches from Garbage for Tijuana
- Labor Department to Spend $1 Million to Increase Gender Equality in Work – in Morocco
- $25 Million NSF Grant to Build Machines Smarter Than Average 3-Year-Old
- Federal stimulus funds paid for new trees in posh Denver neighborhoods
- White House to announce $300M in aid Friday to make Detroit safer, erase blight
- Energy Department loses $42M on clean-energy loan to Mich. van company
- Latino Group Wants to Expand Fraud-Ridden "Obamaphone" Program – BILLIONS
- Gov't Spends $379K Texting Kids to Take a Walk
- Gov't Spends $495-K for False Killer Whale Team to Meet
- $2M NIH Grant to Study Effect of Cultural Stigma on Chinese Homosexual Men
- $5.7M NSF Grant for Card Games, Videos To Teach Public About Global Warming
- U.S. Spending $653K to "Reduce Tobacco Use" Among Brazilian Women
- $1M NIH Grant to Reduce HIV, Domestic Violence in Dar es Salaam, Tanzania
- 78K Fed Study: Did "Climate Change" Cause Decline of the Mayan Civilization?
- NEA Awards $35,000 For "Grow-Sculpture"
- NIH to Spend $200K Studying Teenage Drinking Binges on Social Media
- Obama Spends $20 M Helping Indonesian Kids Get College Degrees
- $10 Million Stimulus Solar Company Can't Take the Heat, Closes
- White House Pays $53 Million for Voter ID in Kenya While Opposing Same in US

- Illegal Immigrant Mother of Seven Given Food Stamps, Meds, Housing and Social Security – For 20 Years
- $2.44M Fed Study: "Deportation and Loneliness" Led Former Illegals to Use Drugs, Whores
- NIH Awards $254K to Study Workforce Safety of Male Prostitutes in Boston
- $21K Dissertation Grant Aims to Help Political Campaigns Motivate Voters
- 1/3 Population of Puerto Rico Gets Food Stamps from U.S. Gov't – $2 Billion in 2012
- Feds Dig Up $98,000 to Study "3rd Millennium BC Mortuary Traditions" in Oman
- $658K Federal Study Tests Hypotheses of Cicada Evolution
- NIH: $357K for Spanish Ad Campaign Convincing Gay Illegal Aliens to Use Free Condoms, Get Treated
- DOT to Spend $1.8 Million to Encourage Kids to Walk, Bike to School
- State Dep't Building $15-Million Women's Dorms in Afghanistan
- $509K Federal Safe-Sex Study Will Text "Gay-Lingo" to Meth Addicts
- U.S. Spends $228K to Find Out Why Gay Kenyans Avoid Free HIV Treatment
- $4.5M Fed Study: Effects of Climate Change on Indoor Air
- Dept. of Education Spent $20.3 Million on 10 Equity Centers to Fight the "Isms"
- Obama Gives $737 Million to Solar Firm Linked to the Pelosi Clan

That's just a drop in the bucket. Former Sen. Tom Coburn's annual government waste report: $30 BILLION BORROWED dollars in 2013 wasted on nonsense, "pork" and more debt. Cut veterans pensions to save $6 billion dollars over ten years, but it's okay, Nancy Pelosi, to rape we the people to the tune of $30 BILLION borrowed dollars in one year alone **to fund insanity**.

The cost of the unconstitutional, grotesque invasions of Iraq and Afghanistan alone have cost upwards of $3 TRILLION BORROWED dollars. Vile politicians who send our troops into undeclared wars then turn right around and penalize them by taking away what they were promised as a condition of their service. BOTH parties. Why? To save money to spend on all the above and more.

Voting for any incumbent who voted for that budget bill is rewarding them for screwing our veterans. Again. Every time you vote for your incumbent in the Outlaw Congress you are rewarding them for destroying this republic by voting for unconstitutional programs stealing us blind. The cupboard isn't bare. The entire house is empty." [9] [End of my column.]

Since I wrote that column, let's see what else Congress has **unconstitutionally** been throwing away YOUR money on:

U.S. Pays Black Comedian to Deliver Anti-White Racist Tirade at Fed Agency, *Judicial Watch*, August 3, 2015

"The U.S. government paid a controversial civil rights activist/comedian to deliver an anti-white racist tirade at a major federal agency during Black History month and Judicial Watch has obtained the disturbing transcript and the shocking video of the offensive political rant....The Census Bureau paid Gregory $1,400 to "share a wealth of history as a Civil Rights Activist," according to the records obtained by JW under the federal public records law known as the Freedom of Information Act (FOIA)."

Feds spent $2 million to study nagging wives, July 9, 2015, *The Washington Times*
$52,293 NIH Study Aims to Reduce Discrimination of LGBT Schizophrenics by Convenience Store Clerks, May 27, 2015, *CNS News*
Feds Spend $471,770 Observing Pregnant Women Walking Around, May 11, 2015, *The Washington Free Beacon*
Feds Award $20 Million to Teach Guatemalan Mothers To Spot a Baby's "Hunger Cues", May 11, 2015, *CNS News*
$169,240 Federal Grant to Build "Educational Pipeline" for LGBT Population Researchers, May 6, 2015, *CNS News*

Gov't Grants $49K to Market "Alpaca Poop Packs", October 8, 2014, *CNS News*
State Dept Spends $357K to Beef up Border Security – in Ukraine,

October 16, 2014, *CNS News*
$39,643,352 worth of NIH funding that could have gone to the Ebola vaccine, October 17, 2014, *Fox News*

"The National Institutes of Health (NIH) has spent more than $39 million on obese lesbians, origami condoms, texting drunks, and dozens of other projects that could have been scrapped in favor of developing an Ebola vaccine. "Frankly, if we had not gone through our 10-year slide in research support, we probably would have had a vaccine in time for this that would've gone through clinical trials and would have been ready," said NIH Director Francis Collins, blaming budget cuts for his agency's failure to develop a vaccine for the deadly virus.

"However, the *Washington Free Beacon* has uncovered $39,643,352 worth of NIH studies within the past several years that have gone to questionable research. For instance, the agency has spent $2,873,440 trying to figure out why lesbians are obese, and $466,642 on why fat girls have a tough time getting dates. Another $2,075,611 was spent encouraging old people to join choirs."

Feds Pay $91K for Bat Population Survey, September 30, 2014, *Weekly Standard*
Feds spend $300,000 to study how to ride bikes, September 28, 2014, *Fox News*
$3.2 million in taxpayer money to get monkeys drunk, September 11, 2014, *The Washington Times*
NIH also has handed out $69,459 to the University of Missouri to study whether text messaging college students before they attend pre-football game tailgates will encourage them to drink less and "reduce harmful effects related to alcohol consumption." September 11, 2014, *The Washington Times*

$300k to Boost "Culturally Appropriate" Gene Studies in Africa, September 9, 2014, *Judicial Watch*
$400,000 To Promote "Pickleball", *The Waste List*

Not a single penny of that spending is authorized under the U.S. Constitution, yet Congress – both parties – **are spending us, our children and grandchildren into poverty**. Cutting benefits for our veterans instead of axing all that unconstitutional spending and more.

Leaked Document: Nearly One-Third of 847,000 Vets with Pending Applications for VA Health Care Already Died, July 13, 2015

WASHINGTON – "More than 238,000 of the 847,000 veterans with pending applications for health care through the Department of Veterans Affairs have already died, according to an internal VA document provided to *The Huffington Post*.

"Scott Davis, a program specialist at the VA's Health Eligibility Center in Atlanta and a past whistle blower on the VA's failings, provided HuffPost with an April 2015 report titled "Analysis of Death Services," which reviews the accuracy of the VA's veteran death records. The report was conducted by staffers in the VA Health Eligibility Center and the VA Office of Analytics. Flip to page 13 and you'll see some stark numbers. As of April, there were 847,822 veterans listed as pending for enrollment in VA health care. Of those, 238,657 are now deceased, meaning they died after they applied for, but never got, health care…

"The best thing President Barack Obama can do, said Davis, is force the VA to allow veterans to upload their so-called DD-214 forms when they apply for health care. The form is a lifelong document that shows a person's military record. If veterans could use it to show their eligibility for health care, and if the VA assigned staff to review all of the pending applications, it would clear the logjam in the system, he said. "The White House has the ability to direct the VA to do this immediately," said Davis. "That would get rid of the pending eligibility issue." [10]

How many times have you seen campaign ads or listened to the same old canned speeches during an election year from your *incumbent* in the U.S. House or Senate that proclaims how much they support our vets? Has it made any difference to our vets? Instead of Congress butting their noses into issues where they have NO legislative authority they should be spending their time fixing problems instead of making noises for the next election.

H.R. 91: Veterans Identification Card Act 2015 was signed into law, July 20, 2015, that will expedite applications as discussed in the article above. A very important first step. Do you know how many

VA employees have been fired since the first whistle blowers brought out the truth almost two years ago?

Bombshell: So Far, Only Three People Have Been Fired After VA Scandal, April 25, 2015, *Townhall*

"The scandal at the Office of Veterans Affairs last year proved that our veterans were being shamelessly ill-treated. Among other atrocities, our former soldiers were forced to wait months to be seen by doctors and, once they were finally admitted, were often treated in unsanitary and dangerous conditions. Politicians demanded change and accountability. VA Secretary Eric Shinseki resigned. Yet, months later, new internal documents prove that the mess is hardly cleaned up at all.

"The documents given this month to the House Committee on Veterans Affairs, which provided them to The New York Times, show that the department punished a total of eight of its 280,000 employees for involvement in the scandal. One was fired, one retired in lieu of termination, one's termination is pending, and five were reprimanded or suspended for up to two months. That means only three people have actually been fired from their positions. Three. Oh, and the only person actually fired, Sharon Helman, the director of the Phoenix VA hospital was not fired because of her role in the scandal, but because she had accepted "inappropriate gifts," according to the *New York Times*." [11]

While more than **238,000 veterans across this country died waiting for their applications to be processed through the VA**, 8 out of 280,000 employees were punished. How? They are mostly civil service who received a slap on the wrist like a letter in their personnel file. How reprehensible.

Can they be more despicable?

VA Manager Says "Thank God" They Don't Have to Hire Veterans, April 13, 2016, *The Daily Caller*

"A Department of Veterans Affairs (VA) hiring manager said in a sworn deposition "thank God" they don't give veterans hiring preference for well-paying jobs....

"Title 38" refers to the pay-grade for doctors working in VA. A Daily Caller News Foundation investigation previously found that, although government-wide, veterans are supposed to be given hiring preference, and VA boasts that one-third of the people it hires are veterans. This is misleading: At VA, vets usually get the worst, lowest-paying jobs — the only job reserved exclusively for veterans is janitor.

"One cause is a provision in the union contract that says preference must be given to current federal employees — union members — for higher-paying and easier jobs, preventing them from even being advertised to the public unless no current VA employee wants a promotion. That leaves only the jobs at the bottom of the totem pole available for veterans, the sole reason for the department's existence."

The VA should be devoted solely to processing necessary paperwork for our veterans as they already do. Help with funerals, getting separation papers, history of service and so on. Veterans should be given medical cards that don't just identify them but allow them to be seen in the private sector. Shut down all the VA hospitals and clinics; sell the buildings and equipment. That wouldn't be difficult for the GAO and put the money in the VA budget.

Medicare recipients have an identification card that is used at the doctor's office or hospital. Veterans could have the same kind so they are treated just like civilians. With that card, health care providers would know the patient is a veteran and covered for their medical needs. All billing would go to the VA. That way veterans have access to any medical facility in this country. They don't have to travel hundreds of miles to a VA hospital when there's a civilian hospital or clinic right in their town.

I live in Big Spring, Texas which is a fairly small rural town. There's a VA hospital here and a civilian hospital and clinic less than a mile apart as the crow flies. Twenty miles from here is a hospital and medical offices. The VA hospital here employs a lot of people. If the hospital were shutdown they can find jobs with the civilian hospital here or go to Stanton which would grow with new patients. If a higher level of care is needed, 40 miles from here is Midland, Texas, with a massive hospital complex and dozens and dozens of doctor's offices for every specialty under the sun. Sixty miles from here is Odessa, Texas. Same thing.

Doctors and health care providers from pace makers, rehab from war injuries, surgery, tests like MRIs or CAT Scans – whatever treatment they need, those health care providers *must* be paid the same rate as they would receive from a civilian patient with health insurance. If you're going to send Americans into a war zone then the people of this country need to understand when hundreds of thousands of them come home broken and maimed they need and deserve the same level of medical care you do from say a car accident, you break your back or need spine surgery.

Doctors and all those involved in the field of health care should not be penalized for treating veterans just like doctors who take Medicare patients shouldn't be paid less. Americans need to think about that the next time they support sending our military to the Middle East to get bogged down in tribal wars or killing off heads of state for geopolitical games. War is business and business has been booming since 9/11 – so has the massive number of veterans returning home with brain injuries, mental health issues and more.

All the doctors, nurses, x-ray technicians, psychiatrists – whatever the field or service – would be picked up in the private sector. With hundreds of thousands of veterans needing proper medical treatment, VA doctors can open their own offices or go to work at hospitals that would expand to accommodate all those new patients. Existing private sector doctor's offices and clinics would expand and hire former VA employees. It can be done. It can't be done overnight, but setting a time frame of say 18 -24 months should get the job done.

How many more of our veterans are going to die waiting for health care treatment? How many more flag draped coffins is acceptable to you?

Every time a new administration is ensconced in Washington, DC and another Congress *filled with the same incumbents*, we hear the same thing **we've already heard for decades**: We're going to reform the VA! We love our veterans and are going to make sure they get the best treatment possible! BULL. When you have more than a quarter MILLION veterans die waiting for treatment all that political rhetoric is nothing but empty promises for votes. **Reform hasn't happened and it won't happen under the current system and if anyone can't see that by now they're either blind or in denial.**

For hundreds of thousands of our veterans and their families it's a real nightmare when it comes to getting them the help they need. Think about that in 2016 when you decide to vote back in your incumbent who has allowed the mess with the VA to continue decade after decade. Continuing to do the same thing over and over that doesn't work is insanity and we the people have been paying for it for decades – so have our veterans.

13

What Everyone Ignores About Planned Parenthood

The continuing war regarding Planned Parenthood accelerated in late summer 2015 when grizzly videos were released showing 'business as usual' transactions such as harvesting baby parts and selling them. Below is my column, September 27, 2015, What Everyone Ignores About Planned Parenthood. It should be the last word from a constitutional and moral position. Links are in the column on line and are important.

Hillary Clinton: I Admire Planned Parenthood Founder Margaret Sanger

> "And here is Hillary Clinton accepting Planned Parenthood's Margaret Sanger Award: Secretary of State Hillary Clinton accepts the Margaret Sanger Award at the 2009 Planned Parenthood Honors Gala in Houston, Texas. 'I admire Margaret Sanger enormously, her courage, her tenacity, her vision,' said Hillary Rodham Clinton, 'I am really in awe of her, there are a lot of lessons we can learn from her life.'"

Sanger's vision was the work of Satan so much admired by Hillary Clinton:

> "We should hire three or four colored ministers, preferably with social-service backgrounds, and with engaging personalities. The most successful educational approach to the Negro is through a religious appeal. We don't want the word to go out that we want to exterminate the Negro population, and the minister is the man who can straighten out that idea if it ever occurs to any of their more rebellious members." Margaret Sanger's December 19, 1939 letter to Dr. Clarence Gamble, 255 Adams Street, Milton, Massachusetts. Original source: Sophia Smith Collection, Smith College, North Hampton,

Massachusetts. Also described in Linda Gordon's *Woman's Body, Woman's Right: A Social History of Birth Control in America*. New York: Grossman Publishers, 1976.

Sanger's vision so greatly admired by Hillary the Hun:

> "Birth control is not contraception indiscriminately and thoughtlessly practiced. It means the release and cultivation of the better racial elements in our society, and the gradual suppression, elimination and eventual extirpation of defective stocks— those human weeds which threaten the blooming of the finest flowers of American civilization." Margaret Sanger, Apostle of Birth Control Sees Cause Gaining Here, *The New York Times*, 1923-04-08, p. XII

Human weeds?

Margaret Sanger, October 1926 *Birth Control Review*.

"[Slavs, Latin, and Hebrew immigrants are] human weeds ... a deadweight of human waste ... [Blacks, soldiers, and Jews are a] menace to the race. Eugenic sterilization is an urgent need ... We must prevent Multiplication of this bad stock."
(https://www.ewtn.com/library/PROLENC/ENCYC068.HTM)

> More of Sanger's writing: *Woman and the New Race*, (1922), New York: Brentanos Publishers. "The most merciful thing that the large family does to one of its infant members is to kill it."

That is the woman Hillary Clinton admires so much: "I admire Margaret Sanger enormously, her courage, her tenacity, her vision."

Hillary Clinton, Nancy Pelosi, Dirty Harry Reid and so many others support the evil Margaret Sanger set into motion. Chapter 68 — *Margaret Sanger Mother of the Sexual Revolution*: "Margaret Sanger was born an innocent baby in 1879 and died a bisexual Demerol and alcohol addict who spawned the most monstrous organization ever conceived, the International Planned Parenthood Federation (IPPF)."

By now most Americans know about the heinous, despicable practice by Planned Parenthood selling body parts of innocent human life, tiny babies.

The morally and ethically bankrupt useful fools in the U.S. Congress who belong to the Democratic Party have joined together to defend such barbarism. Many claim the videos were fake as if shot on some movie lot. The usual tactic used by those who support killing a human being in the womb: Attack the messenger, ignore the message.

Instead of denouncing such barbaric practices, Democrats in Congress want an investigation of the Center for Medical Progress who filmed those videos! Those folks should be given a medal for exposing such demonic "business" practices.

Morally bankrupt men and women across America who support stopping a beating heart have also risen to the occasion with their screams and chants that anyone who opposes funding for Planned Parenthood is a Nazi or part of the **silly propaganda** called the "war on women". Anyone opposed to funding Planned Parenthood surely must hate women. Sadly, millions of women believe such hyped lies.

When I ran for Congress, the Democrats salted the audience during debates with ignorant, foolish women to taunt me because I am for life, not death. But, I was ready for them when ask this question:

Q: Why do you support taking away women's reproductive rights?

A: What do you think getting pregnant is? No one is interfering with a woman's right to reproduce. *You people have it backwards.* What I oppose is you want to kill what you have reproduced, an innocent baby.

Countless women have abortions because they say they don't have the money to feed another mouth. Then keep your knees together. My mother had a fifth child late in life. My step-father's paycheck simply wasn't enough to support five kids, four of them from mother's previous marriage. When I was growing up we ate spaghetti for lunch and dinner or spam and eggs for dinner or just eggs and milk for dinner and cereal in the morning.

We took our lunches to school; mostly baloney between two slices of bread or peanut butter and jelly. I grew up very poor wearing my older sister's hand me down clothes which didn't fit for which I was teased by other girls in high school. But we love each other and we all made it just fine. My mother could no more abort her baby than cut off her own arm.

Planned Parenthood is a private organization, not part of the U.S. government. They provide services for women's health issues, murdering unborn babies and selling their tissue and body parts.

A woman's health issues and family planning for a family are NOT a financial obligation for taxpayers in this country.

A woman's health care is HER personal responsibility, not a male college student working two jobs to get through college paying income taxes. It's not my responsibility to pay for Linda Smith's health care, family planning or an abortion.

It's not a moral obligation for any taxpayer in this country to fund Planned Parenthood nor does the U.S. Constitution in any language authorize the Outlaw Congress to steal the fruits of your labor to pay for any woman or man's health issues or testing at Planned Parenthood. Art. 1, Sec. 8: Scope of Legislative Power for the U.S. Congress.

Shame on women in this country who demand someone else work to pay for their "issues". One has to wonder how women in this country made it on their own without Planned Parenthood for over 300 years.

The current battle to defund Planned Parenthood is just a continuation of an old war:

Get My Wallet Out of Your Vagina, April 17, 2011, excerpts from my column

The recent budget battle for public consumption brought out high political theater and the usual well fed herds of bovine shouting their ignorance for all the world to see. Some of the loudest manure defecated by the vast herds of cattle focused on making sure the Outlaw Congress continues to fund murdering unborn babies and "women's issues" was propped up by males who lie through their teeth because their very paycheck depends on my wallet (and yours).

In lobbying for defeat of a congressional plan that would cut off taxpayer support for the abortion business leading player, Richards claimed [Link]: "If this bill ever becomes law, millions of women in this country are going to lose their health-care access – not to abortion services – to basic family planning, you know, mammograms." But Live Action workers who called 30 Planned Parenthood business locations across the nation said "every single one admitted they could not do mammograms."

I will never have a mammogram, but having one is a personal decision *and* expense. The Outlaw Congress has NO authority to steal the fruits of your labor to fund abortions or mammograms.

Spineless, sissy boy, Sen. Harry Reid, proclaimed he would shut down the General Government if the Outlaw Congress didn't vote to continue breaking the law by funding the vile Planned Parenthood and their abortion mills. Morally depraved, Sen. Chuck Schumer, said that "we will never, never, never" defund Planned Parenthood! Blow a rod, Chuckie?

This short video hosted by the most vacuous female cable host on the boob tube, Joy Behar, demonstrates the absolute stupidity of Americans regarding the U.S. Constitution. Behar proclaimed Planned Parenthood could save your life with a cervical cancer test. Jerry Springer was one of her guests who spouted off how important PP is for women. I suppose he's an expert since his television show broadcasts some of the filthiest and most degrading behavior by women ever seen on the public air waves." [End]

Oh, how feminists and Planned Parenthood supporters went ballistic after I wrote that column. I was flayed and viciously attacked with the most unladylike language one could ever read on a ton of web sites. At that time $363 million dollars was stolen from we the people and given to Planned Parenthood. *Every penny borrowed with the interest slapped on our backs* by the Outlaw Congress and given to Planned Parenthood *without a scintilla of constitutional authority.*

In 2014, a HALF BILLION **borrowed** dollars was unconstitutionally given to that vile organization. In 2014, the congressionally created national debt was $17.8 TRILLION dollars, yet your incumbent and mine authorized raping we the people for another half billion borrowed dollars to fund Planned Parenthood. They just write another hot check and find some foreign country to borrow the money from slapping us with more unpayable debt. Thankfully, the rat who "represented" me in Congress is retiring in 2016.

On September 25, 2015, I jumped over from my oldies station while driving to Sean Hannity's radio show. It was his show but with a guest host. Popular U.S. Rep. Louis Gohmert [R-TX] was speaking on this very subject. He said what needs to be done is completely defund Planned Parenthood but steal even more than a half billion borrowed dollars and give it to entities around the country that provide health services for women.

What Constitution are you reading, Rep. Gohmert? Show me where in that document, the supreme law of the land, where it gives you, a member of Congress, the authority to steal from one American to give to another for women's or men's health issues. *There is no such authorization* but it's obvious the game being played here. Republicans don't want to lose the "women's vote" over Planned Parenthood *by upholding their oath to obey the Constitution*. No, instead keep stealing from us in a larger amount of money, just send it to other organizations.

There's not a damn thing in the U.S. Constitution about women's issues, men's or Latino issues. The whole purpose behind creating the U.S. Constitution was to breathe life into creating a Congress and setting the rules and requirements for elected officials; president, U.S. House and U.S. Senate. Congress's job would be to take care of things that need to be uniform: trade, commerce, the ability to issue a formal declaration of war and so forth, **not social issues.**

The death of a real education in this country has produced such ignorance on what the U.S. Congress can and cannot legislate that worked for centuries **until special interest groups began buying the favors of Congress who would sell their own mother to get reelected.**

Pelosi & her Brassiere Brigade, January 8, 2007, my column

This last pretend election cycle, voters heard the same old recycled mantra from female incumbents and candidates. The Sisterhood of Sycophants relentless carping on "women's issues" in furtherance of "empowering women," "for the children," and "building the community" (pure communism). What absolute bilge. The feminization of Congress has been destroying constitutional government for decades, running America into oceans of unpayable debt and *breeding generations of helpless women, whining for mother government to take care of them and their every need.*

The U.S. Constitution, specifically Article 1, Section 8, specifically enumerates the only areas where Congress can legislate. There are no "women's issues" in that section of the Constitution. That also eliminates education, altering the Second Amendment, after-school programs, studies for breast feeding, child care and a thousand other areas where women in elected office have been unconstitutionally introducing and passing bills for decades. Corrupt presidents sign them into law for votes to keep their party in power. The resultant laws have saddled all of us with unpayable debt.

Once these constitutionally challenged females are sworn in, the first thing they do is play mommy by introducing legislation that's in violation of the supreme law of the land and the prissy, sissy men serving in Congress go along with it because they're so brassiere whipped, they no longer have the courage to stand up to flakes like Senator Patty Pancake Murray.

The communist agenda has been advanced by the Brassiere Brigade in Congress who made a $million promise$ to loot the public treasury and hand it over to struggling women voters, further weaning them onto the government baby bottle. This, of course, makes the voter dependent upon the largess of that Brassiere Brigade member of Congress, ensuring their vote for the next pretend election." [End excerpt from my column.]

Every state in the Union has Medicaid, which provides medical care for the truly poor or those who have fallen on hard times. Private organizations like Planned Parenthood are in it for the money – YOUR money illegally stolen by politicians in both parties for votes. While I have never applied for Medicaid in my life, I do support the small amount of taxes levied *by my state* to help those who absolutely need it. *But, it should only be temporary, not a way of life.*

Women who demand full funding for Planned Parenthood and any member of Congress including that vile man in the White House don't give a tinker's dam about selling baby parts, tissue or murdering the most innocent of souls.

Watch this video (https://www.youtube.com/embed/fKyljukBE70). You will see through modern technology an unborn baby at 32 days is developing arms and legs – *before* most women know they're pregnant. LOOK and see the truth. From conception to birth. Abortion IS murder. *Killing them at two, three months or 20 weeks is infanticide.* Killing them and then selling their tissue or body parts is so horrifying even I run out of words. Why do you think "pro-choice" advocates fight to keep pictures of an abortion away from the public eye?

On November 2, 2015, the person in the White House signed a massive budget with trillions in unconstitutional spending – including Planned Parenthood. That bill takes the budget *past the 2016 elections* for all those phony cons who call themselves pro-life conservatives in the U.S. House and Senate. Despite the grizzly videos of Planned Parenthood selling body parts, PP is going to get funded for another two years. I challenge anyone who has listened to witless females on the boob tube or Internet proclaim PP didn't do what was caught on video, to look at all the videos – unedited – if you can stomach such barbarism: www.centerformedicalprogress.org/cmp/investigative-footage/

Any member of Congress who voted to continue funding Planned Parenthood is guilty of violating the oath they took to uphold the U.S. Constitution. But, it seems no one gives a damn anymore about that document. It's all about votes come every election. That new budget raised the debt ceiling, added $80 BILLION in new "discretionary" funding, hundreds of billions in of all you've read in this book in violation of every member of Congress' oath to uphold the Constitution. **A half billion in more borrowed debt to give to a private corporation worth a billion dollars, Planned Parenthood.**

Every day in this country an average of **3,300** of those tiny little innocents you see in the video above are murdered in their mother's wound with HER consent.

Links:
1. PepsiCo Says It Will Halt Use of Aborted Fetal Cells in Flavor Research
2. Top 12 Reasons to Defund Planned Parenthood Now
3. Twelve Out of Twelve Recent Studies Show Abortion Linked to Breast Cancer
4. Recent Studies Confirm Women Face Depression After Abortion, Other Problems
5. Study Links Abortion With Depression, PTSD, and Drug Abuse

There is only one solution: All federal funding for Planned Parenthood must be stopped. Congress has zero authority to steal the fruits of your labor to give to any private sector organization, group or club. It is precisely this type of unconstitutional spending that has driven this country to the brink of bankruptcy.

14

Fukushima: On-Going Crime Against Humanity

On March 11, 2011, there was a nuclear disaster at the Fukushima Nuclear Power Plant over in Japan which resulted in a nuclear meltdown of three of the plant's six nuclear reactors. It's known as the Fukushima Daiichi Nuclear Disaster.

And it's still a disaster that is devastating both to the surrounding area and the Pacific Ocean. That nuclear plant was hit by a tsunami triggered by a 9.0 earthquake. *The results were predictable due to the location of the plant.* The next day radioactive material began releasing. Although the Chernobyl nuclear disaster in April 1986 has always been considered the worst, many scientists now think Fukushima is worse because of the circumstances. Fukushima was mishandled from day one to the level of gross mismanagement and cover up.

While media coverage here in the U.S. was extensive at the time, it eventually drifted off the front pages of newspapers and cable news networks after a short time. After all, Japanese officials declared things were under control; propaganda that has been repeated all over the Internet for years. Fukushima has pretty much become a forgotten incident. Not for the Japanese people – not after that day and for decades and generations to come. I have prayed for all the lost souls and the citizens over there who will continue to suffer from radiation poisoning. But, should we be concerned? Has or will the effects of Fukushima hit the U.S.?

Why the Fukushima disaster is worse than Chernobyl

"Some scientists say Fukushima is worse than the 1986 Chernobyl accident, with which it shares a maximum level-7 rating on the sliding scale of nuclear disasters. One of the most prominent of them is Dr. Helen Caldicott, an Australian physician and long-time anti-nuclear activist who warns of "horrors to come" in Fukushima. Chris Busby, a professor at the University of Ulster known for his alarmist views, generated controversy during a Japan visit last month when he said the disaster would result in more than 1 million deaths. "Fukushima is still boiling its radionuclides all over Japan," he said. "Chernobyl went up in one go. So Fukushima is worse."

"The official line is that the accident at the plant is winding down and radiation levels outside of the exclusion zone and designated 'hot spots' are safe. 'But many experts warn that the crisis is just beginning. Professor Tim Mousseau, a biological scientist who has spent more than a decade researching the genetic impact of radiation around Chernobyl, says he worries that many people in Fukushima are 'burying their heads in the sand.' His Chernobyl research concluded that biodiversity and the numbers of insects and spiders had shrunk inside the irradiated zone, and the bird population showed evidence of genetic defects, including smaller brain sizes. 'The truth is that we don't have sufficient data to provide accurate information on the long-term impact,' he says. 'What we can say, though, is that there are very likely to be very significant long-term health impact from prolonged exposure." [1]

Here's but a small sample of what we all need to know:

Fukushima radiation detected in bluefin tuna on California coast, May 29, 2012, *CNN*

"The bluefin spawn off Japan, and many migrate across the Pacific Ocean. Tissue samples taken from 15 bluefin caught in August, five months after the meltdowns at Fukushima Daiichi, all contained reactor byproducts cesium-134 and cesium-137 at levels that produced radiation about 3% higher than natural background sources – but well below levels considered dangerous for human consumption, the researchers say. "Cesium-137 has a radioactive half-life of about 30 years, and traces of the isotope still persist from above-ground nuclear bomb tests in the 1950s and '60s. But cesium-134, which has a half-life of only two years, "is inarguably from Fukushima Daiichi," Stanford University marine ecologist Dan Madigan told CNN." [2]

That was in 2012. By August 2013, Fukushima was pouring 300 TONS of contaminated water into the ocean EVERY day:

"In the weeks after the disaster, the government allowed Tepco to dump tens of thousands of tonnes of contaminated water into the

Pacific in an emergency move. But the escalation of the crisis raises the risk of an even longer and more expensive clean-up, already forecast to take more than 40 years and cost $11 billion. The admission further dents the credibility of Tepco, criticized for its failure to prepare for the tsunami and earthquake, for a confused response to the disaster and for covering up shortcomings. "We think that the volume of water (leaking into the Pacific) is about 300 tonnes a day," said Yushi Yoneyama, an official with the Minister of Economy, Trade and Industry, which oversees energy policy." [3]

Tritium soaring in water at No. 1 plant (July 2013): "A Nuclear Regulation Authority official recently said contaminated groundwater from the plant, which is being fed cooling water from outside, may be seeping into the ocean and that the matter must be addressed carefully because data is limited." [4] Tritium is a radioactive isotope of hydrogen.

There's no maybe about it: Toxic groundwater reaching sea: NRA (July 2013)

"The Nuclear Regulation Authority said Wednesday it strongly suspects highly radioactive water at the Fukushima No. 1 nuclear power plant is seeping into the ground and contaminating the Pacific Ocean. "We must find the cause of the contamination . . . and put the highest priority on implementing countermeasures," NRA Chairman Shunichi Tanaka told a meeting of the body's commissioners after they had examined recent studies carried out on groundwater samples at the plant that detected high levels of cesium, tritium and other radioactive contamination." [5]

Radioactive Nightmare - Government turns a blind eye as fallout from Fukushima heads our way, July 5, 2012

"Millions of tons of seawater and fresh water have been used to cool the melted cores and spent fuel rods, generating millions of tons of irradiated water. The Kuroshio Current is transporting a significant amount of this escaping radiation from Fukushima Daiichi across the Pacific toward the West Coast..."NOAA suspended testing in the Pacific for Fukushima radiation last summer after concluding that there wasn't any radiation to be detected. "As far as questions about radiation, we are working with radiation experts within the

Environmental Protection Agency and the Department of Energy," NOAA media liaison Keeley Belva said in a Feb. 10 email interview.

"In other words, no federal agency, department or administration is doing anything to sample and analyze water from the Pacific. Fish aren't being tested for contamination, either. 'NOAA is not currently doing further research on seafood,' Belva added. 'NOAA is doing a study related to radiation that is focused on radiation plume modeling.' This lack of testing is disappointing, according to Dan Hirsch, a UC Santa Cruz nuclear policy lecturer and president of the nuclear policy nonprofit Committee to Bridge the Gap, which exposed the Rocketdyne partial meltdowns above the western San Fernando Valley in 1979 and continues to lead the fight to clean up the area today. 'EPA did some special monitoring for a few weeks after the accident began, then shut down the special monitoring,' Hirsch said. 'What monitoring was done was very troubled. Half of the stationary air monitors were broken at the time of the accident. Deployable monitors were ordered but not deployed.'

"Even when the government testing did work, increasingly high levels of radiation seem to have been ignored. The paper also learned that the California Department of Public Health halted monitoring of Fukushima fallout when its Radiologic Health Branch issued its last report on Oct. 10, 2011." [6]

All of these are after Fukushima. Are all of them just a coincidence? Why so many mysteries after Fukushima?

Scientists Confirm Fukushima Radiation in California Kelp, February 7, 2014

"Part of the ongoing 'Kelp Watch 2014' project, government and academic institutions have begun receiving results from samples of Bull Kelp and Giant Kelp collected along the California coast. Despite attempts by the media to downplay the ongoing disaster, the discovery has only confirmed the continued build-up of radiation in West Coast waters. 'We're trying to figure out how much is there and how much is getting into the ecosystem,' said Dr. Matthew Edwards, a professor from San Diego State University. 'Things are linked a little more closely than sometimes we'd like to think. Just because it is on the other side of the world doesn't mean that it doesn't affect us.'"

"The discovery coincides with statements made by researchers at the Institute for Cross-Disciplinary Physics and Complex Systems in Spain, who predicted the early 2014 arrival of Fukushima radiation along the North American West Coast...."Given radiation's ability to bio-accumulate in sea life, many fear that the massive animal die-off along the west coast is related to the continued consumption of radioactive isotopes. Sea stars and sardines have been especially affected, with other strange anomalies such as the discovery of "never before seen" conjoined gray whale calves off the coast of Northern Mexico, sparking increased worry as well." [7]

Fukushima radioactive contamination is rapidly warming North Pacific seawater, September 2014

"These are certainly record high temperature levels. Bob Tisdale, a manmade climate change skeptic, has an excellent summary of this situation here. In March 2014 there was something very unusual occurring in the Northeast (NE) Pacific that might have substantial consequences for biota in the Gulf of Alaska and southward into the subtropics... we see SST departures of 4.5 standard deviations... The anomaly field covers a large region of the N.E. Pacific... The authors of this article have never seen [such] deviations... Something as extraordinary as a 4.5-sigma deviation requires corroboration." [8]

Six sick sea lions found in Sonoma County, February 25, 2015, *The Press Democrat:* "A crisis among California sea lions that has resulted in nearly 1,000 stranded pups and older animals arriving starved and sick on coastal shores has reached the Sonoma Coast, where six animals have been recovered in recent weeks, according to the Marine Mammal Center near Sausalito." [9] Photos of the stranded babies is absolutely heartbreaking.

Gov't Official: Chilling report from Pacific Ocean... "Silence on the seas" — "Quite literally, there isn't any fish" — Japan Professor: Fukushima posing reproduction risk to marine life, ongoing concern over bio-accumulation of radioactive material

"Senator Penelope Wright, Parliament of Australia, Mar 5, 2015 (emphasis added): "Like many others, I read an article in 2013 by Ivan Macfadyen called "The ocean is broken". It was published in *The Sydney Morning Herald*...He is an experienced sailor, so he had the ability to compare his experience then with...other trips. It was chilling. It was heartbreaking really. He had noticed changes in the last years. Basically, he was confronted by the silence that he heard, the silence on the seas, and he realised that this was attributable to the fact that they saw very, very few birds. They also caught very few fish... two fish."

"Interview with Ivan Macfadyen, Talk Radio Europe, May 24, 2015 (at 14:30 in): "The reality was... if I would have had no spare dry food on the boat — relying on fish this time around — we would have starved to death — because, quite literally, there isn't any fish. There's vast tracks where they're just all gone. Where you could fish reliably, they're just not there... I used to fish here on exactly the same course, at exactly the same time of year... the same ocean, on the same course, into the same place — and I could catch fish every day, and for some reason now 10 years later they're all gone."

'Though not discussed in the above interview, Macfadyen has attributed his statement 'The ocean is broken' to the impact of Fukushima:

'Host: What about sea birds and all of that?

'Macfadyen: As you get closer up to Japan they're all gone, they're not there anymore... Everything's all gone, it's just like sailing in a dead sea... there's nothing...

"Host: After Japan you headed [to] America, did you see any impact from...Fukushima?

"Macfadyen: It's dead. That's where I coined the phrase, "The ocean's broken" – because, for thousands of miles, there's nothing. No birds, no fish, no sharks, no dolphins, no turtles... they're not there... all those beautiful creatures, they're just all gone... We'd seen a whale, round about probably 1,000 miles [off] Japan, just lying on the surface with like a big tumor... just behind its head... it looked like it was going to die... it didn't try to get away, it didn't flap its tail, it didn't do anything...It had such a profound effect on me...Just talking about it makes me feel like I want to cry." [10]

"A record 2,250 sea lions, mostly pups, have washed up starving and stranded in Southern California, a 20-fold increase in the level of strandings averaged for the same three-month period over the past decade, and twice the number documented in 2013, the previous worst winter season recorded for Southern California sea lions." *Natural News*, April 22, 2015

A 1,000 Mile Stretch of the Pacific Ocean Has Heated Up Several Degrees and Scientists Don't Know Why, April 13, 2015, Michael Snyder, *endoftheamericandream.com*

"According to two University of Washington scientific research papers that were recently released, a 1,000-mile stretch of the Pacific Ocean has warmed up by several degrees, and nobody seems to know why this is happening...

"Meanwhile, while this has been going on, scientists have also been noticing that sea creatures in the Pacific have been dying in record numbers. In fact, last summer I wrote an article entitled "Why are massive numbers of sea creatures dying along the west coast right now?" Since then, things have continued to get even worse. For instance, it was recently reported that the number of sea lions washing up on Southern California beaches is at an all-time record high...

"A record 2,250 sea lions, mostly pups, have washed up starving and stranded on Southern California beaches so far this year, a worsening phenomenon blamed on warming seas in the region that have disrupted the marine mammals" food supply. "The latest tally, reported on Monday by the National Marine Fisheries Service, is 20 times the level of strandings averaged for the same three-month period over the past decade and twice the number documented in 2013, the previous worst winter season recorded for Southern California sea lions. "And of course fish are being deeply affected as well. Sardines have declined to their lowest level in six decades, and National Geographic says that a whole host of tiny fish species at the bottom of the food chain are dying off rapidly." [11]

Radiation Expert: Enormous amount of contamination flowing from Fukushima will probably imperil entire Pacific Ocean — Threatens other countries, food chain — Absolutely can reach U.S. and Canadian shores, August 12 2013

Title: Fukushima Radiation Leakage Still Going on / Source: CCTV (China Central Television of Beijing)

"Anand Naidoo, CCTV anchor: From what we know about what is going on at the plant right now, is this going to get worse?

"Dr. Janette Sherman, radiation expert: I hate say this, but yes I think it will. And my concern is the enormous amount of radioactive material flowing with the water into the Pacific Ocean. And we know that the ocean flows northward along Alaska and down the coast of Canada and the United States. And I think it probably will imperil the entire Pacific Ocean, and the sea life that's in it.

"Naidoo: What you're saying here is that this water can actually reach other shores, can reach other countries as well?

"Sherman: Oh absolutely, we already know that.

"Naidoo: The radioactive content in this water — does it dissipate, or does it just stay in the water all the time?

"Sherman: Well, both cesium and strontium have a half-life about thirty years. It takes 10 half-lives for each of these isotopes to decay down to nothing. We contaminate the plankton, and that's eaten by shrimp and oysters and fish and mammals. And as most of these move up the food chain they get concentrated. Particularly strontium-90 gets concentrated in the bones." [12]

NBC: Sea creatures swarming ashore from San Diego to San Francisco, June 19, 2015 [13]

CBS: Millions of dead blanketing miles of coastline, "...like a red carpet... 12-16 inches thick... never seen anything like this" — *ABC*: We wonder if they're sick, or it's something in ocean? Scientists don't have an explanation.

"*NBC* (Weather Channel) transcript, Jun 16, 2015 (emphasis added): "From San Diego to San Francisco, creatures from the sea are swarming ashore... large slugs are showing up on Bay Area beaches... In the San Diego area, local beaches have taken on a reddish tint... crabs have washed ashore."

"*NBC* (Weather Channel), Jun 16, 2015: A pair of bizarre invasions have left California beachgoers perplexed... Large purple blobs... known as sea hares [and] hundreds of miles to the south... tuna crabs washed ashore.

ABC News transcript, Jun 16, 2015: "Like something from a science fiction movie, the invasion of the purple blob... [Experts] tell us it's unusual to see these slugs show up [over] an extended period of time. Morgan Dill: "We've been seeing them wash up since September, going all through winter, and now even more in spring. Perhaps it's because of the warmer water?" The slugs are among the creatures that have been mysteriously showing up on land. A number of whales have been beached in the area recently.'

CBS News, Jun 17, 2015:" Millions of red tuna crabs invade California... overwhelming beaches in Orange County... Ben Tracy says these crabs are trying to tell us something... crabs are so thick in places... "It looked like a red carpet — a good foot-to-16 inches thick. It kinda took me back, [I've never seen anything like this before]."

CBS LA, Jun 16, 2015: "Countless red tuna crabs have washed ashore... covering the Orange County coastline... conditions few [fisherman] have seen in their lifetimes."

10 giant whales found dead in Pacific off US coast — Victims of "mysterious affliction" — Mass die-off of walruses and seabirds reported nearby — Experts: "Something out of the ordinary is happening" — "Really perplexing... We're at a loss... Maybe whales ran into a toxin".

Kodiak Daily Mirror, Jun 19, 2015: "At least nine fin whales have been found floating dead... the exact numbers are still unknown... Daily Mirror columnist Zoya Saltonstall also photographed a dead fin whale at the mouth of Afognak Bay around the last week of May. She said she was told that a "very young fin whale calf" was also found dead, floating nearby. "There were long black and white stripes along the whale's body and it was bloated and swollen," she said.

Prof. Kate Wynne, Univ. of Alaska marine mammal specialist: "It is an unusual and mysterious event... We rarely see more than one fin whale carcass every couple of years... It is really perplexing... They appear to have all died around the same time... We are asking people to watch for, report and photograph dead birds, fish or anything that seems unusual... So far there is no "smoking gun" in this environmental mystery."

Wynne: "The fact that the carcasses are intact, it rules out killer whale predation — but other than that, we're at a loss... It suggests that there's something, maybe a feeding group of fin whales ran into a toxin or bio-toxin."

Wynne: "It is hard to trace a source when dealing only with evidence in the aftermath."

Deborah Mercy, communications coordinator at the University of Alaska Fairbanks: "They don't know exactly how many (whales have died). It's a big mystery."

Bree Witteveen, UAF Sea Grant marine mammal specialist: "It is enough to raise a concern that something unusual, something out of the ordinary is happening."

Andrea Medeiros, U.S. Fish and Wildlife Service: "You don't usually see large mortality events in that area... I don't know if there's a connection or not [between all the bird, walrus, and whale deaths]." [14]

Mass death of seabirds in Western U.S. is "unprecedented" – unexplained changes within ocean to blame, May 19, 2015

OCEAN HEALTH – "In the storm debris littering a Washington State shoreline, Bonnie Wood saw something grisly: the mangled bodies of dozens of scraggly young seabirds. In the storm debris littering a Washington State shoreline, Bonnie Wood saw something grisly: the mangled bodies of dozens of scraggly young seabirds. Walking half a mile along the beach at Twin Harbors State Park on Wednesday, Wood spotted more than 130 carcasses of juvenile Cassin's auklets—the blue-footed, palm-size victims of what is becoming one of the largest mass die-offs of seabirds ever recorded. "It was so distressing," recalled Wood, a volunteer who patrols Pacific Northwest beaches looking for dead or stranded birds. "They were just everywhere. Every ten yards we'd find another ten bodies of these sweet little things."

"Cassin's auklets are tiny diving seabirds that look like puffballs. They feed on animal plankton and build their nests by burrowing in the dirt on offshore islands. Their total population, from the Baja Peninsula to Alaska's Aleutian Islands, is estimated at somewhere between 1 million and 3.5 million. Last year, beginning about Halloween, thousands of juvenile auklets started washing ashore dead from California's Farallon Islands to Haida Gwaii (also known as the Queen Charlotte Islands) off central British Columbia. Since then the deaths haven't stopped. Researchers are wondering if the die-off might spread to other birds or even fish. "This is just massive, massive, unprecedented," said Julia Parrish, a University of Washington seabird ecologist who oversees the Coastal Observation and Seabird Survey Team (COASST), a program that has tracked West Coast seabird deaths for almost 20 years." [15]

Unprecedented emergency statewide fishing closures enacted in Pacific Northwest — "We've never had to do anything like this" — "Very alarming" mass die-offs linked to disease outbreak — Nearly 100% infection rate in some areas — Rotting gills, distended bellies

KTVZ, Jul 16, 2015 (emphasis added): "Restricting fishing in Oregon streams and rivers for the first time ever… Oregon Department of Fish & Wildlife announced it's taking drastic measures… they've never had to do this before… ODFW: "We're starting to see fish kills in more places than we typically do. This is a pretty extreme set of conditions."

Statesman Journal, Jul 16, 2015: "[ODFW is taking] an unprecedented step… The move comes on the heels of multiple fish die-offs… "We've never had to do anything like this before — we're in new territory," said [ODFW"s] Bruce McIntosh."

Mail Tribune (Oregon), Jul 16, 2015: Emergency fishing closures go statewide

Spokesman Review, Jul 17, 2015: "Washington Fish and Wildlife Department officials are enacting fishing restrictions involving 38 rivers… emergency rules take effect on Saturday."

AP, Jul 9, 2015: "Fisheries biologist Rod French said [dead salmon] appeared to have been infected with a gill rot disease".

The Oregonian, Jul 10, 2015: "Scores of dead salmon are washing ashore… mortality rates are rapidly rising for juvenile fish near John Day Dam… [French] said it appears the fish are dying from a bacterial infection… "It's very alarming that we're seeing them this early," he said... [Paul Wagner, NOAA fisheries biologist] called it a head scratcher. The die-offs seem to be associated with disease, he said."

Siskiyou Daily (Calif.), May 19, 2015: "Klamath Fish Health Assessment Team has raised its level of alert... due to an increased detection of a deadly disease.... Chinook salmon tested in two reaches of the Klamath River... reached a 100-percent prevalence of infection [for] one of the deadliest salmon diseases... [Juveniles] have been found with... distended bellies, pale-colored gill and gill erosion... [N]ear the Scott and Klamath rivers confluence... 86 out of 120 showing distended bellies and 87 out of 114 showing pale gills..."

OPB, Jun 9, 2015: "More than half of the 3-inch long Chinook in the [Klamath River] traps are either dead or showing signs of a serious parasitic infection... nearly 100 percent of Chinook caught in this fish trap in early May were infected."

KATU (Portland), Jul 10, 2015: "Salmon and trout, even sturgeon, are dying like never before... on the Deschutes, Santiam, Mackenzie, Clackamas, and other rivers."

KGW (Portland), Jul 7, 2015: "It just seems like it's getting worse... the issue certainly hasn't improved since we reported on it 2 weeks ago... Chinook salmon, even some sturgeon, continue to wash up... Several fishermen I spoke with down here today, well they're worried... Pretty much everywhere you look... dead fish... Starting last month, Chinook salmon began washing up... far short of their spawning grounds... It's all the talk among local fisherman, "I've lived here about 25 years, and I'm an avid fisherman. I've never seen any fish like this on the bank as much as I've seen this year."

KOIN (Portland), Jun 19, 2015: "Is this a really big concern right now? Very much so... "I've never seen it like that before" The Chinook are on their way back from the ocean... Fishermen are coming up empty and are worried." [16]

I lived in California 40 years. Through earthquakes and droughts. Scientists are saying all this could be because of the big drought in California, others are saying warming water in the Pacific Ocean. Can't be Fukushima, so it must be just a coincidence.

Sickened by service: More US sailors claim cancer from helping at Fukushima, December 20, 2013, *FOX News*

"When the USS Ronald Reagan responded to the tsunami that struck Japan in March 2011, Navy sailors including Quartermaster Maurice Enis gladly pitched in with rescue efforts. But months later, while still serving aboard the aircraft carrier, he began to notice strange lumps all over his body. Testing revealed he'd been poisoned with radiation, and his illness would get worse. And his fiancé and fellow Reagan quartermaster, Jamie Plym, who also spent several months helping near the Fukushima nuclear power plant, also began to develop frightening symptoms, including chronic bronchitis and hemorrhaging.

"They and 49 other U.S. Navy members who served aboard the Reagan and sister ship the USS Essex now trace illnesses including thyroid and testicular cancers, leukemia and brain tumors to the time spent aboard the massive ship, whose desalination system pulled in seawater that was used for drinking, cooking and bathing. In a lawsuit filed against Tokyo Electric Power Company (TEPCO), the plaintiffs claim the power company delayed telling the U.S. Navy the tsunami had caused a nuclear meltdown, sending huge amounts of contaminated water into the sea and, ultimately, into the ship's water system." [17]

As of July 21, 2015, three sailors have died. In an interview with the attorney presenting 250+ sailors, Charles Bonner says. "We had one of the sailors who came home and impregnated his wife. They gave birth to a little baby born with brain cancer and cancer down the spine, lived for two years, and just died in March of this year."

Of course they were lied to; they were told it was safe and now sailors are dead. Many more have developed different forms of cancer. It wasn't safe and now our sailors along with all those poor souls over there in Japan who have been suffering and will for decades just to keep the true extent of that disaster from the world. You can watch the interview with Bonner on the Internet. Just type in a search engine: USS Reagan Sailors Sue for Nuclear Justice You Tube

Five years into that disaster and still no one over there seems to know what they're doing. All that contaminated water sitting *in an earthquake zone*. Okuma, Fukushima prefecture, northeastern Japan lies on what's known as the "Ring of Fire" — an arc of earthquake and volcanic zones that stretches around the Pacific Rim. Good place to build a nuclear power plant where 90 percent of the world's quakes occur in that region. On September 19, 2013, a 5.3 magnitude earthquake hit Fukushima. Wait until another 9.0 hits.

WUS 2015 Impacts of the Fukushima nuclear accident: 4 years later. Arnie Gundersen, Chief Engineer at Fairewinds Energy Education, World Uranium Symposium, April 2015 (21:15 in): "[Chernobyl's] core never hit groundwater, that core stayed in the building and remained dry. We have 3 nuclear cores in contact with groundwater." [18]

In May 2015, the UN says TEPCO might have to dump all that contaminated water into the Pacific Ocean. Let us hope countries like the United States and others strenuously objected to such lunacy.

West Coast of North America to be Slammed by 2016 with 80% As Much Fukushima Radiation As Japan, June 10, 2015. "A professor from Japan's Fukushima University Institute of Environmental Radioactivity (Michio Aoyama) told Kyodo in April that the West Coast of North America will be hit with around 800 terabecquerels of Cesium- 137 by 2016. EneNews notes that this is 80% of the cesium-137 deposited in Japan by Fukushima, according to the company which runs Fukushima, Tepco...And we've noted for years that there is no real testing of Fukushima radiation by any government agency." [19]

What's being done over here in the U.S.? The California Coastal Commission is involved in clean-up for which the Japanese government and TEPCO should foot all the bills for cleaning up Fukushima debris where ever it's found. Alaska, Canada, Hawaii, you name it, tons and tons of debris has washed up so far.

Leading Scientist On Fukushima Radiation Hitting West Coast of North America: "No One Is Measuring So Therefore We Should Be Alarmed", January 26, 2014

"Ken Buessler is the head scientist at Woods Hole in Massachusetts, one of the world's top ocean science institutions. Much of Buessler's career has focused on measuring radioactive particles in the ocean, and he's been studying groundwater and ocean samples in and around Fukushima since the accident in March of 2011. Buessler has consistently tried to downplay the risks from Fukushima, and yet even he admits that we won't know unless we test. Buessler noted this week:

"The predictions are rather low and are not of direct concern, but no one makes measurements of these isotopes along the [West] coast. No one is measuring so therefore we should be alarmed. I really try to take the approach that we shouldn't trivialize the risks of radiation and shouldn't be overly alarmed.

"Buessler said last week: What we don't really know is how fast and how much is being transported across the Pacific. Yes, models tell us it will be safe, yes the levels we expect off the US West Coast and Canada we expect to be low, but we need measurements — especially now, as the plume begins to arrive along the West Coast and will actually increase in concentration over the next 1 to 2 years. Despite public concern about the levels, no public agency in the US is monitoring the activities in the Pacific." [20]

Tragically, it appears the worst predictions are underway:

"Mind-blowing" die off of seabirds underway from California to Alaska — Experts: "This is unprecedented... Worst I've ever seen... Why they're dying, I'm still baffled" — "Every bird we're seeing is starving to death... Basically withering away" — "Catastrophic molting" due to unknown cause – a small sampling. (For the full list in the article see Endnotes at back of book)

"San Francisco Chronicle, Oct 15, 2015 (emphasis added): [T]housands of common murres... have been found dead... "all signs point to starvation from a lack of forage fish," [Marine ecologist Kirsten Lindquist] said, adding that the same problem has been documented along the Oregon, Washington and Alaska coastlines... many endemic marine birds and mammals are suffering.

"International Bird Rescue, Sep 22, 2015: An unprecedented number of exhausted, hungry seabirds continue to flood International Bird Rescue's San Francisco Bay Center... The sight of so many starving seabirds has raised red flags among seabird scientists...

"Santa Cruz Sentinel, Sep 25, 2015: A troubling number of starved and weak seabirds are washing ashore on beaches from the Monterey Bay to Alaska... "There's been die-offs in the past, but this is one of the worst ones I've ever seen," said Lupin Egan, an animal technician... "it's been really crazy," said spokesman Russ Curtis. "They're really sick — just feather and bone."

"At Waddell and Greyhound (Rock) beaches, I saw the most murres I've ever seen in 10 years," said Cori Gibble, seabird health coordinator with the UC Davis Wildlife Health Center in Santa Cruz. "You see them on the tide line. They're kind of strewn all over the beaches... It's been a really strange year."

"ABC San Francisco, Sep 22, 2015: The number of birds being delivered to the rescue center daily is the number that usually comes over the entirety of a month, center officials said. "The sheer number of birds we're seeing is pretty mind-blowing" Curtis said. "This is unprecedented. Sometimes we get spikes and it dissipates. But it has not stopped."

"Sacramento Bee, Sep 24, 2015: Rescue center overwhelmed with starving seabirds... Fairfield rescue center has seen 25 times more common murres than normal... Across Northern California... malnourished seabirds have been appearing in alarming numbers, some shrunken to little more than feather and bone... The murres" presence is significant to scientists because they're considered a marker species, whose movements and numbers signal changes in the ocean's food supply... "Our gut tells us there is something going on in the marine environment." Some of the birds that are being brought into the center are showing symptoms of catastrophic molting, where large patches of their bodies are missing feathers, said Kelly Berry, wildlife manager with the center. The cause is unknown."

"Santa Cruz Sentinel, Sep 2, 2015: A huge influx of weak, starving seabirds have been overwhelming a Fairfield bird rescue center... "They're like the canaries in the coal mines," Curtis said, the first ones to tell us if... there's something wrong with our environment."

"KTVU, Sep 25 2015: Up and down the West Coast, thousands of starving sea birds are washing up... [The murres] resemble penguins, but can fly... "They are washing up extremely skinny... They're

starving to death," lead rehabilitation technician Isabel Luevano told *KTVU*... "they're basically withering away" More heron and egret hatchlings have needed care this summer as well." [21]

To even suggest this might be from Fukushima is to invite being called a conspiracy nut. Is he a nut, too?

Nuclear Engineer: "Alarm bells" are going off over Fukushima plume coming to US West Coast — People will be dying from radiation that's flowing across Pacific — Massive amounts of nuclear waste are flowing into ocean every day, and will for more than a century — "We've contaminated the biggest source of water on planet, and there's no way to stop it", enenews.com, March 7, 2016

"Nuclear engineer Arnie Gundersen: Massive amounts of radiation continue to enter Japan's water and air, and the Pacific Ocean, daily… Due to its triple meltdowns and the unmitigable radioactive releases, Fukushima Daiichi will continue to bleed radiation into the Pacific Ocean for more than a century… There is no road map to follow with directions to stop the ongoing debacle."

California's New Desalination Plant Wins International Award, April 24, 2016, *Breitbart*. The new $1 billion-dollar desalinization plant in Carlsbad, California (which I had the opportunity to see) is open and pumping millions and millions of gallons of water out of the Pacific Ocean every day: "The largest seawater desalination plant in the nation, it started commercial operations in December 2015 and is providing the San Diego region with a drought-proof water supply during one of the most severe droughts in California's recorded history."

One problem: Desalinization cannot remove all radiation from the water.

This is also very telling and should concern everyone, October 3, 2015: Unpublished gov't map shows massive plume of Fukushima radioactive material just off West Coast of North America. You'll have to bring it up on your computer. Just type "Unpublished gov't map shows massive plume of Fukushima radioactive material just off West Coast of North America" into a search engine and the enenews.com article and map will come up.

28 Signs That the West Coast Is Being Absolutely Fried With Nuclear Radiation From Fukushima, March 10, 2016, *Global Research*:

"Ultimately, all of this nuclear radiation will outlive all of us by a very wide margin. They are saying that it could take up to 40 years to clean up the Fukushima disaster, and meanwhile countless innocent people will develop cancer and other health problems as a result of exposure to high levels of nuclear radiation. We are talking about a nuclear disaster that is absolutely unprecedented, and it is constantly getting worse. The following are 28 signs that the west coast of North America is being absolutely fried with nuclear radiation from Fukushima". Type the title into a search engine to read the horror.

I have no doubt some testing is going on at universities up and down the Pacific Coast. Private organizations are doing what the U.S. government should be doing. This web site will show you the ongoing spread of radiation across the Pacific and its evolving impacts on the ocean. http://ourradioactiveocean.org/

According to the State of Alaska's Environmental Health: "The U.S. Food & Drug Administration (FDA) is the lead agency on food safety. Both FDA-regulated food products imported from Japan and domestic food products, including U.S. seafood, have been tested. FDA has found no evidence that radionuclides of health concern from the Japanese nuclear power plant disaster are present in the U.S. food supply."

Believe them?

According the much of the mainstream press, radiation from Fukushima has shown up in Canada and the Pacific Ocean but the levels are so low, you shouldn't worry about it. Nothing to see, move on. Really?

"Millions of salmon mysteriously just disappear" off West Coast — Expert: "Literally within 2 days it disappeared, it just crashed… I have never ever seen, nor can I explain" that — "One of the worst seasons ever" — "Disturbing… Serious trouble… Very dramatic", November 4, 2015, *Enenews*

Our oceans provide us with so many wonderful things besides beautiful mammals, heavenly beaches and delicious fish of all kinds for consumption. They also provide critical plant life. Too many do not appreciate the importance of all sea life. **TEPCO and the Japanese government are guilty of a monstrous crime against humanity and they still haven't taken responsibility.**

If you live in California, Oregon, Washington State or Canada (Pacific side), you need to contact your state representative and ask if your state's health department is monitoring and testing things like fish, water, soil and air samples. Is your state working with big universities in their monitoring and testing? What are the results? Why isn't more being publicized to the citizens of those states – especially farmers? Is river water being tested on a regular basis?

This is nothing to smirk at and it's certainly not some "flaky" issue cooked up by conspiracy nuts. There's been a conspiracy alright and it's to keep the American people in the dark. Out of sight, out of mind might seem like a good idea, but a lot of suffering has been going on since that earthquake. As scientists have said, Fukushima is unprecedented. In April 2011, Chernobyl was still leaking. Effects from Fukushima will be felt for a long time to come.

15

Federal Drug Administration (FDA) = Federal Death Administration

The Federal Drug Administration's web site makes the following claim: Protecting and Promoting Your Health

Nothing could be further from the truth. In fact, the FDA is one of the most corrupt, incompetent agencies of the federal government. **They are mass murderers sanctioned by the U.S. Congress.**

The American people have grown up with so many federal alphabet soup agencies, they've become immune to the dastardly deeds done by these unelected officials – except when it hits them personally. When I refer to the FDA, I don't mean the Federal Drug Administration, I mean the Federal Death Administration. That agency derives its jurisdiction from treaties and has been getting away with destroying people's health for decades, and in too many cases, the result is death. The FDA is nothing more than another out of control agency answerable to no one because of big money.

Every year more and more drugs given the stamp of approval by the Federal Death Administration have proven fatal. Only after enough Americans die or thousands have their health destroyed, does the FDA pull some of these dangerous drugs:

October 8, 2007, FDA pulls Drug for Stomach Ills Is Pulled from the Market: Drug for Stomach Ills Is Pulled from the Market: Zelnorm: "WASHINGTON, March 30 — "The maker of Zelnorm, a medicine that treats irritable bowel syndrome, withdrew the drug from the market today after federal drug officials concluded that it could increase the risks of heart attacks and strokes." [1]

Pain Killer Bextra Pulled from Market

WASHINGTON — "The painkiller Bextra was taken off the market Thursday, and the government wants similar prescription drugs to carry the strongest possible warnings about increased risk of heart attack and stroke among the millions of people who rely on them. Pfizer Inc. suspended sales of Bextra in the United States and the European Union at the request of the Food and Drug Administration and European regulators. The company said that the FDA, in seeking Bextra's withdrawal, cited a risk of serious, sometimes fatal, skin reactions to Bextra on top of the risks shared by other similar drugs." [2]

As a matter of fact, in 2014, 35 FDA approved drugs were yanked from the market. Thousands of deaths, heart attacks, strokes, miscarriages. Reading through the list makes you sick. Some of the drugs listed were on the market for decades killing and maiming before the FDA pulled them off the market. [2A]

Parkinson's disease drug pulled from market: "The FDA pulled a Parkinson's drug from the market after reports of heart valve damage in more than a dozen patients. Pergolide is sold under the name Permax and is believed to raise the risk of heart valve damage by 20 percent." [3]

Baycol, a cholesterol-lowering drug: "Why it was taken off the market: Reports of sometimes fatal rhabdomyolysis—a severe muscle condition. All statins cause rare cases of rhabdomyolysis, but Baycol patients experienced it at a significantly higher rate than patients on other statins. The FDA received reports of 31 deaths related to Baycol." [3]

FDA Approves Potentially Disastrous Cholesterol-Lowering Drug, August 19, 2015

"One in three Americans aged 40 and over take a cholesterol-lowering statin drug, and nearly half of people over age 75 are on them, despite their risks, and the fact that "high" cholesterol is not always the enemy it's made out to be. Statins have a long list of side effects, and may even lead to the very problem you're trying to avoid — heart disease — as the drug inhibits both Coenzyme Q10 and vitamin K2. Statins also reduce squalene, which can raise your risk of immune system dysfunction.

"(The depletion of CoQ10 caused by the drug is why statins can increase your risk of acute heart failure. So if you're taking a statin drug, you simply MUST take Coenzyme Q10 or ubiquinol as a supplement. You cannot get enough of it through your diet.) Now, the drug industry is rolling out yet another cholesterol-lowering medication that may turn out to be even worse than statins." [3A] I highly encourage everyone read that article on Dr. Mercola's web site – one of the very best sites on the Internet to get the truth about drugs and natural remedies that actually work instead of more pills.

NeutroSpec: "What it is: NeutroSpec is an antibody labeled with a radioactive marker that was used to diagnose appendicitis in patients that show some but not all of the clinical signs of appendicitis. Why it was taken off the market: While the agent was on the market, 17 patients who received NeutroSpec experienced life-threatening side effects soon after it was injected, including shortness of breath, low blood pressure, and cardiac and pulmonary arrest. Two patients died." [3]

Avandia Maker Hid Risks for Years, Probe Finds

"The maker of controversial diabetes drug Avandia knew for around a decade that the medication increased risks of heart problems in patients but covered up that fact from the public, according to a Senate Finance Committee probe. Internal company emails showed GlaxoSmithKline "attempted to downplay scientific findings about the safety of Avandia as far back as 2000," according to a committee press release.

"According to a New York Times report Tuesday, SmithKline Beecham began testing on the drug in 1999 to see how it compared to a rival pill, the Takeda-manufactured Actos. The results showed signs that Avandia posed a heart risk.

"In a March 29, 2001 e-mail about the study, SmithKline executive Dr. Martin I. Freed wrote: "This was done for the U.S. business, way under the radar. Per Sr. Mgmt request, these data should not see the light of day to anyone outside of GSK." The company became GlaxoSmithKline after a 2000 merger." [4]

Avandia Lawsuits – May 2014

"Serious cardiovascular side effects and potentially life-threatening complications from the diabetes drug Avandia prompted tens of thousands of patients in the United States to file lawsuits against GlaxoSmithKline, the drug's manufacturer. GlaxoSmithKline could face up to $6 billion in liability for side effects litigation. According to a scientist for the U.S. Food and Drug Administration (FDA), Avandia is linked to as many as 100,000 heart attacks. Clinical studies show that the drug increases the risk of heart attack by 43 percent and can double the risk of heart failure after one year of treatment...

"More than 50,000 Avandia lawsuits have been filed in state and federal court across the United States, citing GlaxoSmithKline's failure to inform patients about potentially life-threatening symptoms, including stroke, heart failure, heart attack, bone fractures, vision loss and death, that have been linked to Avandia treatment." [5]

Pfizer Paid $896 Million in Prempro Settlements – June 2012

June 19 (Bloomberg) – "Pfizer Inc., the world's largest drugmaker, said in a securities filing that it has paid $896 million to resolve about 60 percent of the cases alleging its menopause drugs caused cancer in women. Pfizer has now settled about 6,000 lawsuits that claim Prempro and other hormone-replacement drugs caused breast cancer, and it has set aside an additional $330 million to resolve the remaining 4,000 suits, according to a filing with the U.S. Securities and Exchange Commission.

"The reserve means New York-based Pfizer has committed more than $1.2 billion to resolving claims that its Wyeth and Pharmacia & Upjohn units failed to properly warn women about the menopause drugs" health risk...More than 6 million women took Prempro and related menopause drugs to treat symptoms including hot flashes and mood swings before a 2002 study highlighted their links to cancer. Wyeth's sales of the medicines, which are still on the market, exceeded $2 billion before the release of the Women's Health Initiative, a study sponsored by the National Institutes of Health." [6]

April 24, 2007. 70 women die each year from cancer after taking HRT. "But the UK-sponsored Million Women Study now suggests HRT resulted in 1,300 extra cases of ovarian cancer between 1991 and 2005. Of these women, 1,000 died of the disease." [7]

2008: Wyeth, Pfizer ordered to pay $27 million in punitive damages. "A Little Rock, Ark., federal jury found Wyeth Pharmaceuticals and

Upjohn (a Pfizer unit) liable for $27 million in punitive damages to Donna Scroggin, who sued the drug manufacturers in 2004 after developing breast cancer after taking hormone replacement therapy. The award includes $19.3 million from Wyeth and $7.7 from Upjohn.

"Wyeth manufactures Premarin, an estrogen replacement, and Prempro, which is a combination of estrogen and progestin. These, along with Upjohn's Provera, which contains progestin, are commonly prescribed to treat the unpleasant effects of menopause...About 25 million American women use hormone replacement therapy (HRT) to ease the discomfort of menopause. There are about 5,300 similar cases pending across the country for Premarin and Prempro." [8]

Here's a news flash: Those products are still on the market. I've never taken any form of HRT and am truly thankful I was given guidance by a friend (a female surgeon) who educated me how to go through menopause naturally.

The 25 million women who use HRT's in this country just might be "concerned" they will end up dead from breast and/or cervical cancer. I don't understand why anyone would take these drugs **once you read the side effects**: "Long-term treatment with Prempro may increase your risk of breast cancer, heart attack, or stroke." (http://www.drugs.com/prempro.html)

To help with hot flashes? Perhaps women should try natural supplements (Evening Primrose Oil, Dong Quai, Black Cohash) and a good 100% progesterone cream.

(I use what I believe to be the best on the market: ProgesterAll [9] I have to give this disclaimer: I'm not a doctor nor am I making a medical referral here. I wouldn't want armed federal agents from the Department of (Homeland) Fatherland Security to storm my home and charge me with some federal crime, i.e., prescribing natural supplements without approval from ghouls at the FDA.)

As long as we're on health issues, what about fluoride?

I stopped using any products with fluoride in 1994. Back then it wasn't as easy as it is now to find fluoride free toothpaste and mouthwash. Since then our dentists have not used any fluoride products on our teeth or gums by my request. There are a million articles and probably a few hundred books on the dangers of fluoride the U.S. government has known about for longer than I've been alive. Government agencies are experts in keeping the truth from the American people. The case of Dr. William Marcus, Ph.D., employed and fired by the EPA is a prime example.

Why did the EPA fire Dr. Marcus? This is taken directly from the judge's decision and order. You can read the entire document on line by simply typing in the case title below.

Marcus v. United States Environmental Protection Agency, 92-TSC-5 (ALJ Dec. 3, 1992), U.S. Department of Labor Office of Administrative Law Judges 800 K Street, N.W. Washington, D.C. 20001-8002.

"Dr. William Marcus (Complainant) alleges that he was subjected to a hostile work environment and later terminated because of a memo he drafted and released that warned of potential harm from the use of fluoride, contrary to the U.S. Environmental Protection Agency's official position concerning the safety of fluoride use."

The EPA made this man's life hell because he told the truth. The allegations made by the EPA to justify his termination were not sustained by the court. Dr. Marcus was given his job back, back pay and a measly $50,000 for compensatory damages. For all they put Dr. Marcus through, it should have been more. On the FDA's web site is this propaganda: Health Claim Notification for Fluoridated Water and Reduced Risk of Dental Caries

"Recommendation for Using Fluoride to Prevent and Control Dental Caries in the U.S. (Centers for Disease Control, 2001):

"Widespread use of fluoride has been a major factor in the decline in the prevalence and severity of dental caries (i.e., tooth decay) in the United States and other economically developed countries. When used appropriately, fluoride is both safe and effective in preventing and controlling dental caries. All U.S. residents are likely exposed to some degree of fluoride, which is available from multiple sources." (Summary section, page 1)

"Continue and extend fluoridation of community drinking water: Community water fluoridation is a safe, effective, and inexpensive way to prevent dental caries. This modality benefits persons in all age groups and of all SES, ..." (Recommendation section, page 24)

"Oral Health in America: A Report of the Surgeon General (2000):

"Community water fluoridation is safe and effective in preventing dental caries in both children and adults. Water fluoridation benefits all residents served by community water supplies regardless of their social or economic status. Professional and individual measures, including the use of fluoride mouth rinses, gels, dentifrices, and dietary supplements and the application of dental sealants, are additional means of preventing dental caries." (Executive summary)

"Review of Fluoride: Benefits and Risks (Public Health Service, 1991):

"Extensive studies over the past 50 years have established that individuals whose drinking water is fluoridated show a reduction in dental caries. Although the comparative degree of measurable benefit has been reduced recently as other fluoride sources have become available in non-fluoride areas, the benefits of water fluoridation are still clearly evident." (Conclusions section, page 87) [10]

BULL. It's nothing more than propaganda. To say I was shocked when I read the public press release below is putting it mildly, but I thank them for stepping forward with the truth.

That press release is too many pages to reproduce here, but *I highly encourage you to read the entire analysis.* Just type the title in bold below into a search engine.

NTEU Chapter 280 - U.S. Environmental Protection Agency, National Headquarters, Ben Franklin Station, Box 7672, Washington, D.C. 20044, http://www.nteu280.org

"Why EPA Headquarters" Union of Scientists Opposes Fluoridation."

"The following documents why our union, formerly National Federation of Federal Employees Local 2050 and since April 1998 Chapter 280 of the National Treasury Employees Union, took the stand it did opposing fluoridation of drinking water supplies. Our union is comprised of and represents the approximately 1500 scientists, lawyers, engineers and other professional employees at EPA Headquarters here in Washington, D.C...

"The type of cancer of particular concern with fluoride, although not the only type, is osteosarcoma, especially in males. The National Toxicology Program conducted a two-year study in which rats and mice were given sodium fluoride in drinking water. The positive result of that study (in which malignancies in tissues other than bone were also observed), particularly in male rats, is convergent with a host of data from tests showing fluoride's ability to cause mutations (a principal "trigger" mechanism for inducing a cell to become cancerous) and data showing increases in osteosarcomas in young men in New Jersey, Washington and Iowa based on their drinking fluoridated water. It was his analysis, repeated statements about all these and other incriminating cancer data, and his requests for an independent, unbiased evaluation of them that got Dr. Marcus fired.

"Bone pathology other than cancer is a concern as well. An excellent review of this issue was published by Diesendorf et al. in 1997. Five epidemiology studies have shown a higher rate of hip fractures in fluoridated vs. non-fluoridated communities. Crippling skeletal fluorosis was the endpoint used by EPA to set its primary drinking water standard in 1986, and the ethical deficiencies in that standard setting process prompted our union to join the Natural Resources Defense Council in opposing the standard in court, as mentioned above.

"The implication for the general public of these calculations is clear. Recent, peer-reviewed toxicity data, when applied to EPA's standard method for controlling risks from toxic chemicals, require an immediate halt to the use of the nation's drinking water reservoirs as disposal sites for the toxic waste of the phosphate fertilizer industry.

"This document was prepared on behalf of the National Treasury Employees Union Chapter 280 by Chapter Senior Vice-President, J. William Hirzy, Ph.D. For more information, please call Dr. Hirzy at 202-260-4683." [The extensive list of End Note Literature Citations and Other Citations isn't reproduced here for brevity, but you can read them on line: http://www.nteu280.org/Issues/Fluoride/NTEU280-Fluoride.htm]

Vioxx Killed Half a Million? The Facts Are Grim. – Mike Ferrara, *The Legal Examiner*

"It's looking more and more likely that the Merck painkiller Vioxx, the blockbuster drug suspected of having caused more than 55,000 deaths from stroke and heart attack before being withdrawn from the market in 2004, actually killed many more people than we previously thought...."The FDA studies had proven that use of Vioxx led to deaths from cardiovascular diseases such as heart attacks and strokes, and these were exactly the factors driving the changes in national mortality rates."…(Attribution: *The Week*)

"The numbers suggest that Vioxx may have caused more than 500,000 premature deaths. This is so far beyond the 3,468 that were named in Merck's class action settlement for $4.85 billion in 2007 that it boggles the mind. Further investigation is clearly needed to determine just what effect Vioxx had on the almost uniquely elderly population that took it. And Merck needs to be held accountable for the colossal harms it has caused." [11]

All of the above were approved by the FDA and considered safe.

I opened this chapter charging the FDA as mass murderers. Add up all the deaths and believe me, this is just the tip of the ice berg. More people have died as a result of "safe" drugs above approved by the FDA than died on 9/11 and the Viet Nam "era". The numbers don't lie.

On the front page of the FDAs web site, www.fda.gov, there is a box to click on for Recalls. Pages and pages and pages of product and drug recall. While researching this book, I also found on their web site a story titled: FDA China Office's Lixia Wang Wins Award for HHS Locally-Employed Staff with this: "During that time, she also supported the FDA response to emerging problems associated with melamine in dairy and pet products, and worked to address contaminated blood thinner sourced from China."

With massive unemployment here in OUR country, big pharmaceutical companies who are anti-American workers use cheap labor in Communist China. For decades it's been an endless recall not only of tainted pills coming out of Communist China, but dog and cat products killing them here in the U.S.

In 2013, this was one of many headlines: The FDA Has No Idea Why Jerky Treats Are Killing Hundreds of Dogs – 600 dogs and 10 cats have died after eating the treats. "Federal animal health officials announced Tuesday that Chinese jerky treats have caused a mysterious illness outbreak in more than 3,600 dogs (and ten cats) and the death of about 600 pets."

Petco pulls pet treats from China suspected of killing, sickening thousands, January 6, 2015: "Petco said Monday it has removed all remaining Chinese-made dog and cat treats from its website and stores nationwide because of concerns they have sickened thousands of pets and killed more than 1,000 dogs in the U.S. since 2007."

I now have only two dogs; they will be the last dogs in my lifetime due to my age. My beautiful, sweet West Highland Terrier, Miss Muffin, died of kidney failure on May 13, 2016. All my babies are rescue dogs, thrown out on the street like garbage. **I've never fed them anything that comes from communist China**. Go on the Internet and look up "natural dog treats" and you'll find several web sites that give recipes for making doggie treats that are 100% safe for your muggers. Just think of all the money you'll save! Who knows, if enough Americans stop buying any dog or cat treats from communist China, perhaps some of those recipes might end up at PetsMart or Petco **creating even more jobs for Americans instead of communists.**

In August of 2007, Mattell recalled 19 million toys manufactured in Communist China. Toy cars with lead paint. In 2009, this story hit the headlines but you probably didn't see it on your "trustworthy" nightly news: Made in China: Seven toxic imports from The Week, Dec. 11, 2009:

"Toxic dog food – A number of American pet food companies began recalling a wide range of Chinese-made products in March 2007 after discovering that they contained melamine, a chemical that causes kidney failure. According to reports, the melamine was intentionally added by some Chinese companies to boost the appearance of protein in product tests. More than 4,000 Americans reported the death of a dog or cat due to the tainted food....

"Dangerous ginger – In July 2007, the California Department of Health issued a caution to grocery stores and consumers after abnormally high levels of the pesticide aldicarb sulfoxide were found on ginger imported from China. According to the FDA, exposure to aldicarb sulfoxide can cause "flu-like symptoms," including nausea, headache, and blurred vision, while higher levels can cause, among other things, excessive sweating, salivation, and twitching.

Tainted Toys: Virtually all mass market toys in the U.S. are made in China—and in recent years a not-insubstantial portion of them have proved hazardous. In 2007, 467 different types of toys made in China were recalled—including a slew of toys containing lead paint, which can harm brain development in children. Among the most notable were some of the immensely popular Thomas & Friends wooden train engines and cars." [12]

How many more Americans will die, have strokes or suffer life-long medical problems from deadly chemicals and treatments approved by the FDA? The U.S. Congress has oversight of the FDA and EPA and **through decades of endless committee hearings and millions of complaints from the American people NOTHING has changed.**

Too many members in Congress who also own stock in pharmaceutical companies, continue to pass legislation to protect their big $$ donors and dividend checks, while parents try to cope with sick or dying children they love so much damaged by "safe" drugs and vaccines approved by the FDA. Do you not cry for them? Congress has given these drug peddlers immunity more times than you can imagine to protect them from lawsuits.

Is the head of the FDA (past and present) ever held accountable? NO. They just resign and move on to another lucrative job if there's some heat. How about their lackeys? NO. You can sue the federal government, but it's a nightmare. Why should we the people continue paying taxes for settlements when the people who caused the problem (FDA) are never held accountable? The honchos at the FDA who do the approving of these deadly cocktails walk around with impunity because they know from past history that Congress will not hold them accountable.

However, Larry Klayman is about to hold a former FDA Commissioner and others accountable since Congress does nothing but look the other way. For those not familiar with Larry, he's an attorney with an impressive track record going after the liars and crooks in Washington, DC. You can visit his web site at:

www.freedomwatchusa.org/klayman

In January 2016, Larry filed a lawsuit against Former FDA commissioner Hamburg, Johnson & Johnson and others. He filed under the Racketeering and Corrupt Organizations Act (RICO), the Lanham Act, for alleged racketeering and other claims over a dangerous drug called Levaquin.

"According to Klayman, "Obama administration appointee, former FDA Commissioner Dr. Margaret Hamburg, is at the heart of this scandal, and her husband Peter Brown, co-CEO of Renaissance Technologies, L.L.C., a major New York hedge fund. While Dr. Hamburg was head of the FDA, her husband profited enormously from as much as half a billion dollars in Johnson & Johnson stock, the maker of Levaquin, held by Renaissance Technologies."

"The complaint alleges Dr. Hamburg and her husband and others at Renaissance Technologies, L.L.C., conspired with Johnson & Johnson and other defendants to suppress information about Levaquin's harmful effects. "To reveal it would have not only harmed Johnson & Johnson's profits, but invite significant lawsuits, driving Johnson & Johnson stock price downward, thereby financially harming Dr. Hamburg, her husband and Renaissance Technologies" profits. Plaintiffs were unwitting victims, suffering from a variety of medical conditions, some of which were just recently disclosed at an FDA Advisory Committee Hearing November 5, 2015." *PR Newswire.com*

The FDA pulls these deadly drugs off the market. Then, the head of the FDA goes back to business as usual, power lunches in DC with his big pharma house buddies and is NEVER held accountable. I'm sure you've seen TV commercial after commercial for law firms advertising if you've been harmed or have a loved one die from some pill approved by the FDA or "vaginal mesh patch" that's maimed women. Never ending and never a true crackdown or solution by Congress to hold the FDA accountable.

It's long past time to abolish the FDA, period. It is one of the most corrupt, dangerous agencies sucking down billions that has approved drugs that end up killing tens of thousands. I know there are good people who work for the FDA, but as an agency it is rotten and corrupt. For God's sake. Killing 500,000 Americans with a drug approved by that venal agency is mass murder! Has one single person in the FDA been held accountable for that episode of mass murder? Not a chance. **How many more coffins is it going to take for the American people to say enough is enough?**

I don't think Americans have any idea just how many complaints there are about the drugs they approve, how many deaths from drugs they approve or how many lawsuits on behalf of doctors who cure cancer without killing people through chemotherapy have made their way through the courts. No one is suggesting there should be no oversight or testing of drugs.

Just like the VA, the FDA is another out of control agency that will never work. Congress after Congress, president after president have all chanted how they will reform the FDA to be more fair, blah, blah, blah. *It hasn't happened and it won't happen.* No, it's time to get rid of it and I don't care how loud the left bellows, it's time to stop killing Americans with FDA approved drugs. *It's time to stop persecuting alternative medicine doctors who heal people instead of just treat them.* Of course, that's not what the big pharmaceutical companies want because their motto is: **There's no money in the cure, only the treatment – just like the cancer industry.**

It's time to stop withholding experimental drugs from patients who are dying if they want to take them. It's time to stop the heavy handed regulations of the FDA. A drug manufacturer pays the FDA a half million dollars for each new application and can simply deny that application for no good reason.

I can tell you sure as the sun shines that if the FDA isn't abolished, tens of thousands more Americans will die from various drugs and vaccines hustled by the FDA on behalf of the big pharma houses. Do you want to be the next victim of a drug approved by the FDA? Your child maimed by some vaccine like Merck's HPV?

Abolishing the FDA, FDA Policies Keep People Sick and Create a False Sense of Security by Larry Van Heerden, March 1, 2007

"The Food and Drug Administration (FDA) started out as a bulwark against snake-oil peddling. It has since swung back and forth between hostility and subservience to the drug industry. The FDA seems indifferent to the many deaths its own intransigence has caused and imperious when forced to defend its actions in court, resulting in a system that withholds life-saving drugs from the market, approves dangerous drugs, and denies everyone freedom of choice. The time has come to seriously consider abolishing the FDA...

End the FDA

"The first step to correct these problems is to abolish the FDA, stripping the government of the power to approve drugs (and medical devices) for the market or to remove them from the market. Any rule-making for disclosure and lawsuits for fraud should be devolved to the states...

"In the late 1960s the FDA's Drug Efficacy Study examined the effectiveness of drugs that had been on the market before enactment of mandated pre-market drug testing. As a result of the study, around 300 drugs were removed from the market after being judged ineffective. In a market-driven system, such as the one proposed here, what would prevent the reappearance and wide consumption of worthless or even dangerous drugs?

"One answer is private testing and certification of pharmaceutical drugs along the lines of what Underwriters Laboratories does for household appliances. Several writers have discussed how, in the absence of the current FDA monopoly, private firms could adequately and profitably fill this role." [13]

Abolish the FDA; it's insane, July 27, 2011

"Because of the hundreds of millions of dollars needed for approvals. Dendreon has to charge $90,000 a month for Provenge, a prostate cancer drug. Ironwood will have to charge $100,000 a month for its irritable bowel syndrome drug, is my guess. They have to charge these enormous amounts because they need to recoup the costs of getting the drug through the FDA. The actual gross margins on these drugs are over 80% in most case.

"Let's think about this from a macro level. The president sends 18-year-olds to war in Iraq and actually spends our taxpayer money to send them there and many come back dead or stress disorders. No problem. (BTW, Congress, which is the only body with constitutional authority to declare war, has not done so since 1941). And yet we can't give a 65-year old who has six months to live a drug that will save him because we're afraid he might die? This makes no sense to me....

"Right now many companies with good drugs don't even bother getting them approved in the United States. They either give up when they can't raise the money, or they sell the drugs in other countries. I know of at least one powerful drug (saving it for a later article) that's worked in every test in every other country but can't get it approved here because of the money it takes to get through the FDA.

"The FDA itself is a money-sink for the government. You want to cut the deficit? Start with the FDA." [14]

Money sink for the government is right, but it's also financially benefited members of the bandits in Congress. Member of Congress trade stocks in companies while they are making laws that affect those companies. Members of Congress put hookers to shame in the amount of money they take from lobbyists:

"Pharmaceuticals Invested Nearly $2 billion in Campaign Contributions and Lobbying. Pharmaceutical Industry Money Targeted Key Committees and Incumbents. Pharmaceutical industry contributions were targeted at members of the relevant commerce and tax committee's responsibility for industry regulation. The top ten Senate recipients of industry contributions in 2008 served on the key oversight committees: Appropriations, Budget, Finance, or Commerce. Members of the relevant Senate committees received an average of $210,432 in industry contributions, nearly three times the Senate average of $81,891.

"Nine of the top ten targeted House recipients in 2008 served on the Energy and Commerce or Ways and Means Committees, or in House leadership. Targeted Members received an average of $163,280 in industry contributions, six times the House average. Pharmaceutical industry contributions favored incumbents by a factor of nine to one (89%). Pharmaceutical Industry Contributions Pegged to Key Legislation." [15] And, the list goes on and on.

The Federal Death Administration's 2014 budget was $4.7 billion **borrowed** dollars. Abolishing it would eliminate another massive debt for which there is no money to pay for and put it where it belongs under the state for disclosure and lawsuits and into the private sector for testing. Of course, that won't happen if the same incumbents, both parties, continue to get reelected who have done NOTHING to stop the deaths of tens of thousands of Americans and those who now suffer from serious medical conditions the rest of their lives from FDA approved drugs.

16

Vaccines – Silent Destroyers

There's been a war going on in this country for more than a decade over vaccines, their safety and forcing Americans to give up their right to choose for themselves and children. If the FDA (Federal Death Administration) says they're safe, we should simply act like sheep, line up and get jabbed.

Laws making it mandatory for school children to get shot up before they can go to school have become ubiquitous and oppressive. Lawmakers around this country firmly believe we the people are too stupid to understand this medical issue. If one dares challenge ingredients in vaccines, they are labeled the worn-out "conspiracy nuts". Only those who support every vaccine under the sun and politicians whose favors are bought and paid for by mega pharmaceutical houses understand vaccines. The rest of us are just dummies.

In the pharmaceutical world deaths and maiming people for life is considered acceptable risks because the majority will benefit. That's a fact. Which child or father, mother, sister or brother is it okay to sacrifice under the benefit-to-risk ratio? We the people are nothing more than guinea pigs or lab rats to experiment on "for the good of everyone".

I grew up with four brothers and sisters. I ask my mother what vaccines we had as children. Small pox, polio and DPT: diphtheria, pertussis (whooping cough), and tetanus. No measles vaccine. My daughter was born in 1975 and those are the only vaccines I allowed her to have. Today, unless you load your infant/toddler up with a dozen or more by age 2 they cannot attend one of the government's indoctrination centers they call public schools.

During the measles outbreak hysteria last year, the *LA Times* reported on doctors who will no longer see a child if the parent refuses to shoot them up with MMR cocktails. How shameful. I thought the oath doctors took was to do no harm to their patients?

Some pediatricians in this country are refusing to take children as patients unless they've been shot up – even if it's due to religious beliefs of the parents. In Texas, clinics across the state are refusing to see children who haven't been drowned in a dozen vaccines. Those doctors obviously have no understanding of freedom and liberty nor do they care.

Yes, some vaccines have been very effective and safe. But, that is no longer the case for some of them now regardless how many times some bought and paid for member of your state legislature or Congress says otherwise.

Measles vaccines kill more than measles, February 7, 2015

WASHINGTON – "While those opposing mandatory vaccination for measles are widely portrayed as ignorant and even dangerous by some officials, pundits and even news media accounts, Centers for Disease Control records reveal a startling truth – while no one has died of measles in the U.S. in the last 12 years, 108 have died as a result of the adverse effects of the vaccine in that same time period.

"The death statistics are recorded by Vaccine Adverse Event Reporting System, or VAERS, which captures only a small percentage of the actual number of deaths and other adverse reactions to the vaccine. In addition, 96 of the 108 deaths in that 12-year time period were a result of the MMR vaccine, now the preferred shot for measles immunization. In addition, CDC statistic show measles deaths were rare in the U.S. before the vaccine became widely used.

"The adverse reactions to the measles vaccines are much more widespread than death, points out Dr. Lee Hieb, an orthopaedic surgeon and past president of the Association of American Physicians and Surgeons who has studied vaccines and written about them in medical journals.

"In a recent commentary in WND, the author "Surviving the Medical Meltdown: Your Guide to Living Through the Disaster of Obamacare," revealed that since 2005 there have been 86 deaths from the MMR vaccine – 68 of them children under the age of 3 years old.

In addition, there have been nearly 2,000 disabled, according to the VAERS data. As a result of her study, Hieb questions the zealous push for mandatory measles vaccination." [1]

When I was growing up my siblings and I got the measles. We stayed home from school, got over it and went back to school. The outbreak earlier of measles in this country turned into a hysterical circus with politicians and school officials clucking around like the bubonic plague was taking over the country. As a result, hundreds of thousands of parents allowed their children to get yet another unnecessary chemical cocktail.

Back in 2007, our then governor of Texas, Ricky Perry, decided he would force the very dangerous HPV (Human papillomavirus) vaccine on young girls and women in our state. Ricky, who took campaign money from the manufacturer issued an Executive Order in 2007 to force all young girls in this state to take the deadly cocktail known as the HPV vaccine. Our legislature held an emergency session and over rode his EO.

The HPV vaccine known as Gardasil has been touted as safe and absolutely necessary to keep girls and young women from getting cervical cancer. *HPV is a sexually transmitted disease not a communicable disease like tuberculosis and therefore does not affect the general public.* Gardasil was studied less than two years and fast tracked. Has it been safe?

213 Women Who Took Gardasil Suffered Permanent Disability, January 14, 2012, Dr. Mercola

"Naomi Snell, a 28-year-old woman in Melbourne, Australia, is leading a class-action civil lawsuit against drug maker Merck after suffering autoimmune and neurological complications following injections with the HPV vaccine, Gardasil. After receiving the first of three doses of the vaccine, Naomi suffered convulsions, severe back and neck pain, and lost her ability to walk.

"Unfortunately, stories like Naomi's are all too common in relation to Gardasil. One of the vaccine injury cases featured in the movie The Greater Good is that of Gabi Swank, a 15-year-old honor student who decided to get the Gardasil vaccine after seeing a "Be One Less" Gardasil vaccine advertisement on TV. "Like so many young girls, she wasn't warned about any possible side effects when she got the shots, which are given as a series of three injections.

"At the time the documentary was filmed, she had already suffered two strokes and experienced partial paralysis. She also lost part of her vision and today suffers frequent seizures. When she was in high school, many days she had to use a wheelchair to get around school due to muscle pain and chronic fatigue. A similar reaction happened to 13-year-old Jenny Tetlock, who began seeing signs of trouble just one month after she was vaccinated against the HPV virus. Fifteen months later, a degenerative muscle disease left her nearly completely paralyzed.

"The documents obtained from the U.S. Food and Drug Administration (FDA) under the provisions of the Freedom of Information Act (FOIA) detail 26 new deaths reported to the government following HPV vaccination between September 1, 2010 and September 15, 2011. That's 26 reported deaths of young, previously healthy, girls after Gardasil vaccination in just one year." [2]

$47 Mil to Get More Adolescents on Gardasil, October 24, 2013, Judicial Watch

"The continued use of taxpayer dollars to provide this drug is baffling considering its history. The government's own records document dozens of deaths associated with Gardasil—manufactured by pharmaceutical giant Merck—and seizures, blindness, speech problems, pancreatic and short-term memory loss in thousands of cases. Incredibly, the Food and Drug Administration (FDA) fast-tracked Gardasil's approval and the CDC keeps recommending it for girls starting at age 9. Read all about it in a special report published by JW.

"Earlier this year JW uncovered documents from the Department of Health and Human Services (HHS) revealing that its National Vaccine Injury Compensation Program (VICP) has awarded nearly $6 million to dozens of victims in claims made against the very HPV vaccine it is pushing on children. To date 200 claims have been filed with VICP, with barely half adjudicated, according to the documents obtained by JW.

"Nevertheless, the Obama administration continues advocating this dangerous vaccine and lying to the public about its severe repercussions. In fact, just a few months ago the CDC issued a video that outrageously claims Gardasil's side effects are limited to "dizziness and stomach aches." The 13-minuted DVD endorsing the three-dose HPV vaccine series was designed to reach "underserved areas" and minority populations." [3]

HPV Vaccine Mandated for All Rhode Island Middle School Students, August 3, 2015

"The Associated Press has reported that starting this coming school year, middle school students must receive the jab unless they have medical or religious exemptions (both are difficult to obtain): Tricia Washburn, chief of the office of immunization for the Rhode Island Department of Health, said the Centers for Disease Control found no safety concerns with the vaccine.

"The bottom line is that HPV is the most sexually transmitted disease in the U.S." she said. "We are interested in protecting the public health. We feel it shouldn't be treated any differently than any of the other vaccines recommended by the CDC."

"Actually, this vaccine in particular should be treated differently than other vaccines. By different, I mean extra banned – or for a person to have the secured freedom to opt-out. It has been shown to be deadly, injurious, and unnecessary given how the immune system can overcome warts. (Quick facts about HPV) By the summer of 2009, this fast-tracked vaccine already caused more than 15,000 thousand reports of vaccine reactions, including more than 3,000 injuries and 48 deaths...

"So much more can be said about the dangers of the HPV vaccine. At least one documentary is devoted to shining light on the damage this abominable jab has done to ravage young women's lives and rob them of bright futures. Not to mention, it was just reported on mainstream news this past Spring, that Gardasil vaccine can cause infection with higher risk HPV strain. Isn't that akin to giving someone cancer? [4] I encourage parents to read the entire article.

Merck's Former Doctor Predicts that Gardasil will Become the Greatest Medical Scandal of All Time, September 28, 2015, www.healthimpactnews.com

'Dr. Dalbergue (pictured above), a former pharmaceutical industry physician with Gardasil manufacturer Merck, was interviewed in the April 2014 issue of the French magazine Principes de Santé (Health Principles).

Excerpts: 'The full extent of the Gardasil scandal needs to be assessed: everyone knew when this vaccine was released on the American market that it would prove to be worthless! Diane Harper, a major opinion leader in the United States, was one of the first to blow the whistle, pointing out the fraud and scam of it all.

'Gardasil is useless and costs a fortune! In addition, decision-makers at all levels are aware of it! Cases of Guillain-Barré syndrome, paralysis of the lower limbs, vaccine-induced MS and vaccine-induced encephalitis can be found, whatever the vaccine.

'I predict that Gardasil will become the greatest medical scandal of all times because at some point in time, the evidence will add up to prove that this vaccine, technical and scientific feat that it may be, has absolutely no effect on cervical cancer and that all the very many adverse effects which destroy lives and even kill, serve no other purpose than to generate profit for the manufacturers. There is far too much financial interest for these medicines to be withdrawn...

'U.S. law prevents anyone from suing Merck or any other vaccine manufacturer as the U.S. Congress gave them total immunity from civil lawsuits in 1986, and that legal protection which gives them a free pass to put as many vaccines into the market as they want to, was upheld by the U.S. Supreme Court in 2011. In addition, the National Institute of Health receives royalties from the sales of Gardasil.' [5]

Also, this is a *must* read on the same person but with more explosive information:

http://www.collective-evolution.com/2015/01/25/mercks-former-doctor-predicts-gardasil-to-become-the-greatest-medical-scandal-of-all-time/

"One of the best examples (out of many) comes from Lucija Tomljenovic, PhD, from the Neural Dynamics Research Group in the Department of Ophthalmology and Visual Sciences at the University of British Columbia. In 2011 she obtained documents which reveal that vaccine manufacturers, pharmaceutical companies, and health authorities have known about the multiple dangers associated with vaccines but have chosen to withhold them from the public. The documents were obtained from the UK Department of Health (DH) and the Joint Committee on Vaccination and Immunization (JCVI), who advise the Secretaries of State for Health in the UK about diseases preventable through immunizations. You can read those documents here."

I have not had the flu but a few times in my life. In 1993, I got the "flu bug" bad. My husband took me to the doctor in the Denver metro area. He said I had the Beijing flu and was going to give me a shot and some pills. I said no. He was very upset because a couple of people died from it and I must get the shot! I said no and John took me home. For eight days I was really sick, but with bed rest, lots of liquids, vitamins and homemade soup (which I cooked sick as I was) I recovered.

You see, I had just finished reading *"Murder by Injection: The Medical Conspiracy Against America"* and no way was I going to take that shot. That was the last time I had the flu; 23 years ago this December. I've never had a flu shot and never will. That book is free on line:

http://www.bibliotecapleyades.net/archivos_pdf/murderinjection.pdf

The "Measles outbreak – Disneyland" piece mentioned earlier also said this: "Though the vaccines are said to be 99% effective, a recent anti-vaccination movement in the US has falsely linked autism to the vaccines. Scientists have thoroughly decried the claims as false and misleading." Really?

The media has saturated this country, electronic and boob tube, with all the experts and their personal opinions on why everyone should take every vaccine that comes down the pipeline and never ask questions about how safe they are because they're FDA approved. They all cite how science backs up the safety of the dozen or so vaccines forced on infants and toddlers; some on adults if they want to keep their job.

What industry seems to have the most commercials on the boob tube? I would say it's the pill pushers with auto makers coming in second. BIG revenues for *ABC*, *CBS*, *NBC*, *FOX*, *MSNBC*, *CNN* and virtually every other channel on the cable line up.

Why do members of Congress lie about how safe all vaccines are? BIG money. Pharmaceutical companies pour tens of millions into the coffers of congressional incumbents who have allowed the FDA to run amok giving approval for drugs that kill Americans.

The battle over whether or not vaccines can cause autism continues because there's big money at stake. My *personal* opinion after reading a thousand hours of research by qualified individuals *not on the payroll of the U.S. government or one of the big pharma houses* is that they do cause autism. The increase in the number of children who have autism after massive vaccine pushes just isn't a co-incidence. Naturally, my position is the one attacked the most.

One could fill a book on this issue. Many have helped Americans become informed. There are probably thousands of articles and columns on the Internet so parents can research for themselves. The big problem is big media, the "big 3" as well as cable news networks pick and choose what they want you to know.

Since the big pharmaceutical companies paid for the favors of those in Congress to shield them from lawsuits, guess who pays damages for maiming and death as a result of vaccines? You got it – you.

Media Bias Rears Ugly Head in Vaccine Controversy, February 5, 2015, *Accuracy in Media* – very important article

"Going further back in time, consider a program on the link between vaccines and mental problems which was aired by *NBC* in 1994 and featured Katie Couric as a co-host. If there are no problems associated with vaccines, then why did Congress pass the National Childhood Vaccine Injury Act of 1986, which created a national Vaccine Injury Compensation Program?

"Michael Chen of *ABC 10 News* in San Diego reports on one mother whose son suffered a very serious vaccine reaction and was diagnosed with autism, and later Tourette syndrome, obsessive-compulsive disorder and mitochondrial dysfunction. She was awarded $55,000 in damages. Chen reported that since 1988, 15,684 injury and death claims related to vaccines have been submitted to the National Vaccine Injury Compensation Program, and that among those, nearly 4,000 cases received compensation from a federal fund.

"Nearly $2 billion dollars has been paid out to vaccine victims for their injuries. But in response to New Jersey Republican Governor Chris Christie supporting parental choice in vaccines, CNN ran a story saying he had sidestepped "vaccine science."

"*The Washington Pos*t reported in 2008 that candidate Barack Obama had said, "We've seen just a skyrocketing autism rate. Some people are suspicious that it's connected to the vaccines. This person included. The science right now is inconclusive, but we have to research it." The phrase "This person included" was apparently a reference to someone in the audience. Now Obama acts as if all the science is settled. It is total hypocrisy. But the science is not settled." [7]

Say Her Name: Vaccine Victim Hannah Poling, February 10, 2015, *Accuracy In Media* – very important article:

"The number of cases have risen from an estimated one in 5,000 in 1975 to one in 64 today, a more than 600 percent increase. The Centers for Disease Control (CDC) claims it can't identify the cause, but has consistently claimed that the disorder is not linked to the growing number of vaccines required for children...

"There is one name these proponents of mandatory vaccines in the media desperately want to avoid: vaccine victim Hannah Poling. You can search in vain for her name in the recent coverage of alleged vaccine safety.

"Attkisson notes in her book that in 2008, the federal government agreed to pay damages to the family of Hannah Poling, "a child who developed autism after multiple vaccinations." Attkisson explained that the "landmark case" amounted to $1.5 million for the girl the first year and $500,000 each year after. In total, the compensation could amount to $20 million over the child's lifetime. The Poling case was just one of thousands of cases filed in the National Vaccine Injury

Program. But it was selected as a "test case" to evaluate the arguments underlying most of the other vaccine-autism claims.

"Attkisson writes that the case was "ordered sealed, protecting the pharmaceutical vaccine industry and keeping the crucial information hidden from other families who have autistic children and also believe vaccines to be the culprit." But word leaked out. At the time, the head of the federal Centers for Disease Control,which assures the public of vaccine safety, was Dr. Julie Gerberding. After insisting the settlement of the Poling case was not an admission of a direct vaccine-autism link, she left the CDC to become president of vaccines for Merck. Last December she was promoted to executive vice president for strategic communications, global public policy and population health at Merck. [8]

My column: Polio Vaccine, Cancer and Dr. Mary's Monkey, April 26, 2015, my column

One of the reasons I decided to read Dr. Mary's Monkey is because one of my dearest friends, Thelma Taormina, passed away, April 6, 2015, after losing her heroic fight against small cell carcinoma cancer.

Dr. Mary's Monkey is fully footnoted. The author, Edward T. Haslam, went to extraordinary lengths to make sure the reader understands what is speculation and what is fact based on documentation and his research – his personal involvement.

I knew little about monkey viruses until a few years ago. On top of everything else floating around in my head and having had only three vaccines in my life, did I really need to do a bunch of research on monkey viruses? Yes, I did because it's what I do: try to educate and inform my fellow Americans about what is good, what isn't good and why we the people are fed lies about everything affecting our daily lives.

As hardened a cynic as I have become over the past 25 years, Dr. Mary's Monkey truly was frightening. **Why did America suddenly experience a cancer epidemic?** How much do Americans really know about the polio vaccine seventy years ago – about the number of deaths and cover-up and more importantly – why on earth would research scientists use monkey viruses?

Long before I ever heard of Haslam's book, in my research I found the testimony below. I do hope you take the time to read it in full because the American people must know the truth about how we've all been used as guinea pigs while enriching the coffers of prostitute politicians in the Outlaw Congress and morally, ethically bankrupt pharmaceutical companies.

The SV40 Virus: Has Tainted Polio Vaccine Caused an Increase in Cancer? Oral Presentation by Barbara Loe Fisher, Co-founder & President, National Vaccine Information Center, September 10, 2003, Subcommittee on Human Rights and Wellness, U.S. House Government Reform Committee, U.S. House of Representatives, Washington, D.C.: "The SV40 Virus: Has Tainted Polio Vaccine Caused an Increase in Cancer?"

"It was in 1960 that an NIH scientist named Bernice Eddy discovered that rhesus monkey kidney cells used to make the Salk polio vaccine and experimental oral polio vaccines could cause cancer when injected into lab animals. Later that year the cancer-causing virus in the rhesus monkey kidney cells was identified as SV40 or simian virus 40, the 40th monkey virus to be discovered. (Shorter, e. 1987. The Health Century) Sadly, the American people were not told the truth about this in 1960. The SV40 contaminated stocks of Salk polio vaccine were never withdrawn from the market but continued to be given to American children until early 1963 with full knowledge of federal health agencies. Between 1955 and early 1963, nearly 100 million American children had been given polio vaccine contaminated with the monkey virus, SV40. (Institute of Medicine, National Academy of Sciences. 2002. Immunization Safety Review: SV40 Contamination of Polio Vaccine and Cancer. Washington, D.C.: National Academy Press)

"Today, U.S. federal health agencies admit the following two facts: 1. Salk polio vaccine released for public use between 1955 and 1963 was contaminated with SV40; and 2. SV40 has been proven to cause cancer in animals. In fact, at a conference on SV-40 and human cancers held by the National Institutes of Health in 1997, which I attended, there was no disagreement among both government and non-government scientists about these two facts.

"The only disagreement was whether SV40 was actually being identified in the cancerous tumors of children and adults alive today and, if it was, whether the monkey virus was in fact responsible for their cancer. Non-government scientists working in independent labs around the world said, "Yes." But the scientists connected with the U.S. government said "No." (Transcript of FDA, CDC, NIH, NIP, NVPO January 27-28, 1997 Workshop on Simian Virus 40: A Possible Human Polyomavirus)."

Bernice Eddy is covered in Dr. Mary's Monkey. How does that tie in with Lee Harvey Oswald or cancer? What in the world is a Linear Particle Accelerator and what did it have to do with Dr. Mary Sherman's horrible death and Lee Harvey Oswald? Covered in Dr. Mary's Monkey. Available on Amazon.

Americans who seek the truth know that most of the time what evil being done to we the people in America is being done right under our noses. It's just that we don't know what's going on behind the curtain. Like the Infectious Disease Laboratory at the U.S. Public Health Service hospital in New Orleans back in the "60s. How on earth did Lee Harvey Oswald get connected to the secret goings-on - monkey viruses and cancer?

Were there secret experiments going on with the full knowledge of certain individuals in the U.S. government to "develop an anti-cancer vaccine diverted secretly into biological weapons"? My conclusion after reading the book and documents is yes. On page 206, Haslam covers Bernice Eddy's research in a flu vaccine project that morphed into much more dealing with the polio vaccine. Millions and millions of school aged children were given the needle during the time period covered in the book. *The explosion of soft cell cancers and those secret research projects is no coincidence*:

Page 207: "In June 1959 Bernice Eddy, who was still officially assigned to the flu vaccine project, began thinking about the polio vaccine again. This time she was worried about something much deeper than polio. The vaccine's manufacturers had grown their polio viruses on the kidneys of monkeys. And when they removed the polio virus from the monkey's kidneys, they also removed an unknown number of other monkey viruses. The more they looked, the more they found. The medical science of the day knew little about the behavior or consequences of these monkey viruses. But time were changing. Confronted with mounting evidence that some monkey viruses caused cancer, Eddy grew suspicious of the polio vaccine and asked an excruciating question: Had they inoculated an entire generation of Americans with cancer-causing monkey viruses?"

Take the time to read Dr. Mary's Monkey. It will answer so many questions and maybe, just maybe Americans will rise up and tell the Outlaw Congress and members of our state legislatures that we are NOT lab rats. As for the article below, California has recall and should go after every senator in that committee and get them kicked out of the legislature.

"California's SB277 mandatory vaccination bill passes Senate committee after votes rigged, public testimony silenced, April 22, 2015: "After California's vaccine mandate bill SB277 was halted last week with an outcry of public outrage against it, the pro-vaccine mafia machine went to work. Democratic Sens. Ben Allen of Santa Monica and Richard Pan of Sacramento helped pursue a vote rigging agenda to replace seats on the committee with pro-vaccine industry sellouts. A new democrat, Sen. Bill Monning, was chosen to fill a vacant seat, and with his vote in favor of stripping Californians of vaccine exemption rights, SB277 was approved today.

"The California Coalition for Health Choice branded the action as, "a rare act of outright rigging the results..." CCHC's press release also explains, "Adding one vote in favor of the bill wasn't enough. He also removed the Vice Chair of the committee, Senator Huff, an ardent opponent of the bill, and replaced him with Senator Runner." [9]

Tell the Outlaw Congress and our state legislatures we are will NOT line up like cattle to the slaughterhouse for mandatory vaccines and we WILL protect our children and grandchildren against the God-awful cancer epidemic playing out across our country for decades savaging our loved ones to a horrible death.

I do encourage you to read the items below. Just type the title in a search engine (I use www.startpage.com – they don't sell your data like Google and is absolutely secure).

This is MUST read. Truly horrifying: **Exposing the FDA's Vaccine Injury Cover-up: An Interview With Walter Kyle, Esq.**, August 4, 2012

Chemist Says "Media Left Out Horrifying Facts about Measles Shot", Shane Ellison: "One brave father stepped forward to show pictures of his 15-month old son playing with his tool box and scrambling through the house to use them on furniture and toys. Days later he received his MMR shot. 18 years later, he's still in diapers trying to learn his first words.

"I'll risk measles any day over Merck's bullsh*t science. When herd immunity and vaccines are proven failures, you can't use them as evidence to encourage vaccination or to sue a family who refuses to accept the flawed status-quo perpetuated by the pharmaceutically compliant politicians and the media."

Hundreds of children brain damaged by the swine flu vaccine to receive $90 million in financial compensation from UK government, April 20, 2015, *NaturalNews*

Flu shot hoax admitted: "No controlled trials demonstrating a decrease in influenza", January 27, 2015, *Natural News.com*

Big Pharma's Corporate Crimes and Fines: How Can They Get Away With It? February 4, 2015, *NaturalBlaze.com*

How Vaccines Harm Child Brain Development, Dr. Russell Blaylock MD, February 5, 2015: "If childhood vaccines are safe, why are well over half a million vaccinated American children afflicted with autism, while non-vaccinated Amish and Mennonite children rarely suffer from the disorder? Why has the incidence of asthma, allergies, autoimmune disease, Type 1 diabetes and neurological conditions also dramatically increased in vaccinated children? Furthermore, why do obstetricians give pregnant women influenza vaccines that contain a toxic dose of mercury and why are new babies injected with the Hepatitis B vaccine within hours of birth when there is no medical justification for it?"

New Published Study Verifies Andrew Wakefield's Research on Autism – Again (MMR Vaccine Causes Autism), June 21, 2013, *thelibertybeacon.com*

MMR: A mother's victory. The vast majority of doctors say there is no link between the triple jab and autism, but could an Italian court case reignite this controversial debate? June 15, 2010

"At nine months old, Valentino Bocca was as bright as a button. In a favourite family photo, taken by his father, the baby boy wriggles in his mother's arms and laughs for the camera. His parents look at the precious picture often these days. It is a reminder of their only son before they took him on a sunny morning to the local public health clinic for a routine childhood vaccination. Valentino was never the same child after the jab in his arm. He developed autism and, in a landmark judgment, a judge has ruled that his devastating disability was provoked by the inoculation against measles, mumps and rubella (MMR)."

Pharmaceutical Giant –Merck, Has Some Explaining To Do Over Its MMR Vaccination Claims, February 24, 2015

Fast forward, June 11, 2015: **Whistleblowers accuse Merck of withholding info on mumps vaccine**

GAPS Nutritional Program: How a Physician Cured Her Son's Autism, June 31, 2011, *www.articles.mercola.com*. Dr. Campbell is a medical doctor with a postgraduate degree in neurology. She worked as a neurologist and a neurosurgeon for several years before starting a family.

The Real Story Behind the Anti-Vaccine Billboards That Are Going Viral, July 23, 2015

If vaccines don't cause brain damage, why is GlaxoSmithKline paying out $63 million to vaccine victims? July 21, 2015, *Natural News*

Scientist and Stem Cell Expert Says Don't Be So Quick to Believe Vaccines Are Safe, July 24, 2015

What Opened My Eyes to the Problems Vaccines Cause? by: Sherri Tenpenny, DO

March 2015 Settlements in Vaccine Court: 117 Vaccine Injuries and Deaths, September 28, 2015, *healthimpactnews.com*

Study: Flu Vaccine Causes 5.5 Times More Respiratory Infections – A True Vaccinated vs. Unvaccinated Study, September 28, 2015

Former Merck Rep Says Mandatory Vaccination Is For Profit and Not Public Health, August 12, 2015. She will not vaccinate her children.

This one is a long piece but needs to be read. The research and sources are fully footnoted: **VRM: Vaccines Do Contain Aborted Human Fetal Tissue**. Again, just type the title into a search engine and match to the URL: http://vaccineresistancemovement.org/?p=13685

In March 2016, a new documentary, *Vaxxed: From Coverup to Catastrophe*, was released and all hell broke loose. It was to be shown at Robert DeNero's Tribeca film festival but threats and intimidation forced DeNiro to withdraw the showing. DeNero has a son who is autistic – after he was vaccinated. DeNero thought it appropriate that Americans should see all sides of the story. It was the official selection at the 49th Annual Worldfest-Houston International Film Festival, however there would be no showing:

Dear Philippe~ Good Morning…

I wanted you to know that just like DeNiro and Tribeca, we must withdraw our invitation to screen VAXXED! It has been cancelled, and there was no press release about the film… that was scheduled for today, but after very threatening calls late yesterday (Monday) from high Houston Government officials (the first and only time they have ever called in 49 years) – we had no choice but to drop the film. Heavy handed censorship, to say the least… they both threatened severe action against the festival if we showed it, so it is out. Their actions would have cost us more than $100,000 in grants. It does seem a bit of overkill, as I am confident that it will be released Online soon and millions of people can see it.

My Thanks and Best regards, Hunter Todd, Chairman & Founding Director, TEAM WORLDFEST, The 49th Annual WorldFest-Houston

Just what is it the big pharma houses, corrupt members of Congress who line their pockets with big money from pharmaceutical companies and even city governments like Houston don't want you to know? Oh, that's right. All the studies paid for by the very pharma houses that make those deadly cocktails say they're safe!

Is there is solution?

Yes. Vote out any incumbent in your state capitol and Congress who has voted to force toxic vaccines into your body and your children's. Workers all over this country are being threatened with termination if they don't submit to those worthless flu shots. *Your best defense is your natural immune system.*

It's no fun getting old, but I'm so glad I had my daughter before the Gestapo-like crack down on forcing vaccines on children. Truly, I feel for parents today who don't want their child(ren) shot up with dangerous cocktails, but can't afford to home school them.

Despite a massive uproar by we the people over the past 15 years or so regarding the corrupt FDA, all we get from Congress are form letters they will look into it. We hear talk of reform by Congress every couple of years but it hasn't happened and **it won't because of big money** and that's the bottom line.

Abolishing the FDA – Policies Keep People Sick and Create a False Sense of Security, March 1, 2007 – read the entire piece

"In a market-driven system, such as the one proposed here, what would prevent the reappearance and wide consumption of worthless or even dangerous drugs? One answer is private testing and certification of pharmaceutical drugs along the lines of what Underwriters Laboratories does for household appliances. Several writers have discussed how, in the absence of the current FDA monopoly, private firms could adequately and profitably fill this role." [10]

Now, I ask you as so many have in articles and columns: *If all those vaccines are so safe, why did Congress pass the National Childhood Vaccine Injury Act of 1986, which created a national Vaccine Injury Compensation Program?*

Are all the doctors, scientists and other experts who believe some vaccines are dangerous for humans ALL Kool Aids drinkers? Are only those on the government's payroll or who receive federal money right?

Why don't you see anything in the "mainstream" media – including cable networks and the Internet about what you've just read?

All we ever see are cheerleaders for vaccines and any guest who dares bring up an opposing opinion is bitch-slapped and never invited back. This is an election next year. If the same incumbents are reelected for the 5th, 10th or 15th time who support the vaccine disaster nothing will change.

17

Monsanto Must Be Stopped

Monsanto is a huge corporation most Americans don't even think about except when they purchase one of their products. Monsanto manufactures toxic chemicals they swear are safe. Tens of millions of Americans in this country and more around the world use their chemical products without knowing the health hazards.

Monsanto began trying to force genetically modified food crops down the world's throat four years after approval of a patent in 1980, the first of its kind on a living organism. In 1982, the Federal Death Administration (FDA) approved the first GMO altered insulin. In 1994, the first GMO tomatoes hit store shelves. (GMO: genetically modified organisms)

Things rapidly moved from there. Wisely, the European Union in 1997 made mandatory labeling on all GMO food products. Here in the U.S. citizens who fully understand how toxic GMO food is still can't get their states to force mandatory labeling. Why? Big money in the hands of politicians and ignorance. Big money in campaign donations just like TV advertising. Truth doesn't matter. Forget solid science because one mustn't rile those big campaign donors.

By 1999, more than 100 million acres worldwide were planted with GMO seeds. After all, GMO food products have been sold as the way to feed the world! Nothing could be further from the truth.

Because "mainstream" media (*ABC*, *CBS*, *NBC*), including cable networks like *CNN*, *FOX* and *MSNBC,* refuse to cover the atrocities by Monsanto around the world, the majority of Americans know nothing about them. The courts have ruled it's okay for the media to lie to you.

Florida Appeals Court Orders Akre-Wilson Must Pay Trial Costs for $24.3 Billion *Fox* Television; Couple Warns Journalists of Danger to Free Speech, Whistle Blower Protection

"In February 2003, a Florida Court of Appeals unanimously agreed with an assertion by *FOX* News that there is no rule against distorting or falsifying the news in the United States.

"Back in December of 1996, Jane Akre and her husband, Steve Wilson, were hired by *FOX* as a part of the *Fox* 'Investigators' team at WTVT in Tampa Bay, Florida. In 1997 the team began work on a story about bovine growth hormone (BGH), a controversial substance manufactured by Monsanto Corporation. The couple produced a four-part series revealing that there were many health risks related to BGH and that Florida supermarket chains did little to avoid selling milk from cows treated with the hormone, despite assuring customers otherwise.

"According to Akre and Wilson, the station was initially very excited about the series. But within a week, Fox executives and their attorneys wanted the reporters to use statements from Monsanto representatives that the reporters knew were false and to make other revisions to the story that were in direct conflict with the facts. Fox editors then tried to force Akre and Wilson to continue to produce the distorted story. When they refused and threatened to report Fox's actions to the FCC, they were both fired."[1]

It's okay for the media to lie to the American people. Those whistle blowers not only lost their jobs, they were slapped with astronomical trial costs. This is exactly why millions of Americans will spend an extra dollar for a gallon of organic milk: to protect their families from BGH in commercial milk. It's too bad the people in the Tampa Bay, Florida area weren't allowed to see their investigation.

The level to which the compromised media, print and electronic, has fallen is a very sad commentary for the "right to know free press". Take it from a woman kicked to the curb for trying to expose the truth:

Emmy Award Winning Journalist Exposes Corporate Censorship on GMOs and Vaccines in Mainstream Media by Dr. Mercola

"Sharyl Attkisson, a five-time Emmy Award winning investigative journalist whose television career spans more than three decades is one of my personal heroes. She was the reporter who, in 2009, blew the lid off the swine flu media hype, showing the hysteria was completely unfounded and manufactured...

"Intimidation and Harassment of Journalists – True investigative journalists, such as Sharyl, have also become targets of intimidation and harassment. For example, at one point her computer and phone lines were hacked to find out what she was working on.

"I assume there are a handful of journalists who do that sort of critical reporting on the government, and on this administration in particular, that they wanted to watch. They never dreamed I would luck upon the resources to have the computer examined by experts that could find the software they deposited in my computer. This software was proprietary to a government agency, either the Defense Intelligence Agency (DIA), National Security Agency (NSA), Central Intelligence Agency (CIA), or Federal Bureau of Investigation (FBI)…

"They had my keystroke data… They could look at all my files. They used Skype audio – I didn't know this was possible – but they could turn it on invisibly, without you knowing it, to listen into conversations. They could also remove files using Skype… We were able to confirm these highly sophisticated long-term, remote intrusions." [2]

Sharyl Attkisson worked as an investigative correspondent for *CBS News* for 21 years; she resigned on March 10, 2014. She filed a lawsuit in D.C. Superior Court, alleging the U.S. government's "unauthorized and illegal surveillance of the Plaintiff's laptop computers and telephones from 2011-2013." The suit lists as plaintiffs Attkisson, who resigned from *CBS* last year, her husband, James Attkisson, and daughter Sarah Judith Starr Attkisson. Defendants include (former) Attorney General Eric Holder and Postmaster General Patrick Donahoe and "Unknown Names Agents of the United States, in their individual capacities." Those defendants, the suit alleges, violated several constitutional rights, including freedom of the press, freedom of expression and freedom from "unreasonable searches and seizures."

This should NEVER happen here in America. Those who gave their blood to birth this constitutional republic gave we the people the greatest form of government in the history of the world. A Bill of Rights which succinctly state rights we are born with and for which the U.S. government and all of its various cabinets and agencies have no right to violate.

"An able, disinterested, public-spirited press, with trained intelligence to know the right and courage to do it, can preserve that public virtue without which popular government is a sham and a mockery. A cynical, mercenary, demagogic press will produce in time a people as base as itself." Joseph Pulitzer, American Newspaper Publisher

And, so it has come to pass.

But, were Jane Akre and Steve Wilson off-base in their research? People around the globe are sick and dying from a lot of things, but don't know why. Perhaps a 2012 ruling in France might make some re-evaluate their health issues:

LYON/PARIS, Feb 13 (*Reuters*, Feb. 13, 2012) – "A French court on Monday declared U.S. biotech giant Monsanto guilty of chemical poisoning of a French farmer, a judgment that could lend weight to other health claims against pesticides. In the first such case heard in court in France, grain grower Paul Francois, 47, says he suffered neurological problems including memory loss, headaches and stammering after inhaling Monsanto's Lasso weedkiller in 2004."[3]

Now you might think that's just one farmer with health problems looking to make a buck off a mega-billion-dollar company. Not so because it's not just one chemical product sold by Monsanto:

New study reveals how glyphosate in Monsanto's Roundup inhibits natural detoxification in human cells. "(*NaturalNews*, May 2013) "The modern age of industrial agriculture and manufacturing has dumped heavy metals, carninogens, plastics, and pesticides into the environment at alarming rates. These toxins are showing up in most human tissue cells today. One distinct chemical may be trapping these toxins in human cells, limiting the human body's ability to detoxify its own cells. In a new peer reviewed study, this sinister chemical, glyphosate, has been proven to inhibit the human cell's ability to detoxify altogether. Glyphosate, found in Monsanto's Roundup, is being deemed by publishers of the new study "one of the most dangerous chemicals" being unleashed into the environment today."

How glyphosate destroys human cells

"Glyphosate, most commonly found in conventional sugar, corn, soy and wheat products, throws off the cytochrome P450 gene pathway, inhibiting enzyme production in the body. CYP enzymes play a crucial role in detoxifying xenobiotics, which include drugs, carcinogens, and pesticides. By inhibiting this natural detoxification process, glyphosate systematically enhances the damaging effects of other environmental toxins that get in the body. This, in turn, disrupts homeostasis, increases inflammation, and leads to a slow deconstruction of the cellular system. Toxins build up in the gut over time and break down through the intestinal walls, infiltrating blood, and ultimately passing through the brain/blood barrier, damaging neurological function." [4]

More on the study discussed above: Glyphosate's Suppression of Cytochrome P450 Enzymes and Amino Acid Biosynthesis by the Gut Microbiome: Pathways to Modern Diseases states

"Glyphosate, the active ingredient in Roundup®, is the most popular herbicide used worldwide. The industry asserts it is minimally toxic to humans, but here we argue otherwise. Residues are found in the main foods of the Western diet, comprised primarily of sugar, corn, soy and wheat. Glyphosate's inhibition of cytochrome P450 (CYP) enzymes is an overlooked component of its toxicity to mammals. CYP enzymes play crucial roles in biology, one of which is to detoxify xenobiotics. Thus, glyphosate enhances the damaging effects of other food borne chemical residues and environmental toxins. Negative impact on the body is insidious and manifests slowly over time as inflammation damages cellular systems throughout the body. Here, we show how interference with CYP enzymes acts synergistically with disruption of the biosynthesis of aromatic amino acids by gut bacteria, as well as impairment in serum sulfate transport. Consequences are most of the diseases and conditions associated with a Western diet, which include gastrointestinal disorders, obesity, diabetes, heart disease, depression, autism, infertility, cancer and Alzheimer's disease. We explain the documented effects of glyphosate and its ability to induce disease, and we show that glyphosate is the "textbook example" of exogenous semiotic entropy: the disruption of homeostasis by environmental toxins."[5]

3 Studies Proving Toxic Glyphosate Found in Urine, Blood, and Even Breast Milk by Mike Barrett

"Approximately 1 billion pounds of pesticides are sprayed on crops in the United States alone every single year. Thanks to pesticide/herbicide-resistant GMO crops, that number is growing every year. Much of this pesticide spraying contains a toxic ingredient known as glyphosate – the primary poisonous active ingredient in Monsanto's best-selling herbicide RoundUp. Regulators as well as Monsanto claim that this ingredient is excreted from the body, but numerous studies have shown that not only is it causing numerous health problems, but it is showing up in urine samples, blood samples, and even breast milk....

"Very recently, the Organic Consumers Association have demanded that U.S. regulators such as the FDA, EPA, and USDA ban glyphosate as many other communities and even nations have. Why? Because a new piece of research found that the toxic ingredient is actually found in the breast milk of women, leading to damage to underdeveloped human beings." [6]

"On the Offensive" Against Monsanto, France Removes Roundup from Store Shelves

"France will cease over-the-counter sales of agrochemical giant Monsanto's weedkiller brand Roundup, following a recent United Nations report that found the active ingredient, glyphosate, was "probably carcinogenic to humans."

"It's the newest development in the growing international movement against Monsanto in general and Roundup in particular. French Ecology Minister Segolene Royal announced on Sunday that she had instructed garden centers to stop putting the herbicide on the shelves of their self-service aisles, stating, "France must be on the offensive with regards to the banning of pesticides."

"Colombian officials made similar statements in May, when they put a halt to U.S.-backed toxic fumigation of coca fields in the country, noting that a previous ruling by the Colombian Supreme Court called for an end to the aerial spraying program if health concerns over glyphosate were discovered."[7]

More you need to know: GMO Corn – the Poison Plant Everyone Eats

"Jerry Rosman was a pig and cattle farmer, who now is an organic farming consultant as a result of losing his animal-breeding farming business due to GMO corn feedstock interfering with animal husbandry and reproduction—baby piglets and calves. Rosman realized that the GM corn, actually bt-corn, he was feeding his hogs was responsible for sows experiencing false pregnancies. That led to his eventually losing the swine and cattle breeding and farming business. In his ah-ha moment, after realizing what was going on, he said, "If this is happening to our hogs, what's happening to humans?"

"If that's what happened to Mr. Rosman, shouldn't everyone be concerned about GMO bt-corn, which is an ingredient in just about every mass-produced food product sold in the USA? Former pig farmer, now organic farming consultant, Jerry Rosman talks about his experience with GMO corn, the politics of GMOs, and the harassment everyone who speaks out against them receives."[8] Article includes a video interview with Rosman.

Hungary torches 500 hectares of GM corn to eradicate GMOs from food supply

(*NaturalNews*) "When it comes to protecting the public from GMOs, Hungary knows how to get the job done: set fire to the fields growing GM corn!

"Although environmentalists might at first argue about the ramifications of burning so much organic matter right out in the open, the deeper truth is that genetic pollution poses a vastly more serious threat to our world, and burning GM corn is the one sure way to destroy the poisonous genetic code contained in plant tissues...."Lajos Bognar, Hungary's Minister of Rural Development, reported this week that around 500 hectares of GM corn were ordered burned by the government. Hungary has criminalized the planting of genetically modified crops of any kind, and it has repeatedly burned thousands of hectares of illegal GM crops in years past." [9]

Russia Bans GMO Corn Over Cancer Fears as Pressure Builds on Monsanto (*New American Magazine*, October 2012)

"Following an explosive French study suggesting a link between Monsanto's controversial genetically engineered corn and cancer, Russian authorities have temporarily suspended all imports and use of the biotech GMO product until further safety testing can be performed. Officials worldwide are reportedly investigating the matter as well. Russia's consumer-protection agency, known as Rospotrebnadzor, announced the decision last week, saying it had ordered the country's Institute of Nutrition to investigate the recent French university study. The regulatory agency has also reportedly asked the European Union for its views as the European Food Safety Authority vowed to review the research...

"The news out of Moscow quickly prompted headlines around the world as consumer fears over genetically engineered crops reached their highest level yet. But even before Russia's new temporary ban was announced, the embattled American biotech giant was already under attack from California to Europe." [10]

In April 2014, Russia announced it will no longer import any GMO products. Prime Minister Dmitry Medvedev stated: "...the nation has enough space, and enough resources to produce organic food. If the Americans like to eat GMO products, let them eat it then. We don't need to do that; we have enough space and opportunities to produce organic food."

Here is just one example of corporate thuggery by Monsanto against an American farmer. While other countries protect their farmers, here in America hard working family farmers are beaten into the ground:

Corporate Win: Supreme Court Says Monsanto Has "Control Over Product of Life" (May 2013) (Bold emphasis mine)

"The U.S. Supreme Court ruled Monday in favor of biotech giant Monsanto, ordering Indiana farmer Vernon Hugh Bowman, 75, to pay Monsanto more than $84,000 for patent infringement for using second generation Monsanto seeds purchased second hand—a ruling which will have broad implications for the ownership of "life" and farmers" rights in the future.

"In the case, Bowman had purchased soybean seeds from a grain elevator—where seeds are cheaper than freshly engineered Monsanto GE (genetically engineered) seeds and typically used for animal feed rather than for crops. The sources of the seeds Bowman purchased were mixed and **were not labeled**. However, some were "Roundup Ready" patented Monsanto seeds.

"The Supreme Court Justices, who gave Monsanto a warm reception from the start, ruled that Bowman had broken the law because he planted seeds which naturally yielded from the original patented seed products—Monsanto's policies prohibit farmers from saving or reusing seeds from Monsanto born crops. Farmers who use Monsanto's seeds **are forced to buy the high priced new seeds every year**.

"Ahead of the expected ruling, Debbie Barker, Program Director for Save Our Seeds (SOS), and George Kimbrell, staff attorney for Center for Food Safety (CFS), asked in an op-ed earlier this year, "Should anyone, or any corporation, control a product of life?"...The Center for Food Safety released a report in February which shows three corporations control more than half of the global commercial seed market. As a result, from 1995-2011 the average cost to plant 1 acre of soybeans **rose 325%**." [11]

Not only is the consumer hit with higher prices because farmers have to pass along their costs of operation, Americans have become nothing but guinea pigs for mega-corporations who only care about more money:

Genetically modified foods...Are they safe? (Institute for Responsible Technology) December 2013

"The American Academy of Environmental Medicine (AAEM) doesn't think so. The Academy reported that "Several animal studies indicate serious health risks associated with GM food," including infertility, immune problems, accelerated aging, faulty insulin regulation, and changes in major organs and the gastrointestinal system. The AAEM asked physicians to advise patients to avoid GM foods.

"Before the FDA decided to allow GMOs into food without labeling, FDA scientists had repeatedly warned that GM foods can create unpredictable, hard-to-detect side effects, including allergies, toxins, new diseases, and nutritional problems. They urged long-term safety studies, but were ignored.

"Since then, findings include:

Thousands of sheep, buffalo, and goats in India died after grazing on Bt cotton plants

Mice eating GM corn for the long term had fewer, and smaller, babies

More than half the babies of mother rats fed GM soy died within three weeks, and were smaller

Testicle cells of mice and rats on GM soy change significantly

By the third generation, most GM soy-fed hamsters lost the ability to have babies

Rodents fed GM corn and soy showed immune system responses and signs of toxicity

Cooked GM soy contains as much as 7-times the amount of a known soy allergen

Soy allergies skyrocketed by 50% in the UK, soon after GM soy was introduced

The stomach lining of rats fed GM potatoes showed excessive cell growth, a condition that may lead to cancer.

Studies showed organ lesions, altered liver and pancreas cells, changed enzyme levels, etc.

"Unlike safety evaluations for drugs, there are no human clinical trials of GM foods. The only published human feeding experiment revealed that the genetic material inserted into GM soy transfers into bacteria living inside our intestines and continues to function. This means that long after we stop eating GM foods, we may still have their GM proteins produced continuously inside us." [12]

These resources are based on science, but the one recurring theme is the lies by U.S. government agencies to hide the truth from the American people endangering all of us

Altered Genes, Twisted Truth—How GMOs Took Over the Food Supply by Dr. Mercola (Health Freedom Alliance). Reprinted with permission. Dr. Mercola has one of the best web sites on health issues; I purchase some of his supplements.

"Genetically manipulated foods may be one of the most serious threats not only to our environment but to the health and very survival of future generations. Typically, the blame for the promulgation of genetic engineering of our food is placed on chemical companies. But there's actually a hidden back story to how genetically engineered foods were able to reach millions of dinner tables.

"Steven Druker, who you may not be aware of, is the attorney who filed a lawsuit in the late '90s challenging the most important action the U.S. Food and Drug Administration (FDA) has taken in this area: its presumption that genetically engineered (GE) foods are Generally Recognized as Safe (GRAS) and can enter the market without a shred of safety testing.

"However, the evidence clearly reveals that the FDA's GRAS presumption was fraudulent when first announced in 1992 and that it remains fraudulent today. Nonetheless, it has played the central role in allowing inadequately tested GE foods to permeate the American market. There are many components to this story, and Steven is just the man to set the story straight.

"He's written a landmark and historic book *Altered Genes, Twisted Truth*, with the revealing subtitle: How the Venture to Genetically Engineer Our Food Has Subverted Science, Corrupted Government, and Systematically Deceived the Public. If you have even the remotest interest in this topic, I would strongly encourage you to get a copy of this book. It is, without a doubt, the best book on the topic and provides a treasure trove of facts that will help you decimate anyone who believes that GMOs are safe…

"Steven's book goes into that in great depth, and provides an accurate historical record of the irresponsible behavior of many eminent scientists and scientific institutions in the earlier decades of the genetic engineering revolution, long before Monsanto's lackey Michael Taylor and the hordes of revolving door cronies came into the picture.

"It was probably not until about late '94 or '95 that I became aware of genetic engineering, and that it was being used by that point to reconfigure the genetic core of many of our foods. The goal is, ultimately, to reconfigure the genetic core of almost every edible fruit, vegetable, and grain. That's the grand vision. I became very concerned as I learned about this. I've had a long-term interest in eating healthy nutritious food myself, and in protecting the purity of the food. I was involved back in the late 1980s in the campaign to better regulate food irradiation.

"But I too was behind the curve on understanding what was going on with genetically engineered foods, which I think puts things in perspective. So you can see why people still, up to a few years ago, didn't even know that they had been eating genetically engineered food for all these years, and feeding them unknowingly to their kids. It really has blindsided many of us."

Blatant Misrepresentation of US Food Law

"Steven began researching the matter around 1996, and quickly realized that there is a great gap—both then and now—between the claims made by the proponents of GE foods and the actual facts.

"One major concern was the fact that while the US had the strictest and the most rigorous food safety laws in the world in regard to new additives, the FDA had not enforced those laws when it comes to GMOs. Instead, the FDA gave GE foods a free ticket to circumvent the law.

"In May 1992, the FDA made a blanket presumption that GE foods qualified to be categorized "Generally Recognized as Safe" (GRAS). They then said that this meant these foods could be marketed without any safety testing at all.

"That actually is a blatant misrepresentation of US food law, but that was the FDA claim," Steven says. "[They claim] there's an overwhelming "scientific consensus" they're safe, and so safe that they don't need to be tested. Therefore, the FDA let these foods into our market without the requirement of a smidgen of testing."

FDA Scientists Warned of Grave Risks

"Steven decided to launch a lawsuit on his own, and founded a non-profit organization called the Alliance for Bio-Integrity. Fortunately, as word got around, he was contacted by a public interest group in Washington D.C., the International Center for Technology Assessment (ICTA).

"They had a very good legal team and they were very interested in taking this on," he says. "The lawsuit was filed in May 1998, and it quickly accomplished something very major... It forced the FDA, through the discovery process, to hand over more than 44,000 pages of its internal files relevant to the policy that it made on genetically engineered foods."

"It turned out to be a real treasure trove of hidden 'gems' the FDA had undoubtedly hoped would remain hidden for all time. For starters, there were damning memos from FDA scientists assigned to the biotechnology task force, whose job it was to actually analyze and assess genetically engineered foods in terms of both the law and the science, and to do a risk assessment.

"This is probably one of the first scientific risk assessments performed by independent scientists," he notes, adding: "The memos that I was reading were astounding, because...they recognized that there were unusual risks in these foods. I already knew that genetic engineering had the potential to create unexpected and unpredictable new toxins and allergens in these foods. These toxins would be very difficult to detect unless each food was subjected to very rigorous long-term toxicological testing, the likes of which the biotech industry has routinely avoided performing and has been given a pass on by various governments. The surprising thing was not just that they understood these risks, but that they were warning about them in no uncertain terms to their superiors."

FDA Supports Biotechnology Industry as Matter of Policy

"According to the FDA's own admission, the agency has been operating for years under a policy to promote the US biotechnology industry. They decided it was more important to promote the industry and uphold the fragile image of GE foods rather than tell the truth and acknowledge the scientist warnings. So they covered up these warnings. Had Steven not sued, the warnings of the FDA's own scientists still would be unknown to this day.

"We wouldn't know the extent to which the FDA has been lying all these years. But fortunately, we do know now,' he says. 'And what we know is that although the FDA scientists overwhelmingly concluded and warned their superiors that these foods entail unique risks, that they cannot be presumed safe, and that each one of them should be subjected to long-term rigorous toxicological testing, what the public

heard from the FDA was that 'The agency is not aware of any information showing that foods developed by these methods differ from other foods in any meaningful or uniform way."

"Now, it's impossible, I think, for any rational man or woman to read just the sampling of memos from the FDA scientists that are posted on the website of the Alliance for Bio-Integrity... and feel that the FDA's assertion is anything other than a blatant fraud meant to mislead the public, mislead the world, and allow genetically engineered food a free pass to enter the market. It's just an astounding fraud." [13]

[Dr. Mercola's web site is outstanding for accurate information to help all of us better understand these important health issues, www.mercola.com, which is why the government is going after him, again.]

Millions of people around the world have been fighting against GMOs. Success has come slowly. We the people have the absolute right to know about seeds that grow the food we eat. My late husband and I have been eating organic food since 1994; only "free range" beef, poultry and pork. I'm not a pork or beef person, but I do eat a regular diet of fish, chicken and turkey. Cage free eggs. Back then I knew nothing about Monsanto. What I did know from my research convinced me to seek out as much organic vegetables, fruits, dairy and meat/poultry products as I could find.

Back then it wasn't so easy and terribly expensive. As more stores along the Whole Foods concept have opened, even here in W. Texas where I live, organics of all sorts are now available. But, you still have to read the label to make sure they are not GM food stuffs.

The people in Vermont decided the public has the right to know about what they're eating. Their legislature stepped up to the plate by passing legislation requiring GMO labeling and their governor, Peter Shumlin, signed the new law on May 8, 2014. The state was immediately sued by The Grocery Manufacturers Association, the Snack Foods Association, the International Dairy Foods Association and the National Association of Manufacturers claiming the law was unconstitutional. What does that say about the Grocery Manufacturers Association, the Snack Foods Association and the other two above? **It**

says they don't want you the consumer to know the truth about what they're selling. What's unconstitutional about a company putting an accurate ingredient and source list on their product?

Yes, that law does require a change in labeling to inform consumers about product content. Yes, it does cost money as does any new regulation imposed by government and believe me, I'm all for getting rid of thousands of rules and regulations in the states that cripple business in unnecessary costs. However, in this case it's protecting the people of Vermont from consuming food products that are dangerous to the human body – just like "smart" meters. If those defendants are so concerned about costs maybe they should think about in the future not trying to hide the truth about what they're selling.

In April 2015, U.S. District Judge Chritina Reiss ruled against the defendants for a preliminary order to stop the law scheduled to go into effect, July 1, 2016. The decision was actually two-fold: partially granted and also partially denied which means it will probably go to trial.

One more fact here about truth. Because of the Internet, millions and millions of Americans seeking the truth about things like dangerous pesticides and the food eat have been able to get "the other side of the story" about mega-corporations like Monsanto and their products. Naturally, this doesn't sit well with them. Criticize Monsanto and be prepared for attacks:

Monsanto Employee Admits an Entire Department Exists to "Discredit" Scientists by Christina Sarich, *Natural Society*, April 2015:

"Dare to publish a scientific study against Big Biotech, and Monsanto will defame and discredit you. For the first time, a Monsanto employee admits that there is an entire department within the corporation with the simple task of 'discrediting' and 'debunking' scientists who speak out against GMOs....

"In a recent talk attended mostly by students hoping to get decent paying internships in their field, a student asked what the company was doing to negate 'bad science' concerning their work. 'Monsanto's employee, Dr. William 'Bill' Moar, who gives talks on Monsanto's products to reassure everyone that they are safe, perhaps forgot the event was public when he openly revealed that Monsanto had:

"An entire department (waving his arm for emphasis) dedicated to 'debunking' science which disagreed with theirs."

"Likely, this is the first time a Monsanto employee has publicly admitted that they have immense political and financial weight to bear on scientists who dare to publish against them. Of course they don't list this discrediting department anywhere on their website. The company will stop at nothing to discredit and devalue the contributions of unimpeachably respected Lancet and the international scientific bodies of WHO and IARC, among others.

"The stakes are high – after all, an entire industry of GMO seed (for which they currently hold more than a three-fourths monopoly share) is based on being Roundup ready. Glyphosate is their hallmark product, and it accounts for billions in sales when you account for the seed they sell to go with their best-selling herbicide. In a single publicly made phrase, Moar has admitted that the Monsanto-funded science is sheer propaganda – essentially that they indeed have dozens, if not hundreds of employees out making sure that no science which tells the truth about their cancer-causing products ever garners any credibility whatsoever in the information age." [14]

Can anyone possibly think the U.S. Congress hasn't known about this problem for decades? Of course they have. What was their solution to protect the people of this country?

Obama signs "Monsanto Protection Act" written by Monsanto-sponsored senator

"United States President Barack Obama has signed a bill into law that was written in part by the very billion-dollar corporation that will benefit directly from the legislation. On Tuesday, Pres. Obama inked his name to H.R. 933, a continuing resolution spending bill approved in Congress days earlier. Buried 78 pages within the bill exists a provision that grossly protects biotech corporations such as the Missouri-based Monsanto Company from litigation…

"James Brumley, a reporter for Investor Place, explains a little more thoroughly just how dangerous the rider is now that biotech companies are allowed to bypass judicial scrutiny. Up until it was signed, he writes, 'the USDA [US Department of Agriculture] oversaw and approved (or denied) the testing of genetically modified seeds, while the federal courts retained the authority to halt the testing or sale of these plants if it felt that public health was being jeopardized. With HR 933 now a law, however, the court system no longer has the right to step in and protect the consumer." [15]

Act surprised: In a *NY Daily News* piece, March 2013, author of the bill is Roy Blunt, Republican Senator from Missouri who "worked with Monsanto to craft the language in the bill."

We the people do not elect individuals to any elected office much less Congress who allow unelected individuals (likely lawyers in this case) help write legislation, but it goes on all the time. ALEC (American Legislative Exchange Council) is a private entity that writes model legislation for your state house. Right or left, it doesn't matter. You and I elect our state reps and senators to represent us and if they're too ignorant to write a proper bill that doesn't violate your rights, is necessary and constitutional under your state and the U.S. Constitutions, they shouldn't be in office.

Non-elected individuals should not be involved in writing bills that get passed in our state legislatures. Non-elected individuals should not be on "equal" ground with those we vote in office to represent us. That's what elections are for – OUR voice – not some well-funded group we can't vote out of office. That practice will not stop at the state level until the people blast their state capitol: *NO outside companies, counsels or lawyers writing legislation.* Sometimes constituents send in a model bill they want their state rep or senator to introduce and that's just fine since it's our state government and we the people must have a say or simply roll over and let outside forces control our state houses.

That Act was temporary then extended, but it's back:

The Monsanto Protection Act is Back, and Worse Than Ever – Center For Food Safety, June 15th, 2015

(Washington, D.C.) – "The Monsanto Protection Act is back, and it's even worse than before. This bill would strip away a state or local government's basic rights of local control, and hands the biotech industry everything it wants on a silver platter. No Member of Congress that cares about the rights and concerns of his or her constituents should support this bill," said Andrew Kimbrell, executive director at Center for Food Safety.

"Earlier versions of Rep. Pompeo's bill, known as the 'Denying Americans the Right to Know Act' or DARK Act, preempted states' rights to require the labeling of GE foods, and this version continues that: It would overturn state labeling laws that have passed in Vermont, Connecticut, and Maine, and stop any future laws from passing. CFS has been a champion of GE food labeling for over two decades, and in the past 2 years, over thirty states have introduced laws requiring the labeling of GE foods.

"64 countries around the world require GE food labeling and have not reported higher food costs as a result. Last month, a federal court in Vermont resoundingly rejected industry's challenges to Vermont's labeling law, scheduled to take effect next year, becoming the first court to conclude that states do have the right to label GE foods under current law.

"However, that's not all the bill would do: while keeping language preempting labeling, the new Monsanto Protection Act would also forbid states and local governments from any sort of oversight of GE crops, even when the federal government has declined or failed to regulate them." [16]

If Monsanto's Round Up and other products are so safe, why did the U.S. Congress need to pass legislation protecting Monsanto against lawsuits? Just like vaccines. Just like Public Utility Commissions across this country protecting the energy companies and their deadly 'smart' meters. Are all the scientists, geneticists and doctors around the world ALL wrong? Are they all conspiracy nuts? Why is it only scientists who work for big mega corporations approved by the U.S. government, the FDA and USDA are right?

On May 25, 2013 the March Against Monsanto protests were held in 52 countries and 436 cities with an estimated 2 MILLION participants. In Argentina protesters carried signs that read: "Monsanto – get Out of Latin America". Portland, Oregon drew big with about 6,000 protesters and it wasn't just big cities. Other locations in Oregon were Medford, Grants Pass, Coos Bay, Eugene and Redmond.

GMO friendly media claim it's not true so many countries have banned GMO crops. Really? This will require a computer to view: GMO cultivation bans in Europe gives a list of every country of GMO Free regions by country. [17] The list is massive. Here is an example: "In 2005, the Swiss voted by referendum a 5-year moratorium against the commercial cultivation of GM crops and animals. The Swiss government decided to extend this moratorium till 2013. In 2012 the Swiss Parliament voted for a second extension of the moratorium until December 2017."

Why The Netherlands Just Banned Monsanto's Glyphosate-Based Herbicides, May 30, 2015

"The Netherlands has just become the latest country, following Russia, Mexico, and many others, to say no to Monsanto. The sale and use of glyphosate-based herbicides (the most commonly used herbicides in the world) has just been banned for non-commercial use in the country, effective later this year. This means that people will no longer be able to spray RoundUp on their lawns and gardens and will instead have to find another (hopefully more natural) means of pest control. This is definitely a step in the right direction. The move comes as no surprise, considering that the number of countries around the world who are choosing to ban this product is growing at an exponential rate." [18]

Are the governments of all those countries conspiracy nuts or have they analyzed the junk science and decided GMO crops and animals are not good? Here in America our government passes legislation to protect Monsanto from lawsuits and trample on state's rights under the Tenth Amendment. Does anyone see anything wrong with this picture? But, Monsanto isn't done with us yet:

Monsanto to Spend $1 Billion on New Herbicide Following Roundup Cancer Link Now that glyphosate is being rejected worldwide – This is another great piece of investigative reporting by Christina Sarich. June 2015.

"A billion dollars would feed a lot of people for a very long time, but instead, Monsanto will spend this absurd amount of money to build a new plant in Luling, Louisiana to produce weed-killing, and health-damaging dicamba. In an effort to expand its business after glyphosate was declared likely carcinogenic by the WHO, Monsanto has announced that it will focus on an alternative herbicide – dicamba. While the EPA only considers dicamba to be "mildly toxic" thus far, and it has been used since the 1960s, research does link the chemical to colon cancer and lung cancers.

"It is also very similar in its chemical make up to 2,4-D, another herbicide which was recently called 'possibly carcinogenic' by the World Health Organization's International Agency for Research on Cancer (IARC). Though while the warnings for this herbicide were less alarming than those for the other-tested pesticides Lindane and DDT, the researchers did still called 2,4,-D, possibly carcinogenic. They also reported that it caused oxidative stress as well as a suppressed immune response, which are both known health conditions that support the development of cancer.

"Monsanto will likely spend up to $1 billion to create a production facility that can make up for its failed Round Up, which has caused super weeds to grow throughout farms in the Midwest and across the US. The plant is expected to be built over the next three to five years, and will take place in a part of Louisiana that has been responsible for making glyphosate for years. It should be noted that Monsanto still has not taken any responsibility for polluting farms and tables everywhere with glyphosate. Traces of the herbicide have even been found in breast milk and fetal tissues." [19]

Making decisions about the food you eat and feed your family is the most important one you make all day. **Monsanto and OUR Congress do not want you to be informed about how our food is grown and all the toxic pesticides and chemicals being used.** Is that okay with you?

Try this one on for size:

"Undercover footage: Disease-ravaged corpses, birds so genetically modified they can't stand up and bloody feces everywhere", April 19, 2016, *Daily Mail UK*. Type title into a search engine, but I warn you the photos are beyond revolting. Hideous beyond words. The live chickens mashed in with the dead, diseased and deformed.

Ten Reasons Why GE Foods Will Not Feed the World, *organicconsumers.org*

"It is often claimed that genetically engineered crops are the only way to feed a growing world population. Yet close analysis suggests that there are at least 10 good reasons why the widespread adoption of genetic engineering in agriculture will lead to more hungry people – not fewer.

"Feed, Not Food, Engineering for Convenience, Substituting Tropical Cash Crops, Increasing Farm Debt, Promoting Inefficient Farming, Increasing Destitution, Unsustainable Agriculture, Lower Yields, Increased Corporate Control, Misreading the Problem" – just type the title into a search engine to read the facts, not more politics.

On March 28, 2013, despite massive opposition, the current occupant in the White House Signed the Monsanto Protection act thanks to senators like Ted Cruz. Oh, yes, it is protection and just like vaccines, Monsanto will be the ultimate power and given immunity from the US Federal courts.

What's the solution? Part of it is coming from other countries banning it which just might help our **state legislatures** understand this is not some wacko conspiracy fodder. Any state legislature in any state can kick Monsanto and their products out of their state. I would venture to guess too many either don't understand the problem or because they're bought and paid for by Monsanto they won't do what's right. **That's where you the voter come in and make sure they don't serve another term in office.**

I'm sorry for all the good, decent people who work for Monsanto that probably don't know what's going on or perhaps do, but like everyone else, need their paycheck. Monsanto is losing money by the bucket loads. Perhaps their shareholders and board members might demand they get out of the business of poisoning people and strive towards using safe products.

18

Islam: A cancer oozing across America

Every time I do a column on Islam and Muslims I receive the filthiest hate e-mail one can imagine. Not to mention serious death threats in graphic detail. So does just about every other writer opposed to that toxic 'religion' and what it will mean for America if we don't stop more Muslims from coming into this country.

Islam: A cancer oozing across America, July 19, 2010, My column which contains all the internal links.

Until September 11, 2001, most Americans didn't give a thought about Islam or Muslims. As the years have passed, the truth about that *brutal form of government* has become a subject of major discussion in this country. While people continue to refer to Islam as a religion, I do not, which is my absolute right under the First Amendment. My personal opinion is that being a Muslim is nothing more than a being a slave to a violent, barbaric form of totalitarian government which demands everyone must be a Muslim or join all non-believers in death.

By declaring Islam a religion, religious leaders in the Middle East and now here in America, control their believers with the threat of some god named Allah. Allegedly, their "holy" Quran was revealed by a man named Muhammad. I have devoted a great deal of time reading about Islam and Muslims. One web site in particular seems to be very fair in allowing Muslims and non-Muslims to post their views on Muhammad. One of the links from that site led me to this one:

Child marriage and divorce in Yemen

"After visiting their home and seeing Arwa and her 15-year-old sister, he opted for the younger child. Abdul Ali says the man promised he would wait for the girl to reach puberty before calling her to his house but then changed his mind and came to live with them. So why did he sell his daughter to a stranger? "He gave me 30,000 rial ($150, £90) and promised another 400,000 ($2,000). I was really in need of money and thought it was a solution for the family," he explains.

"For seven months, Arwa's husband shared the small room where the family eat, play and sleep. When Arwa fought off his advances, she was beaten. The torment only came to an end when her husband and father quarrelled and Abdul Ali gave her permission to seek outside help. At this point in the narrative, she finds her voice again, describing how she went looking for a neighbour who could lend her money for the journey to court where the judge took pity on her and granted her freedom. A medical examination showed that she had been sexually molested but was still technically a virgin...

"A third girl, Reem is still waiting for the court's decision and says her two ambitions are to get a divorce and go to college. Married at 12, she describes the moment when her 30-year-old husband insisted on sex. When she resisted, he choked and bit her and dragged her by the hair, overwhelming her with force."

Americans support such a putrid culture by being raped in taxes:

"Defense relations between Yemen and the United States are improving rapidly, with the resumption of International Military Education and Training assistance and the transfer of military equipment and spare parts. In FY 2009 U.S. Foreign Military Financing (FMF) for Yemen was $2.8 million, International Military Education and Training (IMET) was $1 million, and Non-Proliferation, Anti-Terrorism, Demining and Related Programs (NADR) was $2.5 million. In FY 2009 Yemen also received $19.8 million in Economic Support Funds (ESF), $11.2 million in development assistance, and $67.1 million in Section 1206 funding."

Nowhere in the U.S. Constitution does it authorize the Outlaw Congress to steal the fruits of our labor to send to Yemen for any reason. More unpayable debt on our backs with an empty treasury.

Child Brides Escape Marriage, but Not Lashes, *NY Times*

"Forced into a so-called marriage exchange, where each girl was given to an elderly man in the other's family, Khadija and Basgol later complained that their husbands beat them when they tried to resist consummating the unions. Dressed as boys, they escaped and got as far as western Herat Province, where their bus was stopped at a checkpoint and they were arrested. Although Herat has shelters for battered and runaway women and girls, the police instead contacted the former warlord, Fazil Ahad Khan, whom Human Rights Commission workers describe as the self-appointed commander and morals enforcer in his district in Ghor Province, and returned the girls to his custody.

"After a kangaroo trial by Mr. Khan and local religious leaders, according to the commission's report on the episode, the girls were sentenced to 40 lashes each and flogged on Jan. 12. In the video, the mullah, under Mr. Khan's approving eye, administers the punishment with a leather strap, which he appears to wield with as much force as possible, striking each girl in turn on her legs and buttocks with a loud crack each time."

If anyone thinks having American troops remain in that country under an illegal invasion (no formal declaration of war by Congress) is going to change their culture, you're in denial. Let's not forget the increasing number of "honor killings" here in America. *Look what we've imported, America.*

According to Islam, if you do not believe the toxic teachings of the Quran, you must die in the name of Allah. If you think I'm kidding, then take a good look at these pictures [Internal links in my column]. They are not photo shopped. Those photos show exactly how much hatred is spewed by Muslims because hate is what their "religion" teaches. Every time I hear or read about 'moderate' Muslims, I want to gag. There is no moderate if you're a Muslim. It's Allah's way or the highway.

If you haven't read the book, *Londonistan* by Melanie Phillips, I strongly suggest you do because she pulls no punches in proving to anyone who can read how dangerous and destructive Muslims have been to Britain. **Her book is a warning to the whole world about Islam and she has been right. It is now and always has been the goal of Muslims to force everyone on this globe to convert to their putrid form of government using religion as the controlling mechanism.** No? How about right out of the mouth of a Muslim leader in the United Kingdom?

"You can't say that Islam is a religion of peace," Choudary told *CBN News*. "Because Islam does not mean peace. Islam means submission. So the Muslim is one who submits. There is a place for violence in Islam. There is a place for jihad in Islam." Choudary is the leader of Islam4UK, a group recently banned in Britain under the country's counter-terrorism laws. He wants Islamic Sharia law to rule the United Kingdom and is working to make that dream a reality. While Islamic radicals in the United States usually prefer to speak in more moderate tones while in public, masking their true agenda, Choudary has no such inhibitions. He has praised the 9/11 hijackers and has called for the execution of Pope Benedict. He also stirred controversy recently when video emerged of him converting a 10-year-old British boy to Islam."

One of the best short works on the history of Islam is by Dr. Peter Hammond. I had the pleasure of having dinner with Dr. Hammond in the Washington, DC. area several years ago along with my dear friend, Gen. Ben Partin. Dr. Hammond is an expert on this issue like few others and his book, *Slavery, Terrorism and & Islam*, **is a must read**. Dr. Hammond points out and history clearly backs up his statement:

"What few Westerners understand is that Muslim leaders who call for the overthrow of governments and the establishment of an Islamic superstate controlling all aspects of life, for every person on earth, are not necessarily extremists on the fringe of Islam. Jihad, the subjugation and forcible conversion of all people to Islam and world domination are, in fact, central tenants of Islam. Jihad is the sixth pillar of Islam."

Muslims and their clerical leaders will not stop until they achieve their goals and **it will be done with violence here in the United States** as has been the case around the world for centuries. If you think Dr. Hammond is some sort of bigot, you would be badly mistaken. Go look at this 2:07 second video of what has happened in Sweden now that the Muslim population has grown to 1/4th of the population. **If you think this isn't coming to this country, you're in denial.** The same cancer is oozing across America and a growing threat.

Islam has no place in America in my opinion, which I am entitled to believe even though you might disagree. Their culture is barbaric and they are trying to shove it down our throats. There is a web site that has horrific pictures of female mutilation of their private parts. One link is to a web site run by a woman who is trying to stop the abuse of women and children under Islam. Unfortunately, she promotes democracy, but perhaps down the line she will learn that form of government is not desired by those who love freedom and liberty. Here is one excerpt:

"A man can marry a girl younger than nine years of age, even if the girl is still a baby being breastfed. A man, however is prohibited from having intercourse with a girl younger than nine, other sexual act such as foreplay, rubbing, kissing and sodomy is allowed. A man having intercourse with a girl younger than nine years of age has not committed a crime, but only an infraction, if the girl is not permanently damaged. If the girl, however, is permanently damaged, the man must provide for her all her life. But this girl will not count as one of the man's four permanent wives. He also is not permitted to marry the girl's sister."

Think cutting young Muslim females only happens in the Middle East? Think again because it's still happening here in the U.S. And, you wonder why I find their "religion" so repugnant?

I highly encourage you to read this interview, by a Danish Psychologist: *Integration of Muslims in Western Societies is Not Possible*. Muslims will not integrate into Western society because it isn't compatible with Islam. They should be stopped from coming to this country until such time that as Dr. Nicolai Sennels says, it can be proven integration is possible. **That would be never.**

What kind of religion forces you to be a believer or face death? Not Christianity. Not Judaism. Only Islam.

While there have been several efforts to stop Sharia Law from destroying OUR Constitution and Bill of Rights, so far efforts have failed because of DAMN foolish PC judges: Federal court blocks Oklahoma ban on Sharia – January 10, 2012

(*CNN*) – "A federal appeals court has blocked an Oklahoma voter-approved measure barring state judges from considering Islamic and international law in their decisions. The three-judge panel at the 10th U.S. Circuit Court of Appeals upheld an earlier injunction preventing State Question 755 from being certified until the free speech questions are resolved. The decision Tuesday allows a lawsuit brought by Islamic-American groups to move ahead to a bench trial.

"The proposed amendment discriminates among religions," said the judges. "The Oklahoma amendment specifically names the target of its discrimination. The only religious law mentioned in the amendment is Sharia law...."In bringing suit, CAIR argued that the amendment violates the establishment and free-exercise clauses of the First Amendment's guarantee of religious freedom. The group's local leader, Muneer Awad, has said the amendment passed in November 2010 under a campaign of fear and misinformation about Islam."

Let's start with the definition of Sharia Law:

"Sharia is the moral code and religious law of Islam. Sharia deals with many topics addressed by secular law, including crime, politics, and economics, as well as personal matters such as sexual intercourse, hygiene, diet, prayer, and fasting. Though interpretations of sharia vary between cultures, in its strictest definition it is considered the infallible law of God—as opposed to the human interpretation of the laws (fiqh).

"There are two primary sources of sharia law: the precepts set forth in the Quran, and the example set by the Islamic prophet Muhammad in the Sunnah. Where it has official status, sharia is interpreted by Islamic judges (qadis) with varying responsibilities for the religious leaders (imams). For questions not directly addressed in the primary sources, the application of sharia is extended through consensus of the religious scholars (ulama) thought to embody the consensus of the Muslim Community (ijma). Islamic jurisprudence will also sometimes incorporate analogies from the Quran and Sunnah through qiyas, though Shia jurists prefer reasoning ('aql) to analogy."

In order for courts to declare Sharia Law is protected under the First Amendment, *shouldn't there be a rational discussion as to whether or not Islam is even a bona fide religion?* I say, yes. When I brought up this argument several years ago, I can't even begin to describe the vicious emails filled with very personal and in your face death threats imaginable. However, that has not deterred me because **Islam is a national security threat.**

Just because Islam has been called a religion for a few thousand years, doesn't make it so. Discussing religion has caused stupid people who lose their temper to have violent arguments. In the case of Islam, it means death and destruction for anyone who criticizes their pedophile prophet Muhammad. Do read:

Islam Is The Religion of Homosexuality and Pedophilia By Walid Shoebat: "Christianity gave me the light. While I attended high-school at Dar Jasser in Bethlehem where the Muslim history was scrubbed of all the debauchery, but truth was whispered at times when teachers would every now and then expressed their concious having run into obvious words in the poetry and the Quran using the word "ghilman" (sex boys) which compelled them to finally tell the obvious."

In America, people are free to worship the religion of their choice whether I agree with them or not. That is why we call it freedom of religion. Islam, however, is a completely different belief system. Islam is all about killing, violence and has enslaved more than a billion human beings. If you do not believe some guy called Allah is the only God you must worship, you are an infidel punishable by death. What kind of religion is that? What kind of religion calls for decapitating someone who criticizes Islam? *What kind of religion trains children to become soldiers?*

Let me quote a few others who also don't believe Islam is a religion; I hope you take the time to read their columns. Simply type titles into a search engine.

Demoting Islam's Religion Status, by Martel Sobieskey, March 21, 2009: "An Impostor Religion – To put it bluntly, Islam's religion status should be rescinded because it is a wolf in sheep's clothing, a Trojan horse, an impostor religion that has arrived on our shore with malicious intent, deathly determined to replace our constitution with the Koran, and turn America into an Islamic nation controlled by Sharia law. Robert Spencer in his excellent book, Stealth Jihad: How Radical Islam is Subverting America without Guns or Bombs, explains how so-called moderate Islam is having greater success at invading America than its counterpart, militant Islam. Shockingly, one may rightly conclude that America is now being conquered without Islam even having to fire a shot. Have we really become that docile, self-complacent and pathetic? The answer is Yes!"

"Sharia law makes Islam much more than a religion. Its broad doctrine and application to non-Muslims make Islam a political entity, a government with goals of global dominion."

www.counterjihadreport.com

Islam and Shariah Banking, Vincent Gioia, August 3, 2010, Family Security Matters.org. "Whoever says Islam is a religion is totally blind to the obvious or is a sympathizer. Islam is a complete authoritarian government-political-business-control enterprise whose only object is total subjugation of mankind and the destruction of western civilization. They invade the host country as a virus by exploiting the host's freedom of speech and religion with political correctness, and eventually demand Shariah law and Shariah banking. As we appease Muslims and accede to their demands we will see the decline of western civilization."

How foolish is it to invite the enemy into our country and then genuflect at their feet while they hide their real agenda behind our First Amendment?

Mosques and the Islamization of America. "Disguised as religion, Islam has penetrated democracies with the aim of replacing civility and liberty with the barbarism of 7th century Islamic theocracy and Sharia law. Islam's multi-pronged attack aims to destroy all that liberty offers."

Jihad in Islam by Abul a'La Maududi. Read page 5 of the 37 pages: "But the truth is that Islam is not the name of a 'Religion', nor is 'Muslim' the title of a 'Nation'. In reality Islam is a revolutionary ideology and programme which seeks to alter the social order of the whole world and rebuild it in conformity with its own tenets and ideals. 'Muslim' is the title of that International Revolutionary Party organized by Islam to carry into effect its revolutionary programme. And 'Jihad' refers to that revolutionary struggle and utmost exertion which the Islamic Party brings into play to achieve this objective."

If you read the whole thing, you'll get a clear understanding of the goals of Islam. It is a party hell bent on forcing every human on this earth to "worship" their putrid ideology.

Is Islam a Religion or Military Ideology? "The question our political czars and Emir (Leader/Prince) Obama should ponder is this: If Islamic scholars state Islam is more of a political, economic, and military ideology above even religion, then should our government not agree and cancel all of their non-profit tax status? Should we not remove the thousands of religious visa given to Muslim leaders? Should we not be taking the words Jihad and Islamic terrorism seriously?"

Type the titles below into a search engine to read the articles:

General: Muslim Brotherhood plots undoing of America – Boykin makes impassioned plea for expose` of stealth jihad

Muslim Brotherhood: "Yes, We Will Be Masters of the World"

The Muslim Brotherhood in the Obama Administration

New Freedom Center pamphlet by Frank Gaffney exposes just how deeply Islamists have infiltrated the White House, *Front Page Magazine*

Smoking-gun document said to prove Obama-Muslim Brotherhood ties, June 7, 2015, *WND*

Islam is a religion of peace is one of the greatest whoppers ever told.

Below are articles linked in my column: **Challenging Sharia Law Means Challenging Islam as a Religion**, Newswithviews.com, October 13, 2012.

Muslim Children's Comic Book publishes detailed step-by-step instruction of how to make a Molotov cocktail

Outraged Muslim shoots 14-yr old girl in head for wanting an education

Islam's Burning Love. COX'S BAZAR, Bangladesh (*Reuters*)— "Hundreds of Muslims in Bangladesh burned at least four Buddhist temples and 15 homes of Buddhists on Sunday after complaining that a Buddhist man had insulted Islam, police and residents said."

Muslim Dad "tied daughter to tree and hacked her to death with an axe because he was ashamed she worked in a beauty salon".

Enter the Gates of Hell. Warning: The photos are real, they are graphic and anyone who says Islam is a "religion of peace" is a damn fool.

Egyptian Cleric Abd Al-Rahman Mansour Gives Guidelines for Wife Beating in Islam – Last year, the thieves in Congress stole the fruits of your labor to give $1.5 BILLION BORROWED to Egypt in unconstitutional foreign aid. Actually, that is the average every year stolen from we the people.

Egyptian Father Kills Three Daughters with Snake for being girls (Yes, they are heathens)

Muslims (The Religion of Peace) Burn Fifty (50) Christians Alive

Muslim Rape Gangs Have Been a Problem in Europe For Years

UK Muslim Gang Rape 100 Teenage Girls

Now those savage animals have come to America. Headline– Police: "One of The Most Horrific Sexual Assaults I Ever Saw" in Colorado Iraqi Gang Rape Case

Pentagon Indoctrinating U.S. Soldiers with Islamic Propaganda. "... the U.S. Army has published a special handbook for soldiers that appears to justify Islamic jihad by describing it as the 'communal military defense of Islam and Muslims when they are threatened or under attack."

How about Muslims continuing to kill our soldiers in the never ending unconstitutional invasions of countries in the Middle East?

Afghan soldier turns his gun on American troops, killing two in shooting — Worst Loss for Marine Squadron VMA-211 Since Wake Island

"The U.S. Marine Corps has suffered its worst air squadron catastrophe since Vietnam. The VMA-211 squadron has taken its worst hit since the defense of Wake Island in World War II. On Friday, September 14, at around 10:15 p.m. local time, a force of Taliban gunmen attacked Camp Bastion, in Helmand Province — the main strategic base in southwestern Afghanistan.

"Fewer than two dozen insurgents wearing U.S. Army uniforms, divided into three teams, breached the perimeter fence and assaulted the airfield. That includes the U.S. Camp Leatherneck and the U.K.'s Camp Bastion where Prince Harry, an AH-64 Apache pilot is stationed. The Taliban reportedly are anxious to get Prince Harry, who would prefer to be treated just like anyone else.

"The attack killed VMA-211 squadron commander Lt. Col. Christopher Raible and destroyed or permanently disabled eight of the ten top-of-the-line Harrier AV-8B attack aircraft in his squadron. The Harrier has been out of production for more than a decade, and the aircraft can never be replaced."

"I waited until they took off their body armor off... and then I shot them dead." Chilling account of "green on blue" attack by Afghan who killed two U.S. soldiers

3 US troops gunned down by Afghan soldier they were training

For what, I ask you? For every one of the examples above, I can give you a thousand more.

So, I ask you again: Is Islam a religion? *How could anyone who hasn't had their brain polluted with political correctness believe Islam is a religion, never mind a peaceful one?* **Stopping Sharia Law must be a priority in this country in our state legislatures**:

- Minnesota Under Attack from Sharia Law — Short video everyone should watch

- American Muslims Stone Christians in Dearborn, MI – Video that will make you puke. When Muslims become enough in numbers, countries are ruined.

In the blink of an eye, this type of violence will come to your city or town and Muslims will claim protection of religion under the First Amendment. Mark my words: **The Trojan Horse shoved down our throats is named violence and hatred**. Violence is never the answer no matter how much you disagree with someone. For Muslims, it is a way of life.

Someone emailed suggesting all Muslims be deported. That is not only impossible, but not legal. I don't know the exact number, but millions of Muslims born in this country to parents who are U.S. citizens are

Americans by birth. Immigrant Muslims who have come here *legally* become U.S. citizens and must take the oath.

There are exceptions to some of the language like service in the Armed Forces and 8 C.F.R. 337.1 provides that the phrase "so help me God" is optional and that the words "on oath" can be substituted with "and solemnly affirm". Also, if the prospective citizen can prove such commitments are in violation with his or her religion.

That's how Muslims think they can get away with demanding Sharia Law – they don't take the oath of citizenship to become an American. They take it to use the First Amendment as a shield to protect the ultimate goal of Islam. They cannot have taken the oath honestly to "support and defend the Constitution and laws of the United States of America" since the goal is to establish Sharia Law over the U.S. Constitution and state constitutions. Remember: **Muslims are taught lie to infidels about their true purpose and goals.**

I feel very sorry for men, women and children who have bought into the propaganda about Islam as a religion or forced into by virtue of where they live instead of understanding it is nothing more than a brutal totalitarian form of government denying them even the most basic of human rights. However, Muslims in this country should be made to understand in no uncertain terms that this is America. **The supreme law of our land is the U.S. Constitution and it will never be Sharia Law.** If you break our laws, you go to prison, not to some mosque where you can further plan the destruction of America.

Sharia in America

"Omar M. Ahmad founder of CAIR said: "Islam isn't in America to be equal to any other faith, but to become dominant" he said. "The Koran, the Muslim book of scripture, should be the highest authority in America, and Islam the only accepted religion on Earth,' he said."

"Since slavery will be allowed government can open slave markets to sell its 20% share of the captured women. Captured women/slave-girls can provide affordable domestic help for house wives and clean enjoyable sex for their husbands."

"Since men will be allowed four wives and unlimited number of slave girls, population boom will result in making the fastest growing religion grow even faster. All non-Muslims will live under dhimmi rules and pay heavy Jizya. Budget deficits will be a thing of the past.

"Stoning of adulterers, whipping of alcohol drinkers, cutting of hands and feet of thieves and beheadings of apostates can be carried out after Juma prayers on Fridays in the local stadium. Gate charge for this gory and exciting weekly spectacle can generate a lot of revenue".

"Marriage age for girls can be lowered to 6 years. That will reduce the burden of support of large poorer families and also promote a sunna, the tradition set by the holy prophet (peace be up on him)."

This eight-minute video will be an eye opener and should be watched. People must understand what Sharia Law means; it's ugly:

Islam: Most important video I have ever seen on Islam.

Now, do you want Sharia Law allowed in this country and protected under the First Amendment? It is a toxic poison that must be stopped before we're all forced to drink it.

States can continue to pass legislation and get it signed into law, or like Oklahoma, put it to the voters. However, unless and until the real question of whether or not Islam is a religion is settled, the will of the people will continue to be overthrown by politically correct federal judges.

That very important question is the one state legislatures should be addressing. **If you play by the enemy's rules, you'll lose every time.** Muslims are hiding behind the First Amendment. I say we pull back the curtain and take away that protection because Islam is not a religion even under the most liberal definitions. Of course, it takes courage to take a stand and question the legitimacy of Islam as a religion. Only massive pressure from we the people will make it happen.

Important Links:

1- Muslim Inbreeding: Impacts on intelligence, sanity, health and society

2- Muslims Leaving Islam in Droves

3- Campbell's Soup catering to Islam [End]

As time has progressed since I wrote those two columns, the situation has worsened. **Multiculturalism is a poisonous cancer that does NOT work and it will not work here in America.** Muslims come to this country and demand we flush our traditions, our laws and our culture to suit them. **I say go back to where you came from if you hate this country so much.**

We the people are NOT going to get on our knees and surrender to your toxic agenda disguised as a religion. But, it's going to be an uphill battle as the current occupant of the White House has done nothing but bend over for Muslims and pack his administration with individuals tied to a known terrorist organization, the Muslim Brotherhood. THAT is a fact.

Wake up. **This has nothing to do with a religion.** Those vile people are determined to set up a world caliphate and **the first person's head on the chopping block is going to be yours.** Have you never heard the saying: And they who cried: "Appease, Appease!" Are hanged by men they tried to please.

FACTS and the truth are not hate speech, but when it comes to Muslims, guess what? YOUR God-given rights and constitutional protections are being flushed.

Federal Attorney Warns Negative Posts Against Islam Could Get You Prosecution & Imprisonment, June 1, 2013, *Freedom Outpost*

"If you have seen the stories around the globe of how cartoonists, journalists and people simply posting tweets or Facebook posts has gotten them in hot water with Islam and even the government, then you have probably said, "That can't happen in America," right? Well hold on to your seat my friend because you are in for a rude awakening...

"However, the criminal Attorney General Eric Holder seems to be backing Killian and Moore. *Judicial Watch* reports,

> *" In its latest effort to protect followers of Islam in the U.S. the Obama Justice Department warns against using social media to spread information considered inflammatory against Muslims, threatening that it could constitute a violation of civil rights.*

"The move comes a few years after the administration became the first in history to dispatch a U.S. Attorney General to personally reassure Muslims that the Department of Justice (DOJ) is dedicated to protecting them. In the unprecedented event, Attorney General Eric Holder assured a San Francisco-based organization (Muslim Advocates) that urges members not to cooperate in federal terrorism investigations that the "us versus them" environment created by the U.S. government, law enforcement agents and fellow citizens is unacceptable and inconsistent with what America is all about.

"Muslims and Arab Americans have helped build and strengthen our nation." [1]

Muslims have helped build our nation? What a bald faced lie. You don't continue to appease your enemy and the American people had damn well better wake up and understand **Islam and their damnable Sharia laws are American's enemy**. THAT is their goal – sedition through Sharia law – and it's being implemented with the help of imbeciles who sit on the federal bench.

Judges and media who don't want the American people to know about the violence by Muslims in this country that is going to worsen, mark my words.

Woman Beheaded in Oklahoma by Muslim Convert, September 27, 2014, *Fox Nation*

"A fired employee who had been trying to convert co-workers to Islam stabbed two female colleagues – beheading one of them – before an off-duty officer shot him, police have said. Alton Alexander Nolen, 30, was fired from Vaughan Foods, a food distribution center in Moore, Oklahoma on Thursday before returning to his car and smashing it into another vehicle. He then climbed out and entered the building, attacking the first two people he encountered with a knife, Moore Police Sergeant Jeremy Lewis said. After beheading Colleen Hufford, 54, and stabbing Traci Johnson, 43, multiple times, Nolen was shot by off-duty officer Mark Vaughan, who was working at the business." [2]

Muslim parents accused of facilitating daughter's rape – Exclusive: Daniel Akbari explains incident of "ghayra violence," Islam-sanctioned sex, April 28, 2015

"A teenager's mom and dad dragged her, screaming and crying, to a man's apartment and threw her in to have sex, according to a report last week by *FOX 10 News* in Arizona. Police say the man, Muhammad Abdullahi, age 30, punched the teenager in the eye, started to strangle her, tore off her clothes, slapped her and bit her, sexually assaulted her and finally barred the door of his apartment to stop her from leaving when he went to sleep. Once again, Phoenix has been rocked by shocking Islamic ghayra violence." [3]

In Arizona, not Iraq. One case. How many go unreported because it's all justified under their "religion"? Do we want to see this cancer spread to where OUR country looks like Somalia or Afghanistan?

Poor Mrs. Hufford was an infidel who had to have her head chopped off because Nolen couldn't convert her.

Judge seals file in Somali-Muslim suspects' murder trial, August 14, 2015, *WND*

"Freddy Akoa, a 49-year-old health-care worker, was killed in his apartment Sunday, allegedly by three Somali-Americans whose families came to the United States through the United Nations-U.S. State Department refugee resettlement program. Authorities in Portland, Maine, have arrested three Somali-American men in connection with the brutal killing of a man inside his apartment, then moved quickly to seal the case from public view…

"Of all the countries participating in the U.S. refugee resettlement program, Somalia has the worst record. Countless Somalis resettled in America have been investigated, arrested and convicted of violent crimes and terrorism-related charges. More than 50 have left the U.S. to join the ranks of ISIS, al-Shabab and al-Qaida, the FBI has confirmed. Yet, the Obama administration, with the full support of Congress, continues to infuse American cities with a steady stream of Sunni Muslim 'refugees' from Somalia. They arrive in the U.S. at a rate of 7,000 to 10,000 per year, or about 600 to 800 a month, according to records obtained by WND through a search of State Department databases." [4]

Muslim refugee charged with raping 10-year-old girl, October 8, 2015, *WND*

"A 34-year-old Muslim immigrant has been arrested and charged with brutally raping a 10-year-old girl in Minnesota and the local media in Minneapolis has refused to identify the man as a refugee from Somalia. *KSTP 5*, an *ABC* affiliate in Minneapolis, referred to the suspect, Ahmed Hersi Abdi as "A Minneapolis man." *CBS* affiliate *WCCO 4* used the same description, giving no mention of the man's background or how he arrived in the U.S. The attack occurred Sunday evening in an apartment complex in the city's Cedar Riverside neighborhood, also known as "Little Mogadishu" for its high concentration of Somali refugees imported from United Nations refugee camps in Africa." [5]

Those people do not belong in America. **Somali Muslims have been shipped into this country in massive numbers.** They don't speak a word of English, they have no jobs and are immediately put into a federal welfare system. Since we don't know anything about them, it's a severe national security risk. They do not assimilate as shown in the article above, "Little Mogadishu". **They have nothing to contribute to this country and if someone doesn't like me saying that, too bad.**

DHS caught busing in illegal Somalis from Mexican border – Immigration official: "Asylum" is the new password, May 13, 2015

"The U.S. is bringing in 100,000 Muslims every year through legal channels such as the United Nations refugee program and various visa programs, but new reports indicate a pipeline has been established through the southern border with the help of the federal agency whose job it is to protect the homeland. They are coming from Somalia and other African nations, according to a Homeland Security official who was caught recently transporting a busload of Africans to a detention center near Victorville, California.

"Somalia is the home base of al-Shabab, a designated foreign terrorist organization that slaughtered 147 Christians at a university in Kenya just last month. It executed another 67 at the Westgate Mall in Nairobi, Kenya, in 2013, and has put out warnings that it will target malls in Canada and the U.S. Dozens of Somali refugees in the U.S. have been arrested, charged and convicted of providing support to overseas terrorist organizations over the past few years.

"Libya is also awash in Islamist terror following the death of Moammar Gadhafi in 2011. ISIS beheaded 21 Coptic Christians on a Libyan beach in February. So when Anita Fuentes of OpenYourEyesPeople.com posted a video of a U.S. Department of Homeland Security bus pulling into a Shell station in Victorville, on the night of May 7, admitting he had a busload of Somalis and other Africans who had crossed the southern border, it raised more than a few eyebrows among those concerned with illegal immigration and national security." [6]

100,000 Muslims a year! According to a new November 2015 analysis by the highly respected Center for Immigration studies: "On average, each Middle Eastern refugee resettled in the United States costs an estimated $64,370 in the first five years, or $257,481 per household." Multiply that by 500,000. **All stolen from us by both parties in Congress without any constitutional authority.**

Not only do we not know how many terrorists are in the numbers coming here, we are being forced to *pay astronomical amounts of money we don't have* to import more illiterate refugees who don't speak our language, a culture that is NOT compatible with ours, who do not assimilate, who follow Sharia Law, not the U.S. Constitution and massive welfare. This is insanity. *Is this okay with you because it sure as hell is not okay with me and the blame lies squarely with both political parties who refuse to stop the lunatic in the White House.*

How quickly Americans forget our soldiers murdered in March 1993 and dragged down the streets of Mogadishu, Somalia naked. Cheered on by barbarians – including women. Have you seen the horrific pictures on the Internet of Staff Sgt. William David Cleveland bloodied with his genitals exposed? Do you think his family suffered even more pain because those photos were plastered around the world?

How Barack Obama Is Using Taqiyya to Fuse Islam with America, January 13, 2013

"When people have immigrated to America in the past, it was assumed that they wanted to become Americans, and assimilate into the America way of life. My people came from Ukraine to America in the early 1900's. They were excited to learn the language and to become Americans. To them, America was the land of freedom. They were ecstatic about finally being in a country where they would be free. That is not the case with Muslims. I would call their objective "infiltration" more than immigration. They come to countries to bring sharia law, and to live separate lives in their Muslim communities. This is just part of the larger plan. Those who have studied the Qur'an know that Islam is truly a totalitarian political regime, cloaked in the robes of religion so as to fool the world — especially it seems, the liberal media of all countries...

"The ultimate goal of Islam is worldwide domination. The Muslims who follow the Qur'an number over 300 million. Europe has been overrun with Muslims, and many of the countries now have 'No Go' zones. If these zones were named correctly, they would be called 'Sharia zones.' But political correctness reigns in the liberal media and in our liberal White House, so they bow to these people, and accommodate them at every turn. When I think of these sharia zones, I think of a cancer growing out of control, and finally overtaking the entire body. This IS the goal of fundamentalist Muslims — make no mistake about it." [7]

That author is absolutely right. Muslims don't want to assimilate and they don't. Detroit's Muslim population has grown to about 30%; many Americans who are able to afford it have moved out of the area. If you think I'm just blowing smoke, you are dead wrong. Arabic is the fastest growing language in this country because of Muslims and they are working to get Sharia Law to replace OUR U.S. Constitution and Bill of Rights:

Minnesota Muslims brutally honest: "We want Shariah", May 29, 2015, *WND*

"The Cedar Riverside section of Minneapolis is home to the University of Minnesota, some tasty ethnic foods and brutally cold winters. It's also a known hotbed of Islamic terror recruitment. Al-Shabab, the Islamist group based in Somalia, has had a field day there over the past six or seven years.

"Dozens of young Muslims have left the streets of Cedar Riverside, referred to by some Minnesotans as 'Little Mogadishu' for its high concentration of Somali refugees, to travel abroad and fight for terrorist groups. Some have joined Somalia's notorious al-Shabab, which slaughtered 147 Christians at a university in Kenya last month, while others have opted for ISIS in Syria. Their goal is the same – to join their brothers in the fight to establish a Shariah-compliant utopia known as a caliphate. But one would expect those who walk the streets of this quiet neighborhood to be a bit less fanatical in their views, right?" [8]

During the filming on the street the overwhelming response was they want to live under Sharia Law. From the article above: "Shariah law, it says that if you steal something, they cut off your hand," the boy said, making a cutting motion with one hand against the other." Do we want such barbaric "laws" to replace ours? "Is it right to kill someone who insults the prophet?" "Yes," said the bearded man with the animated personality."

For years now, politically correct nitwits running government indoctrination centers they call public schools have been working overtime in an attempt to force American children to embrace the toxic tenants of Islam. Thankfully, parents with the backbone to stand up to those idiots are making their voices heard.

Islam quiz has U.S. parents "outraged" – "They're not teaching 10 Commandments" but Muslim prayers allowed, September 29, 2015

"Hundreds of irate parents are planning to attend the Walton County, Georgia, school board meeting Oct. 10 to convey their outrage over their children being taught the religious beliefs of Islam in middle-school social studies. The outrage erupted over a quiz handed out to students asking them to answer questions related to the five pillars of Islam, the Quran as the "holy" book of Muslims, and the conversion prayer known as the "shahada," which states, "There is no god but Allah and Muhammad is his messenger." Perhaps most disturbing to Christian parents was the "correct" answer that the Muslim god Allah is the "same god" that is worshiped by Christians and Jews. [9]

Textbook Praises Islam, Denigrates Christianity, July 29, 2013, *Townhall*

"A world history book used in an Advanced Placement class is under review by a Florida school board over allegations it favors Islam at the expense of Christianity and Judaism. State Rep. Ritch Workman told Fox News the Prentice World History textbook rewrites Islamic history and presents a biased version of the Muslim faith. "The book has a 36-page chapter on Islam but no chapters on Christianity or Judaism," Workman said. "It's remarkably one-sided."

"Workman said he received a copy of the book and he said it's clear the authors 'make a very obvious attempt not to insult Islam by reshaping history. 'If you don't see it from the eyes of a parent, kids are going to take this book as gospel and believe that Christians and Jews were murderous barbarians and thank God the Muslims came along and the world is great,' he said. For example, Workman said a reference to Mohammed and his armies taking over Medina states, 'people happily accepted Islam as their way of life.' It leaves out that tens of thousands of Jews and non-believers were massacred by Mohammed's armies,' he said. 'It's a blatant deception.'" [10]

If anything should be taught about Islam is exactly what is covered in Dr. Hammond's book I cited earlier. FACTUAL history of nothing but violence and oppression.

What can be done?

First, it's critically important to decide whether or not we are going to allow Muslims to use OUR First Amendment citing a religion as justification for doing to America what they have done in every country where they're become a majority. Some countries actually "get it" after seeing history repeat itself:

Kuwait & Israel Admit They Refuse to Take "Refugees" Because Migrants Don't Assimilate, September 11, 2015

"While Europe is preparing to take in potentially millions of migrants from African and Middle Eastern countries, politicians in Israel and Kuwait admit that their policy of refusing refugees is because the migrants fail to assimilate and pose a huge threat to social cohesion and democracy. Appearing on Middle Eastern television, a Kuwaiti politician stated, "In the end you cannot accept people from a different ethnicity, culture and environment."

"Striking a similar tone, an Israeli politician asserted, "We'll bring in a million Africans, half a million Filipinos, 2 or 3 million Chinese, and that's the end of it for Israel. [11]

Fort Hood gunman had told US military colleagues that infidels should have their throats cut, November 8, 2009

"[Hassan] once gave a lecture to other doctors in which he said non-believers should be beheaded and have boiling oil poured down their throats. He also told colleagues at America's top military hospital that non-Muslims were infidels condemned to hell who should be set on fire. The outburst came during an hour-long talk Hassan, an Army psychiatrist, gave on the Koran in front of dozens of other doctors at Walter Reed Army Medical Centre in Washington DC, where he worked for six years before arriving at Fort Hood in July. Colleagues had expected a discussion on a medical issue but were instead given an extremist interpretation of the Koran, which Hassan appeared to believe." [12]

What stopped those attending doctors to Hassan's murderous rant from reporting him? Political correctness. He's a Muslim. Instead, 13 American soldiers murdered by another savage.

Have people forgotten Muhammad Youssef Abdulazeez, who shot and killed four US Marines in July 2015 was a Muslim from Kuwait? I can tell you the families of those Marines haven't forgotten. The pain will be with them the rest of their lives.

Muslim on US Navy Nuclear Aircraft Carrier Attempted to Sell Secrets, August 18, 2015

"More problems with the religion of Muhammad surface as a naturalized American citizen, who worked for the US Navy, has been arrested after attempting to sell secret technological information to and agent of the Egyptian government. Mostafa Ahmed Awwad, 35, was indicted by a grand jury on December 3, 2014, according to Department of Justice Documents. The agent he attempted to sell the secrets to was a federal undercover agent, who was working for the FBI.

"*The Navy Times* reports: According to a redacted affidavit from federal agent James Blitzer, Awwad was born in 1979 in Saudi Arabia. He married a US citizen in May 2007 in Cairo, Egypt, and later became a US citizen. At the time of his indictment, Awwad, of Yorktown, Virginia, was working as a civilian engineer in the nuclear engineering and planning department of the Norfolk Naval Shipyard, where he had been hired in February. He had been given a clearance of Secret.

"The indictment and affidavit provide details of how, on Sept. 18, an FBI undercover agent speaking in Arabic contacted Awwad by phone and asked to meet the following day. Awwad subsequently agreed to copy and turn over diagrams and schematics of the carrier, many marked 'NOFORN,' meaning no distribution to foreign citizens." [13]

Trojan Horse. Become a citizen. Lie your way into a position to commit crimes against our country and national security. And who was to be the recipient? Why, one of our allies, of course: Egypt. From the same article above:

"Today, Mr. Awwad is being held responsible for attempting to steal the valuable plans for the USS Ford and to provide them to a foreign government,' said U.S. Attorney Boente. 'This office is committed to safeguarding our nation's sensitive defense information, and we will bring to justice those who seek to steal it. I want to commend our partners at the FBI Norfolk and NCIS Norfolk for their excellent work on this case. 'This case underscores the persistent national security threat posed by insiders stealing critical national defense information in order to benefit foreign governments,' said Assistant Director Coleman."

How much money was stolen from we the people and given to Egypt *in violation of the U.S. Constitution* in 2014? $1.5 BILLION BORROWED dollars in "foreign aid".

Does this sound familiar: Offended Muslims erupt on school board, September 22, 2015

"A school-board meeting in New Jersey descended into chaos when a room full of angry Muslim parents were denied a last-minute request by its members. Tempers were so raw last Thursday when the Jersey City Board of Education decided not to close schools for the Muslim holiday of Eid al-Adha that officials had to order security to 'take charge.' The holiday falls on Sept. 24. **'We're going to be the majority soon!'** said one woman into a microphone, *WNBC-TV* reported Sept. 17." [14]

Is everyone who works for the U.S. government and mayors around this country so stupid they simply don't understand the agenda here? **Yes.** Are they so damn dumb they can't see sucking the teat of political correctness regarding refugees is endangering this country? **Yes.** Then there are those in the U.S. government who have an agenda.

Mosques are popping up all over this country like mushrooms – *even when communities don't want them*. Once again, this goes to the heart of the matter: Muslims claiming Islam is a religion. It's Muslim mosques that are breeding grounds for terrorists and they are here in America. Hasn't anyone noticed when some Muslim who has killed Americans, like the one who beheaded an American in Oklahoma – the first place the FBI goes it to the local mosque?

Second is stop all immigration and refugees of Muslims into this country. There's nothing that can be done about Muslims who have already been given citizenship or born to Muslim parents who are citizens. One can only hope they become good Americans because I hold no ill will towards those who come to this country legally and want to embrace America, *our* culture and *our* history. But I don't believe that's possible if they are Muslims, believe Islam is some sort of religion and that Sharia Law must take precedence over our Constitution.

100,000 Muslims have been allowed into this country year after year and it has to stop. **For God's sake, only a fool would continue to invite the enemy into their own backyard.**

Next we have yet another massive human invasion of countries by refugees who expect other countries to take them in and pay their way – just like the unrelenting human invasion pouring in from our southern border. Those refugees we are seeing on the boob tube and Internet feel they can simply invade other countries and demand those citizens pay their way.

And, after tens of thousands have pushed their way into European countries with tragic results many countries have closed their doors because they simply cannot accommodate all those refugees and neither can we: Kerry: USA to Take 200,000 More Refugees, September 20, 2015

Why Don't Syrians Go to the Gulf Arab States?" Question. Answer: The Gulf States Don't Want Them

"Some European countries have been criticized for offering sanctuary only to as small number of refugees, or for discriminating between Muslims and Christians. There's also been a good deal of continental hand-wringing over the general dysfunction of Europe's systems for migration and asylum. Less ire, though, has been directed at another set of stakeholders who almost certainly should be doing more: Saudi Arabia and the wealthy Arab states along the Persian Gulf. As Amnesty International recently pointed out, the "six Gulf countries — Qatar, United Arab Emirates, Saudi Arabia, Kuwait, Oman and Bahrain — have offered zero resettlement places to Syrian refugees."

There has been one response to those allegations: Saudi Arabia "has taken in 2.5m Syrians", claims minister

"Oil-rich Saudi Arabia has come under criticism for not offering to take in Syrian refugees, however, Turki bin Mohamed bin Saud Alkabeer, Saudi deputy minister for multilateral relations, told reporters in New York that the accusations were 'unfair'. 'We have welcomed 2.5 million Syrians – not as refugees, but as residents,' bin Saud Alkabeer said. 'They are allowed to have education, they are allowed to have access to work and to medical care ... No other country has done what we have done.' He noted that 100,000 Syrian students are currently enrolled in Saudi schools.'"

Good. **That's right where they should be since they are culturally compatible.** Now, if the other oil rich countries listed above would do their part, a lot of suffering will be alleviated.

A lot of those refugees have headed for wealthier countries, many of them using stolen passports or papers. "Muslim migrants target nations with higher wages". That's right. **While we have 94 MILLION unemployed Americans, let's continue importing more poverty and jobs that belong to Americans will end up going to foreigners because they will work for cheap.**

Revealed: Four Out of Five Migrants Are NOT from Syria, September 29, 2015: "One cause of the spike is the number of Afghans lodging asylum claims. They are up four-fold, from 6,300 to 27,000. Another 17,700 claims were made by Albanians, whose country is not at war but does share a European border. A further 13,900 applicants came from Iraq which, like neighbouring Syria, is being smashed by the Islamic State terrorists."

German Police Shoot Asylum Seeker Terrorist Dead, Wasn't Deported Because of EU Human Rights Law, September 18, 2015. "Yesterday morning German police shot dead a knife-wielding terrorist on the streets of Berlin after he stabbed a female police officer in the neck. The Iraqi citizen was a convicted terrorist and an asylum seeker who Germany had been powerless to deport because of his "human rights."'

America is drowning in debt. In July 2015, Rep. Brian Babin (R-TX) reported 500,000 Muslims have been re-settled since the person in the White House took office. He also said 3 out of 4 refugees are on government welfare – *unconstitutional spending*. Not only is this an economic hardship for we the people slapped with more and more taxes, *it's a severe national security risk*. Statistics are showing a huge number of those refugees are male between the ages of 18 and 30. Just the right age for terrorists.

Refugees: Another One for the "Not Our Problem" File, September 9, 2015, Ann Coulter

"Fazliddin Kurbanov, or 'Idaho man,' as he is dutifully described in the American media, was brought to the U.S. as a refugee in 2009, joining hundreds of other Uzbeks in Boise, Idaho. He came with his wife and young child, his sister and his two ailing parents." (What an economic powerhouse that family must be. Marco Rubio is right: We're making all kinds of money off of immigrants!)

"So grateful was Kurbanov to America for rescuing his entire family from 'persecution' that he spent the next few years conspiring to commit jihad against us. As he cheerfully told his terrorist buddies back in Uzbekistan: 'We are the closest ones to infidels. We have almost everything. What would you say if, with the help of God, we implement a martyrdom act? ... There are military installations right here, targets, and vehicles are available as well.'"

"Kurbanov had plenty of time on his hands to plot terrorist attacks in the U.S. because he was being supported by you, taxpayer. As the *Lewiston Morning Tribune* (Idaho) reported: He was 'struggling' to find a job – preferably something that involved either marketing or killing all the Jews. Last month, Kurbanov was convicted of various terrorism charges, based on his possession of Tannerite, ammonium nitrate, bullets and aluminum powder, as well as his stated intention, in conversations recorded by the FBI, to bomb military bases in Idaho and Texas.'"

Go ahead, read the entire article about more poor refugee *scum who bragged about killing Americans who were then relocated to this country*. It is pure insanity and the States of the Union had better buck up and tell Obama and John Kerry, another grossly failed Secretary of State: We will not take any refugees, period. Don't send them because they will not be allowed off the planes, trains or buses in our state.

In June 2014 Syria had elections and Assad was reelected. The Syrian rebels didn't want Assad to run for reelection and openly said they would disrupt the elections including bombing government controlled areas as well as polling places. Those wonderful rebels killed 50 innocent voters with their shelling. Those weapons likely paid for by the sweat off your back.

There were multiple candidates on the ballot for that election. Those rebels didn't like it that Assad was reelected by the people of Syria. Fine. Instead of causing so much death and destruction, you work towards getting your candidate elected in the next election. Sometimes it takes a while, but educating a population as to why things can be better under a new leader takes time. No, instead let's just keep a bloody civil war going causing more death, destruction and unbearable conditions for your own fellow country men and women. And much of that death and destruction, America, has been funded by YOU and me with more debt.

Now the truth emerges: How the US fueled the rise of Isis in Syria and Iraq, June 3, 2015, *www.theguardian.com* [Emphasis mine]

"In reality, US and western policy in the conflagration that is now the Middle East is in the classic mould of imperial divide-and-rule. American forces bomb one set of rebels while backing another in Syria, and mount what are effectively joint military operations with Iran against Isis in Iraq while supporting Saudi Arabia's military campaign against Iranian-backed Houthi forces in Yemen. However, confused US policy may often be, a weak, partitioned Iraq and Syria fit such an approach perfectly.

"What's clear is that Isis and its monstrosities won't be defeated by the same powers that brought it to Iraq and Syria in the first place, or whose open and covert war-making has fostered it in the years since. **Endless western military interventions in the Middle East have brought only destruction and division. It's the people of the region who can cure this disease – not those who incubated the virus.**"

I hope you will also contact your governor, attorney general and a good idea to include your mayor: Refuse to take any refugees from any countries in the Middle East for all the reasons above. **If we do nothing, nothing will get done**. Unless we the people stand up and demand our states refuse those refugees don't start crying about your next tax bill or when a football stadium, mall or big hospital is blown to smithereens – and, mark my words – it's coming.

Don't look to the gutless weenies in the Outlaw Congress to take action because so far they've allowed the State Department and Hussein Obama to shred the Refugee Act of 1980.

Syrian surge! "Refugees" flood into U.S. at rate of 358 per week – "Obama is doing everything within his power to advance an Islamic invasion", April 12, 2016, *WND*

"A flood of Muslim refugees from Syria, an average of 358 per week to be exact, is expected to arrive in the United States between now and the end of the fiscal year on Sept. 30. The Obama administration has decided to implement a "surge" in Syrian refugees, fast-tracking the arrival of those fleeing civil war in that country to make good on its commitment of bringing 10,000 by the end of fiscal 2016."

This is INSANITY. Coupled with the mass INVASION going on right now on our southern border – tens of thousands of illegals flooding across every month – we ARE being invaded. No verifiable background checks. Terrorists crossing the border and what are American's hopping up and down about? Tom Brady is going to have to sit out four games this season or endless coverage about Kim Kardasian's sizeable rear end; don't get me started on those witless females.

I am a devout Christian and I am truly sorry for the people over in Syria. The killing can stop but those rebels funded with the sweat off your back **don't want it to stop.** I am truly sorry for the heinous and murderous rampage in the Middle East and all the innocent people suffering at the hands of Satan's Soldiers, ISIS. What's going on with ISIS and other terrorist groups in Middle Eastern countries is EXACTLY why Americans cherish the Second Amendment and why we will NOT give in to the gun grabbers.

Please think back to Bush, Sr.'s invasion of Kuwait:

"The Invasion of Kuwait, also known as the Iraq–Kuwait War, was a major conflict between Ba'athist Iraq and the Emirate of Kuwait, which resulted in the seven-month-long Iraqi occupation of Kuwait, and subsequently led to direct military intervention by US-led forces in the Gulf War and the setting alight by Iraq of 600 Kuwaiti oil wells.

"In 1990 Iraq accused Kuwait of stealing Iraqi petroleum through slant drilling, although some Iraqi sources indicated Saddam Hussein's decision to attack Kuwait was made a few months before the actual invasion. Some feel there were several reasons for the Iraqi move, including Iraq's inability to pay more than US$80 billion that had been borrowed to finance the Iran–Iraq war, and Kuwaiti overproduction of petroleum which kept revenues down for Iraq. The invasion started on 2 August 1990, and within two days of intense combat, most of the Kuwait Armed Forces were either overrun by the Iraqi Republican Guard or fell back to neighboring Saudi Arabia and Bahrain. The Emirate of Kuwait was annexed, and Saddam Hussein announced a few days later that it was the 19th province of Iraq." *Wikipedia.*

Back then, Saddam Hussein was a good buddy to the ruling elite in Washington, DC; oil, you know. Prior to that show of American imperialism did we have all these problems with Muslims? Prior to the undeclared "war" and invasion of Iraq killing millions and the invasion of Afghanistan did we have all this trouble with Muslims and terrorist groups? We did not.

We have the absolute right to defend our country. If we were invaded over a lie and some foreign country was dropping tons of ordnance on our people wouldn't we fight back?

It's a terrible double edge sword. Sane people do not want war. Those who profit from it welcome more killing and bloodshed.

Former Congressman Ron Paul regularly spoke and wrote about "blow back" – our actions have consequences. It was not a popular opinion because of 9/11 and the massive hype about Hussein and his alleged stockpile of weapons of mass destruction. Oh, that's right. Bush, Jr., said we went to Iraq to liberate the people!

Well, the blow back is in our face and anyone who thinks violence by Muslims in this country isn't going to get worse simply doesn't believe history **because that's all Muslims bring to any country.** The hatred against Americans by Muslims is right there for anyone to see. **How many more decades are we going to unconstitutionally occupy countries in the Middle East chasing down terrorists the shadow government helped create through our military actions in those countries?**

Don't we have our hands full already without taking in more people when we don't even know who they really are? Haven't people seen the film clips of women training with ISIS to torture and murder anyone who gets in their way? A Muslim serving in the military who slaughters 13 of our best. A Muslim trying to steal plans for one of our submarines. So-called 'honor killings' in this country as well as an American beheaded by a Muslim. Some Muslim woman screaming at a school board they will soon be the majority.

As I write this chapter, London(istan) has just committed national suicide by electing a Muslim for mayor. It's all but about over for them. In ten years they will be ruled under the toxic Sharia Law. They will be the minority. They will be dead.

It is neither xenophobic or bigotry to recognize there is an agenda going on that is to totally transform this constitutional republic into a nightmare. **Nor is it hate speech when one writes factual information about any subject just because someone else doesn't like the truth.** I am so sick and tired of gutless sissies in this country too afraid to stand up and speak the truth for fear of being slapped with some label.

Tell your mayors and city councils: NO mosques in your city or town.

Publius Huldah Explains Why Islamists Don't Have the Right to Build Mosques, Proselytize or Institute Sharia Law in America, April 9, 2013

"Publius Huldah, a retired attorney, Constitutional scholar and a gracious contributor to Freedom Outpost, addressed the Act for America Chapter in Fayetteville, Tennessee recently and demonstrated that the First Amendment does not give Islamists the right to build mosques, proselytize, and institute Sharia law in the United States. She also took time to point out that multiculturalism is not and that Islam is not a peaceful religion.

"We face a grave threat," she began. "Islamists are infiltrating our country and taking over. Our Federal, state and local governments won't even acknowledge the threat."

"Publius Huldah points out that the "Islamists seek to replace our Constitution, our religion and our culture with Sharia, their totalitarian political, economic, military, social and legal system. They are making progress and conquering our country because we are not resisting. We are not resisting because people actually believe Islamists have "constitutional rights" to build mosques and proselytize here and that those who oppose them are haters, racists, xenophobes (someone who hates and fears other cultures), and intolerant." [15]

On October 23, 2015, FBI Director James Comey told a bunch of intelligence officials there are close to 1,000 investigations pending against suspected "Islamic State" inspired operations. That included some rag tag "home grown violent extremists" of which there are in this country. Comey did say the vast majority involved ISIL who I call Satan's Soldiers. He also said it was unclear whether or not the FBI had enough money to go after them all. *He's talking about here in the U.S., not some country in the Middle East.* Recruiting of young males is growing through social media campaigns. **So, why are we importing more of them?**

As I said in my column above it's up to we the people to tell our governors, state reps and senators and mayors and your city council: We do not want any more Muslim refugees regardless of what country the UN wants to send them from, send them someplace else. Thankfully, it looks like that's starting to happen:

U.S. state draws line in sand against Islamization, November 12, 2015, *WND*.

"A third South Carolina county has barred the door to any Third World refugees being resettled in their community, and at least two others are considering the same move. The Berkeley County Council unanimously passed a resolution Monday that bars any refugee funds from flowing into that county. The resolution calls for "all South Carolina public officials to immediately cease and desist" from helping to resettle Middle Eastern refugees anywhere in the state until the legislature can act on the issue and pass legislation reflecting the will of the people."

"Anderson and Pickens counties already passed similar resolutions. Two more counties – Greenville and York – are expected to vote soon on similar resolutions. South Carolina is the only state that gives local governments the option of rejecting, not necessarily the refugees, but the state and federal tax dollars that flow to their aid when they are resettled in a city."

And, where is the U.S. Congress? All they have to do is pull the funding plug. Instead, it's politics and tolerance while America is put at grave risk and it's coming.

19

In Closing

Everything you have read in this book is true. I've worked very hard over the past 26 years to maintain my credibility and be sure of facts before I write my columns or appear on talk radio. I spent days checking links, attributions and quotes for accuracy in this book. All writers go through it at the end.

Millions of Americans are suffering because incumbents in the U.S. Congress – both parties – have destroyed this country with their lies, greed and patently un-American agendas. The single worst treachery is to bring these united States of America into a one world government where we have no borders and would answer to a world body. How those who spilled their blood to birth a new nation, America, must be spinning in their graves.

I do no exaggerate when I say millions of "Americans", 61 million now foreign born in this country, care absolutely nothing for the very documents that gives them so much freedom, the U.S. Constitution and the Bill of Rights. They come here with no allegiance to America as did my grandparents from Palermo, Sicily and Munich, Germany.

When both sets of my grandparents came to America, they literally kissed the ground at Ellis Island. They were so grateful to have a chance at a new life after coming here legally; waiting their turn which illegal aliens don't give a damn about. It's not that my grandparents forgot about where they came from but they came to become Americans. Not Italian-American or German-American, but American, period.

America, a nation drowning in unpayable debt, continues to import third world illiterates who demand WE bow down to their customs and a political party called Islam masquerading as a religion hell bent on establishing their toxic caliphate in this country. They demand we pay their way for everything from medical care, education to welfare.

The government indoctrination centers they call public schools have deliberately dumbed down America's precious school children. Thousands of schools across this country no longer teach the history of this country. Instead they promote the toxic poison called globalism.

Kindergartners: "We pledge allegiance to international flag"– Exclusive: Chuck Norris blasts "anti-American, unpatriotic sentiment" pervading schools, *WND.com*, March 6, 2016

"We pledge allegiance to an international flag"? Hannity.com reported on Friday, "Kindergarten students from PS75, a public school in New York City, recently took part in a class project in which the children were made to create an American flag with the flags of 22 other nations superimposed over the stripes. Below the flag read the words, "We pledge allegiance to an international flag..."

In violation of federal law, 18 US code §700 – Desecration of the flag of the United States; penalties. Author Chuck Norris adds more: "In 2010, a 13-year-old Northern California student was told by officials from his middle school that he could not ride onto campus with a U.S. flag on his bike...

"In 2013, a Texas high-school student was punished for refusing to recite the Mexican pledge of allegiance, so she filed a federal lawsuit against her school and her teachers.

"In 2014, *WND* reported that another northern California school's officials ordered students not to wear U.S. flag-themed shirts on Cinco de Mayo, in fear that Hispanic students would retaliate. Their ban was upheld by a federal appeals court. And when a small group of protesters waving the American flag stood in front of the school, they were considered "racists."

"In 2015, the University of California-Irvine student government voted to remove all flags, including the "offensive American flag," from its main lobby and "inclusive space."

Most Americans have zero knowledge of the Communist Party International. Through repeated propaganda, millions of Americans think communism is dead. They couldn't be more wrong. These are the ones not listed in the education chapter:

Communist Goals (1963), Congressional Record– Appendix, pp. A34-A35, January 10, 1963, Extension of Remarks of Hon. A.S. Herlong, Jr., of Florida in the House of Representatives, Thursday, January 10, 1963. Some were covered in 11 on education. Here are more:

Permit free trade between all nations regardless of Communist affiliation and regardless of whether or not items could be used for war.

Provide American aid to all nations regardless of Communist domination.

Promote the U.N. as the only hope for mankind. If its charter is rewritten, demand that it be set up as a one-world government with its own independent armed forces. (Some Communist leaders believe the world can be taken over as easily by the U.N. as by Moscow. Sometimes these two centers compete with each other as they are now doing in the Congo.)

Capture one or both of the political parties in the United States.

Gain control of key positions in radio, TV, and motion pictures.

Continue discrediting American culture by degrading all forms of artistic expression. An American Communist cell was told to "eliminate all good sculpture from parks and buildings, substitute shapeless, awkward and meaningless forms."

Eliminate all laws governing obscenity by calling them "censorship" and a violation of free speech and free press.

Break down cultural standards of morality by promoting pornography and obscenity in books, magazines, motion pictures, radio, and TV.

Present homosexuality, degeneracy and promiscuity as "normal, natural, healthy."

Infiltrate the churches and replace revealed religion with "social" religion. Discredit the Bible and emphasize the need for intellectual maturity which does not need a "religious crutch."

Eliminate prayer or any phase of religious expression in the schools on the ground that it violates the principle of "separation of church and state."

Discredit the American Constitution by calling it inadequate, old-fashioned, out of step with modern needs, a hindrance to cooperation between nations on a worldwide basis.

Discredit the American Founding Fathers. Present them as selfish aristocrats who had no concern for the "common man."

Belittle all forms of American culture and discourage the teaching of American history on the ground that it was only a minor part of the "big picture." Give more emphasis to Russian history since the Communists took over.

Support any socialist movement to give centralized control over any part of the culture – education, social agencies, welfare programs, mental health clinics, etc.

Discredit the family as an institution. Encourage promiscuity and easy divorce.

Emphasize the need to raise children away from the negative influence of parents. Attribute prejudices, mental blocks and retarding of children to suppressive influence of parents. [End]

Every one of those goals have been fully accomplished here in America while people are lined up for blocks to buy the latest cheap tech gadget made by slave labor in communist China or drowning themselves during happy hour at some local watering hole while they spout off about democracy.

"But between a balanced republic and a democracy, the difference is like that between order and chaos." — John Marshall (1755-1835) was a U.S. House Member, Secretary of State became 4th Chief Justice of the Supreme Court

On April 28, 2016, presidential candidate, Donald Trump, spoke at a rally in Costa Mesa, California. Likely some of the protesters were Mexican illegal aliens waving Mexican flags, beat bloody Trump supporters, destroyed a police car and created mayhem. Some held signs claiming we stole their land referring to the southern border states. Because they're uneducated, *they don't even know the history of their own country*, much less ours:

Treaty of Guadalupe Hidalgo, Library of Congress

"The Treaty of Guadalupe Hidalgo was signed by the United States and Mexico on February 2, 1848, ending the Mexican War and extending the boundaries of the United States by over 525,000 square miles. In addition to establishing the Rio Grande as the border between the two countries, the territory acquired by the U.S. included what will become the states of Texas, California, Nevada, Utah, most of New Mexico and Arizona, and parts of Colorado and Wyoming. In exchange Mexico received fifteen million dollars in compensation for the territory and the U.S. agreed to assume claims from private citizens of these areas against the Mexican government."

The U.S. paid the Mexican government $15 MILLION dollars. Back in 1848 that was a ton of gold. So, you see, we did not steal anything from Mexico and *if Mexicans have a problem with that treaty they should take it up with their corrupt government* and stop their destruction of OUR country.

Donald Trump wears a bullet proof vest. A presidential candidate in 2016. How absolutely shameful. Paid agitators and politically correct morons in this country who have zero command of the facts nor do they care a whit about the truth plan violence at the Republican Convention in July in Cleveland, Ohio (which is why I won't attend to cover that event; I can't afford body guards). All because they want to keep the gravy train supplying their every want and need.

America will elect a new president this November. However, a president is not – despite the best efforts of the current occupant of the White House – a king. A president under OUR constitution is limited in the scope of what he can and cannot do under Art. II:

Section 2.

The President shall be commander in chief of the Army and Navy of the United States, and of the militia of the several states, when called into the actual service of the United States; he may require the opinion, in writing, of the principal officer in each of the executive departments, upon any subject relating to the duties of their respective offices, and he shall have power to grant reprieves and pardons for offenses against the United States, except in cases of impeachment.

He shall have power, by and with the advice and consent of the Senate, to make treaties, provided two thirds of the Senators present concur;

and he shall nominate, and by and with the advice and consent of the Senate, shall appoint ambassadors, other public ministers and consuls, judges of the Supreme Court, and all other officers of the United States, whose appointments are not herein otherwise provided for, and which shall be established by law: but the Congress may by law vest the appointment of such inferior officers, as they think proper, in the President alone, in the courts of law, or in the heads of departments.

The President shall have power to fill up all vacancies that may happen during the recess of the Senate, by granting commissions which shall expire at the end of their next session.

Section 3.

He shall from time to time give to the Congress information of the state of the union, and recommend to their consideration such measures as he shall judge necessary and expedient; he may, on extraordinary occasions, convene both Houses, or either of them, and in case of disagreement between them, with respect to the time of adjournment, he may adjourn them to such time as he shall think proper; he shall receive ambassadors and other public ministers; he shall take care that the laws be faithfully executed, and shall commission all the officers of the United States. [End]

The silent majority has again risen up against tyranny, corruption and the near and complete destruction of our beloved republic. However, one must remember that all spending bills must originate in the U.S. House of Representatives. A sitting president has no constitutional authority to spend the people's purse without Congress passing a bill reconciled by both the House and Senate and sent to a president to either sign or veto.

Sadly, as we go to press, over 95% of incumbents from both parties have won their primaries (more still to come) and will go on to win in November. I'll ask again as I have said so many times: **Do people expect change and problems solved by reelecting the same incumbents who never got the job done in all the years they've been in Congress?**

With 95% or higher of the same incumbents who have refused to cure the cancer instead of treat the symptoms and have done nothing to stop the massive illegal invasion, correct the disabilities of our monetary system and all you've read in this book – **how does anyone think there will be any change or problems solved by reelecting those same incumbents to go back to Washington, DC and continue destroying this country?** And, please, don't tell me "it's the other party".

Legislation to shut down our borders, abolish the unconstitutional "Fed", stop all unconstitutional foreign aid, abolish the unconstitutional Obamacare – **all has to come from Congress, not the Oval Office**. Certainly a president has limited use of Executive Orders, can overturn Executive Orders and can use the power of the 'bully pulpit' to try to get Congress to act, but the same incumbents winning in November is going to put the situation at a standstill because it will be party politics first, not solutions.

I have given you the truth in this book. I hope you will share it with other Americans trying desperately to save our country. If you belong to a tea party chapter or other groups in this country fighting to take back America, the publisher of this book is giving good bulk discounts. Please help spread the truth because *you can't solve a problem if you don't really understand how it started.* How well I know!

This book is full of resources, but I would leave you with two more I feel very strongly everyone should watch. For full disclosure I receive no compensation in any form for recommendations in this book and the two below:

DVD: *Cultural Marxism – The Corruption of America* is free on the Internet. Full length, just type the title into a search engine. "A love affair with collectivist ideologies has led to ever bigger government and the welfare-warfare state. Lead by a Marxist splinter group called the 'Frankfurt School' – 'the long march through the institutions' has infiltrated every corner of Western culture to corrupt traditional Christian values with 'political correctness,' another name for 'cultural Marxism.'"

The Purse and the Sword. A 4 DVD set that every member of Congress who isn't a socialist or Marxist and every state representative and senator must watch if they are going to do their constitutional duty. Of all the DVDs I've seen over the decades, this one featuring Dr. Edwin Vieira, Jr., Ph.D., J.D., is the most powerful:

"In this one-of-a-kind presentation Dr. Vieira utilizes his 'Visual Constitution' to demonstrates both the government's and the people's unique capacities to remedy both these and other crisis in accordance with the law of the Constitution. The clarity and common sense approach that Dr. Vieira utilizes to explain these very complex issues in a way that anyone can understand makes this DVD set truly a MUST SEE for all Americans." Order on line or snail mail: Heritage Research Institute, The Purse & The Sword DVD, 4723 Hasslick Rd, North Branch, MI 48461.

http://www.heritageresearchinstitute.org/PurseSwordPage.htm

We live in the most dangerous time since the Revolutionary War. Our fate, the fate of our country and the future of our children and grandchildren is at stake. Nothing is more important than taking back our country from the forces determined to destroy us. It is now up to we the people.

"The liberties of our country, the freedom of our civil constitution, are worth defending at all hazards; and it is our duty to defend them against all attacks. We have received them as a fair inheritance from our worthy ancestors: they purchased them for us with toil, danger and expense of treasure and blood, and transmitted them to us with care and diligence. It will bring an everlasting mark of infamy on the present generation, enlightened as it is, if we should suffer them to be wrested from us by violence without a struggle, or be cheated out of them by the artifices of false and designing men." Samuel Adams, American revolutionary leader.

Endnotes & Additional Resources

Chapter 1

[1] – Overstock Holds 3 Months Of Food, $10 Million In Gold For Employees In Preparation For The Next Collapse, Tyler Durden, October 25, 2015
http://www.zerohedge.com/news/2015-10-24/overstock-holds-3-months-food-10-million-gold-employees-preparation-next-collapse

[2] –National debt sees one-day record increase after debt limit suspended, November 4,2015, MSN
http://www.msn.com/en-us/money/topstories/national-debt-sees-one-day-record-increase-after-debt-limit-suspended/ar-BBmQkxi?li=AAa0dzB

Chapter 2

[1] - There is No Such Thing as a Fair Tax, December 12, 2005
https://mises.org/library/there-no-such-thing-fair-tax

[2] - There is Still No Such Thing As a Fair Tax
https://mises.org/library/there-still-no-such-thing-fair-tax

[3] - Fair tax is a trap: Demand NO vote on H.R. 25, August 9, 2010
http://www.devvy.com/new_site/fair_tax_080910.html

[4] - The Flat Tax Is Not Flat and the Fair Tax Is Not Fair, April 3, 2009
https://mises.org/library/flat-tax-not-flat-and-fairtax-not-fair

[5] - US to Give $125 Million to Upgrade Pakistan's Power Sector. October 29, 2009
http://www.wsj.com/articles/SB125673882918513095

[6] - U.S. pays for Indonesians' master's degrees - Obama expanding program with $16-$20 million

http://www.wnd.com/2012/02/u-s-paying-for-indonesians-masters-degrees/

Chapter 3

[1] - NAFTA at 20
http://www.citizen.org

[2] - NAFTA and CAFTA – And now OUTSOURCING! They're all bad for Americans
http://aoafa.org/nafta-and-cafta-and-now-outsourcing-theyre-all-bad-for-americans/

[3] - U.S. taxpayers expected to upgrade communist Vietnam, November 9, 2014, WND
http://www.wnd.com/2014/11/u-s-taxpayers-expected-to-upgrade-communist-vietnam/

[4] - Rand Paul to Obama: "Prioritize" Passage of Trans-Pacific Partnership, November 3, 2014, The New American
http://www.thenewamerican.com/usnews/politics/item/19439-rand-paul-to-obama-prioritize-passage-of-trans-pacific-partnership

Facts about the TransPacific Partnership (TPP) and more:

Canada Claims It Will Back Out of TPP to Protect Its Sovereignty, July 17, 2015, The New American
http://www.thenewamerican.com/usnews/foreign-policy/item/21270-canada-claims-it-will-back-out-of-tpp-to-protect-its-sovereignty

Stop the North American Union/SPP, August 27, 2007, My column
http://www.newswithviews.com/Devvy/kidd298.htm

Connecting the Americas 2022, September 22, 203, My column
http://www.newswithviews.com/Devvy/kidd605.htm

10 Reasons Why You Should Oppose TPP and TTIP, June 5, 2015, The New American

http://www.thenewamerican.com/usnews/constitution/item/21010-10-reasons-why-you-should-oppose-obamatrade

Just Another Factory Closing, September 23, 2015, Hanover, ILL. All 100 jobs in that small town are heading for Mexico
http://www.theatlantic.com/business/archive/2015/09/factory-closure-private-equity/406264/

No wonder Obama won't let us read TPP, June 15, 2015, WND
http://www.wnd.com/2015/06/no-wonder-obama-wont-let-us-read-tpp/

Why the Seventeenth Amendment must go:

Here's how much corporations paid US senators to fast-track the TPP bill, May 27, 2015, The Guardian
http://www.theguardian.com/business/2015/may/27/corporations-paid-us-senators-fast-track-tpp

Trump: I'd Break NAFTA, It's "A Disaster", September 25, 2015, NewsMax
http://www.newsmax.com/Newsfront/NAFTA-TRUMP-BREAK-DEAL/2015/09/25/id/693391/

Obamatrade Undermines Intellectual Property, Crushes Freedom of Expression, October 10, 2015, Brietbart
http://www.breitbart.com/big-government/2015/10/10/report-obamatrade-undermines-intellectual-property-crushes-freedom-expression/

Border crisis linked to North American Union, August 13, 2014, WND
http://www.wnd.com/2014/08/border-crisis-linked-to-north-american-union/

Stop TPP - TransPacific Partnership like NAFTA on Steroids
http://stoptpp.org/

Chapter 4

[1] --Warning sign: Tech companies of All Sizes and Ages Are Starting to Have Layoffs, October 19, 2015, David Stockman
http://davidstockmanscontracorner.com/warning-sign-tech-companies-of-all-sizes-and-ages-are-starting-to-have-layoffs/

[2] - Ignore the Media Bullsh*t - Retail Implosion Proves We Are in Recession, October 14, 2015, *TheBurningPlatform.com*
http://www.theburningplatform.com/2015/10/14/ignore-the-media-bullsht-retail-implosion-proves-we-are-in-recession/

[3] - None Is So Blind As He Who Will Not See, Congressional Record. House of Representatives January 15, 1962
http://www.devvy.com/utt_20020410.html

[4] - Congressman Mike Rogers Introduces Bill to Get U.S. Out of UN, June 12, 2015, *The New American*
http://www.thenewamerican.com/usnews/congress/item/21058-congressman-mike-rogers-introduces-bill-to-get-u-s-out-of-un

[5] --Detroit Pension Cuts From Bankruptcy Prompt Cries of Betrayal, February 4, 2015, *Bloomberg Business*
http://www.bloomberg.com/news/articles/2015-02-05/detroit-pension-cuts-from-bankruptcy-prompt-cries-of-betrayal

[6] - State high court strikes down pension reform, May 8, 2015
http://www.chicagobusiness.com/article/20150508/BLOGS02/150509835/state-high-court-strikes-down-pension-reform

[7] - Teacher pensions: The math adds up to a crisis, January 28, 2015, *CBS Money Watch*
http://www.cbsnews.com/news/teacher-pensions-the-math-adds-up-to-a-crisis/

[8] - Large pension fund files plan to cut retiree benefits under new law, October 7, 2015, *MSN Money*
http://www.msn.com/en-us/money/retirement/large-pension-fund-files-plan-to-cut-retiree-benefits-under-new-law/ar-AAfbeQN?li=AAa0dzB

[9] - California's farmers left high and dry by drought, environmental regs, October 7, 2015, *FOX News Science*
http://www.foxnews.com/science/2015/10/07/california-farmers-left-high-and-dry-by-drought-environmental-regs.html?intcmp=hplnws

Recommended Reading:

The Echo Bubble in Housing Is About to Pop, September 29, 2015, Charles Hugh Smith
https://www.lewrockwell.com/2015/09/charles-hugh-smith/pop-3/

Clear Signs That The Great Derivatives Crisis Has Now Begun
http://etfdailynews.com/2015/10/07/clear-signs-that-the-great-derivatives-crisis-has-now-begun/

Almost a Third of Those with Savings Have Less Than $1,000 for Retirement, April 22, 2015, Breitbart (A national tragedy)
http://www.breitbart.com/big-government/2015/04/22/almost-a-third-of-savers-have-banked-less-than-1000-for-retirement/

National epidemic: Public employees "spiking" pensions - Taxpayers "squeezed and abused in every imaginable way", WND
http://www.wnd.com/2014/01/national-epidemic-public-employees-spiking-pensions/

Major U.S. Retailers Are Closing More Than 6,000 Stores, May 2, 2015
http://www.infowars.com/major-u-s-retailers-are-closing-more-than-6000-stores/

Another Government Housing Bubble. Government Using Subprime Mortgages to Pump Housing Recovery – Taxpayers will Pay Again, May 6, 2015
http://www.theburningplatform.com/2015/05/05/government-using-subprime-mortgages-to-pump-housing-recovery-taxpayers-will-pay-again/

GAO: Union Pension Insurance Fund "Likely To Be Insolvent"

Within Decade, February 24, 2015, CNS News
http://www.cnsnews.com/news/article/barbara-hollingsworth/gao-union-pension-insurance-fund-likely-be-insolvent-within

We Are About To Witness Orchestrated Financial Destruction And Social Unrest That Is Beyond Imagination, March 9, 2015
http://kingworldnews.com/witness-orchestrated-financial-destruction-social-unrest-beyond-imagination/

The Economy Is Not Recovering - Get Prepared, December 28, 2014, My column packed with important information and data
http://www.newswithviews.com/Devvy/kidd665.htm

The 401(k) crisis is getting worse, October 21, 2015, by Carol Hymowitz
http://www.msn.com/en-us/money/retirement/the-401-k-crisis-is-getting-worse/ar-BBmhbUd?li=AA4Zjn

The Six Too Big To Fail Banks In The U.S. Have 278 TRILLION Dollars Of Exposure To Derivatives, April 13, 2015, Michael Snyder
http://theeconomiccollapseblog.com/archives/the-six-too-big-to-fail-banks-in-the-u-s-have-278-trillion-dollars-of-exposure-to-derivatives

Chapter 5

[1] - Understanding why Americans' insurance plans are being canceled, *PBS Newshour*, November 12, 2013
http://www.pbs.org/newshour/bb/government_programs-july-dec13-health_11-12/

[2] - Obamacare Skyrockets Cancer Patient's Meds to $14,000, February 24, 2014, *Brietbart*
http://www.breitbart.com/big-government/2014/02/24/obamacare-skyrockets-cancer-patient-s-meds-to-14-000-for-8-week-supply/

[3] - Hawaii's $205 Million Obamacare Exchange Implodes, May 12, 2015

https://www.atr.org/hawaii-s-205-million-obamacare-exchange-implodes

[4] - Almost 80% of Hawaii Obamacare Enrollees Have Failed to Pay Premiums in 2015, Americans For Tax Reform
https://www.atr.org/almost-80-hawaii-obamacare-enrollees-have-failed-pay-premiums-2015

[5] - Vermont's Giving Up On Single-Payer Health Care Over Ballooning Costs, December 17, 2014, *The Daily Caller*
http://dailycaller.com/2014/12/17/vermonts-giving-up-on-single-payer-health-care-over-ballooning-costs/

[6] - Incompetence, Mismanagement Plague California's Obamacare Insurance Exchange
http://dailysignal.com/2015/04/20/incompetence-mismanagement-plague-californias-obamacare-insurance-exchange/

[7] - Insiders Detail Culture of Secrecy at California's Obamacare Exchange - Part 2
http://dailysignal.com/2015/04/21/whistleblowers-detail-culture-of-secrecy-at-californias-obamacare-exchange/

[8] - Obamacare Insurance Premiums to Jump, up to 51%, May 25, 2015, Breitbart
http://www.breitbart.com/big-government/2015/05/25/obamacare-insurance-premiums-to-jump-up-to-51/

[9] - CBO Now Says 10 Mil Will Lose Employer Health Plans Under ObamaCare, January 27, 2015, Investors.com
http://news.investors.com/ibd-editorials-obama-care/012715-736559-cbo-says-obamacare-will-push-10-million-of-employer-plans.htm<>

[10] - Feds Can't Verify $2.8 Billion in Obamacare Subsidies, June 16, 2015, *The Washington Free Beacon*
http://freebeacon.com/issues/feds-cant-verify-2-8-billion-in-obamacare-subsidies/

[11] - Because Of Obamacare, 123-Year-Old Major Health Insurance Provider Set To Close Its Doors, May 6, 2015, *Western Journalism*
http://www.westernjournalism.com/because-of-obamacare-123-year-old-major-health-insurance-provider-set-to-close-its-doors/

[12] - Mercy Health Fires 347 Workers Due to Obamacare, June 25, 2015, *Breitbart*
http://www.breitbart.com/big-government/2015/06/25/mercy-health-fires-347-workers-due-to-obamacare/

[13] - 7 Companies That Have to Lay Off Employees to Deal With Obamacare, August 23, 2013, *Policy.mic*
http://mic.com/articles/60661/7-companies-that-have-to-lay-off-employees-to-deal-with-obamacare

[14] - Obamacare brings $273 billion bonanza for paper pushers, May 28, 2015, *MSN News*
http://www.thefiscaltimes.com/2015/05/28/Obamacare-s-273-Billion-Bonanza-Paper-Pushers

[15] - Boehner profits from Obamacare stocks - Medical, insurance investments continue to prosper, January 2015, *WND*
http://www.wnd.com/2015/01/boehner-profits-from-obamacare-stocks/

[16] - How Five Republicans Let Congress Keep Its Fraudulent Obamacare Subsidies, by Brendan Bordelon May 7, 2015, *National Review*
http://www.nationalreview.com/article/418055/how-five-republicans-let-congress-keep-its-fraudulent-obamacare-subsidies-brendan

[17] - Obamacare Effect? 9 Companies Exit Nebraska's Health Insurance Market
http://www.foxnews.com/politics/2013/10/11/obamacare-effect-companies-exit-nebraskas-health-insurance-market.html

Chapter 6

[1] - Non-Ratification of Seventeenth Amendment - Why It's So Important - Max Farrand, The Records of the Federal Convention of 1787
http://oll.libertyfund.org/titles/1057/95683

[2] - The Papers of John Jay
https://dlc.library.columbia.edu/jay

[3] - Why should we repeal the 17th Amendment and forfeit our right to vote for U.S. senators?
http://www.liberty-ca.org/repeal17/states/montana2003oneil.htm

[4] - The Seventeenth Amendment: Should It Be Repealed? Why Direct Election of Senators May Have Been A Serious Mistake
http://writ.corporate.findlaw.com/dean/20020913.html

[5] - Rethinking The 17th Amendment by Trenton Hansen, Mary 13, 2009
http://www.conservativefront.com/2009/05/13/rethinking-the-17th-amendment/

[6] - Zell Miller: Dump 17th Amendment
http://www.wnd.com/2004/04/24390/

Chapter 7

[1] - America First Latinos
http://hosted-p0.vresp.com/869711/61c201ace2/ARCHIVE

[2] - Growing number of Hispanic Texans pushing for tougher immigration laws. March 24, 2015, *Fox News Latino*
http://latino.foxnews.com/latino/news/2015/03/24/hispanic-activists-organizing-in-support-tougher-immigration-laws/

[3] - Illegal Alien Minors Spreading TB, Dengue, Swine Flu. July 8m, 2014, *Judicial Watch*

http://www.judicialwatch.org/blog/2014/07/illegal-alien-minors-spreading-tb-ebola-dengue-swine-flu/

[4] - Nurse: Illegals' baggage includes TB, leprosy, polio, July 9, 2014, *WND*
http://www.wnd.com/2014/07/nurse-illegals-baggage-includes-tb-leprosy-polio/

[5] - Obama gives illegals massive health-care plan - *WND*
http://www.wnd.com/2015/08/obama-gives-illegals-massive-health-care-plan/

[6] - It's Okay for Illegals to Steal Your Identity!, December 14, 2006, *Newswithviews.com*
http://www.newswithviews.com/Devvy/kidd236.htm

[7] -- Identity Theft, Document Fraud, and Illegal Employment By Ronald W. Mortensen, Center for Immigration Studies
http://cis.org/mortensen/identitytheft

[8] - TX Taxpayers Pay Billions for Illegal Aliens to Use State Services, January 16, 2014, *Breitbart*
http://www.breitbart.com/big-government/2014/01/16/exclusive-report-texas-taxpayers-paying-billions-of-dollars-to-fund-illegal-aliens-in-state/

[9] - Illegal immigrants send home $50 billion annually but cost taxpayers more than $113 billion, October 29, 2014
http://immigrationreform.com/2014/10/29/illegal-immigrants-send-home-50-billion-annually-but-cost-taxpayers-more-than-113-billion/

[10] - California DMV Ordered to Overlook Identity Theft by Illegals, January 27, 2015, *Breitbart*
http://www.breitbart.com/california/2015/01/27/exclusive-california-dmv-ordered-to-overlook-identity-theft-by-illegals/

[11] - ISIS Camp a Few Miles from Texas, Mexican Authorities Confirm, April 14, 2015, *Judicial Watch*

http://www.judicialwatch.org/blog/2015/04/isis-camp-a-few-miles-from-texas-mexican-authorities-confirm/

[12] - Father of slain QT clerk: why was criminal migrant free? April 7, 2015, *AZ Central*
http://www.azcentral.com/story/laurieroberts/2015/04/07/steve-ronnebeck-speaks-out/25381993/

[13] - More Than 347,000 Convicted Criminal Immigrants At Large In U.S., July 7, 2015, *Breitbart*
http://www.breitbart.com/big-government/2015/07/07/more-than-347000-convicted-criminal-immigrants-at-large-in-u-s/

[14] - Mexican Criminal Alien Slaughters Motorists Who Tried to Help Him, August 4, 2015, *Newswithviews.com*
http://www.newswithviews.com/NWV-News/news455.htm

[15] - U.S. released thousands of immigrant felons last year. May 15, 2014, *CBS News*
http://www.cbsnews.com/news/report-u-s-released-thousands-of-immigrant-felons-last-year/

[16] - Two Illegals Plead Guilty to Baseball Bat-Machete Murder of Teen, May 5, 2015, *CNS News*
http://www.cnsnews.com/news/article/brittany-m-hughes/two-illegals-plead-guilty-baseball-bat-machete-murder-teen

[17] - Illegal Alien Crime Accounts for over 30% of Murders in Many States, August 8, 2015, *Breitbart*
http://www.breitbart.com/big-journalism/2015/08/08/illegal-alien-crime-accounts-for-over-30-of-murders-in-some-states/

[18] - Illegal alien crime wave in Texas: Nearly 3,000 homicides since 2008, July 24, 2015, *American Thinker*
http://www.americanthinker.com/blog/2015/07/illegal_alien_crime_wave_in_texas_nearly_3000_homicides_since_2008.html

[19] - Immigration Stabilization Act [S.1351]
https://www.govtrack.us/congress/bills/103/s1351

[20] - Filmmakers' Claim: Illegals Were Told To Vote Democrat, Or Be Deported
http://www.westernjournalism.com/claim-democrats-using-shocking-lie-maintain-support-illegals/

[21] - Endless wave of illegal immigrants floods Rio Grande Valley, July 14, 2014, *Fox News*
http://www.foxnews.com/us/2014/07/14/night-time-on-border-endless-wave-illegal-immigrants-floods-rio-grande-valley/

[22] - Birthright Citizenship and Dual Citizenship: Harbingers of Administrative Tyranny
http://imprimis.hillsdale.edu/birthright-citizenship-and-dual-citizenship-harbingers-of-administrative-tyranny/

[23] - Obama Handed 166,000 Criminal Illegals A Free Pass. The Reason Will Outrage You, March 2, 2015, Western Journalism Center
http://www.westernjournalism.com/obama-admin-releases-166000-criminal-illegal-aliens/

Text of the Immigration Stabilization Act of 1993. S 1351 introduced by Dirty Harry Reid who is now retiring from the U.S. Senate.
https://www.govtrack.us/congress/bills/103/s1351/text

Chapter 8

[1] - Congressionally Duped Americans, November 6, 2013, *Frontpage Magazine*
http://www.frontpagemag.com/fpm/209851/congressionally-duped-americans-walter-williams

[2] - Massive Debt, Budget Deal Introduced In Dead of Night, Vote Violates Another Boehner Pledge, October 27, 2015, Brietbart
http://www.breitbart.com/big-government/2015/10/27/massive-debt-budget-deal-introduced-in-dead-of-night-vote-violates-another-boehner-pledge/

[3] - GOP Reps. Pushing to End "Double-Taxing by the Federal Government", January 14, 2013
http://www.theblaze.com/stories/2014/01/22/gop-reps-pushing-to-end-double-taxing-by-the-federal-government/

Chapter 9

<> [1] - Trustees: Social Security Will Run $84 Billion Deficit in 2015, September 1, 2015, *CNSNews.com*
http://www.cnsnews.com/news/article/barbara-hollingsworth/trustees-social-security-will-run-84-billion-deficit-2015

[2] - Can The US Economy Keep Up With This Exponential Chart? July 22, 2013, *Zero Hedge*
http://www.zerohedge.com/news/2013-07-22/can-us-economy-keep-exponential-chart

[3] - Medicare Lawsuit Update
http://thefundforpersonalliberty.org/medicare-lawsuit-update/

Chapter 10

[1] -Smart Meters: A Surveillance and Control Con Job Revealed
http://www.newswithviews.com/NWVexclusive/exclusive127.htm

[2] -Cindy Sage, MA, Sage Associates, Environmental Consultants, Letter of Comment on Smart Meter Report, January 17, 2011
http://sagereports.com/smart-meter-rf/?p=343

[3] - American Academy of Environmental Medicine - Proposed Decision of Commissioner Peevy (Mailed 11/22/2011)
 - BEFORE THE PUBLIC UTILITIES COMMISSION OF THE STATE OF CALIFORNIA
http://www.healthandenvironment.org/docs/AAEMResolution.pdf

[4] - National and Kapodistrian, University of Athens, Faculty of Biology, Department of Cell Biology & Biophysics, Electromagnetic Biology Laboratory, Professor Lukas H. Margaritis,

January 16, 2011
http://sagereports.com/smart-meter-rf/docs/letters/Margaritis_Official_letter_by_Margaritis-Fragopoulou.pdf

[5] -Dr. Magda Havas, S.Sc., Ph.D., Environmental and Resource Studies Program to California Council on Science and Technology (CCST, October 10, 2010)
http://www.wirelesswatchblog.org/wp-content/uploads/2001/11/Declaration-of-Dr.-Magda-Havas.pdf

[6] - Hebrew University - Hadassah School of Public Health and Community Medicine Unit of Occupational and Environmental Medicine,
January 26, 2011 - Letter of Comment on Smart Meter Report
http://sagereports.com/smart-meter-rf/docs/letters/Eli_Richter_CCST_-final.pdf

[7] - Comments on California Council on Science and Technology's Smart Meter Report, January 2011 Nancy Evans, Health
 Science Consultant, San Francisco
http://sagereports.com/smart-meter-rf/docs/letters/Nancy_Evans,_CCST_Smart_Meter_report_NancyEvanscomments.pdf

[8] - The Green Sheen Wearing Thin- How Corporate Environmental Organizations are Providing Cover for the
Mounting Ecological Catastrophe of the "Smart Grid"
http://stopsmartmeters.org/2011/07/26/the-green-sheen-wearing-thin-how-corporate-environmental-organizations-are-providing-cover-for-the-mounting-ecological-catastrophe-of-the-%E2%80%9Csmart-grid%E2%80%9D/

[9] -Olle Johansson, Assoc. Professor, Karolinska Institute, Dept of Neuroscience, July 9, 2011 to the California Public Utilities Commission
http://electromagnetichealth.org/electromagnetic-health-blog/letter-johansson-smart-meters/

[10] - Radio Frequency Radiation: The Invisible Hazards of "Smart" Meters by Dr. Ilya Sandra Perlingieri – August 2011
http://www.globalresearch.ca/radiofrequency-radiation-the-invisible-hazards-of-smart-meters/26082

[11] -Elihu D. Richter MD, MPH (Assoc Professor), Hebrew University-Hadassah, School of Public Health and Community Medicine, Unit of Occupations and Environmental Medicine to Susan Hackwood, Ph.D., Executive Director, California Council on Science and Technology. Letter of Comment on Smart Meter Report
http://sagereports.com/smart-meter-rf/?p=278

[12] - Witness Statement, Andrew Goldsworthy, Lecturer in Biology (retired), Imperial College, London
http://thermoguy.com/wp-content/uploads/Declaration-of-Dr.-Andrew-Goldsworthy.pdf

[13] -Overloading of Towns and Cities with Radio Transmitters: A hazard for the human health and disturbance of eco-ethics.
Karl Hecht, Elena N. Savoley, IRCHET International Research Center of Healthy and Ecological Technology, Berlin, Germany
http://www.hese-project.org/hese-uk/en/niemr/hechtvortrag070724englisch.pdf

[14] -Comments on California Council on Science and Technology's Smart Meter Report, January 2011, Nancy Evans, Health Science Consultant, San Francisco. United States District Court – District of Oregon – Portland Division – June 2011
http://sagereports.com/smart-meter-rf/docs/letters/Nancy_Evans,_CCST_Smart_Meter_report_NancyEvanscomments.pdf

[15] -Comments on the Draft Report by the California Council on Science and Technology "Health Impacts of Radio Frequency from Smart Meters" by Daniel Hirsch.
http://www.committeetobridgethegap.org/pdf/110212_RFrad_comments.pdf

Chapter 11

[1] - "Underfunded" Baltimore schools among best funded in nation
http://www.wnd.com/2015/05/underfunded-baltimore-schools-among-best-funded-in-nation/

[2] - The New England Primer - Religious Roots
http://familyphonics.com/ab/ab1/history.htm

[3] - We Are At War For Our Children's Mind and Soul
http://www.newswithviews.com/iserbyt/iserbyt129.htm

[4] - School districts spending millions on "white privilege" training for employees
http://eagnews.org/school-districts-spending-millions-on-white-privilege-training-for-employees/

[5] - Father Protests Islamic Indoctrination in Florida Curriculum – School District Justifies It with Support of Terror Group
http://freedomoutpost.com/2015/02/father-protests-islamic-indoctrination-florida-curriculum-school-district-justifies-support-terror-group/

[6] - Common Core would make any communist regime proud
http://www.renewamerica.com/columns/miller/131021

[7] - Valerie Jarrett's Communist Ties Confirmed by Judicial Watch
http://www.thenewamerican.com/usnews/politics/item/21133-valerie-jarretts-communist-ties-confirmed-by-judicial-watch

[8] - Global Citizen Festival returns even bigger, bolder, September 27, 2015
http://www.msnbc.com/msnbc/global-citizen-festival-returns-even-bigger-bolder

[9] - United States Is Being Turned Into a Communist Country, July 6, 2015, Newswithviews.com
http://www.newswithviews.com/iserbyt/iserbyt138.htm

[10] - State threatening anti-Common Core parents with jail? - Fight over federalized testing escalates, April 29, 2015
http://www.wnd.com/2015/04/state-threatening-anti-common-core-parents-with-jail/

[11] - Union enrollment plummets for Wisconsin teachers under tough law, October 19, 2014
http://www.foxnews.com/us/2014/10/19/one-third-wisconsin-teachers-have-dropped-union-since-gov-walker-ended/

[12] - Common Core School Assignment FORCES Students to Make Islamic Prayer Rugs, Recite Muslim Prayers
http://toprightnews.com/common-core-school-assignment-forces-students-to-make-islamic-prayer-rug-recite-islamic-prayers/

[13] - Federal Reserve Blames Gov't Aid for Driving up College Tuitions, August 7, 2015
http://www.breitbart.com/big-government/2015/08/07/federal-reserve-blames-govt-aid-for-driving-up-college-tuitions/

[14] - Wyo. Catholic College Latest to Abstain From Federal Student Loan Program, April 16, 2015
http://www.cnsnews.com/news/article/barbara-hollingsworth/wyo-catholic-college-latest-abstain-federal-student-loan-program

I strongly urge you to read the columns below. YOUR child is in grave danger and it is now being shoved in the face of private Christian schools as well as non-religious private schools. Simply type the title in a search engine and you should see the URL address match up.

At Anti-Bullying Conference, Middle Schoolers Learn About Lesbian Strap-On Anal Sex, Fake Testicles
http://www.infowars.com/at-anti-bullying-conference-middle-schoolers-learn-about-lesbian-strap-on-anal-sex-fake-testicles/

The College Bubble 2.0, August 15, 2015

https://www.lewrockwell.com/2015/08/tyler-durden/college-bubble-2-0/

The Student Loan Racket: Ron Paul Right Again, October 23, 2011
http://tomwoods.com/blog/the-student-loan-racket-ron-paul-right-again/

Why not just give out steak dinners on the taxpayers dime while you eat mac and cheese?

USDA Expands $500 Million Summer Meals Programs to Sites Outside of School, June 18, 2015
http://www.cnsnews.com/news/article/penny-starr/usda-expands-500-million-summer-meals-programs-sites-outside-school

How Student Loan Debt Is Turning Us into Serfs, October 5, 2015
http://www.thedailysheeple.com/how-student-loan-debt-is-turning-us-into-serfs_102015

Ripping Off Young America: The College-Loan Scandal, August 15, 2013
http://www.rollingstone.com/politics/news/ripping-off-young-america-the-college-loan-scandal-20130815?page=2

The Nazi Model for Outcome-Based Education, By Berit Kjos - 1996
http://www.crossroad.to/text/articles/tnmfobe1196.html

4th Grade Reading Assignments: Black Panthers, Police Brutality, Need for Amnesty, February 6, 2015
http://www.breitbart.com/big-government/2015/02/06/4th-grade-reading-assignments-black-panthers-police-brutality-need-for-amnesty/

College Board to rewrite US history exam after critics blast anti-America language, August 4, 2015
http://www.foxnews.com/us/2015/08/04/criticism-prompts-college-board-to-rewrite-us-history-exam-to-put-america-in/?intcmp=hpbt3

OR High Schools Adding "13th Grade" to Boost State's On-Time Graduation Rate, October 24, 2014
http://www.cnsnews.com/news/article/joseph-perticone/oregon-high-schools-adding-13th-grade-boost-time-graduation-rate

FAIL: Only 18% of 8th-Graders Proficient in US History, May 4, 2015
http://www.breitbart.com/big-government/2015/05/04/fail-only-18-percent-of-8th-graders-proficient-in-us-history/

Feds look to control kids "womb to workforce" - "Democrats, Obama, are working with Republicans to get this thing passed" (They did)
http://www.wnd.com/2015/02/feds-look-to-control-kids-womb-to-workforce/

Looking Behind the Curtain in Texas Education Reform, May 30, 2015
http://www.newswithviews.com/guest_opinion/guest288.htm

(Bill) Gates-Funded Group Pushes Common Core on Catholic Schools, Targets Cardinal Newman Society
http://www.breitbart.com/big-government/2014/09/24/gates-funded-lobbying-group-pushes-common-core-on-catholic-schools-targets-cardinal-newman-society/

"Student loan debt has surpassed $1.3 trillion and the American taxpayer is now on the hook. At least 30% of the outstanding debt is already in default or deferral. The students are left with a debt burden that can't be written off by declaring bankruptcy, very few jobs in their fields of study, wages that can barely cover the debt payments, and no chance of ever owning a home. They were told by their parents, politicians, and the mainstream media that college was the path to prosperity. They were lied to."

http://www.theburningplatform.com/2015/04/21/they-said-go-to-college/

21 States Will Take DL If You Don't Pay College Loans

http://www.alternet.org/economy/21-states-will-take-away-your-drivers-license-if-you-cant-pay-your-college-loans-activists

How Student Loans Create Demand for Useless Degrees
http://www.infowars.com/how-student-loans-create-demand-for-useless-degrees/

Chapter 12

[1] - Vets Die Waiting for Obama VA Action, December 29, 2012
http://www.newswithviews.com/Lloyd/rees137.htm

[2] - Veterans Affairs workers reap bonuses despite claims backlog
http://www.foxnews.com/politics/2013/08/26/veterans-affairs-workers-reap-bonuses-despite-claims-backlog/?test=latestnews

[3] - 40 U.S. veterans die while on Phoenix VA hospital's cost-cutting secret wait list, April 24, 2014
http://www.nydailynews.com/life-style/health/40-veterans-die-va-hospital-secret-wait-list-report-article-1.1767284

[4] - Isolated. Harassed. Their personal lives investigated. That's life as a VA whistle blower
http://www.washingtonpost.com/blogs/federal-eye/wp/2015/04/14/isolated-harassed-their-personal-lives-investigated-thats-life-as-a-va-whistleblower-employees-tell-congress/

[5] - Homeless Veteran Commits Suicide Outside Phoenix VA
http://www.phoenixnewtimes.com/news/homeless-veteran-commits-suicide-outside-phoenix-va-7324999

[6] - VA Makes Little Headway in Fight to Shorten Waits for Care
http://www.military.com/daily-news/2015/04/09/va-makes-little-headway-in-fight-to-shorten-waits-for-care.html

[7] - Report: Wait Lists for Vets Even Longer Today Than Last Year - VA also faces a budget shortfall of nearly $3 billion

http://news.yahoo.com/report-wait-lists-vets-even-longer-today-last-020512653--politics.html

[8] -VA under fire for tossing claims in trash, September 19, 2015"
https://specialoperationsspeaks.com/current-news/va-under-fire-for-tossing-claims-in-trash

[9] -Cutting veterans pensions vs cupboard is bare
http://www.newswithviews.com/Devvy/kidd622.htm

[10] - Leaked Document: Nearly One-Third Of 847,000 Vets With Pending Applications For VA Health Care Already Died, July 13, 2015
http://www.huffingtonpost.com/2015/07/13/veterans-health-care-backlog-died_n_7785920.html

[11] - Bombshell: So Far, Only Three People Have Been Fired After VA Scandal, April 25, 2015, *Townhall*
http://townhall.com/tipsheet/cortneyobrien/2015/04/25/bombshell-so-far-only-three-people-have-been-fired-after-va-scandal-n1989994

[12] - Veterans Administration Dishonesty: The Truth Emerges
http://www.newswithviews.com/Clausen/barry118.htm

Chapter 13 – No endnotes

Chapter 14

[1] - Why the Fukushima disaster is worse than Chernobyl, August 29, 2011
http://www.independent.co.uk/news/world/asia/why-the-fukushima-disaster-is-worse-than-chernobyl-2345542.html

[2] - Fukushima radiation detected in bluefin tuna on California coast, May 29, 2012, CNN
http://eatocracy.cnn.com/2012/05/29/fukushima-radiation-turns-up-in-bluefin-tuna-on-california-coast/

[3] - Fukushima: 300 tons of radioactive water leak everyday
https://www.yahoo.com/?err=404&err_url=http%3a%2f%2fnews.yahoo.com%2fjapan-government-joining-efforts-contain-fukushima-toxic-water-033418884.html

[4] -Tritium soaring in water at No. 1 plant
http://www.japantimes.co.jp/news/2013/07/07/national/tritium-soaring-in-water-at-no-1-plant/#.Vb6PrPngG71

[5] - Toxic groundwater reaching sea: NRA
http://www.japantimes.co.jp/news/2013/07/10/national/toxic-groundwater-reaching-sea-nra/#.Vb6QgPngG72

[6] - Radioactive Nightmare - Government turns a blind eye as fallout from Fukushima heads our way, July 5, 2012
http://www.enviroreporter.com/investigations/fukushima/radioactive-nightmare/

[7] - Scientists Confirm Fukushima Radiation in California Kelp
http://www.storyleak.com/scientists-confirm-fukushima-radiation-california-kelp-2/

[8] -Fukushima radioactive contamination is rapidly warming North Pacific seawater, September 2014
http://optimalprediction.com/wp/fukushima-radioactive-contamination-is-rapidly-warming-north-pacific-seawater/

[9] - Six sick sea lions found in Sonoma County, February 25, 2015, The Press Democrat
http://www.pressdemocrat.com/news/3574302-181/six-sick-sea-lions-found?page=1

[10] - Gov't Official: Chilling report from Pacific Ocean… "Silence on the seas"
http://enenews.com/govt-official-chilling-report-pacific-ocean-silence-seas-very-very

[11] - A 1,000 Mile Stretch Of The Pacific Ocean Has Heated Up

Several Degrees And Scientists Don't Know Why
http://endoftheamericandream.com/archives/a-1000-mile-stretch-of-the-pacific-ocean-has-heated-up-several-degrees-and-scientists-dont-know-why

[12] - Radiation Expert: Enormous amount of contamination flowing from Fukushima will probably imperil entire Pacific Ocean — Threatens other countries, food chain — Absolutely can reach U.S. and Canadian shores, August 12 2013

Here is the live interview with Dr. Janette Sherman:
https://www.youtube.com/watch?v=KIZEmpkgXmc

[13] - TEPCO Concedes Failure of Fukushima Ice Wall, August 20, 2014
http://cleantechnica.com/2014/08/20/tepco-concedes-failure-fukushima-ice-wall/

[14] -NBC: Sea creatures swarming ashore from San Diego to San Francisco, June 19, 2015
http://enenews.com/nbc-sea-creatures-swarming-ashore-san-diego-san-francisco-cbs-millions-dead-crabs-blanketing-miles-shoreline-like-red-carpet-foot-to16-inches-thick-ive-never-anything-like-abc-wondering-whats-wr

[15] -10 giant whales found dead in Pacific off US coast — Victims of "mysterious affliction"
http://enenews.com/10-endangered-whales-found-dead-pacific-coast-victims-mysterious-affliction-dozens-walrus-hundreds-seabirds-die-nearby-ordinary-happening-loss-whales-ran-toxin-audio

[16] -Mass death of seabirds in Western U.S. is "unprecedented" – unexplained changes within ocean to blame, May 19, 2015
https://theextinctionprotocol.wordpress.com/2015/05/19/mass-death-of-seabirds-in-western-u-s-is-unprecedented-unexplained-changes-within-ocean-to-blame/

[17] -Unprecedented emergency statewide fishing closures enacted in

Pacific Northwest
http://enenews.com/emergency-statewide-fishing-closures-pacific-northwest-unprecedented-weve-never-anything-like-before-disease-causing-very-alarming-mass-die-100-infection-rate-areas-rotting-gills-distended

[18] -Sickened by service: More US sailors claim cancer from helping at Fukushima, December 20, 2013, *FOX News*
http://www.foxnews.com/us/2013/12/20/sickened-by-service-more-us-sailors-claim-cancer-from-helping-at-fukushima/

[19] - Tokyo Electric executives to be charged over Fukushima nuclear disaster, July 31, 2015, *Reuters's*
http://www.reuters.com/article/2015/07/31/us-japan-nuclear-prosecution-idUSKCN0Q50FJ20150731?feedType=RSS&feedName=topNews&utm_source=twitter

[20] - No more half-baked plans for decommissioning Fukushima reactors, June 17, 2015
http://ajw.asahi.com/article/views/editorial/AJ201506170050

[21] - WUS 2015 Impacts of the Fukushima nuclear accident : 4 years later
https://www.youtube.com/watch?v=8af-4QSbfWw&feature=youtu.be&t=1275

[22] -West Coast of North America to be Slammed by 2016 with 80% As Much Fukushima Radiation As Japan, June 10, 2015
http://www.washingtonsblog.com/2015/06/west-coast-of-north-america-to-be-slammed-by-2016-with-80-as-much-fukushima-radiation-as-japan.html

[23] - Leading Scientist On Fukushima Radiation Hitting West Coast of North America: "No One Is Measuring So Therefore We Should Be Alarmed", January 26, 2014
http://www.washingtonsblog.com/2014/01/leading-scientist-

fukushima-radiation-hitting-west-coast-north-america-one-measuring-therefore-alarmed.html

[24] - Mind-blowing die off of seabirds underway from California to Alaska
http://enenews.com/mind-blowing-die-seabirds-underway-california-alaska-experts-unprecedented-theyre-dying-im-baffled-every-bird-starving-death-basically-withering-away-catastrophic-molting-observed-due-unknown

Chapter 15

[1] - Drug for Stomach Ills Is Pulled From the Market - *NY Times*
http://www.nytimes.com/2007/03/30/us/30cnd-Drug.html?_r=2&adxnnl=1&oref=slogin&adxnnlx=1191770183-crvAN5sgYoNoBljCfYyl3A&

[2] - Pain Killer Bextra Pulled From Market
http://www.nbcnews.com/id/7418345/ns/health-arthritis/t/painkiller-bextrapulled-market/#.VhrTDSvgG70

[2A] - 35 FDA-Approved Prescription Drugs Later Pulled from the Market
http://prescriptiondrugs.procon.org/view.resource.php?resourceID=005528

[3] - FDA's Biggest Blunders
http://www.doctorbob.com/danger_meds_fda_blunders.html

[3A] -FDA Approves Potentially Disastrous Cholesterol-Lowering Drug, August 19, 2015
http://articles.mercola.com/sites/articles/archive/2015/08/19/pcsk9-inhibitors-cholesterol-lowering-drugs.aspx?e_cid=20150819Z1_PRNL_art_1&utm_source=prnl&utm_medium=email&utm_content=art1&utm_campaign=20150819Z1&et_cid=DM83073&et_rid=1080161126

[4] - Avandia Maker Hid Risks for Years, Probe Finds

http://www.cbsnews.com/news/avandia-maker-hid-risks-for-years-probe-finds/

[5] - Avandia Lawsuits - May 2014
http://www.drugwatch.com/avandia/lawsuit.php

[6] - Pfizer Paid $896 Million in Prempro Settlements - June 2012
http://www.bloomberg.com/news/articles/2012-06-19/pfizer-paid-896-million-in-prempro-accords-filing-shows-1-

[7] - 70 women "die each year from cancer after taking HRT"
http://www.dailymail.co.uk/news/article-449420/70-women-die-year-cancer-taking-HRT.html

[8] - 2008: Wyeth, Pfizer ordered to pay $27 million in punitive damage
https://tuesdayshorse.wordpress.com/2012/03/10/premarin-the-consequences-of-deception-a-litany-of-litigation/

[9] - Bioidentical Progesterone / Natural Progesterone Cream - Dr. John Lee, M.D.
http://www.progesterall.com/more_progesterall.html

[10] - Health Claim Notification for Fluoridated Water and Reduced Risk of Dental Caries
http://www.fda.gov/food/ingredientspackaginglabeling/labelingnutrition/ucm073602.htm

[11] - Vioxx Killed Half a Million? The Facts Are Grim. - Mike Ferrara, *The Legal Examiner*
http://cherryhill.legalexaminer.com/fda-prescription-drugs/vioxx-killed-half-a-million-the-facts-are-grim/

[12] - Made in China: Seven toxic imports from The Week, Dec. 11, 2009
http://theweek.com/articles/498611/made-china-seven-toxic-imports

[13] - Abolishing the FDA, FDA Policies Keep People Sick and Create a False Sense of Security
http://fee.org/freeman/abolishing-the-fda/

[14] - Abolish the FDA; it's insane, July 27, 2011
http://blogs.marketwatch.com/thisisinsane/2011/07/27/abolish-the-fda-its-insane/

[15] - Pharmaceuticals Invested Nearly $2 billion in Campaign Contributions and Lobbying
http://www.acrreform.org/research/money-in-politics-prescription-drugs/

Chapter 16

[1] - Measles vaccines kill more than measles
http://www.wnd.com/2015/02/measles-vaccines-kill-more-than-measles/

[2] 213 Women Who Took Gardasil Suffered Permanent Disability
http://articles.mercola.com/sites/articles/archive/2012/01/24/hpv-vaccine-victim-sues-merck.aspx-

[3] -$47 Mil to Get More Adolescents on Gardasil
http://www.judicialwatch.org/blog/2013/10/47-mil-to-get-more-adolescents-on-gardasil/

[4] -HPV Vaccine Mandated for All Rhode Island Middle School Students
http://www.thelibertybeacon.com/tag/cdc/page/3/

[5] -Merck's Former Doctor Predicts that Gardasil will Become the Greatest Medical Scandal of All Time,
http://healthimpactnews.com/2014/mercks-former-doctor-predicts-that-gardasil-will-become-the-greatest-medical-scandal-of-all-time/

[6] - Merck Paid 3,468 Death Claims to Resolve Vioxx Suits
http://www.bloomberg.com/news/articles/2010-07-27/merck-paid-3-

468-death-claims-to-resolve-vioxx-suits

[7] -Media Bias Rears Ugly Head in Vaccine Controversy
http://www.newswithviews.com/Kincaid/cliff881.htm

[8] - Say Her Name: Vaccine Victim Hannah Poling
http://www.newswithviews.com/Kincaid/cliff883.htm

[9] - Polio Vaccine, Cancer and Dr. Mary's Monkey
http://www.newswithviews.com/Devvy/kidd674.htm

[10] -Abolishing the FDA - Policies Keep People Sick and Create a False Sense of Security
http://fee.org/freeman/abolishing-the-fda/

Chapter 17

[1] - Florida Appeals Court Orders Akre-Wilson Must Pay Trial Costs for $24.3 Billion *Fox* Television; Couple Warns Journalists of Danger to Free Speech, Whistle Blower Protection
http://www.projectcensored.org/11-the-media-can-legally-lie/

[2] - Emmy Award Winning Journalist Exposes Corporate Censorship on GMOs and Vaccines in Mainstream Media
http://articles.mercola.com/sites/articles/archive/2015/04/26/media-obstruction-intimidation-harassment.aspx

[3] - Update 2-Monsanto guilty of chemical poisoning in France
http://www.reuters.com/article/2012/02/13/france-pesticides-monsanto-idUSL5E8DD5UG20120213

[4] - New study reveals how glyphosate in Monsanto's Roundup inhibits natural detoxification in human cells - Natural News
http://www.naturalnews.com/040482_glyphosate_monsanto_detoxification.html

[5] - Glyphosate's Suppression of Cytochrome P450 Enzymes and Amino Acid Biosynthesis by the Gut Microbiome: Pathways to

Modern Diseases
http://www.cornucopia.org/2013/05/glyphosates-suppression-of-cytochrome-p450-enzymes-and-amino-acid-biosynthesis-by-the-gut-microbiome-pathways-to-modern-diseases/

[6] - 3 Studies Proving Toxic Glyphosate Found in Urine, Blood, and Even Breast Milk by Mike Barrett
http://naturalsociety.com/3-studies-proving-toxic-glyphosate-found-urine-blood-even-breast-milk/

[7] - "On the Offensive" Against Monsanto, France Removes Roundup from Store Shelves
http://www.commondreams.org/news/2015/06/15/offensive-against-monsanto-france-removes-roundup-store-shelves

[8] - GMO Corn – the Poison Plant Everyone Eats
http://www.activistpost.com/2015/06/gmo-cornthe-poison-plant-everyone-eats.html

[9] - Hungary torches 500 hectares of GM corn to eradicate GMOs from food supply
http://www.naturalnews.com/040525_Hungary_GM_corn_burning_fields.html

[10] - Russia Bans GMO Corn Over Cancer Fears as Pressure Builds on Monsanto
http://www.thenewamerican.com/world-news/europe/item/13050-russia-bans-gmo-corn-over-cancer-fears-as-pressure-builds-on-monsanto

[11] -Corporate Win: Supreme Court Says Monsanto Has "Control Over Product of Life" (May 2013)
http://www.commondreams.org/news/2013/05/13/corporate-win-supreme-court-says-monsanto-has-control-over-product-life

[12] -Genetically modified foods…Are they safe? (Institute for Responsible Technology) December 2013
http://www.responsibletechnology.org/posts/gmo-health-dangers/

[13] -Altered Genes, Twisted Truth—How GMOs Took Over the Food Supply by Dr. Mercola (Health Freedom Alliance) https://www.organicconsumers.org/news/altered-genes-twisted-truth%E2%80%94how-gmos-took-over-food-supply

[14] -Monsanto Employee Admits an Entire Department Exists to "Discredit" Scientists by Christina Sarich, Natural Society, April 2015 http://naturalsociety.com/monsanto-employee-admits-an-entire-department-exists-to-discredit-scientists/

[15] - Obama signs "Monsanto Protection Act" written by Monsanto-sponsored senator http://www.globalresearch.ca/monsanto-protection-act-signed-by-obama-gmo-bill-written-by-monsanto-signed-into-law/5329388

[16] - The Monsanto Protection Act is Back, and Worse Than Ever - Center For Food Safety, June 15th, 2015 http://www.centerforfoodsafety.org/press-releases/3961/the-monsanto-protection-act-is-back-and-worse-than-ever#

[17] - GMO cultivation bans in Europe http://www.centerforfoodsafety.org/press-releases/3961/the-monsanto-protection-act-is-back-and-worse-than-ever#

[18] - Why The Netherlands Just Banned Monsanto's Glyphosate-Based Herbicides, May 30, 2015 http://www.collective-evolution.com/2015/05/30/why-the-netherlands-just-banned-monsantos-glyphosate-based-herbicides/

[19] - Monsanto to Spend $1 Billion on New Herbicide Following Roundup Cancer Link Now that glyphosate is being rejected worldwide http://naturalsociety.com/monsanto-to-invest-1-billion-on-producing-dicamba-herbicide-chemicals/

Chapter 18

[1] - Federal Attorney Warns Negative Posts Against Islam Could Get You Prosecution & Imprisonment, June 1, 2013, Freedom Outpost
http://freedomoutpost.com/2013/06/federal-attorney-warns-negative-posts-against-islam-could-get-you-prosecution-imprisonment/

[2] - Woman Beheaded In Oklahoma By Muslim Convert, September 27, 2014, Fox Nation"
http://nation.foxnews.com/2014/09/26/women-beheaded-oklahoma-muslim-convert

[3] - Muslim parents accused of facilitating daughter's rape - Exclusive: Daniel Akbari explains incident of "ghayra violence," Islam-sanctioned sex, April 28, 2015
http://www.wnd.com/2015/04/muslims-accused-of-facilitating-daughters-rape/

[4] - Judge seals file in Somali-Muslim suspects' murder trial, August 14, 2015, WND
http://www.wnd.com/2015/08/judge-seals-file-in-somali-muslim-suspects-murder-trial/

[5] - Muslim refugee charged with raping 10-year-old girl, October 8, 2015, WND
http://www.wnd.com/2015/10/muslim-refugee-charged-with-raping-10-year-old-girl/

[6] - DHS caught busing in illegal Somalis from Mexican border - Immigration official: "Asylum" is the new password, May 13, 2015
http://www.wnd.com/2015/05/dhs-caught-busing-in-illegal-somalis-from-mexican-border/#Sj4378RbibzQwEOo.9

[7] - How Barack Obama Is Using Taqiyya To Fuse Islam With America, January 13, 2013
http://www.nowtheendbegins.com/blog/?p=29881

[8] -- Minnesota Muslims brutally honest: "We want Shariah", May 29, 2015, WND

http://www.wnd.com/2015/05/minnesota-muslims-brutally-honest-we-want-shariah/

[9] - Islam quiz has U.S. parents "outraged" - "They're not teaching 10 Commandments" but Muslim prayers allowed, September 29, 2015
http://www.wnd.com/2015/09/islam-quiz-has-u-s-parents-outraged/

[10] - Textbook Praises Islam, Denigrates Christianity, July 29, 2013, Townhall
http://townhall.com/columnists/toddstarnes/2013/07/29/textbook-praises-islam-denigrates-christianity-n1651503

[11] - Kuwait & Israel Admit They Refuse to Take "Refugees" Because Migrants Don't Assimilate, September 11, 2015
http://www.infowars.com/kuwait-israel-admit-they-refuse-to-take-refugees-because-migrants-dont-assimilate/

[12] - Fort Hood gunman had told US military colleagues that infidels should have their throats cut, November 8, 2009
http://www.telegraph.co.uk/news/worldnews/northamerica/usa/6526030/Fort-Hood-gunman-had-told-US-military-colleagues-that-infidels-should-have-their-throats-cut.html

[13] - Muslim on US Navy Nuclear Aircraft Carrier Attempted to Sell Secrets, August 18, 2015
http://sonsoflibertymedia.com/2015/08/muslim-on-us-navy-nuclear-aircraft-carrier-attempted-to-sell-secrets/

[14] - Offended Muslims erupt on school board, September 22, 2015
http://www.wnd.com/2015/09/offended-muslims-go-berserk-on-school-board/

[15] - Publius Huldah Explains Why Islamists Don't Have the Right to Build Mosques, Proselytize Or Institute Sharia Law In America, April 9, 2013
http://freedomoutpost.com/2013/04/publius-huldah-explains-why-islamists-dont-have-the-right-to-build-mosques-proselytize-or-institute-sharia-law-in-america/